The Practice Turn in Contemporary Theory

Edited by **Theodore R. Schatzki**,
Karin Knorr Cetina and
Eike von Savigny

London and New York

First published 2001
by Routledge
11 New Fetter Lane, London EC4P 4EE

Simultaneously published in the USA and Canada
by Routledge
29 West 35th Street, New York, NY 10001

Routledge is an imprint of the Taylor & Francis Group

Typeset in Times by
BOOK NOW Ltd
Printed and bound in Great Britain by TJ International Ltd, Padstow, Cornwall

British Library Cataloguing in Publication Data
A catalogue record for this book is available from the British Library

Library of Congress Cataloging-in-Publication Data
The practice turn in contemporary theory / edited by Theodore R. Schatzki, Karin Knorr
Cetina, and Eike von Savigny.
    p.   cm.
Based on a conference held Jan. 4–6, 1996 at the University of Bielefeld.
Includes bibliographical references (p.) and index.
1. Practice (Philosophy)—Congresses. I. Schatzki, Theodore R. II. Knorr Cetina, K.
(Karin) III. Savigny, Eike von.

B831.3 P33 2000
128′.4–dc21

          00–055820

ISBN 0-415-22813-1 (hbk)
ISBN 0-415-22814-X (pbk)

The Practice Turn in Contemporary Theory

It is through action and interaction within practices that mind, rationality and knowledge are constituted and social life is organized, reproduced and transformed. During the past two decades, practice theory has emerged as a potent challenger to prevalent ways of thinking about human life and sociality, which have until now focused either on individual minds and actions or social structures, systems and discourses. *The Practice Turn in Contemporary Theory* is the first volume to bring together philosophers, sociologists and scholars of science to explore the significance of practices in human life.

The essays focus on three overall themes: the character and establishment of social order, the psychological basis of human activity and contemporary posthumanist challenges. Philosophers such as Wittgenstein and Heidegger who have been influential in the shaping of practice theory are also discussed. In examining these themes and thinkers the essays document how practice theory stands opposed to prominent modes of thought such as individualism, intellectualism, structuralism, systems theory, and many strains of humanism and poststructuralism.

The Practice Turn in Contemporary Theory will be invaluable to all those interested in the role that practices play in our lives and across a large number of disciplines including philosophy, sociology, science studies, cultural theory, history and anthropology.

Theodore R. Schatzki is Professor of Philosophy at the University of Kentucky. **Karin Knorr Cetina** is Professor of Sociology and **Eike von Savigny** is Professor of Philosophy, both at the University of Bielefeld.

Contents

List of contributors   vii
Acknowledgements   xi

Introduction: practice theory   1
THEODORE R. SCHATZKI

PART I
Practices and social orders   15

1   **Practice as collective action**   17
    BARRY BARNES

2   **Human practices and the observability of the 'macro-social'**   29
    JEFF COULTER

3   **Practice mind-ed orders**   42
    THEODORE R. SCHATZKI

4   **Pragmatic regimes governing the engagement with the world**   56
    LAURENT THÉVENOT

5   **What anchors cultural practices**   74
    ANN SWIDLER

PART II
Inside practices   93

6   **Wittgenstein and the priority of practice**   95
    DAVID BLOOR

7   **What is tacit knowledge?**   107
    H. M. COLLINS

  8 **Throwing out the tacit rule book: learning and practices**   120
     STEPHEN TURNER

  9 **Ethnomethodology and the logic of practice**   131
     MICHAEL LYNCH

PART III
Posthumanist challenges   149

10 **How Heidegger defends the possibility of a correspondence
     theory of truth with respect to the entities of natural science**   151
     HUBERT L. DREYFUS

11 **Practice and posthumanism: social theory and a history
     of agency**   163
     ANDREW PICKERING

12 **Objectual practice**   175
     KARIN KNORR CETINA

13 **Two concepts of practices**   189
     JOSEPH ROUSE

14 **Derridian dispersion and Heideggerian articulation: general
     tendencies in the practices that govern intelligibility**   199
     CHARLES SPINOSA

     Bibliography   213
     Index   231

Contributors

Barry Barnes is Professor of Sociology at the University of Exeter, a founding figure in contemporary sociology of knowledge, and author, among other works, of *Interests and the Growth of Knowledge* (Routledge, 1977), *The Nature of Power* (Polity Press, 1988), and (with David Bloor and John Henry) *Scientific Knowledge: A Sociological Analysis* (University of Chicago Press, 1996).

David Bloor is Reader in the Philosophy of Science in the Social Studies Unit, University of Edinburgh, and he is another founding figure in contemporary sociology of knowledge. Among his works number *Knowledge and Social Imagery* (Routledge and Kegan Paul, 1976), *Wittgenstein: A Social Theory of Knowledge* (Columbia University Press, 1983), and *Wittgenstein: Rules and Institutions* (Routledge, 1997).

H. M. Collins is Distinguished Research Professor of Sociology and director of the Centre for the Study of Knowledge, Expertise and Science at the University of Cardiff. Most prominent among his publications are *Artificial Experts: Social Knowledge and Intelligent Machines* (MIT Press, 1990), *Changing Order: Replication and Induction in Scientific Practice* (University of Chicago Press, 1992), (with Trevor Pinch) *Frames of Meaning: The Social Construction of Extraordinary Science* (Routledge and Kegan Paul, 1982), and (with Martin Kusch) *The Shape of Actions: What Humans and Machines Can Do* (MIT Press, 1998).

Jeff Coulter is Professor of Sociology at Boston University and author of numerous books, including *The Social Construction of Mind* (Rowman and Littlefield, 1979), *Rethinking Cognitive Theory* (Macmillan, 1983), and *Mind in Action* (Polity Press, 1989).

Hubert L. Dreyfus is Professor of Philosophy at the University of California, Berkeley, author of *What Computers Still Can't Do: A Critique of Artificial Intelligence* (Harper and Row, 2nd edn 1979) and *Being-in-the-World: A Commentary on Heidegger's Being and Time, Division I* (MIT Press, 1991), and coauthor (with Paul Rabinow) of *Michel Foucault: Beyond Structuralism and Hermeneutics* (University of Chicago Press, 2nd edn,

1983), (with Stuart Dreyfus) of *Mind Over Machine* (The Free Press, 1986), and (with Charles Spinosa and Fernando Flores) of *Disclosing New Worlds* (MIT Press, 1996).

Karin Knorr Cetina is Professor of Sociology at the University of Bielefeld, former member of the Institute for Advanced Study at Princeton University, author of *The Manufacture of Knowledge: An Essay on the Constructivist and Contextual Nature of Science* (Pergamon, 1981) and of *Epistemic Cultures: How the Sciences Make Knowledge* (Harvard University Press, 1999), and coauthor of several volumes, including (with Aaron V. Cicourel) *Advances in Social Theory and Methodology: Toward an Integration of Micro- and Macrosociologies* (Routledge and Kegan Paul, 1981) and (with Michael Mulkay) *Science Observed: New Perspectives on the Social Study of Science* (Sage, 1983).

Michael Lynch is Professor of Science and Technology Studies at Cornell University, author of *Art and Artifact in Laboratory Science: A Study of Shop Work and Shop Talk in a Research Laboratory* (Routledge and Kegan Paul, 1985) and of the award-winning *Scientific Practice and Ordinary Action: Ethnomethodology and Social Studies of Science* (Cambridge, 1993), and coauthor (with David Bogan) of *The Spectacle of History: Speech, Text, and Memory at the Iran–Contra Hearings* (Duke, 1996).

Andrew Pickering is Professor of Sociology at the University of Illinois, Champagne-Urbana, former member of the Advanced Institute at Princeton University, author of *Constructing Quarks: A Sociological History of Particle Physics* (University of Chicago Press, 1984) and *The Mangle of Practice: Time, Agency, and Science* (University of Chicago Press, 1995), and editor of *Science as Culture and Practice* (University of Chicago Press, 1992).

Joseph Rouse is Professor of Philosophy and of the Science, Medicine, and Culture Program at Wesleyan University and author of *Knowledge and Power: Toward a Political Philosophy of Science* (Cornell University Press, 1987) and *Engaging Science* (Cornell University Press, 1996).

Eike von Savigny is Professor of Philosophy at the University of Bielefeld and author of numerous books, including *Die Philosophie der Normalen Sprache* (Suhrkamp, 1974), *The Social Foundations of Meaning* (Springer, 1988), *Wittgensteins "Philosophische Untersuchungen"* (Klostermann, two volumes 1988 and 1989), and *Der Mensch als Mitmensch: Studien zu Wittgensteins "Philosophische Untersuchungen"* (Deutscher Taschenbuch Verlag, 1995).

Theodore R. Schatzki is Professor of Philosophy and codirector of the Committee on Social Theory at the University of Kentucky, author of *Social Practices: A Wittgensteinian Approach to Human Activity and the Social* (Cambridge University Press, 1996), and contributing coeditor and series coeditor of a series of multidisciplinary volumes in social theory published by Guilford Press.

Charles Spinosa is Head of Research at Vision Consulting and author of "Derrida and Heidegger: Iterability and Ereignis", in Hubert Dreyfus and Harrison Hall (eds) *Heidegger: A Critical Reader* (Blackwell, 1992), and coauthor (with Hubert Dreyfus) of "Two Kinds of Anti-Essentialism and their Consequences," *Critical Inquiry,* 22 (1996), 735–63 and (with Hubert Dreyfus and Fernando Flores) of *Disclosing New Worlds: Entrepreneurship, Democratic Action, and the Cultivation of Solidarity* (MIT Press, 1997).

Ann Swidler is Professor of Sociology at the University of California, Berkeley, author of *Organization without Authority* (Harvard University Press, 1979), the important article "Culture in Action: Symbols and Strategies" (*American Sociological Review,* 1986), and *Talk of Love: How Culture Matters* (University of Chicago Press, 2001), and coauthor (with Robert Bellah et al.) of both *Habits of the Heart* (University of California Press, 1985) and *The Good Society* (Vintage, 1992).

Laurent Thévenot is Professor in the Groupe de Sociologie Politique et Morale at the Ecoles des Hautes Etudes, one of the originators of the "new French school" of sociology, author, among other works, of *Sociologie pragmatique: les régimes d'engagement* (forthcoming), and coauthor (with Luc Boltanski) of *De la justification* (Gallimard, 1991).

Stephen Turner is Distinguished Research Professor at the University of South Florida, author of numerous books, including *Sociological Explanation as Translation* (Cambridge University Press, 1980) and *The Social Theory of Practices* (University of Chicago Press, 1994), and coauthor of several volumes, including (with Mark L. Wardell) *Sociological Theory in Transition* (Allen and Unwin, 1986) and (with Regis A. Factor) *Max Weber: The Lawyer as Social Thinker* (Routledge, 1994).

Acknowledgements

This anthology originated in a conference, 'Practices and Social Order,' that was held at the Center for Interdisciplinary Studies (ZiF) at the University of Bielefeld, Germany, on January 4–6, 1996. We would like to thank the Center for its hospitality and generous financial support, as well as the German Research Council (Deutsche Forschungsgemeinschaft) for its considerable financial assistance. We would like to thank, further, all the conference's participants, especially those whose contributions did not find their way into this volume.

The production of the volume would not have been possible without the assistance of Jeffery Nicholas and Katie Barrett in Lexington and Gisela Diekmeier and Hendrik Wortmann in Bielefeld. The entire book has benefited from the comments of anonymous reviewers.

Introduction
Practice theory

Theodore R. Schatzki

Thinkers once spoke of 'structures,' 'systems,' 'meaning,' 'life world,' 'events,' and 'actions' when naming the primary generic social thing. Today, many theorists would accord 'practices' a comparable honor. Varied references to practices await the contemporary academician in diverse disciplines, from philosophy, cultural theory, and history to sociology, anthropology, and science and technology studies.

Underlying many such references are impulses to move these disciplines beyond current problematic dualisms and ways of thinking. For instance, philosophical practice thinkers such as Ludwig Wittgenstein (1958), Hubert Dreyfus (1991), and Charles Taylor (1985: part one) contend that practices at once underlie subjects and objects, highlight nonpropositional knowledge, and illuminate the conditions of intelligibility.[1] For their social theoretical brethren Pierre Bourdieu (1977, 1990), Anthony Giddens (1979, 1984), and the ethnomethodologists (see Lynch 1993), talk of practices bespeaks such desires as those to free activity from the determining grasp of objectified social structures and systems, to question individual actions and their status as the building-blocks of social phenomena, and to transcend rigid action–structure oppositions.[2] For cultural theorists Michel Foucault (e.g., 1976, 1980) and Jean-François Lyotard (1984, 1988), among others, to speak of practices is to depict language as discursive activity in opposition to structuralist, semiotic, and poststructuralist conceptions of it as structure, system, or abstract discourse. And among, finally, the purposes animating the practice theoretical study of science and technology (e.g., Rouse 1996b; Pickering 1995a) are the development of concepts of science as activity as opposed to representation and the reconsideration of humanist dichotomies between human and nonhuman entities.

In moving the above disciplines in such directions, practice theorists are making decisive contributions to contemporary understandings of diverse issues. These include the philosophical and social scientific significance of human activity; the nature of subjectivity, embodiment, rationality, meaning, and normativity; the character of language, science, and power; and the organization, reproduction, and transformation of social life. In making these contributions, practice approaches thereby oppose numerous current and recent paths of thinking, including intellectualism, representationalism, individualisms (e.g., rational choice theory, methodological individualism, network analysis), structuralism, structure-functionalism, systems theory, semiotics, and many strains of humanism and poststructuralism.

Given this multiplicity of impulses, issues, and oppositions, it is not surprising that there is no unified practice approach. Most thinkers who theorize practices conceive of them, minimally, as arrays of activity. Not only, however, do their conceptions of activity and what connects activities vary, but some theorists define practices as the skills, or tacit knowledges and presuppositions, that underpin activities (e.g., Turner 1994; Dreyfus 1991). Most theorists, moreover, above all those in philosophy and the traditional social sciences, identify the activities involved as those of persons: practices are arrays of human activity. A significant 'posthumanist' minority centered in science and technology studies avers, however, that the activities bound into practices also include those of nonhumans such as machines and the objects of scientific investigation. Although, finally, most practice theorists would agree that activity is embodied and that nexuses of practices are mediated by artifacts, hybrids, and natural objects, disagreements reign about the nature of embodiment, the pertinence of thematizing it when analyzing practices, the sorts of entities that mediate activity, and whether these entities are relevant to practices as more than mere intermediaries among humans.

Despite this diversity, practice accounts are joined in the belief that such phenomena as knowledge, meaning, human activity, science, power, language, social institutions, and historical transformation occur within and are aspects or components of the *field of practices*. The field of practices is the total nexus of interconnected human practices. The 'practice approach' can thus be demarcated as all analyses that (1) develop an account of practices, either the field of practices or some subdomain thereof (e.g., science), or (2) treat the field of practices as the place to study the nature and transformation of their subject matter.[3] Note that this demarcation makes the notion of a field of practice the linchpin of the practice approach.

A central core, moreover, of practice theorists conceives of practices as embodied, materially mediated arrays of human activity centrally organized around shared practical understanding. The point of the qualifier 'embodied' is that, as many late twentieth-century thinkers (above all feminists) emphasize, the forms of human activity are entwined with the character of the human body. Practice theorists who highlight embodiment typically believe, further, that bodies and activities are 'constituted' within practices. Foucault (1976: 138), for example, described how the constitution of present-day activity centrally consists in the fashioning of bodies (e.g., their aptitudes) within disciplinary practices. According to these practice theorists, practices are the chief and immediate context within which the preponderance of bodily properties crucial to social life are formed, not just skills and activities but bodily experiences, surface presentations, and even physical structures as well. Of course, the idea that 'the body' is 'constituted' within some social matrix is not unique to practice theory. This approach nonetheless helps mark the frontiers of contemporary thought on the body–activity–society complex.

All practice theorists, meanwhile, acknowledge the dependence of activity on shared skills or understandings (which are typically viewed as embodied). Disagreement reigns on what, if anything, beyond shared understandings is necessary to explain practices. This disagreement notwithstanding, the prominence of practical understanding underwrites the proposition that the maintenance of practices, and thus the persistence and transformation of social life, rests centrally on the successful inculcation of shared embodied know-how. As will be discussed below, the skilled body commands attention in practice theory as the common meeting point of mind and activity and of individual activity and society.

Practice theory also joins a variety of 'materialist' approaches in highlighting how bundled activities interweave with ordered constellations of nonhuman entities. Indeed, because human activity is beholden to the milieus of nonhumans amid which it proceeds, understanding specific practices always involves apprehending material configurations. Ethnomethodologists, for instance, examine the immediate settings within which activity propagates, while students of science and technology map the wider human–nonhuman networks that form and orient activity within them. Philosophers ponder how the meanings of material contexts depend on human practices, while sociologists study how the stability of practices and meanings partly reflects the solidifying inertia of material layouts.

In social theory, consequently, practice approaches promulgate a distinct social ontology: the social is a field of embodied, materially interwoven practices centrally organized around shared practical understandings. This conception contrasts with accounts that privilege individuals, (inter)actions, language, signifying systems, the life world, institutions/roles, structures, or systems in defining the social. These phenomena, say practice theorists, can only be analyzed via the field of practices. Actions, for instance, are embedded in practices, just as individuals are constituted within them. Language, moreover, is a type of activity (discursive) and hence a practice phenomenon, whereas institutions and structures are effects of them. Needless to say, practice theorists have different understandings of these matters. What is more, some posthumanist practice theorists claim that nonhumans do not just mediate, but themselves propagate practices: practices, in their eyes, comprise human and nonhuman activities. This thesis challenges attempts to analyze the social via practices, as well as the very notion of the social itself.

The present volume illustrates both the variety and scope of contemporary practice theories. Before describing its contents, I want briefly to explicate the expression 'practice theory.' 'Theory' means, simply, general and abstract account. A theory of X is a general and abstract account of X. A theory is of the practice variety, consequently, when it either (1) proffers a general and abstract account of practices, either the field of practices or some subdomain thereof, or (2) refers whatever it offers a general and abstract account of to the field of practices. This definition of theory obviously departs from both the once dominant conception that ties theory to explanation and prediction and the more colloquial and still prevalent notion that theories are hypotheses. Systems of generalizations (or universal statements) that back explanations, predictions, and research strategies are theories. But so, too, for example, are typologies of social phenomena; models of social affairs; accounts of what social things (e.g., practices, institutions) are; conceptual frameworks developed expressly for depicting sociality; and descriptions of social life – so long as they are couched in general, abstract terms. The current introduction exemplifies this conception of theory; it also signals it by using the expressions 'practice theory,' 'practice thinking,' and 'the practice approach' interchangeably. It is in this sense of 'theory,' furthermore, that the expression 'social theory' has lately established itself outside sociology. I should add that, although practice thinkers fashion theories of this sort, they are generally suspicious of 'theories' that deliver general *explanations* of why social life is as it is.

Practices and social order

Social order is a preeminent concern of modern social thought. Thomas Hobbes inaugurated this theme by proclaiming sovereign power the only escape from an abject state of total war, therewith equating order with peace and security. During the past two centuries, other notions of order have arisen alongside his that reflect the explanatory and analytic concerns of social science. These notions treat order as a generic ontological feature of the layout of social life (cf. Parsons's [1949: 91] definition of factual order as cognizable organization). The most prominent such features are regularity or pattern, interdependent functioning (systemic relatedness in some versions), stability, and orderliness. A crucial issue is the nature of macro orders: regularities and interdependencies, etc., in social affairs that encompass myriad individuals and their interactions.

Accounts of what is responsible for order are as varied as conceptions of it. Individualist approaches attribute the layout of social affairs to features of individuals and their direct interactions – for example, agreements (Hobbes); shared internalized norms (Durkheim, Parsons, and Habermas); skills, mutual understandings, and reciprocal interpretations (ethnomethodology); communication, negotiation, and mutual adjustment (symbolic interactionism); and coercion and domination. Another idea, prominent among advocates of rational choice or game theory, is that social orders (e.g., markets) are unintended byproducts of actions governed by rational calculations.

Nonindividualist accounts attribute social order to phenomena that are something more than features of individuals and their immediate interactions. Typically, these phenomena determine order either by affecting the actions that produce it – causing them, constraining them, forming them, organizing the contexts in which people proceed – or by directly determining order independently of human activity (as when one macro state of society causes another). A currently popular nonindividualist order-instituting entity is discourse (abstract webs of linguistically articulated meaning), to which some discourse theorists attribute the formation of discursive behavior. In the middle of this century, similarly, regularity, stability, and interdependence in both activities and macro institutions were widely seen as established by underlying abstract structures. The even longer history of wholism (e.g., Hegel, Malinowski, Parsons, and Luhmann) attributes the ordering of activities and macro institutions to social wholes, usually societies, which determine the actions and interactions occurring within them by way of shaping societal subdomains and institutions.

Practice approaches to social order refer order, however conceived, to the field of practices. This means, first, that order is understood as (a) feature(s) of this field and, second, that components and aspects of the field are deemed responsible for the establishment of order. Although accounts of exactly how this works are as diverse as theorists' depictions of the field of practices, these accounts all undermine the traditional individual–nonindividual divide by availing themselves of features of both sides. Practice thinkers usually acknowledge the structuring and coordinating import of agreements, negotiations, and other interactions, as well as the undergirding significance of skills and interpretations. They treat these phenomena, however, as features of or as embedded in practices, hence as subject to or as constitutive of the latter. As a result, interactions, skills, and interpretations determine orders (and are themselves ordered) *qua* features of practice. Practice approaches also tend to reduce the scope and ordering power of reason. They do this by abandoning the traditional conception of reason as an innate mental faculty and reconceptualizing it as a practice phenomenon: as (1) a way of being dependent upon and thus varying among practices or (2) ways of operating within practices, e.g., rational procedures and argumentation (cf., Winch 1977; Toulmin 1958, 1972).

At the same time, although practices, as Barry Barnes argues in his contribution, do not reduce to individuals, *qua* activity arrays they are much more closely tied to individuals than are the orders and order-establishing phenomena of much macro social thought. Although practices, for example, resemble macro phenomena in constraining individual activity and organizing the contexts in which people act, they never possess the *sui generis* existence and near omnipotence sometimes attributed to structural and wholist phenomena. Practice thought also never countenances macro determinations that are impervious to the intervention of individuals. In sum, the attribution of order to practice nexuses differentiates practice thinking from both the individualist and traditional nonindividualist camps. As might be expected from an approach that treats the social as a nexus of activity, it appropriates in transfigured form a variety of individualist *explanantia*, while grounding these in a supraindividual phenomenon that differs significantly from those of conventional social thought (e.g., societies and systems).

Treating the social as a field of practices also opens up new questions concerning order. One set of issues addresses the distinction and relations between micro and macro. As Jeff Coulter suggests in his essay, practice theory can depart from the usual construal of the micro as individuals and their interactions and instead conceive of it as the field of practices. Practice approaches can then analyze (a) communities, societies, and cultures, (b) governments, corporations, and armies, and (c) domination and coercion as either features of, collections of, or phenomena instituted and instantiated in practices. A second set of issues focuses on the ordering of the field of practices itself, that is, the patterns and interdependencies (etc.) that appear there. Ann Swidler's investigation of whether some practices anchor and organize others illustrates this second area of research. Individual practices, finally, also exhibit interdependence, orderliness, and the like. A further problem sphere, consequently, pursued in Laurent Thévenot's, my own (and Joseph Rouse's) contributions, is what orders individual practices.

The opening pair of essays in Part 1 examines ontological relations between, on the one hand, practices such as vegetarianism, riding in formation, and the use of particular linguistic expressions and, on the other, individuals or macro phenomena. Barry Barnes begins by arguing that practices are genuine collective entities immune to individualist analysis. He first challenges one familiar practice approach that attributes shared activity to nothing but individual capacities identical across people (e.g., shared skills). Without denying the significance of shared capacities, he argues (not unlike Thévenot's and my own contributions) that accounting for practices requires invoking other phenomena, in particular, goals, propositional knowledge, and active monitoring of the setting of action. Barnes then explains how the lean practice approach he criticizes, like Stephen Turner's attribution of practices to the habits of individuals (see his essay in this volume), is a form of individualism. Practices, he counters, are collective possessions and accomplishments sustained through interaction and mutual adjustment among people. Jeff Coulter follows with a 'praxiological resolution of the micro–macro problem.' He first examines the micro accounts of macro phenomena found in Max Weber and interactionism, faulting both for oversimplification and inter-actionism in addition for a residual reification of macro things. Conceiving the micro as the realm of practices, he ties the existence of macro things to everyday practices of (legitimately) assigning individuals and actions to macro categories. Macro phenomena, he claims, exist in and through their praxi-ological instantiations; that is, they exist primarily in and through the occasions when it is relevant and legitimate to characterize people and actions with macro categories.

Following this, I address the organization of practices and the nature as well as establishment of social order. I first argue that order should not be con-ceived of as regularities, but instead as arrangements of people, artifacts, and things. I contend next that social practices govern both the meanings of arranged entities and the actions that bring arrangements about, and that this governance is the basis of social order. To substantiate these theses, I (1) analyze practices as open sets of nonregularized actions that are organized by practical understandings, rules, and teleoaffectivity and (2) show how practices so conceived determine order by governing the meanings and establishment of arrangements. In the succeeding essay, Laurent Thévenot similarly contests those practice theories that construe practices as custom-like regularities and ground activity solely in shared habits or dispositions. Such approaches, he (not unlike Barnes) claims, ignore how the world responds to human intervention and thereby orders human activity. They also reduce, wrongfully, the conceptions of the good governing human activity to social norms which actors follow. To rectify these difficiencies, Thévenot presents his notion of a pragmatic regime. A pragmatic regime joins a mode of mutual exchange between actor and world with a conception of the good that governs human activity. Thévenot suggests that social order arises from the sharing of pragmatic regimes, through which modes of human coordination are established. He also concreticizes these contentions via an examination of three particular such regimes.

Part 1 concludes with Ann Swidler's examination of the organization of the field of practices. After first showing how practice theory solves persistent problems in the sociology of culture, she argues that practices lie behind every aspect of social causation. Following this, Swidler asks whether some practices organize, anchor, or constrain others. Through a trio of case studies, she examines two categories of ordering practice: those that constitute discourses, activity patterns, and social relations by enactively anchoring 'constitutive rules' definitive of agents and phenomena, and those that coordinate wide domains of activity in social life.

Inside practices

Part 2 examines a psychological aspect of the conception of embodiment that is central to many practice approaches. Over the past three decades, a radical change has occurred in what analysts view as the principal psychological basis of activity. Whereas philosophers and social investigators once cited mental entities such as beliefs, desires, emotions, and purposes, practice theorists instead highlight embodied capacities such as know-how, skills, tacit understanding, and dispositions.

To some extent the adoption of these alternative determining factors is part of a general anti-Cartesianism in contemporary academic culture that sees 'mental states' as irredeemably contaminated by the 'Cartesian' interpretation of them as occupants or aspects of a distinct space or realm. It also reflects the particular traditions out of which practice analysis emerged. Two key influences upon Giddens's account of practice, for instance, are Wittgensteinian philosophy and a mix of Schützian and Heideggerian phenomenologies. These same philosophical sources of the picture of a fundament of understandings-skills have also shaped the work of Dreyfus and the ethnomethodologists. A further formative context is American pragmatism (e.g., John Dewey and George Herbert Mead), which grounded human activity in habits.

Practice theory's embrace of embodied cognitive capacities was also a response to structuralism and subjectivism. Declining to attribute human activity either to Lévi-Straussian abstract structures or to Sartrean projections of human subjectivity, Bourdieu, for instance, conceives practices as self-organizing and -propagating manifolds of activity. He seeks, however, to anchor these manifolds in the individuals who perform their constituent activities, while also dismissing mental states as subjective epiphenomena. The *human body*, accordingly, offers itself as the point of connection between individuals and social manifolds. And therewith habitus (practical understanding) becomes the ideal determining phenomenon, sufficiently psychological to avoid physical determinism, sufficiently nonpsychological to be embodied, and adequately supple to account for much if not all human activity. Practice theory's embrace of embodied understanding is rooted in the realization that the body is the meeting points both of mind and activity and of individual activity and social manifold.

This appeal to skillful practical understanding raises the question: can an array of activity be adequately explained by shared skills alone? Practice approaches diverge on this issue. Opposing Bourdieu's affirmation of the adequacy of habitus, for example, is Barnes's (and Giddens's and others') insistence that skills be supplemented by some combination of perception, propositional knowledge, reasons, and goals. Some theorists also claim that explicit rules must be brought into the mix. This is a tricky issue because practice theorists resoundingly oppose the idea that explicit rules govern much, if not most, social activity. They also resist accounts that defend rule ubiquity by construing practical understanding as the observance of tacit or hidden rules (the application of implicit propositions). Animating this resistance is, above all, Wittgenstein's observation in the *Philosophical Investigations* that contents of any sort (e.g., linguistic or mental) are unable by themselves, i.e., in the absence of established ways of using/applying them, to govern activity determinately. Some theorists follow Wittgenstein (1958: sections 86, 139–41) even further in maintaining that practical understanding cannot be adequately formulated in words – either by social investigators or, as Michael Lynch emphasizes in this volume, by actors themselves.[4] (As H. M. Collins points out in his essay, this claim must be distinguished from the empirical observation that, in a given domain of practices such as science, explicit formulations ride atop an embodied practical dimension that is *de facto* unformulated and of which it would be unreasonable to expect, given the practices involved, that it would be formulated.) For these theorists, no representation of the skills involved in performing appropriate human activity can be adequate.

It must be stressed that these claims about practical understanding deny neither the existence nor the efficacy of explicit formulations in ongoing activity. Skills and explicit propositions work in tandem. What is more, differ-ent mixes of these reign in different practice arenas. Practice approaches instead emphasize two central points in this context. The first is the priority of understanding: skills are not just omnipresent in human activity, but the capacity of formulations to guide what people do rests on abilities to use and understand them. The second point is that skills are shared, that is, they are the same in different individuals. Nexuses of activity are rooted in, though not for most theorists exclusively in, shared understandings.

Since the prominence of practical understanding is tied to the body's mediative positions between mind and activity and between individual activity and social manifold, understanding is stretched between two poles: the body on the one side and the social world on the other. Although thinkers disagree about whether practical understanding possesses causal power, they typically concur that it exists only as embodied in the individual. An individual possesses practical understanding, however, only as a participant in social practices (see David Bloor's essay). Practical understanding is, thus, a battery of bodily abilities that results from, and also makes possible, participation in practices. It follows that because social orders rest upon practices that are founded on embodied understanding, they are rooted directly in the human body.

The essays in Part 2 cover many of these issues. David Bloor begins by bringing G. E. M. Anscombe's account of reflexive action to bear on Witt-genstein's groundbreaking remarks on rule-following. On the basis of meticulous textual interpretation, he argues that Wittgenstein understands following a rule to be an institution, one that encompasses patterns of behavior as well as normative verbal 'accounting.' Analyzing rule-following as an institution, Bloor further contends, at once (1) consolidates the wider thesis that society is a set of such institutions and (2) dissolves one of the central obstacles to the sociology of knowledge, namely, its inability to offer a convincing analysis of rule-following (and, thereby, mathematics and logic). Following this, H. M. Collins examines three approaches to tacit knowledge pursued by sociologists of scientific knowledge: the motor-skills metaphor, the rules-regress model, and the form of life approach. He argues that the tacitness that these approaches attribute to much human knowledge does not reflect the nature of knowledge as such, but instead follows from how humans are built. This fact, whatever its philosophical significance, does not negate the momentous difference the recognition of tacit knowledge has made to the study of scientific practices. Collins concludes his discussion by contending that what is opaque to both computer and neural-net models of human activity is the embedding of knowledge and action within social contexts (cf. Collins 1990).

In the next essay, Stephen Turner extends arguments of his recent book (Turner 1994) against explaining practices *qua* behavioral regularities by reference to shared tacit rules. On the background of connectionist accounts of the learning of grammar, he suggests that any account of practices is constrained by the fact that practices have a learned component. His account of learning highlights the quantity and structuring of information in given practice domains together with the varying purposes and experiential histories of the different individuals mastering them. The resulting minimalist conception of social practices has them arising entirely from convergences in what people learn (information and habits). Part 2 concludes with Michael Lynch's demonstration that, although the 'methods' actors employ in carrying off social life can be represented by describing what people do (in accomplishing this), it is impossible to capture these methods in abstract, rule-like formulations that spell out the logic of practice. Examples of such formulations are the rules of scientific method and the rules and models that conversation analysis attributes to speakers. Lynch's strategy is to expose the gaps that repeatedly arise between methods and abstract formulations. Examining an interrogation episode from the first O. J. Simpson trial, he shows that the infirmity of formulation attends not just formulations of social scientists, but also those participants offer when investigating their own practices.

Posthumanist challenges

By any account, a key defining characteristic of modern Western thought is humanism, humanity's 'self-assertion' (cf. Blumenberg 1983). This cultural stance arose in Europe during the 1500s and 1600s to celebrate Man as thinker, creator, and actor. Its exaltation of the human reflected growing sentiment that human beings are beholden neither to God, the chain of being, or the implacable order of the universe – they can create and take responsibility for conceptual and material structures whose splendor honors their capabilities and power. Later, more militant atheisms dispensed entirely with God or Nature and proclaimed Man the unique source of meaning, value, truth, and being.

Humanism remains a potent cultural position at the beginning of the twenty-first century. The idea that human beings create meaning, value, and truth persists in diverse intellectual contexts, including morality, as in renewed attempts to link morality to rationality; epistemology, as in the panoply of relativisms or 'internal' realisms; science, in the conviction that humans can fathom nature; and social thought generally, where humanity remains the central and, for many thinkers, exclusive focus. Various self-proclaiming 'posthumanisms,' however, have arisen to challenge different aspects of the modernist creed.

Two varieties of posthumanism intersect practice theory. The first might be called 'objectivism.' Objectivism alerts theorists overly fixated on human beings and their relations to the founding presence of nonhumans in human life. Humans and nonhumans, it proclaims, codetermine one another; what is more, humans do not master, conceptually or causally, either the entry of nonhumans into or their impact upon the human world. Andrew Pickering's and Karin Knorr Cetina's contributions to this volume illustrate one line of objectivist research: studying the role of nonhumans and their agency in directing human practices and in forming and stabilizing human worlds. Note that by acknowledging nonhumans as components and determinants of the arrangements that encompass people, this line of research problematizes the concept of the social and challenges traditional renderings of it as relations between people.

Today, practice theorists of many stripes acknowledge that nonhuman entities help constitute human sociality. Practices, as indicated, are generally construed as *materially mediated* nexuses of activity. In thinking thus, however, most practice theorists continue to focus on the human. They do not follow their posthumanist colleagues in (a) upholding something like Callon and Latour's (e.g., Callon 1986; Callon and Latour 1992) principle of symmetry, on which concepts hitherto reserved for humans – agency, intention, purpose, knowledge, voice, etc. – also apply to nonhumans; and/or (b) seeing humans and nonhumans (their powers and properties) as equally emergent from a prior matrix or plane called 'practices' (Rouse 1996b, Pickering 1995a). For these humanist theorists, practices are arrays of activity, and the activities involved are those of humans. Their accounts, consequently, also presume the relative unity and integrity of human agency. Humanist theorists might buy sufficiently into posthumanism to acknowledge that human agency both arises from bodily systems and is tied to 'external' arrangements of humans and nonhumans. According to them, however, these facts neither replace human agency with, nor fragment it into, the actions of these systems or arrangements. The bulk of practice theorists might also accept other posthumanist-sounding theses, for instance, that human activity is not completely mastered by the self-conscious subject of modernist lore, and that nonhumans are agents in some sense of the word.

A second posthumanist agenda widely pursued in practice theory is the prioritization of practices over individuals (or individual subjects). For example, many features of individuals are claimed to arise from the incorporation of humans into social practices. More generally, there come to be people, that is to say, humans with activities, minds, identities, and genders through this incorporation.[5] This thesis is instantiated in, among other things, the idea that the forms of individual activity depend on the practices in which people participate. It also expresses itself decisively in a rejection of the modern conviction that mind is the central phenomenon in human life: the source of meaning, the receptacle of knowledge and truth, the wellspring of activity, and the co- or sole constitutor of reality. According to practice theory, mind is at least to a significant extent 'constituted' within practices. However much the contents and properties that compose and define mind have biophysiological sources and continuous neurophysiological underpinnings, they depend, both causally and ontologically, on participation in social practices (e.g., Coulter 1989). As a result, the status of human beings as 'subjects' (and 'agents') is bound to practices. Practices, in sum, displace mind as the central phenomenon in human life.

This prioritization of practices over mind brings with it a transformed conception of knowledge. As indicated, knowledge (and truth) are no longer automatically self-transparent possessions of minds. Rather, knowledge and truth, including the scientific versions, are mediated both by interactions between people and by arrangements in the world.[6] Often, consequently, knowledge is no longer even the property of individuals, but instead a feature of groups, together with their material setups. Scientific and other knowledges also no longer amount to stockpiled representations. Not only do practical understandings, ways of proceeding, and even setups of the material environment represent forms of knowledge – propositional knowledge presupposes and depends on them.

As suggested, practice thought also joins other contemporary currents in undercutting individual subjects as the source of meaning and normativity (value too). Practice theorists claim, instead, that practices are the source and carrier of meaning, language, and normativity.[7] The generation, maintenance, and transformation of these phenomena are achievements of extant practices that are realized in the public realm of actions and interactions that practices open up. Individuals, instead of effecting and sustaining norms, meaning, and language out of their own resources, are integrated (to varying degrees) into the ways of proceeding that characterize extant practices, where these matters are conserved and novelty and transformation take their start. Since practices are almost always, as a matter of fact, social in the minimal sense of embracing multiple, to varying extents interacting participants, normativity, meaning, and language (of all sorts) are at bottom social phenomena. Notice, as Rouse emphasizes in his essay, that the positioning of language, meaning, and normativity in practices open these phenomena to determination by the social factors that affect practices, for example, power and politics. The practice approach to these topics is summed up in its forceful opposition to representational accounts: meaning and language, arising from and tied to continuous activity, cannot be telescoped into representations or mental contents, which themselves acquire the property of being about something by virtue of how people use and react to them.

Part 3 begins with an idea fundamental to posthumanist objectivism: the independence of (some) objects from human activity and conceptualization. Hubert Dreyfus argues, in his contribution, that the practice approach is compatible with a robust form of realism. His main target is the 'deflationary realism' of, for instance, Donald Davidson (as understood by Rouse), according to which practices, meanings, objects, and mental contents are inextricably intertwined, so that the very idea of things as they are in themselves is incoherent. The basis of his richer alternative is Heidegger's account of equipment, breakdown, and objects in *Being and Time*. Dreyfus distinguishes the capacity of practices to constitute objects from their capacity to access them and analyzes the latter capacity through Heidegger's notion of formal designation. He then uses an experience called 'defamiliarization' to develop three features that scientific practices must possess to be able to access the functional components of the universe as they are in themselves.

The two following essays address objectivism. Andy Pickering commences by reissuing his call for a posthumanist social theory that recognizes – from the start – the mutual constitution of material and human agency. He envisions a history of agency that would study key sites of encounter between the material and the human, and in his essay considers three examples: the nineteenth-century synthetic dye industry, the railroad, and post-World War II cybernetics, in particular, the human–computer interface. Such examples illustrate, Pickering argues, both the coevolution of the material, conceptual, and social and the poverty of contextual explanations in the human sciences. Karin Knorr Cetina follows with an analysis of the knowledge-based practices that have become prominent in contemporary knowledge societies, above all in science. She argues that theories that anchor practices in human skills/ habits and conceive practices as routines are unable to give a felicitous analysis of the jagged character of these epistemic practices. She proposes that the 'backbone' of such practices is, instead, a 'relational dynamics' that links subjects and objects. In science in particular, the objects involved are 'epistemic objects' characterized by an incompletion of being and the capacity to unfold indefinitely. Because such objects point toward further explorations and unfoldings, they, together with the libidinal structuring of wanting they determine, govern the advance of practice and the transformation of the subject–object relations at its core.

The final two essays examine the prioritization of practices over individuals. Joseph Rouse begins by distinguishing two conceptions of practice: as regularities of behavior or belief and as arrays of activity that answer to norms of behavior. Opposing Turner's version of the first conception, he explores what normativity looks like as a feature and determinant of practices and plumbs the significance of language within practices. Turning to science studies, Rouse then outlines the philosophical conceptions of language, knowledge, and power that follow from treating human activities (including science) as normative practices. The essay concludes with reflections on the reflexive position of science studies. Charles Spinosa wraps up the volume by examining how individuals do not control the development and fate of practices. Spinosa argues that all practices exhibit general tendencies to their own elaboration regardless of the intentions of their participants, where 'elaboration' means greater refinement along with the addition of new practices to core ones. His essay discusses two possible such general tendencies: one on which elaboration is a discontinuous and decisionistic process (Derrida) and one on which it is the gradual articulation of an implicit telos (Heidegger). Spinosa favors Heidegger's account on the grounds that it offers a better analysis of how practices – in particular, marginal practices – underwrite local stability in social life.

Practice theory is one horizon of present social thought. This introduction has sought to articulate this approach as a loose, but nevertheless definable movement of thought that is unified around the idea that the field of practices is the place to investigate such phenomena as agency, knowledge, language, ethics,[8] power, and science. Despite this shared conviction, practice thought encompasses multifarious and often conflicting intuitions, conceptions, and research strategies. This volume charts some of the diversity in practice thinking about order, the explanation of practices, and various issues tied up with posthumanism. In doing so, it also seeks to demonstrate the increasing power and scope of practice theory.

Notes

This introduction has been greatly improved by the comments of Harry Collins, Bert Dreyfus, Karin Knorr Cetina, Joe Rouse, and Steve Turner.

1　Wittgenstein, of course, does not use an expression translatable as the count noun 'practices'. His usage of *Sprachspiele* simply points toward the phenomenon of practices. Dreyfus's and Taylor's views, incidentally, are deeply informed by Heidegger (1978).

2　For a discussion of the impact of Bourdieu's and Giddens's work, see Ortner (1984).

3　Examples of (1) are Bourdieu (1977, 1990), Giddens (1979, 1984), and Rouse (1996b). Examples of (2) include Swidler's (1986) account of culture as practice (as opposed to belief, idea, or value) and Boltanski and Thévenot's (1991) analysis of justification as practices.

4　For discussions of the implications of Wittgenstein's remarks for norms and rules as determinants of practices, see Stern (1994), Barnes (1995: Chapter 2), Pleasants (1996), Schatzki (1996: Chapters 2 and 5), and Bloor (1997).

5　The idea that people are constituted by the incorporation of human bodies into something social is advocated in streams of contemporary thought other than practice theory. For general discussion, see Schatzki and Natter (1996).

6　This thesis unites a broad collection of thinkers, not all practice theorists, for example, Knorr Cetina (1981), Bloor (1983), Hacking (1983), Latour (1987), Lave (1988), Pickering (1992a), and Rheinberger (1997).

7　Cf. Heidegger's (1978) and Mead's (1934) conceptions of the practical meanings of things, Wittgenstein on meaning as use, Mead's gestural account of the origin of language, Lyotard's (1984) and Foucault's (1976) conception of language as discursive practices, and Brandom's (1994) theory of normativity (see Rouse's article in this volume). For some, the priority of practice also means that pragmatics takes precedence over semantics and syntax. Very different examples include Brandom's theory and von Savigny's (1988) account of the social foundation of linguistic meaning.

8　The current introduction has no space to examine how practice notions reinforce the conception of ethics as Hegelian *Sittlichkeit* as opposed to Kantian *Moralität*. See, for example, MacIntyre (1981) and Oakeshott (1992). For conceptions of politics informed by notions of practices consult Oakeshott (1975), Mitchell (1991), and Spinosa, Flores, and Dreyfus (1996).

Part I
Practices and social orders

1 Practice as collective action

Barry Barnes

References to shared practices or to agreement in practice have long figured in the discourse of sociologists, but in recent years they have taken on an enhanced importance. Social systems have been characterized as ongoing, self-reproducing arrays of shared practices, and structured dispositions to generate such practices have been made central to the understanding of social and cultural phenomena of every kind. In extreme extensions of approaches of this kind, it may even be argued that as far as the sociologist is concerned practice is all there is to study and describe. An unkind account of this development might regard 'practice' as part of the debris produced by the disintegration of Marxism, a concept carried by refugee theorists who have found new homes in various 'post-Marxist' forms of sociology and social theory. But a much kinder account of the basis of the current interest in practice can be given, and should indeed be accepted. Accounts of societies as practices may be regarded as attempts to remedy the technical deficiencies of the idealist forms of theory that hitherto were dominant in this context.

One of the central tasks of theory in the social sciences is to specify what distinguishes the members of a culture or a collective from outsiders, and on what basis they sustain orderly activities and relationships amongst themselves. Often this is seen as equivalent to identifying what members have in common, or what they share with each other and not outsiders. One approach is to describe the shared theories, ideas, beliefs or abstractly specified rules or norms that allegedly 'govern' their behavior. Two major difficulties are routinely associated with this approach. One is that ideas, beliefs, norms, and so forth are conceived of as being internal to individuals, and hence as invisible entities, all descriptions of which are bound to be highly conjectural. The second is the fact that these entities almost invariably serve as the basis of questionable passive actor theories of order and agreement: the entities are presumed to have fixed and definite implications, which those who cleave to them are obliged to enact. In contrast, to insist that the bedrock of all order and agreement is agreement in practice is to cite something public and visible, something that is manifest in what members do. Moreover, accounts of order and agreement that refer to practice presume not passive actors but active members, members who reconstitute the system of shared practices by drawing upon it as a set of resources in the course of living their lives. It is now generally recognized that accounts of this kind are more satisfactory empirically than passive actor theories.[1]

I am myself in sympathy with the turn to 'practice' I have just described, and in particular with the implied reaction against idealism. But for all its merits the relevant literature remains unsatisfactory, even in the most elementary respects. It fails to make clear just what social practices are. And its vision of the scope and power of 'theories of practice' is nowhere adequately justified. Mindful that this is the first contribution to the volume, the argument here will focus on these elementary issues. It will seek to set out just what a shared practice consists in. It will emphasize that no 'theory of practice' can be a sufficient basis for an understanding of human behavior, or even that part of it which is orderly and routine. But it will conclude by showing that a correct understanding of the nature of shared practices is necessary notwithstanding, if that is our goal.

Examples of practices

The overall argument of this paper leads to clear recommendations concerning how shared practices should be understood and defined. But people may agree to differ on matters of verbal definition, when nothing substantial has been shown to be at stake. Hence it is best to begin not with definitions but with examples, with exemplary instances that almost everyone is likely to accept as instances of practices. Consider then, as a first example, vegetarianism. This particular example nicely points up the difficulties that arise from treating shared activity as 'governed' by ideas or theories. Vegetarians do not employ scientific experts or modern laboratory techniques to separate the animal and the vegetable. Nor does one vegetarian community necessarily follow the same dietary prohibitions as another. Nor is it possible to provide an algorithm for vegetarianism, as it is expressed in any particular vegetarian community: vegetarianism is not a matter of behaving in ways that can be exhaustively specified by abstract verbal rules. Nonetheless vegetarianism is routinely recognizable as coherent social activity; we encounter it as custom and practice, and acknowledge that membership of a specific vegetarian community will involve acceptance of its distinctive customs and shared practices.

As a second example let us turn to an esoteric technical activity. Acupuncture is now routinely employed in Western countries as a way of achieving anesthesia, in dentistry for example. Consider that dentists may share the practice of acupuncture, pass it on to trainees as a skill, and yet have no elaborated verbal theory of what it is or how it works. Here is a nice example for those who would define practice in contrast with theory, seen as no more than a rationalizing gloss laid upon it, as it were. In its move from the context of its development into Western medicine, acupuncture lost its theoretical baggage and acquired a different overlay of glosses. Or so they might wish to say. For there is an alternative conception, according to which acupuncture is now two different practices, two different bundles of practical activity and linguistic activity, one Western one Eastern, each of which may now develop and grow in different directions.

Finally let us take an example from a military context. Consider the members of a company of cavalry. They too might be said to be the possessors of a shared practice: manifest in their riding, in their use of weapons, and generally in the business of mounted combat. Such practices may be acquired through an extended military training and sustained and developed as part of a military culture transmitted from generation to generation. The reason for the choice of this example will become clear later. For the moment, simply note that to master the practice of mounted combat in a cavalry company is to participate in something done by a group.

I shall rely heavily on these examples in what follows, but whilst ostension will remain my favored method of addressing practices it may be worth supplementing it with a rough and ready verbal statement. Let practices be socially recognized forms of activity, done on the basis of what members learn from others, and capable of being done well or badly, correctly or incorrectly. This is a very broad description, but it nonetheless fails to encompass many ways of understanding practices encountered in the literature and it may prove useful for just that reason.

On the scope of theories of practice

If we move on now, and use the examples to explore what accounts of practice can and cannot do, we shall at the same time become more familiar with practices and with the problems involved in describing them adequately. As Ted Schatzki has remarked (this volume), practice is now frequently identified as 'the primary generic social thing.' Indeed it is sometimes said to be the only social thing. And there are 'theories of practice' wherein this assertion plays an essential role, and its oxymoronic character seems to go wholly unremarked. Perhaps it is typical of newly introduced theories that exaggerated claims are made for their scope. In any event, it is important to recognize that exaggeration is involved here, and that a more modest account of the scope of 'theories of practice' must be accepted. In particular, it must be recognized that: (a) no simple either/or contrast can be made between 'theory' and 'practice'; (b) no indefeasible distinction can be established between visible external practices and invisible, internal states; (c) any attempt to give a satisfactory description of social life must make reference to much else besides practice; and (d) practice does not account for its own production and reproduction.

Let us take the four points in order. The acupuncture example is a good basis for dealing with the first point. It beautifully illustrates the flaw in any view which places theory prior to practice and sees the latter as somehow 'implied by' the former. But whilst it is indeed important that the sticking-in of needles is not seen purely as the expression of a theory of the body, as an effort to balance ying and yang in the patient for example, it is equally wrong to invert the relationship. The practice of acupuncture is not the sticking-in of needles without thought. The practice should be treated as involving thought and action together, and in so far as this is the case, embodied theory, as it were, is a part of practice itself. This, of course, is a standard point, but it is an important one. Indeed, if the practice of acupuncture is understood in this way it will serve also as a reminder of the way that agreement in practice characterizes collectives in many other esoteric technical fields, including even the 'pure' natural sciences. Thomas Kuhn's identification of scientific paradigms as the crucial foci of agreement in scientific communities is consistent with this. Paradigms are not theories but practices, 'accepted examples of actual scientific practice – examples which include law, theory, application and instrumentation together; they are examples selected as model achievements, ways of solving problems known to work in one case and available to guide practice in other cases' (Kuhn 1970: 10). In operating on the basis of a shared paradigm scientists in a given field agree in their practice. It is perfectly possible for them to press forward cooperatively on the basis of this agreement, whilst being in radical disagreement with each other at the level of 'philosophy' or in their abstract theoretical ideas.

With regard to the second point, it is a great virtue of accounts of social practices that they are based on something observable. But it is important not to be tempted into a positivist or phenomenalist or behaviorist justification of them. Practices are forms of action, and all the familiar arguments about the difference between action and behavior are relevant here. Descriptions of social life as practice are, in the last analysis, as 'theory laden' as any other descriptions. It is worth pointing out also, indeed it is probably the more important point, that ordinary members take a theoretical perspective in orienting to each other's practice. When one member successfully engages in a practice, what this invariably betokens to others is the possession of a competence or a power. The inference from performance to capacity is made. Thus, the membership as a whole conies to know itself not as a performing membership but as a membership with the power to perform – as, that is, a set of competent members. And the use of these two last words indicates that many social theorists themselves see social life in much the same way, not merely as members doing things but as members able to do a range of things. In the last analysis, talk of practices is talk of powers – and all the difficulties associated by theories of social power have to be faced by accounts of practices.[2]

To engage in a practice is to exercise a power. This equivalence is worth bearing in mind in considering the third point made above. Powers are exercised at need by active agents; they are, as it were, switched on and off as expediency or inclination or whatever else requires. Practices are enacted in the same way. Or rather, what is called the active exercise of a power may equally be called the enactment of a practice. But a whole range of further sociologically interesting factors are material to understanding the exercise of powers. A cavalry charge is a fearful unleashing of powers. It may unfold as a practiced routine, a manifestation of a shared social practice, but the target of the charge and the signal that unleashes it are further features of equal sociological interest. Both these things are extrinsic to the 'shared practice' itself, and need to be understood by reference to 'members' knowledge' in a broader sense. The company of cavalry knows that it should charge on the signal of its commanders.[3] The commander selects the target of the charge mindful partly of the lie of the land and the enemy dispositions, partly of an accepted and authoritative body of knowledge of military strategy, partly of memories of past charges. Notice too how the company of cavalry may stand fast and not charge at all, and even conceivably decide the course of the battle by standing fast, by its latent powers being taken into account in the calculations of the commanders of other military formations and thereby affecting their strategies. This indeed is a nice symbol of the necessity of references to knowledge and experience in making sense of social activities.

A charge of cavalry must be understood not as the mere enactment of a practice, but as its knowledgeable, informed and goal-directed enactment. It is necessary to make reference to more than practice itself in order to understand it. It is true that idealist writers have sometimes overlooked the role of practice altogether in contexts like this, and described military engagements purely by reference to the ratiocination of generals (and their outcomes by reference to the 'genius' of one and the 'stupidity' of another). But to react against excesses of this kind by giving attention exclusively to the role of practice is merely to indulge in another form of excess. It amounts to an ungrounded prejudice in favor of know-how at the expense of know-that, in favor of skill and competence at the expense of information and representation. In the vocabulary of psychology, wherein valuable empirical studies of both exist, it amounts to an exclusive concentration on procedural memory and a corresponding neglect of descriptive memory. Both of these forms of memory need to be taken into account; both are socially structured and both are implicated in social action.

The same example will serve as the basis for the discussion of the fourth and final point. Practices are often cited in order to explain things, including notably their own enactment. It may be said, for example, that something is done because it is traditionally done, or routinely done, or done because it is part of the practice of the collective. The problem of why human beings should enact the practice is thereby completely glossed over. It is as if the cavalry has to charge, twice a week perhaps, simply because it can charge, as if there is something automatic and compelling about the enactment of practices which makes it unnecessary to consider what moves or inspires the human beings involved.[4]

What are shared practices?

Practices are enacted by people, and simply because of this they are an insufficient basis for an understanding of the ongoing pattern of social life that they constitute. It is always necessary to ask what disposes people to enact the practices they do, how and when they do; and their aims, their lived experience and their inherited knowledge will surely figure amongst the factors of interest here. But it is not just a matter of asking what contingencies incline people to enact, or not to enact, practices, as if they exist like tools in a toolbox and it is merely a matter of explaining when and why one or another is picked out. The relationship of practices and people is far more intimate and profound than this. The next part of the discussion is concerned precisely with this relationship, but to appreciate what it involves it is necessary first to probe more deeply into the nature of shared practices.

An extended and detailed analysis by Stephen Turner (1994) has high-lighted the difficulties that have to be faced in this context. If there are shared practices, then what is it that is shared? Turner confronts us with the horns of a dilemma: is a shared practice a single object (an essence, it is tempting to say, although Turner does not), when the problem of how the object/essence is transmitted and disseminated pure and unchanged must be faced; or is shared practice merely an aggregate of separate individual elements, when reference to practice ceases to have any fundamental theoretical interest? Turner notes that sociological theorists are especially prone to treat shared practice as a unity, a single object. They explain other things by reference to a shared practice conceived of as a real collective entity. Durkheim and Sumner are cited as examples here, and Turner emphatically rejects their collectivist approach, which speaks of 'society' or 'custom' or 'the mores' as a single object with causal powers. There is neither ground nor evidence for belief in the existence of shared practice as a unitary object, says Turner, and no theory of cultural transmission and dissemination which allows us to understand how such an object could pass from person to person unchanged. What we refer to as shared practice is actually a composite: it is constituted of so many separate individual habits, habits sufficiently alike for us to get along together on the basis of them, but individual entities nonetheless, and not collective ones. Hence, references to practice should be discontinued and social theory should focus instead upon habit and habituation.

Turner's book offers a radically individualistic critique of social theory that would have profound implications if accepted. It would not just be 'shared practice' that belonged in the waste bin; 'tradition,' 'form of life,' 'habitus,' 'tacit knowledge,' and many other 'collective' terms would have to be con-signed there as well, or so we are told. Nonetheless, we should surely accept Turner's first claim. Shared practice cannot be treated as a single real object in the usual sense; certainly it cannot be treated as an essence. It can no more be treated in this way than can 'rule' or 'norm' or 'ideas'; the familiar formal arguments against essentialism in relation to these entities will extend routinely to shared practice. Indeed, it is easy to illustrate the problems here by direct reference to examples. Consider the shared practice of our company of cavalry. What happens if the horses, or the saddles, or the swords of the members are all switched around? A diminution of fighting power is the immediate consequence, at least temporarily. For each member is attuned to a particular sword and a specific horse: the 'shared practice' of the company is apparently made up of different skills and competences, differently manifested in different performances. References to shared practice here seem to mask a motley of distinct individual capabilities.

Turner suggests that the relevant individual capabilities here are habits, and that social theory should concern itself not with practice but with habits and habituation. He is not, of course, referring to addictive habituation here, of the kind induced by cigarette smoking or heroin injection. Rather, he is speaking of things that people have learned by repetition so that they can do them smoothly, easily and competently. Habits are individual competences for Turner, not individual compulsions. His objective is to redescribe 'shared practice' as clusters of individual habits which, precisely because they are individual, all differ in detail from each other. He wants us to see routine practice at the collective level as just so many distinct individuals behaving in their own habituated ways, ways sufficiently similar through shared teaching to fit with each other for given purposes, but nonetheless distinct and different.

It is surely correct that a very careful detailed account of 'shared practice' would reveal all kinds of differences in individual behavior. And a first response to this could well be the thought that Turner's account must be correct, that shared practice can actually be nothing more than habituated individual behavior. Recourse to examples, however, quickly reveals the inadequacies of this radically individualistic approach. Consider some routine activity that might, prima facie, be counted part of the 'shared practice' of a company of cavalry, say the routine practice of riding in formation. Can this be reconceptualized as a collage of individual actions, each intelligible as an expression of habit? Certainly, references to the habituated skills of individuals will contribute to an understanding of the routine practice: without the relevant individual skills riding in formation is unlikely to be possible. On the other hand, the mere following of habit is most unlikely to result in performance of the routine. A plausible account of riding in formation must surely refer to calculation, and even creative imagination, on the part of riders actively involved in the business of remaining coordinated with each other: constant adjustment and modification of habit will be required of them to make this possible. We must imagine individual riders taking account of variations in terrain, monitoring the actions of others and adapting accordingly, even perhaps imagining future scenarios, for example the consequences of a possible slow-down at the front as a slope is encountered, well before they occur. Only in this way will coordination be retained and a shared practice enacted. Only in this way will a social power be exercised. The successful execution of routines at the collective level will involve the overriding and modification of routines at the individual level. Practice at the collective level is not a simple summation of practices at the individual level (habits). Shared practice is, as the ethnomethodologists say, a collective accomplishment.

It might be objected that the example cited is not an example of routine practice at all, that by definition something is routine only when it involves no active calculative intervention and proceeds automatically. But this would be a perverse definition. Scarcely anything (routinely) regarded as routine at the collective level could plausibly be made out as routine on this basis. Next to nothing of the 'routine practice' of a collective could be so described. (Indeed it is interesting also to reflect that scarcely anything in the way of routine individual behavior could be so described. Even at this level a distinction must be marked between the automatic/habitual and the routine: starting the day with coffee, walking down the stairs to the street, catching the bus to work, may be daily routines for an individual, but their accomplishment will require constant active modification of what comes automatically or habitually. 'Habit' actually faces all the problems identified by Turner as confronting 'shared practice.')

Turner's argument merits detailed attention because it articulates a very widely held conception of the basic difference between individualist/psychological and collectivist/sociological approaches to social activity. The former speaks of aggregates of separate individuals and individual actions; the latter refers to unitary collective entities. A standard exemplification of the difference is the contrast between rational choice theory and theories of societies as systems of social norms. Indeed many theorists are likely to think of this contrast when they read Turner, and see the horns of his dilemma as akin to these two alternative forms of theory. But this very widely held conception is in truth a misconception, which fails to grasp the nature of a properly sociological approach to social life. The horns of Turner's dilemma are merely alternative expressions of a fundamentally individualistic mode of thought. In the explicitly individualistic view of practice as diversity, there are so many independent individuals moved by habits. In the alternative allegedly 'collectivist' view of practice as a unity there are so many independent individuals moved by a single object or essence. Neither view can throw light on a simple collective routine like riding in formation. What is required to understand a practice of this kind is not individuals oriented primarily by their own habits, nor is it individuals oriented by the same collective object; rather it is human beings oriented to *each other*. Human beings can ride in formation, not because they are independent individuals who possess the same habits, but because they are interdependent social agents, linked by a profound mutual susceptibility,[5] who constantly modify their habituated individual responses as they interact with others, in order to sustain a shared practice.

In formulating the horns of his dilemma Turner overlooked this genuinely sociological way of understanding human activity, just as it has been overlooked in many other contexts of debate. As Zygmunt Bauman has rightly complained, far too many theorists have contrasted the individual and the societal and forgotten altogether about the social (1989 p. 179). Once this lapse is remedied it is possible to move to an adequate understanding of shared practices. They are indeed not stable unitary essences, but neither are they clusters of habitual individual actions. Shared practices are the accomplishments of competent members of collectives. They are accomplishments readily achieved by, and routinely to be expected of' members acting together, but they nonetheless have to be generated on every occasion, by agents concerned all the time to retain coordination and alignment with each other in order to bring them about. Although they are routine at the collective level, they are not routine at the individual level. This is why there is point in referring to a practice as the shared possession of a collective. (There is a sense, of course, in which the shared practice imputed here is a reification, derived from performances all accomplished slightly differently in varying conditions and circumstances; but it is a useful reification and a harmless one, akin to such useful notions as 'skill,' for example, at the individual level.)

It might be objected that a great deal has been made of a single, possibly atypical example, that of cavalry riding in formation, and that there is a need to check on the scope of the argument. The first thing to note by way of reply here is that examples of shared practices collectively executed, like riding in formation, are legion: they include fighting together, hunting together, sailing together, singing together, even, in the present-day world, doing science together. No wholly individualistic account will succeed in accounting for these examples. Individual habits will diverge over time, however rigorously they are initially inculcated, and cannot in any case account for the constant coordination of actions that is evident in examples of the routine practice of an interacting collective.

There are, however, many practices that are carried out solo. Acupuncture is normally administered by a single dentist. A vegetarian meal can be eaten alone. How is this distinct class of practices to be addressed? The answer proposed here is that they should not be treated as a distinct class at all: the need is to see these examples as just like the example of riding in formation. If riding in formation is an example nicely designed to expose the limitations of individualism, these further examples will serve to reveal those limitations as universal ones manifest in all its applications.

Both riding in formation and acupuncture are practices learned from other people, in these instances from fellow occupants of specific occupational roles. And in both instances learning continues after the initial acquisition of 'competent member' status, as part of the business of participation in practice itself. It is part of the nature of a shared practice that learning what it is and enacting it are inseparable. This is one reason why shared practices change. The cavalry company gets better at riding in formation as it rides, even to the extent perhaps that what it counts as riding in formation changes and last year's adequate efforts are this year accounted failures and causes for concern. Shared practices like acupuncture develop similarly, so that acupunctural techniques change over time and what counts as the administration of acupuncture changes. Not every well-intentioned prod with a needle is acupuncture: some prods fall outside the practice, some are more or less adequate expressions of it, some few may be so remarkable that they play major roles in extending existing conceptions of what the practice is.[6]

Thus although acupuncture is individually administered it is administered as acupuncture by a member who, in realizing that shared practice, has to be sensitive to what other practitioners are doing. The acupuncturist must interact with fellow practitioners, and be both cognizant of and disposed to move in the direction of their practice in order to be a practitioner herself. It is only through the interaction of a membership characterized by mutual intelligibility and mutual susceptibility that something identifiable as shared practice can be sustained, and its correct enactment distinguished from what is defective or incompetent. Indeed we might use this as a neat way of distinguishing habit and practice: habit is not enacted well or badly, but practice is. Thus the difference between riding in formation and administering acupuncture is only the contingent one that the necessary interactions for the maintenance of practice are more concentrated and immediately apparent in the former case. Acupuncturists we might say merely operate in a more spread-out mode than cavalry.

It is, of course, when practice is manifest in the actions of isolated individuals that individualistic misconceptions of what is involved are most plausible. Not only habit-individualism but rule-individualism, norm-individualism, and other idealist forms of individualism, are deployed to describe what is involved. All alike are unsatisfactory. Individuals who privately follow rules, for example, will be liable to diverge in their practice over time just as individuals who privately follow habit will. Rules can never be sufficiently informative or well exemplified to keep instances of rule-following behavior relevantly identical in all the diverse situations wherein rules are followed. Only agents actively concerned to modify their idiosyncratic rule-following activities appropriately are able to sustain a shared sense of what it is to follow a rule. Whatever is accounted agreement in the following of a rule is produced by the membership that follows it, not by 'the rule itself.'[7]

Thus, in conclusion, we can see that the adoption even of an apparently simple and anodyne account of social life as practice has profound theoretical implications. These are well brought out by considering Turner's challenging criticisms of 'theories of practice.' Not only does Turner demolish a number of shoddy examples of such theories, much more importantly he allows us to see that no invocation of 'shared practice,' however carefully conceived, is compatible with individualism. An individualist will readily perceive the merits of such a contribution. But an anti-individualist may also be thankful for it. From that perspective, Turner demonstrates that the notions of 'shared practice' and 'agreement in practice' can only be defended as components in a genuinely sociological account of social life, one wherein they feature as accomplishments of those human beings collectively engaged in the task of sustaining them. Such human beings cannot be understood as independent calculative individuals; they stand revealed in their practice as profoundly interdependent, mutually susceptible social agents.

Notes

1   The contribution of ethnomethodology has been decisive here. See Garfinkel (1967) and Heritage (1984). Among the conventional sociological theories to build upon their work is that of Giddens (1984).

2   What a membership is able to do as a matter of routine practice is a tolerable first-order description of its power, i.e. of the power constituted in and as it (Barnes 1988). It is interesting to note here that the social power of a membership typically greatly exceeds the sum of the powers or capacities inherent in members considered as independent individuals, because those individual powers may be combined and coordinated to constitute what otherwise would be nonexistent powers or capacities. This is why the old zero-sum theory of social power has long been discredited. Power is emergent out of order: being a variable dependent on the degree and nature of the order in the collective it cannot be treated as a fixed quantity which can only be concentrated at one point or be put at the discretion of one member by being drawn off from another point or removed from the discretion of other members. Thus, social power is not so many individual powers or capacities separately accounted. It is powers or capacities collectively constituted and visibly expressed in the ongoing routine practice of the membership. In the most profound sense, it is shared practice.

3   The power of the commander to instigate the charge is a consequence of the distribution of knowledge across the army. See Barnes (1988) for a discussion of 'power over' of this kind as related to a distribution of self-referring knowledge – knowledge, incidentally, which cannot be rendered as practice.

4   There are accounts at the most general 'macro' level of social theory that apparently circumvent this problem (Giddens 1984). They emphasize the general dependence of members on the existing repertoire of practices in their society. Members may have innumerable objectives and interests, and very many different beliefs and theories, but whatever their objectives and whatever their beliefs about how to attain them, they will have to draw on that existing repertoire. There is nothing else. Hence the system of practices will in effect reproduce itself by being drawn upon, and this can confidently be predicted without any knowledge of what prompts the specific actions wherein it is drawn upon. Its very existence will indeed account for its continuation: practice will account for practice. This argument, however, is hard to square with the uncontroversial observation that the repertoire of practices changes over time. This evident mutability clearly implies that practices do not self-reproduce, and that to the extent that they are reproduced this must be understood by reference to contingencies external to practices, arguably contingencies to do with the human beings who reproduce them.

5   In this paper it suffices to speak of the interdependence of social agents. Elsewhere I insist that this interdependence takes the form of mutual susceptibility and is *causal*. The link must be made causally, rather than via reason, because it is necessary to account for coordinated understanding as well as coordinated action, and links mediated by reason (i.e. verbal communications rationally addressed) presume coordinated understanding and cannot occur until it exists. See Barnes (1995, 2000).

6   A more satisfactory exposition of these points is part of MacIntyre's brilliant discussion of practices (1981). His definition of 'practice' is, however, much narrower than the one adopted here to suit the needs of the present paper and this is why I have not made use of his highly distinctive but wonderfully insightful account.

7   The argument against 'practice individualism' in this paper parallels familiar arguments against 'rule individualism' and on behalf of collectivist accounts of rules (Wittgenstein 1958; Kripke 1982; Bloor 1997). Rule collectivism is a view I myself advocate, for example, in Barnes (1995). It is a view that follows naturally from a finitist understanding of the nature of rules and meanings, such as that given in Barnes et al. (1996).

2 Human practices and the observability of the 'macro-social'

Jeff Coulter

Garfinkel's remarkably innovative vision of a mode of sociological analysis he termed 'ethnomethodology'[1] has in recent years become detached from its historical relationship to key issues in social theory, in large measure due to the success of the technical field of 'conversation analysis' which owes its genesis to many of his theoretical contributions. However, an abiding issue within ethnomethodology broadly conceived has been the nature of social order and social organization and the appropriate methods for investigating the properties of these phenomena. Among the primary problems confronted by contemporary social theorists has been the development of an adequate conceptual framework for the depiction of the nature of 'macro-social' phenomena. I submit in this essay that various theses advanced within ethnomethodology permit us to cast this issue in a novel fashion and enable us to approach some viable solutions to the problems which are generated by contemplations of the nature of macro-social phenomena and their relationship(s) to quotidian human conduct.

The 'micro–macro' linkage problem, as it is called in contemporary sociological theory,[2] is an issue which requires intensive logical analysis. However, notwithstanding various current treatments which it has received, I believe that a proper logical solution has not (yet) been forthcoming, and if it has, I am not aware of it. It is the purpose of this essay to argue for what I shall claim is a contribution to the solution of the core problems. Identifying what constitute the 'core problems' will itself require detailed discussion. In my view this must involve, and in the first instance, an analysis of the ontological problems arising out of a consideration of the nature of macro- (as well as micro-) social phenomena, from the solution of which significant methodological implications may be derived. I have visited this issue before,[3] although this earlier treatment was almost certainly considered (by those whom it sought to engage) as merely a reiteration of what was then taken to be a conventional 'ethnomethodological' position. In what follows, I shall advance a series of arguments designed to show that the proper route to a solution to the 'micro–macro' relationship problem is to be found in a systematic elucidation of the logic of our ordinary practices (including our communicative practices) in our ordinary life circumstances. If this means that we must revisit the earlier 'ethnomethodological' themes, then all I can say is: better late than never.

'Macro-social' phenomena

Reflecting upon the results of their intellectual–historical investigation of the concept of 'society,' itself in the classical traditions of sociology, Frisby and Sayer concluded that:

> To the question, then, 'Does sociology need to ground itself in a concept of society?' an empirical answer would have to be resoundingly in the negative. Sociology can apparently get by perfectly well without society. Indeed a more than plausible case can be made for saying that socio-logical knowledge has progressed to the extent that the discipline has at last liberated itself from fruitless speculation on society as such – however conceived – and turned its attention to the empirical study of *real instances of human sociation*.[4]

While a good case may be made for this assessment of classical sociological work in relation to 'society' as its putatively central phenomenon of study, it is abundantly clear that many other 'macro categories' enjoy a rich life in the research and theorizing of contemporary sociologists. Many of these modern macro-level inquiries do not lend themselves generally to description as 'empirical stud[ies] of real instances of human sociation' in Frisby and Sayers's terms. What are the putative 'macro-social' phenomena within modern sociological discourse? Any list of such phenomena would be bound to include at least the following: states, nations, governments, legal systems, health systems, corporations, firms, banks, universities, hospitals, armed forces, gangs, crowds, revolutions, social classes, and the like. Efforts to conceptualize modern (usually industrial) societies as holistic 'social systems' may have waned since Parsons (with the exception of some of the 'neofunctionalists' such as Luhmann and Alexander with their somewhat diverse emphases, as well as the neo-Marxist tradition with its sustained treatment of capitalism as a 'system'), but there is still much study of the 'stratification system.' Also, analyses of bureaucracy, large-scale social organizations, the state, the military, the capitalist market (whether construed nationally – or internationally, especially after Mandel and Wallerstein, among others) abound. The 'macro' level of inquiry is alive and well, and takes many forms.

One long-standing tradition of 'macro'-level analysis in sociology is the 'comparative historical' approach, which traces its roots to the comparative institutional analyses of Max Weber. Often considered a classical proponent of 'methodological individualism,' Weber's actual investigations show clearly that his central category of ('multicausal') analysis was not 'the individual' actor, but the concept of the *Träger* (the bearer or 'carrier' of patterned action orientations). In our reanalysis of the micro–macro linkage issue, we shall have occasion to return to this concept, albeit in a somewhat different sense than that employed by Weber. For Weber, as Kalberg has commented, 'carriers stand at the very center of his multicausality; he repeatedly calls attention to them.'[5] Thus, in giving his account of the emergence of the distinctively 'formally rational' capitalist social organization of the Northern European countries, Weber focused upon the 'carriers' of the doctrines of ascetic Calvinist Protestantism. In discussing the persistence of Confucianism for two millennia in China, he stresses the role of the patrimonial bureaucracy and the literati stratum; and in accounting for the persistence of Hinduism in India, he focuses upon the Brahmins as its carrier stratum.[6] Rather than postulate mere 'material conditions' (in Marxist fashion or disengaged 'ideational elements' as moving forces in history [after Hegel]), Weber identifies the living, human embodiments of concrete action orientations in specific groups of people. These groups range from named individuals, (such as, *inter alia*, Franklin and Baxter in *The Protestant Ethic* thesis) to concretely identifiable, 'self-conscious' social 'strata' (such as political parties, churches, sects, states, or voluntary enterprises comprising individuals too numerous – and frequently too distant in history – to identify enumeratively). Kalberg observes that in Weber's accounts:

> The doctrine of early Islam was deeply penetrated by the status ethic of its original carrier stratum: a knightly order of disciplined crusaders and conquerors. Christianity's belief system was shaped significantly in Antiquity by its original carriers: itinerant artisan journeymen, petty-bourgeois merchants, and more generally, urban civic strata.[7]

For Weber, 'methodological individualism' meant eschewing the reification of 'structural entities' by referring whatever 'macro categories' were being used to their actual bearers, even though these were not always nameable nor enumerable. Weber warned against the proclivity to reify structural concepts in sociology in the early passages of his magnum opus, *Economy and Society*. Discussing the categories of 'state,' 'nation,' 'corporation,' 'family,' and 'army corps,' he wrote:

> These concepts of collective entities which are found both in common-sense and in juristic and other technical forms of thought, have a meaning in the minds of individual persons, partly as of something actually existing, partly as something with normative authority. This is true not only of judges and officials, but of ordinary private individuals as well . . . Thus, for instance, one of the important aspects of the existence of a modern state, precisely as a complex of social interaction of individual persons, consists in the fact that the action of various individuals is oriented to the belief that it exists or should exist, thus that its acts and laws are valid in the legal sense.[8]

A little further on, he remarks that:

> It is vital to be continually clear about this in order to avoid the 'reification' of these concepts. A 'state,' for example, ceases to exist in a sociologically relevant sense whenever there is no longer a probability that certain kinds of meaningfully oriented action will take place.[9]

We shall explore the ramifications of this point of view further, and take note of certain revisions to it, which our analysis will be found to entail.

In a related tradition of sociological inquiry, the 'micro' level has long been characterized as the domain of the many modes of analysis of social (inter-personal) interaction, from the quantitative variety of 'social-psychological' studies to the (Chicago-inspired) ethnographic analyses of everyday inter-actions in diverse settings. Blumer's programmatics for what he called 'symbolic interactionism' contained several attacks upon conventional macro-level modes of analysis, especially the practice of 'operationalisation' of ordinary 'macro' concepts and the depiction of domains of social life as 'variables.'[10] For most symbolic interactionists, all 'macro' phenomena are either abstractions from, or actually consist in, patterns of social interaction between people.[11] Some of the more 'radical' among them would argue that 'macro categories' of analysis are essentially linked to Durkheimian or Marxist-inspired modes of structural investigation and theorizing, and are occasionally claimed to be nothing more than 'reifications' (i.e., fallacious concretizations). No existential or ontological status is to be accorded to any 'macro categories,' since all that exists sociologically is said to be social interaction in all of its forms. 'Macro-social' phenomena are illegitimate objectifications of interactional processes from a strictly sociological point of view, no matter what their status is within the confines of everyday, commonsense reasoning. They would assert that only the micro level exists.

Ethnomethodology has often been located at the 'micro' end of the spec-trum, but this characterization, as I shall argue at some length in this discus-sion, is misleading. Indeed, to the contrary, ethnomethodology's abiding interest in revealing the logic of peoples' practical conduct (including the logic of their everyday reasoning within and about their social environments) can be usefully elaborated so as to undermine the very initial generic dichotomy of 'macro' and 'micro' social phenomena here at issue. Indeed, much of the talk of 'macro-social phenomena,' as emergent from microinteractional processes, strikes me as misplaced. This metaphorical construction presupposes the possibility of a discrete identification of different 'levels' (one level somehow emerging from the [lower?] level), raises more questions than it settles, and obscures an adequate characterization of the various ways in which 'macro' phenomena are actually featured in our social world.

A major step in elucidating this issue is afforded by considering, first, the ways in which people routinely and unproblematically use 'the language of the macro level' in the context of living their lives as practical, social agents. It is, above all, immediately apparent to any user of the ordinary language, that instances of so-called 'macro' phenomena exhibit significant differences between how their properties could be conceptualized, and to what their 'existence' actually amounts. Almost all of the macro categories used by sociologists are ordinary-language concepts: such notions as 'army,' 'bank,' 'state,' 'legal system,' 'class,' 'bureaucracy,' etc., are not (or not in the first instance) technical concepts whose meanings intentionally depart from their vernacular usage.[12] Consequently, inspecting the rules of use of these categories will illuminate the logic of their conceptualization. Emphatically, this is not an effort to avoid the ontological issues in favor of 'linguistic' ones. The issue, as I will argue, is that the examination of members' vernacular ways of conceptualizing 'macro'-social phenomena will be instructive for us in dissolving ontological misconceptions often entertained by theorists (within both 'micro' and 'macro' sociology). By way of this analysis we obtain a clearer view of both the issues which divide 'micro' and 'macro' sociology and of how these may be handled.

The 'observability' of macro phenomena

Because many of our macro-social concepts designate institutions which are linked to geographical/architectural structures (e.g., cities, banks, universities, hospitals, police departments, etc.), an ambiguity can readily arise concerning the ways in which such macro-social phenomena are actually observable in the world of everyday life. There is one sense, of course, in which one may 'see' a city (e.g., by flying over it), a college, a bank, or a hospital (by walking around or through its grounds and inspecting its building[s]) but, sociologically speaking, the social institutions of cities or colleges, companies, or consulates (etc.), are clearly not observable in this way. The tendency has been to envisage macro-social phenomena linked to identifiable material structures as 'contained' by or within such material structures. Once this move is made, however, puzzles arise. For example, in what sense is the 'social institution' itself visible within such material domains as geographical areas and/or architectural structures? What we locate there, after all, are people saying and doing a great variety of things, not all of which remotely instantiate 'city-ness,' 'bank-ness,' or 'university-ness.' It can readily appear as though the symbolic interactionists and methodological individualists are correct to propose that such social structures are abstractions from human interactions of specific sorts, and have no genuinely 'independent existence' as such. This move, however, is made too quickly. Changing the example, for a moment, one can actually observe 'crowds,' 'riots,' 'demonstrations,' 'armies' on the march, 'platoons' on the attack, etc., and these are surely no 'abstractions' from things that people are collectively engaged in. What is it then for a 'nation,' a 'religious order,' a 'city,' a 'university' or a 'bank' to *do* something?

Consider the following: Bill Clinton announces from within the Oval Office of the White House to a gathering of journalists from the international press corps that 'the United States is prepared to invade Haiti unless the junta steps down.' Clearly, these are the words of a single individual, but, under the auspices of the relevant identification categories (rules and circumstances of utterance) it is the United States declaring its policy. There is no polling of 250 million people. To think that this would be necessary, in weighing how it is that action predicates can be assigned to collectivities, is to commit the 'fallacy of large numbers.' Consider, further, Karol Woytyla who asserts (again according to specific rules and in very specifically circumscribed circumstances) that 'the Catholic Church will maintain its historic opposition to abortion.' It is not Woytyla, *per se*, who is declaring this, it is the Church reaffirming/announcing its position. Nor are all of these cases simply ones of individuals acting as 'spokespeople' for their respective institutions. This is a very different identification or membership category, and its associated praxis is governed by quite distinct rules. When the telephone rings and the caller says, 'This is Bay Bank. Are you interested in our new money market account?', the person calling may be Jane Doe, but it is not Jane Doe calling. Although Jane Doe is clearly operating as its representative, it is Bay Bank calling. In not all cases in which one or more people do something logically connected to 'macro structure,' however, is it a matter of their behaving as spokespersons or 'representatives.' Rather, on many occasions, their conduct instantiates that of the relevant macro phenomenon. When Mayor Tom Menino and his financial advisers announce 'the City of Boston is determined to lower property taxes,' and then these same personnel fix the rates and have them officially approved by the relevant ratifying body, this is the City of Boston lowering property taxes. The examples can be ramified. Under specific ranges of circumstances, when certain persons do and/or say specific sorts of things according to specific rules (rules constituting also under what identification auspices their conduct is to be construed – e.g., 'Mayor,' 'President,' 'Pope,' etc.), then these cases instantiate the conduct of macro phenomena. They bring these phenomena to life. They realize them, in *occasioned* ways, such that they (again, recurrently) enter into our lives as part of our structures of relevant orientation. Perhaps these are examples of the kind of roles that Weber would have assigned to his *Träger* in his comparative institutional analyses.

Note, however, that in the case of many macro-social phenomena, such *Träger* are either unavailable or only contestably available as such. (Many of the critics of Weber's own 'Protestant Ethic Thesis' accused him of selectively and, thus, contentiously identifying Calvinism's *Träger*). For example, whose deeds constitute the 'proletariat's' doing something, or the 'bourgeoisie's' having decided to X or to do Y, are matters of quite extensive contention; largely because for these macro concepts there are no formal *Träger*, and no 'formal' spokespeople or representatives. Marx's famous distinction between a '*Klass-an-sich*' and a '*Klass-für-sich*,' exhibits a sensitivity to this issue. For Marx, the transition from the former to the latter is largely a matter of the emergence of collective 'self-consciousness' (and, for Lenin, in the case of the 'proletariat,' the rise of the 'Vanguard Party'). Of course, many groups, collectivities, and institutions in contemporary societies comprise self-membershipping organizations (from the 'Hell's Angels' to the 'SPD,' from the 'Chrysler Motor Corporation' to 'Oxford University,' and from the 'British Medical Association' to the 'Church of Scientology'), with more or less circumscribed but broadly known and subscribed-to rules, credentials, role allocations, and the rest of the familiar apparatus of 'self-conscious' collectivities. Other kinds of collectivities and institutions are nonself-membershipping, in the sense that membership itself is not such as to require or presuppose any actual self-conscious 'self-organization' such as character-izes the various self-membershipping collectivities. These latter would include 'genders,' 'ethnic groups,' 'social classes,' 'nations' (excluding the phenomena of 'naturalization'[13]), 'religions' (excluding the phenomena of 'baptism' or 'conversion'[14]), and so on. In Jayyusi's terms, we confront quite diverse 'social organizations of categorical incumbency'[15] among these different collectivities. How do these distinctions relate to our general theme of the 'praxiological' instantiation of 'macro-social' phenomena?

In order to address this question, we shall have to introduce some aspects of Harvey Sacks's logical analysis of 'membership categorization practices.'[16] This will comprise my major theme in this argument.

Sacks observed that any person is a possible incumbent of an indefinitely large array of equally but alternatively correct identification categories. Thus, a given 'adult male' can be correctly identified – although differentially for diverse purposes and in different contexts – as, alternatively, 'a lawyer,' 'a taxpayer,' 'a Protestant,' 'a liberal,' 'an American,' 'a black [Afro-American],' 'a veteran,' 'a bookworm,' 'a father,' 'a son,' 'a socialite,' a 'member of the middle class,' 'a customer,' 'a divorcé,' and so on. Among the many categories of personal identification are the 'collectivity categories' which may, also differentially, be ascribed to (and on occasion avowed by) people. E.g., 'he's French,' 'she's a Rotarian,' 'they are Moslems,' 'we are members of the faculty,' etc. Sacks drew a crucial distinction, then, between 'categorization' of a person and 'relevantly correct categorization' of a person (or persons), arguing that the satisfaction of criteria of correctness could not suffice to account for any actual case of membership categorization. This is because, for example, as I write this paper, whilst it is in some sense 'formally correct' to classify myself as 'a father' (I do indeed have a biologically related daughter), that could not serve as the operationally relevant identification of me for this setting and for this activity. For this setting and for this activity, I am relevantly categorizable as, *inter alia*, and minimally, 'an academic,' perhaps 'a professor,' 'an intellectual,' or a 'sociologist.' It is *qua* 'sociologist,' etc., but *not qua* 'father,' that I am engaged right now in carrying out this intellectual activity. (Indeed, at least in Anglo-American culture, were you to report that you wit-nessed a 'father' produce a piece of written discourse, it would most naturally be heard to be a report on some kind of religiously relevant literature).

Having sketched the bare essentials of (some of) Sacks's arguments, let us see to what extent they can be brought to bear upon the issue before us: the 'praxiological resolution of the micro–macro issue.' First of all, as we noted earlier, it would only be a gratuitous insistence upon the 'fallacy of large numbers' that might prohibit someone from agreeing that when Karol Woytyla 'asserts Papal doctrine' it is the Catholic Church's position that is enunciated. (No poll of the 600 million-odd practicing Catholics is at issue here.) Provided that his papal incumbency has been legitimately brought about, this relation holds for that sort of activity on his part. Note, of course, the normative element at work here. Some people do and say things expecting to instantiate whole organizations or even whole 'peoples' where their widespread recognized *illegitimacy* either render the claim ambiguous or downright absurd. Recall how long it took for Presidents Nelson Mandela and Yasser Arafat to become widely acknowledged (and not without some continuing dissent) as the 'legitimate leaders' of the defined populations of the black South Africans and Palestinian Arabs respectively. There will, clearly, be contestable and borderline cases, cases fraught with struggle, political, religious, professional, and ethical, in respect of their actual or potential ratifiability. However, none of this gainsays the central point being advanced here: indeed, such instances merely reinforce its cogency. Collectivities have their life in through their praxiological instantiations, and especially through the occasions that make relevant the instantiating membership categories. Thus, it really isn't 'Jane Doe' calling 'Jeff Coulter' when it is 'Bay Bank' calling me, just as it really isn't 'Karol Woytyla' *qua* private citizen who instantiates Catholicism on those occasions when the enunciations are formally produced. Jane Doe, and Karol Woytyla, may say and do a host of things in their lives, but only on occasions bounded by specific sorts of rules do their saying/doings make relevant those categories such as to instantiate the action of a collectivity. Armies can plan *coups d'état*, companies can fix prices, governments can declare wars, and so forth, only insofar as the practices and praxis-relevant identities of persons, sometimes few and occasionally many, are recognizably invocable.

The 'occasional relevance' of the macro-social order

Much of the foregoing will be anathema to theorists who subscribe to 'structuralist' conceptions of the macro-social order, or to modes of sociological model-building we could call 'externalist.' After all, the argument appears to posit nothing at all 'behind' or 'over and above' the properties of situated practices and the praxis-relevant identifications of their agents. Surely, it may be objected, macro-level phenomena 'exist' even when no single member is engaged in any kind of macro-instantiating conduct of the kind discussed here? Is this not merely an 'immanentist' argument?

Suppose that no soldier in a given army engages for an entire day in, e.g., 'saluting,' 'drilling,' 'weapons cleaning,' 'combat maneuvers,' even 'combat' itself, and so on, throughout the entire array of action predicates logically related to the category of 'army.' Would this entail the disappearance or 'dissolution' of the 'army' itself? This seems to be an absurd consequence. However, we may approach a resolution of this issue in the following way.

Consider the case of the 'soldier' who enters a store and becomes, for the purpose of a transaction, a 'customer.' Does this mean that he is no longer a 'soldier'? Or consider the case of the 'soldier' who is off duty and is having a domestic quarrel about his family's finances with his wife. Isn't the 'husband' who is doing the quarreling also, and simultaneously, still a 'soldier' (i.e., an incumbent of a 'macro-level' category – the armed forces, the army, etc.)? Our intuitions are perhaps ambiguous on this issue. What may contribute to confusion is the fact that 'soldiers' (unlike 'husbands' and 'customer') are typically uniformed when behaving under such category auspices, and thus they are incumbents of a restricted class of 'membership categories': those which are routinely 'emblematically assignable,' or 'perceptually recordable' at a glance, so to speak. (Policemen, nuns, hospital physicians, traffic wardens, firemen, etc., would be other instances.) Feminists, likewise, speak of the 'omnirelevance' of gender categories, and some others make this claim for (certain) 'racial' or 'ethnic' categories.

The perceptual assignability of categories, however, does not entail their operational relevance. Unless the perceptually assignable membership category is somehow made or rendered operational in and through specific courses of action/activities, then claims for its relevance are either false or, at best, undecidable. Some psychological theorists are adamant that everything we do is a function of some assignable 'personality type,' but similar arguments apply here as well.[17]

Where does this leave us in respect of the question: 'is a soldier still a soldier when he is (e.g.) a 'customer' or a 'husband,' and, if so, then in what does this identity consist?' This is a tricky issue, but I think that it can be resolved. 'Being' a soldier is a matter of being able legitimately and relevantly to claim such a status, as well as a matter of others being able legitimately and relevantly to invoke it in ascriptive practices. In the first person, it is an issue of a legitimate capacity, which is exhibitable independently from the many other manifestations we could call 'soldiering.' In the sense in which a legitimate capacity can be said to 'exist' independently from any local praxiological exhibition of it, then, in that specific sense, of course, one can be a soldier when off duty, not 'soldiering,' and so on. And, similarly, 'armies' can be said still to 'exist' when no soldier at all is engaged in manifesting army membership or army-relevant practices. Note, however, that being stripped of, or abandoning, the capacity of legitimate claim, if instantiated *en masse*, so to speak, does dissolve – render nonexistent – the 'army' and all of its 'soldiers' (as when an army completely 'demobilizes,' or is forcibly dissolved, after a war). Such a collectivity has its 'existence' in these ways. And so do many others, although not all of them.

The central issue before us, then, is this: in what social circumstances can a (lay or professional) observer/reporter, who respects the logic of social situations, invoke collectivity categories in assigning some such to an agent of an activity? It is to this issue that I shall now direct my attention.

'Category-boundedness' as a constraint upon the 'relevance' of the 'macro level'

In elaborating upon his analysis of the logic of the identification of persons in everyday life, Sacks[18] noted that any universe of human activities or practices may be partitioned into those which are 'categorically bound' to some specific (or restricted set of) membership categories, and those which are 'categorically open' (in the sense that no relevant identity is entailed by the performance of the practice). Thus, for example, we can ascertain the category-bound status of an activity or practice by noting how straightforward it is to make an inference from the characterization of an activity to a characterization of the relevant identity of its 'doer.' The simplest pronoun substitution test will suffice. Consider the following as serious and literal locutions produced in social-communicative relations: 'He sentenced him to ten years' imprisonment,' 'She diagnosed lymphoma,' 'He arrested them for disturbing the peace,' 'She fired him on the spot.' In these cases, one can discern the relevant membership categories which apply to the persons represented purely pronominally in the examples, namely, 'judge,' 'physician,' 'cop,' 'employer,' or their cognates, respectively. Contrast such cases to the following: 'He committed suicide,' 'She interrupted them' and 'He complained about the heat.' No specific identification categories can be inferred in these instances (the pronominal exhibition of gender aside). 'Committing suicide,' 'interrupting' and 'complaining' are categorically open activities. Of course, there are some cases which resist such a clean-cut partitioning, such as, e.g., 'saluting' or 'teaching,' where in many cases the *conventional* ties between saluting and being a military person and between teaching and being a teacher do not constitute ties of strict categorical boundedness, since nonmilitary personnel can salute others (and in various ways) and parents can teach their kids but not be 'teachers,' etc. These complications aside, it is reasonably clear that many practices are quite simply institutional practices, presupposing and/or instantiating the operations of macro-social phenomena, whilst others (most others, in fact) are not. I refer to this as the phenomenon of the 'occasional relevance' of the macro-social level to our everyday lives, and offer it as a sharp contrast to perspectives and modes of theorizing which insist upon the omnirelevance of a macrosociological 'contextualization' for everything we do.

Newspaper reportage[19] is replete with efforts to contrive linkages between macro-social identities and categorically open practices. 'Ex-Green Beret goes on rampage,' 'Black youths loot local video store,' 'Government official caught with prostitute,' and so on, exemplify this form of contrived linkage, where the 'relevance' of the selected categorical identifications is clearly not derivable from criteria of correct identification alone, and is certainly not an invocation of a relationship of 'category boundedness.' In referring to su‿ linkages as 'contrived,' I do not mean to suggest that no relevance whatsoever can be attached to the categories selected to identify the producers of the activities in question. As an account unfolds, efforts may be made (and often enough successfully) to argue for, demonstrate, or portray the possible relevance of the selected categories (as when, e.g., it is revealed that the identification of the 'john' in the 'prostitution' example as a 'Government official' has been made simply on the grounds that he is a 'public figure,' or, more strongly perhaps, on the grounds that the prostitute he has been caught with has connections to a foreign intelligence service, etc.). On the other hand, however, the possibilities for 'gratuitous' linkages remain wide open. For example, the youths who looted the store were indeed 'black,' but they were also, *inter alia*, 'unemployed,' 'homeless' and 'hungry.' These are, exactly, issues within practical sociological reasoning.

In the space allotted to me, I cannot aspire to do justice to the full complexity of the issues which are enjoined when a fresh perspective is adopted for construing the micro–macro linkage issue in the social sciences. I shall, therefore, conclude this essay with some brief, but hopefully suggestive, points, which I believe should be borne in mind when this issue arises in our intellectual work as sociologists and behavioral scientists.

Concluding remarks

Max Weber's 'methodological individualism' and Herbert Blumer's 'symbolic interactionism' both advocated de-reifying solutions to the problem of conceptualizing 'macro-social' phenomena, but neither adequately appreciated the complexity of the grammars of our macro-social concepts. In particular, and notwithstanding their occasional programmatic declarations, neither furnished clear solutions to the problem of the relationship between everyday human conduct and the macro-social order, because neither addressed the fundamental problem of the *relevance* of such concepts/phenomena to the organization of our everyday activities and our practical reasoning about such activities. In particular, an adequate appreciation of the role of the 'macro-order' in our everyday lives reveals that such phenomena are variously instantiated in what we say and do and also that our conduct is by no means omnirelevantly linked to 'macro-level' considerations.

What needs to be addressed in this regard at a later point is the nature and role of 'economic' phenomena, a topic I cannot address in this schematic discussion. A first move in the right direction here is, I believe, a rejection of the notion that 'the economy' is a 'system' of interdeterministic 'parts' which works according to principles that can be discerned in complete ('exogenous') independence of our everyday (economic) practices of monetary reckoning, 'embedded' decision-making, and sundry other contingencies so systematically neglected in economic models of our economic behavior. Developing this argument, however, is something I cannot pursue adequately here.

Notes

Based upon the paper of the same name in *Zeitschrift für Soziologie* 25, October 5, 1996: 337–45.

1 Harold Garfinkel (1967).
2 As this issue is identified in, e.g., Jeffrey Alexander, Bernhard Giesen, Richard Munch, and Neil J. Smelser (eds) (1987). For an earlier discussion of this issue see Randall Collins (1981).
3 Jeff Coulter (1982). In this paper, I argued for the position that the clarification of the nature of 'macro-social' phenomena requires a fuller elucidation of the grammar of macro concepts than has been entertained in the many controversies that have been stimulated by the putative 'macro–micro relationship' problem. For a more recent version of the ethnomethodological approach to the 'problem of linkage' see Hilbert (1992: 189–97). Hilbert remarks that members of society 'themselves orient to a macrostructural order and [. . .] reify and reproduce it in the course of their interpretive work, imposing its reality on each other as they go' (*ibid.*: 192). I shall claim further on that such a view glosses over the essentially occasioned character of the relevance to members of a 'macro' order, as well as imputing a fallacious mode of objectification to us all as practical agents (after all, 'reification' is the fallacy of *misplaced* concreteness).
4 David Frisby and Derek Sayer (1986: 122, emphasis added).
5 Stephen Kalberg (1994: 58).
6 See Kalberg's discussion of these issues in 'Social Carriers' (Kalberg 1994: 58–62).
7 *Ibid.*: 60.
8 Max Weber (1921, 1978 edn: 14).
9 *Ibid.*: 27.
10 Blumer's famous essays on these issues were reproduced in his landmark collection (1969), but they are (regrettably) seldom addressed or discussed these days by modern macro-level analysts in sociology. A more recent, albeit related, conception of the micro–macro linkage is that of Randall Collins, who argues that 'macro' phenomena are 'emergent' from the 'micro-level' interactions between people (Collins 1981). I dispute this 'emergence' thesis in the main text of this essay.
11 John Searle arrives at a very similar position (although he nowhere references the sociological tradition of symbolic interactionism) in his recent book (Searle 1995). On p. 57, Searle writes: 'What we think of as social *objects*, such as governments, money, and universities, are in fact just placeholders for patterns of *activities*. I hope it is clear that the whole operation of agentive functions and collective intentionality is a matter of ongoing activities and the creation of the possibility of more ongoing activities.' We shall see further on that Searle's conception of such macro-social phenomena as comprising merely 'placeholders' for patterns of activities misrepresents the logic of the linkage(s) between human practices and such macro-level phenomena.
12 One of the most succinct articulations of the theoretical consequences of the standpoint is to be found in the paper by Egon Bittner (1965: 239–55). Here, Bittner tracks down some of the implications of treating concepts such as 'organization' and 'bureaucracy' as components of members' everyday practical resources for making sense of various events and for undertaking courses of practical action within which such concepts have their places.
13 It is worth taking note of the form of the word 'naturalization': it is as if the *natural* state of a nation-state citizen were one of a person being born into such a role, with immigrants who are legally permitted to join such a 'nationhood' (and its role of 'national citizen') being somehow rendered 'natural' by the requisite legal and ceremonial procedures.

14 One can, after all, simply be 'brought up as a Catholic (etc.).'
15 See Lena Jayyusi (1984: Chapter 2).
16 Harvey Sacks (1992: Parts 3 and 5). See also Sacks (1972, 1974, 1979) and Sacks and Schegloff (1979).
17 For a fuller discussion of this matter, see my 'Praxis and Personality' in Coulter (1989: Chapter 5).
18 Harvey Sacks (1974).
19 For a fascinating discussion of the utility of such reportage to illuminate many properties of membership categorization practices in everyday life, see Peter Eglin and Stephen Hester (1992: 243–68).

3   Practice mind-ed orders

Theodore R. Schatzki

This essay defends two principal theses: (1) that social order is established within the sway of social practices, and (2) that mind is a central dimension of this 'process.' The first claim is a large one and cannot be fully substantiated here. It primarily serves as a context for developing the second thesis. The path to the latter end, moreover, leads through an analysis of the organization of practices. It is the role that a socially constituted mind plays in structuring practices that certifies practices as the place of social order.

Social order(s)

Building on Talcott Parsons's distinction between factual and normative order, Dennis Wrong (1994) has recently distinguished two problems of order. One, the 'mere' cognitive problem of order, concerns the formation and maintenance of stable, regular, and predictable patterns of behavior. The second, genuine problem of order asks what holds society together, that is, what ensures relatively stable, nonovertly violent human coexistence. This second problem, which Parsons dubbed the 'Hobbesian Problem of Order,' is certainly an important issue. Wrong infelicitously underplays, however, the sort of phenomenon to which the first problem calls attention. For practical solutions to the Hobbesian problem implicate establishment of a deeper type of order, one on a par with, though different from, the ones Wrong builds into the definition of the cognitive problem. This seems true even according to his own position, since nonviolent human coexistence likely requires at least some behavioral regularity.

Should, however, cognitive, or in Parsons's terms 'factual,' order be tied to regularity? Like many thinkers, Wrong assumes that factual order – the disposition and hanging together of entities – is the same as regularity. I suspect he thinks this on the grounds that scientific cognition, if not human cognition generally, proceeds by grasping regularities. In recent decades, however, the assimilation of order and cognition to regularity and its apprehension has come under suspicion. Wittgenstein's (1958: sections 65–79) remarks on family resemblances, like Derrida's (e.g., 1988a) reflections on sameness over difference, exemplify considerations that show that order *per se* cannot be identified with regularity *qua* repetition of the same. Recall Wittgenstein's example: a variety of different activities count as games, and in this sense compose an order, even though what in the world corresponds to this state of order is not the uniform repetition of specific features, but a tangle of samenesses and similarities among the activities involved. Observations such as this suggest that there is more both to the ordering of things and to cognition (including scientific cognition) than regularities and their apprehension.

Wittgenstein's remarks, like those of Derrida and also Foucault (1972) and Kuhn (1977), do not just reveal the inadequacy of the widespread equation of order with regularity. They also disclose the elaborate tangle of resemblance and difference that characterizes the phenomena falling under any given concept of natural language. Their discernment of dispersion at the alleged place of regularity thus suggests that a viable conception of order must accommodate manifolds of variably similar and divergent entities as ordered phenomena. Now, one conception of order that does this while also building upon the complex and variable connections that exist among things, construes order as *arrangements*. An arrangement is a layout of entities in which they relate and take up places with respect to one another. On the basis of this intuitive conception, *social* order can be defined as arrangements of people and the organisms, artifacts, and things through which they coexist. An example is an arrangement of teacher, students, desks, chalkboard, plants, and seeing eye dog in a classroom. In this arrangement, the cited entities relate spatially, causally, intentionally (via mental states), and prefigurationally (roughly, by enabling and constraining one another's activities). They thereby take up positions with regard to one another that combine aspects of these four dimensions. As elements of the arrangement, these entities also possess identities (who someone is) or meanings (what something is). For something's meaning/identity is a function of its relations, just as conversely its relations are a function of its meaning/identity. Teachers, for example, face and lecture to students because of who they all are, just as who they are depends on this orientation and activity. Incidentally, I do not claim that the conception of social order as arrangements is the only definition that both declines to assimilate order to regularity and does justice to dispersion and interconnectedness. In the present context, however, I will not defend it against alternatives.

I tie meaning and identity to social order and focus on them in later remarks because meaning and identity do stead for being. To proclaim the interrelated meanings and identities of arranged items a key component of social order is to declare being central to order. It is to acknowledge, first, that there are no arrangements that are not arrangements of somethings and, second, that social somethings, perhaps somethings in general, *are* somethings as parts of arrangements. This latter thesis does not allege that being derives solely from positionality in arrangements. As will be discussed, being also springs from contexts in which arrangements exist. This thesis simply avers that people (and some organisms) possess identities, and that artifacts, things, organisms, and people bear meanings, as elements of arrangements. To use a familiar Heideggerian example: hammers and nails are tools with which (*inter alia*) to pound and fasten – relative to one another, as part of a nexus of equipment for building and repairing, and in relation to humans who use or know how to use them thus in carrying out building and repair activities. What is more, people perform acts of hammering, prying, gauging, measuring, and so on, and acquire such identities as handymen, Sunday bumblers, and skilled carpenters, both through their use of such tools when repairing and building things and through relations with other people within these and further family, recreational, and employment activities.

Congruent with the widespread attention lavished in the past century on meaning *qua* founding dimension of social existence, a variety of contemporary thinkers have focused on the order–meaning–being axis in discussing social order (though their texts often do not mention order by name). The following two examples help prepare the ground for the discussion of practices in the second and third sections. In *Hegemony and Socialist Strategy* (1985: Chapter 3), Ernesto Laclau and Chantal Mouffe define discourses as totalities of systematically and interrelatedly meaningful actions, words, and things.[1] As an example, they cite the builder and assistant example from the second paragraph of Wittgenstein's *Philosophical Investigations*. The discourse described in this paragraph is composed of a variety of building stones, a limited repertoire of words that, for example, designate these stones, and the actions of calling for and bringing stones. Laclau and Mouffe use the word 'positions' to designate the meanings involved in a discourse or, more accurately, entities *qua* bearers of these meanings. Examples of the positions in the building discourse are slab, pillar, the word 'slab,' and calling for a slab (as opposed to the hunks of granite, sounds, and bodily movements that bear these meanings). Positions are defined, moreover, through their differences from one another: for example, blocks are blocks because of their differences from pillars, slabs, beams, and the words as well as actions that pertain to them. Positions also constitute being: what entities are. A discourse is thus a structured totality of systematically related, being-articulating positions, something highly similar to a social order as defined above.

Similarly, in 'Interpretation and the Sciences of Man' (1985) Charles Taylor pronounces semantic spaces a central feature of the social. A semantic space embraces three fields of meaning, one each for (1) people's states of being (e.g., their desires, feelings, emotions), (2) the situations they confront (thus the people, events, and things with which they deal) and (3) their behavior in those situations. According to Taylor, to say that an item of one of these three sorts (states of being, situation, behavior) occurs in a field of meaning is to say that it has meaning only in relation to the meanings of other items in that field. For example, deferential behavior is deferential only in relation to respectful, cringing, ironic, insolent, provocative, and rude, etc., behavior. What is more, the three fields of meaning that make up a semantic space are interwoven. That a situation is shameful, for example, ha together with people both feeling shame and going on in certain ways in Indeed, the three fields are really one, for meaning is tied to language: the meanings that items of the above sorts can have for a group of people are the meanings marked by the vocabulary these people use to describe themselves and their situations. A group's states, situations, and behaviors thus form a web that is woven together by a set of linguistically marked meanings. Like Laclau and Mouffe, furthermore, Taylor connects meaning to being, in part by contending that a group's semantic spaces help constitute the social reality in and through which it lives. These spaces of meaning also subtend social orders *qua* meaning-imbued arrangements. For a consequence of living in and through these spaces is that actors, along with the entities through and to which they relate, form arrangements of interconnectedly meaningful beings.

Setting up the argument

One of the claims this essay advances is that social order is instituted within practices. Although neither Taylor nor Laclau and Mouffe speak specifically of social orders, their semantic spaces and discourses are closely connected to practice. Examining these connections identifies several aspects of practice pertinent to the establishment of order.

Whereas discourses for Laclau and Mouffe are structured totalities of meaningful entities, practice – if I understand them right – is movement and change. Discourse, in other words, is being, while practice is the becoming from which discourses result and to which they eventually succumb. Conversely, discourses are the precarious fixities that precipitate from human practice and from which further practice arises. The latter formulation is preferable in Laclau and Mouffe's eyes because practice has form (being) only in so far as it issues from extant discourse. Erupting from a discourse that imparts to it form, practice dislocates existing positions (meanings) by rearticulating them, thereby establishing transformed discourses. Consider the discourse composed of building stones along with words and actions that pertain to them. Although Wittgenstein does not mention what Laclau and Mouffe call practice in specifying his example, the practice connected to this discourse would be, first, the activity from which the discourse arose in the past and, second, any future activity that rearticulated its arrangement of stones, words, and actions. An example would be the assistant seizing a slab as a weapon and attacking the builder. Laclau and Mouffe maintain, further, that no position is ever secure: recent and enduring fixations of meaning alike are always susceptible to dislocation through practice. Indeed, any entity can bear indefinitely many meanings and enter indefinitely many discourses. Laclau and Mouffe dub the overflow of signification beyond any partial fixation the 'field of discursivity' and in some passages identify this field as the place of the social.

For Taylor, by contrast, practices are not simply becoming (activity), but in addition a site, or context, where activity occurs. This is because practices house the semantic spaces discussed above. Consider Taylor's example, negotiation practices. Negotiation practices carry a range of meanings for behaviors, states, and situations. This space is marked by the language used within it, thus by expressions such as 'entering into negotiations,' 'bargaining in good faith,' 'hoping to reach an agreement,' 'wanting to realize one's maximal demands,' 'time to make a counteroffer,' and so on. Particular acts of entering into negotiation and bargaining in good faith, etc., are moments of the practice; and their meanings as such acts are drawn from the practice's semantic space. Like Laclau and Mouffe, consequently, Taylor believes that human activity has form *qua* embodiment of meaning. Contrary to their account, however, (1) the meaning of an action does not derive from its differences from other elements of a specific order and (2) practice is not a particular – and rare – form of activity that dislocates meaning by reestablishing it. Rather, human activity is meaningful as an instantiation of meanings that are carried in semantic spaces; and practices are open-ended sets of action that carry such spaces. Thus, whereas Laclau and Mouffe treat practice as order-transforming activity and tie meaning to concrete orders, Taylor views practices as the site where human activity occurs and ties meaning to an abstract dimension of them.

Both Taylor and the Laclau/Mouffe team pinpoint key features of practices that are pertinent to their forming the context of social order. Laclau and Mouffe emphasize practice as activity. Moreover, in attributing the transformation of discourses to practice, they declare human activity causally responsible for social orders (as suggested by their references to 'social forces' that transform discourses). Taylor, meanwhile, highlights practices as site and not just as activity: Practices are contexts where actions are carried out. He suggests, further, that the meanings that are instantiated in the arrangements established within a given practice are drawn from the possibilities contained in the practice's semantic space. He thereby links the establishment of social order to abstract contexts. Taylor also, finally, anchors a practice's semantic space in the distinctions marked by the language used in it. For Taylor, as for many contemporary theorists, language is an essential constitutive dimension of social reality – and also of practices and social orders as a result.

I agree with Laclau and Mouffe that practices are human activity and that causality in social affairs is centered in such activity. (Artifacts, organisms, and things also make a contribution, though I will not consider this further.) But I also think Taylor is right that practices are the chief context of human activity – and of social orders. I will substantiate this thesis in two steps. The first is to specify two types of 'determination,' other than the intervention of action in the world, that are pertinent to social orders. This task is carried out in the remainder of the current section. The second step, to be taken in the fourth section, is schematically outlining how practices shape these two types of determination. My overall argument is, thus, that social orders are established within the sway of social practices because practices mold the forms of determination that are responsible for them. In the third section, meanwhile, I outline an account of practices.

One additional type of determination is the specification of what people do. What I mean is not whatever mechanisms might be causally responsible for the carrying out of bodily doings that constitutes the performance of actions (cf. the discussion of doings and actions in the third section). Rather, I mean the specification of x – and not y or z – as the action a person intentionally and knowingly (seeks to) carry out at a given moment (via his or her bodily doings). The actions that people intend knowingly to perform are those that make sense to them to perform. I call the state of affairs that action makes sense to someone to do 'practical intelligibility.' People almost always, I contend, do what makes sense to them to do; more elaborately, they are almost always performing bodily doings that, in the current circumstances, constitute the actions that make sense to them to perform. I should explain that practical intelligibility is not the same as rationality. What makes sense to people to do is, intrinsically, neither what is nor what seems rational to do. Although on many occasions what makes sense coincides with what is or seems rational, on other occasions (such as when one person strikes out at another in anger) what makes sense to someone to do is not what it is rational to do. As will be discussed in the third section, practical intelligibility is determined by the mental phenomena of teleology and affectivity, by orientations toward ends and by how things matter. Both the pursuit of ends and how things matter can divert a person from doing what is rational. Incidentally, in governing activity practical intelligibility specifies the form of human activity. It thus corresponds to Aristotle's formal cause, whereas the bodily mechanisms that bring about bodily doings correspond to what he called moving causes (or rather, the later interpretation of these as efficient causes). Once the bringing about of social states of affairs is recognized as centering in action, as Laclau and Mouffe (and many others) urge it should be, the governing of action through practical intelligibility becomes relevant to the establishment of order.

The second additional type of determination is the institution of meaning. What institutes meaning is whatever in the realm of intelligibility is responsible for people and things bearing such and such meanings and not others. Plato, for example, identified the something concerned as the Forms, whereas Husserl identified it as transcendental intentionality and many contemporary theorists such as Taylor think language does the trick. Note that the institution of meaning is not simply an issue of possible meanings, *à la* Taylor's semantic spaces. It is more directly an issue of what establishes, as a matter of intelligibility, that a piece of behavior constitutes such and such an action and not another, that something is a particular object or event and not another, that someone's identity is such and such and not this and that, in general, that the meanings and identities borne by the components of a particular arrangement are a, b, and c and not x, y, and z. Whereas causality is the bringing about of something that bears a particular meaning, the institution of meaning is the establishment of the fact *that* it bears that meaning.

As noted, Taylor's notion of semantic spaces suggests that some sort of abstract context is pertinent to meaning. I do not want to follow him further and to anchor the institution of meaning essentially in language, but this is a topic for another essay. The fourth section will, instead, simply identify a feature of practices different from semantic spaces as the abstract phenomenon that institutes meaning. In any event, I can now formulate my argument more precisely: practices form the chief context of social orders by molding action and meaning – that is, by helping to shape the practical intelligibility that governs activity and by carrying that, in accordance with which the meanings of arranged entities are instituted.

Practices and their mental organization

Practices are organized nexuses of activity. Examples are cooking practices, rearing practices, political practices, farming practices, negotiation practices, banking practices, and recreational practices. Each, as an organized web of activity, exhibits two overall dimensions: activity and organization.

A practice is, first, a *set of actions*. For instance, farming practices comprise such actions as building fences, harvesting grain, herding sheep, judging weather, and paying for supplies. Generally speaking, moreover, the actions that compose a practice are either bodily doings and sayings or actions that these doings and sayings constitute. By 'bodily doings and sayings' I mean actions that people directly perform bodily and not by way of doing something else. (These 'behaviors,' as I label them, are basic actions in the sense Arthur Danto [1965] gave this term.)[2] Examples are hammering, handing over money, turning a steering wheel, running, watching, looking, uttering words, and writing them. Examples of the actions these bodily doings and sayings might constitute are building a house, paying for supplies, making a left turn, hurrying home, whiling away time, checking for faults, ordering someone to stand, and composing a poem. To say that actions are 'constituted' by doings and sayings is to say that the performance of doings and sayings amounts, in the circumstances involved, to the carrying out of actions.

The asseveration that practices embrace activity is truistic. What more is there, however, to a practice than activity? One might propose that actions compose a practice by virtue of causal connections between them. According to this proposal, acts of, for example, negotiation, making an offer, and buying help compose the practice of economic exchange by way of inducing and responding to one another (cf. Habermas's [1987: Chapter 6, Section 2] conception of systems, as opposed to social, integration). I set this suggestion aside for a number of reasons, the most relevant being that causal connections between actions are mediated by what I contend organizes practices, namely, mind. Consider, then, the idea that practices are organized mentally. Stephen Turner (1994) has recently mounted arguments against this idea and suggested (p. 117) that the only acceptable use of the expression 'practices' is to refer to patterns of behavior. He reaches the latter conclusion in three steps. He first claims that many writers have conceptualized practices as shared, causally effective mental objects such as tacit knowledge and pre-suppositions (that are hypothesized to lie behind behavior). He next stages arguments against the intelligibility and explanatory power of such shared mental entities. He concludes, finally, that the only thing the term 'practices' can designate is patterns of behavior.

Note first that practices cannot be composed of patterns alone. The actions that make up, say, farming or banking practices are not simply those that form patterns: irregular, ad hoc, and even unique actions can also be elements of the activity manifolds that are farming or banking. More importantly, Turner's arguments against the mental organization of practices simply assume that mental states are causally effective objects. This conception of mentality, however, is not universal. Indeed, it is probably mistaken. Diverse contemporary theories of mind hold that the conditions designated by common locutions of mentality are neither objects nor causal determinants of behavior. Examples include all theories that argue that teleological or reason explanations of action are not causal explanations. (For two recent examples, see Brandom [1994] and Heal [1995].) Another example is the account of mind deriving from Wittgenstein that is utilized in the following.

According to this account,[3] mental phenomena such as desiring, hoping, feeling, believing, expecting, seeing, and being in pain are not states or processes of either an abstract or a real and underlying apparatus. Rather, they are states of one's life: ways things stand or are going for oneself in one's ongoing involvement with the world. For example, desiring chocolate ice cream is chocolate ice cream's being (to oneself) something to possess (cf. Sartre's [1962] analysis of emotions). Similarly, believing x is x's being to oneself the case, just as being annoyed is something's annoying one. As these formulations suggest, mental states, instead of being objects or processes, are *states of affairs* that obtain with respect to a person: that such and such is annoying, the case, or something to possess or realize. Such states are how things stand or are going for that person in his or her involvement in the world.

One important feature of mental states so conceived is that they are *expressed* in behavior, where 'expressed' means that behavior manifests or signifies them (as when joy is manifested in crying and belief in God is signified by praying). A second important feature is that these states do not inform activity by causing it. Rather, they inform activity by determining what makes sense to people to do. An end, for instance, can combine with beliefs and emotions to specify a given action as what makes sense to their possessor to do. For instance, receipt of greater parental attention being something to achieve can combine with a brother having received a new train for his birthday and the brother having done a number of annoying things the previous day, to specify breaking the train as the action that now makes sense to a younger brother to perform. (*Ceteris paribus*, moreover, the younger brother proceeds into action.) I should reiterate that practical intelligibility is not the same as rationality, though the actions singled out as the ones to perform can coincide with those that rationality advocates. If the younger brother believes that he will be punished for destroying his brother's train, smashing it might not be the rational thing to do. His annoyance at the brother's earlier escapades might be such, however, that smashing it is still specified as the action to perform. The dictates of practical intelligibility diverge from those of rationality especially (but not only) when emotions, moods, and hopes help determine what makes sense to people to do.

The upshot of this discussion of mentality is that to attribute mental conditions to someone is not, *pace* Turner, to declare that certain hidden objects caused this and that phenomenal behavior. Rather, it is to articulate how things stood and were going for this person who performed such and such behaviors in these particular circumstances. Mind, consequently, does not comprise such representational entities as tacit knowledge that cause behavior, but instead consists in practical intelligibility-determining states of affairs that are expressed in behavior.

It is not necessary to develop this thumbnail sketch further. The important point is that mind need not be conceptualized as a thing or apparatus that causes behavior. As a result, Turner's arguments against the intelligibility and explanatory potency of shared, causally effective mental objects fail to show that practices cannot be organized, *inter alia*, through mentality. For these arguments pass by all defenses of such an organization that work with a non-substantive and noncausal conception of mind. Hence, they fail to refute the possibility that mind is a medium through which the activities that compose a practice are *noncausally* organized.

How, then, does mind organize a set of doings and sayings as a practice? I work toward answering this question by first explaining that a practice is a set of doings and sayings that is organized by a pool of understandings, a set of rules, and something I call a 'teleoaffective structure.'

By 'understandings' I do not mean the sort of practical sensibility that certain prominent practice theorists cite to explain much, if not all human behavior in its finely tuned sensitivity to immediate setting and wider context. Examples of this sort of sensibility are Bourdieu's (1990) habitus (practical sense) and Giddens's (1984) practical consciousness. Bourdieu and Giddens disagree about the range of human activity these sensibilities determine. Whereas Bourdieu maintains that actors' 'sense for the game' determines all human activity, Giddens claims that practical consciousness determines routine actions alone. Uniting them is the intuition, however, that that function of governing human activity which was traditionally assigned to mind can instead be ascribed, generally, to some practical sensibility.

Crediting a practical sensibility with the determination of which actions people always or routinely perform is problematic. To begin with, practical understanding is somewhat nonexplanatory. To say that John x-ed in situation z either because he knows how to go on in z or because he has a 'feel for the game' played there does not explain why he x-ed. It says only that he is proficient at getting about in situations like z and that this proficiency saw him through once again. In other words, it does not indicate what specifically it was about John and z such that someone who is conversant with z-situations as John is would x; and John's x-ing in z is determined by these uncited features of John and z, not by his knowing how to go on. What is more, knowing how to go on can account for *whatever* John does. It fails, consequently, to explain why he x-ed instead of y-ed, moreover why he did anything at all. Finally, the perfunctoriness of explaining people's actions by repeatedly invoking their habitus or practical consciousness sits uneasily alongside the garden variety fact that people can explain almost all their actions in great detail (which is not to say that their explanations are never wrong). In short, practical sense and practical consciousness lack the multiplicity required for crediting them very often with the determination of which specific actions people carry out.[4]

The understandings that link the actions composing a practice are better construed as abilities that pertain to those actions. One such ability is knowing how to x, where x is one of the practice's constituent actions. By 'knowing how to x' I mean knowing which of the doings and sayings of which one is capable would constitute x-ing in current circumstances. A person knows how to build a fence, for instance, when s/he knows which such behaviors as hammering, lifting a board, eyeing the fence line, and inserting a post into a hole would constitute building a fence in the immediate circumstances. Two other important abilities in this context are knowing how to identify x-ings and knowing how to prompt as well as to respond to x-ings. The actions that compose a given practice, consequently, are linked by the cross-referencing and interdependent know-hows that they express concerning their performance, identification, instigation, and response. The actions that compose farming practices, for example, are linked by expressed abilities to perform, identify, prompt, and respond to acts of herding sheep, judging weather, gathering hay, setting up irrigation, building fences, purchasing supplies, and the like.

Understanding sometimes helps determine what specifically makes sense to people to do. Knowing, for instance, what another person is doing helps determine how to respond to him. Understanding also ubiquitously subtends activity without determining practical intelligibility by enabling an actor behaviorally to carry out the actions that make sense to him to perform. Practical intelligibility, however, is primarily determined, not by understanding, but by rules, teleology, and affectivity. By 'rules' I mean explicit formulations that enjoin or school in particular actions. Such formulations must not be thought of simply as articulations of preexisting understanding. Although some formulations – for instance, rules of grammar – approximate this status, others do not – for instance, those conceived and introduced either to bring about specific actions or to regulate existing activities. Statute law, 'rules of thumb,' and explicit normative enjoinings exemplify what I mean by 'rule.' What people do often reflects formulations of which they are aware. For what makes sense to them to do often reflects their understanding of (or desire to circumvent, etc.) specific rules. Indeed, practices harbor collections of rules that practitioners (or subsets thereof) are supposed to observe. Farming practices, for instance, embrace different, though overlapping sets of directives and instructions for farmers, hired help, and children. So the actions composing a practice are linked, second, through the collection of rules that they observe; more precisely, through understandings of these rules that they express.

Rules, however, only intermittently and never *simpliciter* determine what people specifically do. A more omnipresent determinant of practical intelligibility is thus called for. I incline toward drawing on Aristotelian–Heideggarian intuitions and identifying this third factor as a mix of teleology and affectivity. Teleology, as noted, is orientations toward ends, while affectivity is how things matter. What makes sense to a person to do largely depends on the matters for the sake of which she is prepared to act, on how she will proceed for the sake of achieving or possessing those matters, and on how things matter to her; thus on her ends, the projects and tasks she will carry out for the sake of those ends given her beliefs, hopes, and expectations, and her emotions and moods. Practical intelligibility is teleologically and affectively determined.

The previous sentence but one suggests, I hope, that the teleological and affective determination of practical intelligibility is in fact a mental determination. The determination of intelligibility by mattering, for instance, is a determination via emotions and moods. Moreover, the specification of how someone will proceed for the sake of certain ends is tied to her beliefs, hopes, and expectations. And what it is for a person to pursue ends and to carry out projects and tasks for the sake of those ends is for the sought-after states of affairs and pursued activities to be objects of her desires, hopes, and intentions. An example should help clarify these claims. In the previous section I described a case in which a child's desire to gain greater parental attention combined with his annoyance at a brother's earlier behavior and his belief that the brother has received a new train for his birthday to specify breaking the train as the action that makes sense to him to perform. In this example, receiving greater parental attention is the child's end, and breaking the train is the action he intends to and, *ceteris paribus*, in fact carries out for the sake of this end, given his belief. His desires, beliefs, and intentions thus house the teleological determination of practical intelligibility. The child's annoyance, meanwhile, is the element of affectivity which also helps determine what makes sense to him to do. In ways such as this, all mental determinations of practical intelligibility can be cashed out teleologically and affectively – and, conversely, all teleological and affective determinations of intelligibility can be cashed out mentally. The two ways of talking are simply overlapping and otherwise congruent discourses for articulating the self-same phenomenon of practical intelligibility.

Taking teleology and affectivity as a clue, the third dimension of the organization of a practice can be specified as a normative 'teleoaffective structure,' a range of acceptable or correct ends, acceptable or correct tasks to carry out for these ends, acceptable or correct beliefs (etc.) given which specific tasks are carried out for the sake of these ends, and even acceptable or correct emotions out of which to do so. Farming practices, for example, embrace a range of acceptable or correct combinations of such ends as increasing profit, preserving the land, and feeding one's family; such projects as seeding, gathering, and building fences; and such beliefs as that farmland should be burned and that barns should be built in certain forms. Unlike rearing practices, however, farming practices do not reveal much in the way of affectual structuring. The actions composing a practice are thus linked, third, by a teleoaffective structure.

In sum, a practice is a set of doings and sayings organized by a pool of understandings, a set of rules, and a teleoaffective structure. Not just the doings and saying involved, incidentally, but the understandings, rules, and teleoaffectivities that organize them, can change over time in response to contingent events. Of course, practices reveal further 'structural' features, for instance, regularities in and causal connections between their constituent actions, as well as layouts and linkages between the material settings in which they transpire. But it is by virtue of expressing certain understandings, rules, ends, projects, beliefs, and emotions (etc.) that behaviors form an organized manifold. Since, furthermore, the organizing phenomena resolve into mental conditions, mind is a 'medium' through which practices are organized. With this conception of practices and its mental organization in hand, I conclude this essay by returning to the thesis that social order is established within practices.

The establishment of order

Social orders, recall, are arrangements of people and of the artifacts, organisms, and things through which they coexist, in which these entities relate and possess identity and meaning. To say that orders are established within practices is to say that arrangements – their relations, identities, and meanings – are determined there. One crucial aspect of this determination is the bringing about of arrangements through human activity. Another is the institution of the meanings and identities that humans and nonhumans possess as components of arrangements. Both 'processes' depend on the organization of practices. I should mention, by the way, that arrangements are established, not just within individual practices, but also across them. Whereas arrangements within practices rest on the actions and organizations of individual practices, arrangements across them rest on the actions and organizations of different practices. Arrangements are established across practices when, for instance, individuals who are carrying on different practices, say, farming and commercial ones, interact and thus form an arrangement at, say, the general store; or when chains of action pass through different practices, for example, those of farming, commerce, cooking, and state surveillance, and thereby set up arrangements that embrace farmers, shop owners, spouses, and Internal Revenue Service officers.

As Laclau and Mouffe emphasize, social orders are brought about (largely) through human activity. Indeed, human activity brings about most of those interdependencies and sedimentations, the existence of which are marked in expressions for social systems, institutions, and structures, for example, 'economy,' 'state,' and 'kinship.' As discussed, moreover, what people do is governed by what makes sense to them to do. Implicit in my discussion in the previous section is the fact that when people participate in a particular practice their actions express understandings, rules, teleologies, and affectivities that number among those organizing the practice. This means that what makes sense to them to do is determined – at least in part – by these phenomena. For instance, what makes sense to farmers when carrying on farming practices is determined by such ends as increasing profit, preserving the land, and feeding one's family, such tasks as seeding, gathering, and building fences, and such beliefs as that farmland should be burned and that barns should be built in certain forms. Often, however, some of the factors that determine what makes sense to people to do are not contained in the organization of the practice they are currently carrying on. The farmer, for instance, might plant an extra field as a way of impressing the widow who lives across the county. In any event, when people carry on a practice, the organization of the practice is partly responsible for what they do and, thus, for the orders they effect. People, however, are always carrying out this or that practice. Indeed, actions presuppose practices (see Schatzki 1996: Chapter 4, Section 2). It follows that both what people generally do and the orders their activities generally bring about are beholden to practice organization. So practices establish social order, first, because they help mold the practical intelligibility that governs their practitioners' actions and thereby help determine which arrangements people bring about. And to repeat: because understanding, rules (i.e., understandings thereof), and teleoaffectivity are 'mental' phenomena, mind is pivotal to the elaboration of order within practices.

I wrote in the second section that what institutes meaning is whatever in the realm of intelligibility is responsible for entities possessing particular meanings (and not others). As examples of the something concerned, I cited Platonic Forms, Husserlian intentions, and hermeneutic–poststructural languages. According to my Heideggerian–Wittgensteinian intuitions, by contrast, the something concerned is conceptual understandings. For a conceptual understanding of x is an understanding of what x is; and it is on the background of understandings of what x, y, and z, etc., are that something can be and is a x, a y, or a z. Something can be a barn or a crop, for instance, only given what a barn or a crop are. I contend that the conceptual understandings, given which the elements of arrangements have specific meanings and not others (i.e., given which *what* action-effected arrangements are composed of is x, y, and z and not a, b, and c), are features of practices. So practices are the context of social order, second, in encompassing that which institutes the meanings of arranged entities.

Wittgenstein's texts suggest that understanding the concept of x is knowing how to identify x's and to react (appropriately) to the phenomena that qualify as x's. In other words, conceptual understanding is a know-how. This know-how is expressed, moreover, in uses and explanations of the expression 'x,' together with actions taken toward the phenomena to which 'x' applies (e.g., Wittgenstein 1967: Section 513; 1980a: Section 910). As discussed in the previous section, the understandings that help organize practices comprise various know-hows, including knowing how to x, knowing how to identify x-ings, and knowing how to prompt and respond to such acts. Notice that the know-hows that make up conceptual understandings of actions are among those that organize practices. More specifically: conceptual understandings of the actions that compose a practice are contained in the understandings that organize the practice. As noted, for example, farming practices are organized by abilities to perform, identify, prompt, and respond to such acts as herding sheep, judging weather, and gathering hay. In being such, these practices automatically embrace understandings of what these actions are. Moreover, since carrying on practices also involves acting toward and speaking about both the people performing and the things bound up with the practice's actions, practices also carry understandings of the meanings of those humans and nonhumans that are indigenous to the practice and its arrangements (in farming practices: farmers, hired help, barns, crops, crop damage, farm implements, crop dusters, etc.). In short, contained in the understandings that organize a practice are those conceptual understandings, given which the meanings of the entities arranged in the practice are instituted. This is only part of the story, however, about how individual practices institute the meanings of entities within them.

How the meanings of those entities that are scattered among multifarious practices are also instituted in practices, is likewise a further story. This is enough, however, to suggest that the chief context of social order, the place where it is established, is a complex and evolving nexus of interwoven practices.

Notes

1 I acknowledge that the authors would today no longer defend the positions described here.
2 A saying, incidentally, is a doing that says something about something.
3 For detailed discussion of the topics of the third section, see Schatzki (1996: Chapters 2 and 4).
4 These criticisms, I should add, do not apply to Dreyfus's (1991: Chapters 4 and 11) account of skills, at least when this account is expanded to embrace Heidegger's analysis of worldhood. This is because skills, in Dreyfus's Heideggerian hands, possess a teleoaffective *Ausgerichtheit* that sidesteps the problems just identified and renders his account largely compatible with the analysis offered here.

4 Pragmatic regimes governing the engagement with the world

Laurent Thévenot

'We play at paste,
Till qualified for pearl,
Then drop the paste,
And deem ourself a fool.
The shapes, though, were similar,
And our new hands
Learned gem-tactics
Practising sands.'

The Collected Poems of Emily Dickinson,
(New York: Barnes and Noble, 1924: 19)[1]

The social sciences have benefited greatly from the elaboration of a concept of 'practice' that contrasts sharply with the model of rationally calculated action. 'Practice' brings into view activities which are situated, corporeal, and shaped by habits without reflection. This notion has been extraordinarily successful and has now been extended to cover every sort of human activity. Not surprisingly, this success has generated debate and revealed problems in this extended usage which covers an enormous diversity of behaviors designated by that term. From one branch of the social sciences to another, the specific character of what counts as a practice differs significantly. Yet, applied with decreasing rigor, the category serves today as a sort of cement for the social sciences. It may be said that the felicity of the concept comes from its extraordinary breadth. It points equally well to agency of the most personal or intimate kind and to agency that is collective, public, or institutional. But the obvious cost of this extension is that it hinders the detailed clarification of differences between types of agency. This is important because these differences are a major feature of our contemporary societies.

The differentiation of 'pragmatic regimes' is the main part of my research I want to clarify in this paper. In order to characterize a concept of pragmatic regime and the way it differs from practice, I shall work through two basic questions which I find insufficiently addressed by most usages of practice. One concerns what I shall refer to as a lack of realism: theories of practice typically do not provide good accounts of our dynamic confrontation with the world. The other concerns the moral element in practice which shapes the evaluative process governing any pragmatic engagement. I begin this essay with some reasons why I am concerned to differentiate regimes. This will bring me to comment on the two problems raised by the concept of 'practice' as a way to introduce the most basic elements of my own approach.[2] A second part of the essay offers a more concrete picture of the type of pragmatic versatility required in everyday life in contemporary society. Three common-place and related scenes, ranging from the most intimate to the most public, will help us to see how best to characterize the configurations of activity. The third part advances the general features of my analytical framework, organized around a differentiation of three main pragmatic regimes: familiarity, regular planning, and justification. This allows us to bring out into the open the ways we detach ourselves from proximity and enter a public space where critique and legitimate justifications hold sway. It will make clear the benefits and the costs of such a move in contrast to the possibilities offered by more local regimes.

Why do we need to recast the concepts of practice and action in social sciences?

The concepts of practice or action constitute the elementary bricks of any construction in social sciences. Reforming these concepts is a serious undertaking. Nonetheless, many social scientists are today involved in such a task. The Sociology of Science and Knowledge (SSK) greatly contributed to this enterprise, with the help of some philosophers of science and knowledge. I have followed a different road to arrive at a political and moral sociology of an 'equipped' or 'furnished' humanity (Thévenot 2001a).[3] Therefore, my approach involving the plurality of pragmatic regimes is driven by an effort to relate them to a variation of scope in the delimitation of what is good. However, by contrast to most political and moral philosophers, I am deeply concerned by the various ways the natural and artificial equipment of the human world is involved in diverse conceptions of the good. I shall defend a kind of realist orientation which departs from many philosophical views but also from major trends in social constructivism.

The versatility of agency in contemporary societies: engaging in a plurality of pragmatic regimes

It is not only the variety of activities covered by the term 'practice' which poses a problem. In addition, one must also take into account figures of action which, beyond showing habit and the body, point towards intentions and plans, or towards forms of activity that require reflective argumentation. I am concerned with the fact that in our contemporary societies human beings constantly need to change the scope of their engagement, shifting along a scale between greater or lesser generality. The differentiation of pragmatic regimes illuminates this necessity of moving between modes of intervention and agency engaged in local or individual circumstances and those modes oriented towards the general or the public.

One of the canonical debates in the social sciences distinguishes between macrosocial structures and microsocial behaviors. This has elicited various attempts to integrate these two levels – notably by Bourdieu and Giddens – by way of conceptual schemes that show the circulation between reciprocally 'structuring' and 'structured' elements. Like other researchers, I have given special attention to the contribution made by agents in this integration. My research first examined the agents' capacities to move from particularized situations to general forms according to operations of 'investment of form' (Thévenot 1984) which are grounded in a relation to things and their transformation. These operations shape the world by forging likeness and contribute to homogenization, across contexts, in the treatment of people and things (classifications, codes, standards, etc.).[4] Having identified these operations of making people and things general, it became necessary to relate these 'invested forms' to certain modes of coordinated action which are conceived as more legitimate than others and for which these 'shaped beings' are qualified. The next step was realized in collaboration with Luc Boltanski. We related these operations of generalization to the issue of legitimate evaluation, that is to the problem of ranking people and things in relation to conceptions of the common good within a public regime of critique and justification.

I introduce here my subsequent research. It returns to the issue of practice and action. I want to situate a public regime in a variety of more local regimes of engagement, in order to analyze this demanding and strenuous pragmatic versatility which is required by our contemporary societies.

The lack of realism: which reality is engaged?

Sociologists have heavily relied on practices viewed as habits, dispositions, routines, customs and traditions to account for static perpetuation and reproduction of social order. There are some exceptions.[5] The inheritors of pragmatism emphasize the dynamics of practice and creativity (Joas 1993). De Certeau was concerned to elaborate such a dynamics and thereby oppose the rigidity of Bourdieu's habitus (1972) and Foucault's disciplinary arrangements (1975). He opened the path to 'a science of everyday life' which acknowledges the creative character of disseminated tactics and usages that resist the 'monotheism' of panoptical and formal disciplines (de Certeau 1990).

My approach aims to account for not only the movements of an actor but also the way his environment responds to him and the way he takes into account theses responses. That is what I refer to as the 'realism' of each regime. Most conceptions of practice pay little attention to this type of responsiveness. In my view, it is a matter of central importance. As long as the practice is seen as regular and stable, it can hardly be viewed as a realistic adjustment to a resistant, changing and transformed world. Thus, it becomes important for me to conceive of the dynamic aspects of activities, even where these are accounted for in the static terms of practice, routine, or habit. Worry over this kind of realism has been disqualified by sociologists who discarded the conception of a reality 'out there,' and who have spent much effort to elaborate the alternative concept of a 'constructed social reality.' But the dynamics of this material engagement between an agent and his environment is a central issue in my conception of pragmatic regimes. Differentiating regimes brings to light variations in the relevant reality which is put to a test in the dynamics of each kind of pragmatic engagement. The relevant reality depends on the different ways one has to 'take hold' of the environment.[6]

The absent moral element: which good is engaged?

The second problem concerns the force that governs each pragmatic regime. Too many candidates present themselves: value, norm, belief, interest, disposition, etc. In my view, the force is based on some conception of the good. This conception differs from one regime to the other. The moral element is crucial. It is the reason why pragmatic regimes are social. It drives both the agent in his conduct and determines the way other agents take hold of or 'seize' this conduct. This element might also be called 'making sense of' if we are clear that much more is at stake than meaning, language, and understanding.[7] It originates in a notion of the good that grounds each regime. In fact, my aim is to re-moralize sociology. It would be easy to misunderstand what is meant by this, so I raise a flag of caution. For, by the moral element I mean various conceptions of the good, and these appear in places where social scientists usually identify causal factors such as interests or dispositions and not only in 'morality' in the narrowed sense.

This brings us face to face with a main problem of modern social sciences. The question of the good is inadequately addressed. I contend that the previously mentioned candidates for governing practice, or action, are avatars of the good which result from the modeling of social sciences on the pattern of natural sciences. With its inaugural rupture from political and moral philosophy, sociology distanced itself from ideas of good. As a result, sociologists tend to mistrust such ideas because they are reminiscent of the moral and political philosophy from which they believe they have liberated themselves. They replaced them with concepts – like 'norms' or 'values' – which are supposed to be neutral and descriptive. This has led to the strange situation in which most sociologists, while deeply concerned with political and moral issues (sometimes overtly, sometimes not), generally offer accounts of the social world which poorly acknowledge actors' preoccupation with the good.[8]

Worry over the good – whatever might be its definition and scope – has been currently transformed into a category of 'social norm.' Thus, this category offers an opportunity to examine the reduction of the good to a law-like regularity, within the frame of a classical conception of social practice.

'Social practice' designates a model of human behavior which is congruent with the Durkheimian perspective: regular conduct to which the members of the same collective conform. The realism of this social practice is the kind of objectivity which is typical of what Durkheim called a 'social fact.' This objectivity holds as much for the researcher as for the person implicated in the practice. For the sociologist, it is expressed when the regularity and the collective character of practices is translated into scientific laws with the help of social statistics. What about the good of social practices? Mauss conflates social practices with institutions (Mauss 1927) and the concept of institution suggest some connection to a common good. But Mauss does not elaborate such a good. The superposition of regularity and collective in the notion of institution has been formerly made in two steps. First, Quetelet's construction of *'l'homme moyen'* in emerging social statistics (Desrosières 1998) equated the mean of a series of human beings with the moral ideal. Second, Durkheim gave a twist to Rousseau's political philosophy and assimilated his conception of a civic general interest with a factual collective. Laws created by human beings become laws of regular and therefore objective behaviors (Thévenot 1994a). Grounded by the operation of the statistical mean, 'norm' appeared in sociological theory as a powerful way to incorporate within an objective account of behavior the significance of 'the good' even while radically reducing its moral force. This approach was consistent with the project of the social sciences to adopt the bases and models of natural science (Thévenot 1995b).

Linking the reality and the good engaged: regimes of engagement

The problem may be summarized as follows. The category of 'social norm' closely follows the definition of the social; but the social also supports objectivity; hence, the sociological avatar of the good happens to be very similar to sociological objectivity so that both categories are easily collapsed into the single core notion of 'social.'

Therein lies the problem. This reduction obliterates the main tension that human beings have to resolve and which I view at the basis of all regimes. This general tension is between some kind of good which governs the intervention and some sort of response that comes back to the agent from reality. I employ the term engagement precisely because it captures the link between these two orientations. When used in theories of practice, it usually signifies a material adjustment with the world. But it has a second acceptance which points to a moral or political covenant.[9]

This second aspect makes explicit the agent's commitment to some kind of good. I contend that the kind of pragmatic articulation between the two orientations, the engaged good and the engaged reality, is what makes for the force of each regime. The notion of good needs to be put to a reality test where it is realized in the evaluation of some performance. Symmetrically, the capture of relevant pieces of reality depends on the outline of some good.

This interdependence is precisely what turns a mode of adjustment into a common regime. And this is eventually the characterization I would offer of the social.

From personal convenience to collective conventions

I now turn to a concrete story which deploys different modes of engagement with the environment to illustrate the way human beings are compelled to shift from one mode to the other. I will highlight the kind of good which governs the engagement (varying from personal and local convenience to collective and legitimate conventions) and the kind of realism which orients the way to treat the environment.

A scenario of pragmatic versatility

Personal and local convenience

When I have to present my research on pragmatic regimes to a new audience, I often develop my account by starting from a widely shared set of 'practices' which might be covered by the phrase 'inhabiting a home.' I ask people to give very concrete examples of the reason why their home is personally convenient, and to point to how they accommodate a familiar environment.[10] To provide such examples in public is not an easy task; indeed this difficulty is part of the issue I want to address. People feel embarrassed to publicize practices which they rightly view as part of their intimate personality. What we call *pudeur* in French, or what the British have refined with the spatial and moral conception of 'decency,' hinders such publicity. Elias and Goffman devoted a large part of their work to the study of public civility and to the management of the self in public. But we need to pay as much attention to the familiar engagement which is wrecked by the publicization process.

People meet another interesting difficulty in their testimonies. The everyday use of language, which is such an efficient means to carry an event by a discursive representation, is not very suitable to picture these familiar practices. Persons would do better to show me photographs or invite me to visit their home and refrain from anything but a very indexical use of language. Young people are more inclined to disclose the gestures of accommodation by which they aim at a personal and local convenience. A Russian student admits, blushing slightly, that he puts most of his clothes on an old armchair now entirely dedicated to the usage normally reserved to a shelf. A Mexican girl refers to the way she arranged a table with piles of books supporting a board. An American graduate mentions tinkering with his rickety car, with an adjustable wrench in place of a missing door handle. A French man mentions the peculiar way he found to hold the match and simultaneously press the gas button to turn on his old water-heater.

'Intimate' familiarization evokes a direct corporal implication, the idea of a tight union between bodily gestures and an environment which makes for highly local convenience. The dynamics of the relationship between the human and nonhuman entities which compose familiar surroundings are highly dependent on personal and local clues that were made out as salient features for adjustment in the commerce with all these familiar beings. In this regime, agents are guided by a wide range of sensorial data, including not only visual but also tactile, auditory, and olfactory clues, as well as indications from spatial positioning (Conein and Jacopin 1993). Such clues are very widely distributed in the web of connections which sustain familiarity.

None of this familiar accommodation is 'social' in the sense of 'social practices' which designate collectively aligned gestures. Other persons might get accustomed to my home if they cooperate in accommodating this habitat into a convenient setting. It does not follow that they have identified the same clues for their own use, since these marks depend strongly on the person and on his or her 'path-dependent' process of learning. The resulting 'collective,' if we can speak of any, spreads from one person to the next and is deeply supported by the familiarized environment. The arduous and gradual task of becoming capable of living with another person's environment does not actually consist in 'sharing' objects or practices. It requires getting accustomed to another personality through connection with that other person's used habitat and familiar world. This process involves weaving and extending the web of all these idiosyncratic linkages with an entourage. By contrast, the clues which have been deposited during the tuning process are not available to any unfamiliar visitor who might enter the appropriated habitat. Such mannerisms will appear bizarre to any observer lacking the intimate knowledge that has been learned through a long process of accommodation. This intrusion of an 'outsider' leads us to the next scene which is governed by a more conventional arrangement of the world.

Conventional utility

When speaking to a young audience, I usually refer to a painful but common experience which introduces the critical encounter between the regime of familiarity just considered and the one we shall consider in this section. I ask them to recount the scene when they were asked by their parents, as children, to put their room into order. Indeed, it is part of the empirical methodology developed by Boltanski and myself to work on such critical situations, paying close attention to the kind of tensions which are at stake.[11]

Such critical situations induce the agents to disclose the pragmatic requirements of each regime in terms of the engaged good and reality. Young people are very loquacious when it comes to such upsetting happenings. They are inclined to criticize an undue authority or rule which reduces their local arrangement and even their personality by calling it a 'mess.' To facilitate a more balanced view on both regimes and distance from the heteronomous imposition of an order, I would ask my students to imagine the following move from the first to the second scene: 'leaving your home for an internship, you propose that a friend comes to live in your room during this period.' Most people arrive quickly at the following point. However convenient our familiar belongings are for us and other cohabitants, we cannot leave the environment in a state which, from the newcomer's point of view, appears to be nothing but a mess. To allow an unfamiliar visitor a conventional utilization, the first thing to do is to put our home and belongings in a different sort of order, one that is appropriate for a regime of engagement based on regular action and utility. To do this, we must destroy a fair amount of the familiar capacity of the complex web of our habitat. In addition, we need to restore to their normal state the things that were heavily used, in spite of the fact that we had found ways and clues to handle them with great success. The armchair regains its utilization for sitting, the books are made available for reading, the car handle is fixed to serve as a conventional handle, detailed instructions are added to the water-heater.

However, this configuration of conventional utility and regular action includes substantial latitude within the particular way to achieve the action and concerning the state of the object. What counts as 'good working order' is supposed to be common knowledge, but no warranty of any sort can lead to a more precise qualification. Everyday narrative use of language, with its loose denomination of actions and objects, is sufficient to monitor the propriety of the engagement. This is in marked contrast with both the 'personal and local convenience' of the first scene and 'collective conventions' to which we come in the third and last scene.

Legitimate conventions of qualification

In which circumstances does the previous regime of engagement happen to be insufficient to handle an agent's commerce with people and things? When do we have recourse to a more conventionalized way to seize beings and their relationships? The following answer, frequently given by someone among the audience, offers a good opportunity to explore the shift to a third regime governed by conventions with the highest degree of legitimacy. The new situation is created when the home is rented. The extension of the good which governs the engagement goes a step further, resulting in a more convention-alized handling of persons and things. We imagine that things are not going well for the tenant. An accident occurs because the newcomer to the home did not know how to handle adequately one of the appliances. Such mishaps normally result in nothing more than polite and mutual apologies for misuse and misinformation concerning the appliance. But perhaps the guest or the host are particularly acerbic people, or the accident is serious enough to raise questions about responsibility. The format of 'conventional utility' used to capture things and their relations to people was fine while everything was running smoothly. It is not sufficient when a dispute arises, however, because it assumes a large tolerance concerning the regular utilization of objects.

Should the dispute grow, both parties would go beyond the implicit assumptions of an object in 'good working order.' They would begin to refer to general principles of efficiency (of the car handle), or safety (of the water-heater), or market price (of the books), or patrimony (of the antique armchair), to justify their claims. They would ground their arguments on broad conventional requirements that human or nonhuman entities need to satisfy in order to 'qualify' for being offered as evidence of the argument. If the issue is efficiency, the 'qualification' is clearly different from the case where price is at stake. And things or persons are put to different tests. For instance, by referring to operating instructions, disputants question the action of the user. They may attempt to identify 'misuse' and thereby disqualify the other party as incompetent. Or they might point to the 'deficient behavior' of the object in terms of efficiency to identify a 'defect' and thus disqualify the object. By contrast, efficiency would not be a good test if the market value of a torn book is at stake. In that case, qualification would be based on price. Each characterization indicates that the thing is relevant for some general form of evaluation which orients the kind of repair appropriate to the incident. The dispute leads the parties to make reference to the most legitimate collective conventions. The arguments and the evidence which back up their claims rely on conventionalized linguistic terms and entities.

I chose to locate the scenario in a home space but I could as well have placed it on a different stage, for example the commerce with a ticket-selling machine in a public space (Bréviglieri 1997), or the workplace. In this latter case, conventional qualifications would commonly be more prevalent, while personal and local convenience are less commonly taken into account.[12]

Lessons to be drawn from observed pragmatic versatility

The three scenes discussed above offer a first way of seeing the plurality of modes of engaging the world. I am now in a better position to comment on the analytical options introduced in the first section and to confront them with other orientations in the literature on practice.

The relation between human agency and material environment

I share with a series of authors in the sociological tradition a main interest in the relation between human agency and material environment. Unlike Durkheim, Mauss's notion of practice goes beyond a consideration of social sanctions to take into account bodily gestures, or *techniques du corps*, and the agents' dependence on a local environment (Mauss 1934). This figure stresses an agent's ability to adjust his gestures to a natural or artificial environment. This interest in what will be called later an 'ecological' approach to activity is illustrated, for instance, by Mauss's regrets that telegraph workers do not generally climb the 'primitive' way, with the help of a belt around the pole and their body (Mauss 1934). Mauss's interest in a dynamics of adjustment which encompasses gestures, objects, and natural elements of the environment was a guiding inspiration for all the work of Leroi-Gourhan – who pointed to the risk of 'pouring the social realm into material realm' (Leroi-Gourhan 1964: 210) – and Haudricourt (1987). Among sociological literature, works on the sociology of scientific knowledge (SSK) have been unusually concerned with the relation between human agency and material environment and have traced many avenues of research in this direction. The sociology of scientific controversies developed by Latour (1987) and Callon (1986) pictures human agency as the *a posteriori* attributions that result from the network linkage between human beings and non-human entities (Callon and Latour 1981). Recent literature on the role played by the material environment in action and cognition (Conein, Dodier, and Thévenot 1993; Conein and Thévenot 1997) connects with perspectives in cognitive anthropology and cultural studies that stress the fact that human cognition is strongly dependent on the environment of objects (Lave 1988; Norman 1989). Karin Knorr Cetina considers laboratories as sites of both enhanced nature and enhanced agents (1992). Extending her work on the 'manufacture of science' (1981), her studies of the 'ontologies of organisms and machines' in experimental arenas (1993) looks for 'symbolic repertoires' through which 'the structure of things is reset in an epistemic practice.' In her theory of practice, Knorr Cetina refers to the active element as 'tinkering' (Knorr Cetina 1981). Pickering discusses this element under the term 'tuning,' which designates the 'delicate material positioning' so important to practice. This idea supports his argument that 'material agency' is temporally emergent in relation to practice (Pickering 1995a). Ethnomethodologists have been particularly attentive to the settings of action and to the methodological devices which produce a meaningful world (Garfinkel 1967). Cicourel's cognitive sociology illuminated the way the actor perceives and interprets his environment, recognizing what is 'familiar' or 'acceptable' (1974a). Material devices such as photographs and schemas strongly contribute to the scientist's alleged synthesizing capacity (Lynch 1985).[13]

I see a risk in the characterization of the relation between the agent and his environment in terms of symbolic work, meaning, understanding, interpretation, etc. This risk is increased by researchers seeking a 'comprehensive sociology' which conceptualizes *the social* as starting from common frames of understanding rather than pragmatic engagements. It leads to that particular antirealism of which social constructionist views are often accused.[14]

The social character of the relation between human agency and material environment

My own approach is different and it goes this way. First, I situate each kind of human agency within a particular way of engaging with the material environment. I am not only concerned with bodily adjustments. Since human beings live in social relationships with others, my second step is to examine their ways of adjusting to the world in light of a particular mode of coordination. My contention is that coordination with other human beings (and oneself, from one moment to the next) presupposes that the agent makes use of models of activity to take hold of what happens. What is at stake is not simply a matter of 'representation' or 'interpretation': these models are used to monitor one's own conduct and are put to the test of effective coordination with other beings (or oneself) and with the material world. Then, I include in the analysis the agent's modeling which contributes to coordination.[15] The third step is the elucidation of what makes certain modes of coordination commonly enforced and, as such, 'social.' Let us consider this last step in more detail.

The familiar gestures of the first scene, with all their singularity, clearly move us away from the idea of 'social' action in the sense of an act oriented towards other people. They also break with the idea of a 'social practice' which derives from customs, beliefs, symbols, or dispositions shared at the core of a collectivity. Although Bourdieu expressed an initial interest in familiarity, my view on familiar engagement differs from what he says in *Outline of a Theory of Practice* (1977). The notion of habitus, which Bourdieu elaborated as the centerpiece of his theory of the reproduction of social order, short-circuits the analysis of the personalized and localized dynamics of familiarity.[16] Bourdieu was too concerned to make a solid connection between the level of bodily habits and the Mauss–Durkheim level of regular and collective 'social practices.'[17] All the dynamics and personally inventive adjustments are fundamentally impeded by the assumed collective alignment and permanence of habitus which are needed to explain the reproduction of order. Also referring in his own way to the classical notion of habitus, Merleau-Ponty captures more precisely the personal process of familiar accommodation between the human agent armed with a perceiving body and the objects in his or her environment. He considers senses as 'apparatuses to make concretions from an inexhaustible material' (Merleau-Ponty 1964: 245), the body being 'a system of holds on the world' (1964: 53).

Personal and local convenience shows that the social character of the relation between human agency and material environment cannot result from an idea of a collective of shared practices. This relation is supported by idiosyncratic and path-dependent gestures. What is shared is not the gesture which might be hardly understandable, but the mode of engagement from which this gesture gets its propriety (Thévenot 1990b).[18] The three scenes recounted above presented variations of the kinds of propriety which govern the relation between human agents and their environment. I used terms from the root *convenir* (which means literally 'to go with') to designate these variations: personal and local convenience, conventional utilization, collective conventions.[19] Obviously, I do not intend the classical conventionalist approach which is often involved in social constructivism. Propriety does not imply the conformist alignment of practices but leaves a place for creative dynamics.[20] At the heart of propriety is the kind of evaluation which governs these dynamics.[21] As was stated in the first section and exemplified in the second, a notion of the good specifies the relevant reality.

This connection between realism and evaluation requires a significant move from the clear-cut classical fact/value distinction.[22] The next section is dedicated to this issue and to the presentation of the main features through which I identify and differentiate a range of pragmatic regimes.

Ways of engaging the world

The notion of pragmatic regime and its main features

Each pragmatic regime that I analyzed is adopted as a common stance to capture events and agents for the purpose of active intervention. In that sense, it is 'social.' A full account of this adoption would require more space than the present essay permits. Thus, I shall provide just a sketch of the line of argument here. Pragmatic regimes are social devices which govern our way of engaging with our environment inasmuch as they articulate two notions: (a) an orientation towards some kind of good; (b) a mode of access to reality. Let me now summarize the main characteristics of regimes (see Table 4.1).

Every regime is built on a delineation of the good. This notion is used to evaluate the state of people and things and judge whether they are appropriately engaged. The extension of the good varies according to the regime. When the evaluation has to meet the requirement of public justification, the good has to be a legitimate common good. The good might be significantly more limited and mundane when it appears in the achievement of some regular planned action. It might be even more personal and localized when it involves some kind of usual attunement with well-known and near-by surroundings. The three scenes sketched in the section entitled 'A scenario of pragmatic versatility' illustrated such variations of the scope of the good.

Table 4.1 Pragmatic regimes of engagement

	Regime of familiarity	*Regime of regular planned action*	*Regime of justification*
Which good is engaged? With what evaluation?	Personal and local *convenience*, within a familiar milieu	Successful *conventional* action	Collective *conventions* of the common good
Which reality is engaged? With what capacity?	Usual and used surroundings providing a distributed capacity	Functional instrument	'Qualified' object
What is the format of relevant information?	Local and idiosyncratic perceptual clue	Ordinary semantics of action	Codification
Which kind of agency is construed?	A personality attached to his or her entourage	Planner	'Qualified' person

The relevant *reality* which puts the engagement to a test is connected to the outline of some good. Two consequences result from this view on the agents' realism. In accord with the pragmatist tradition, I deal with a reality which cannot be detached from some sort of activity or intervention (Cartwright 1983; Hacking 1983). In contrast to many pragmatists, however, I do not hold to a uniform notion of action when figuring out human interventions which encounter the resistance of reality. A familiar manipulation will not give access to the same kind of reality as a regular planned action which involves a functional environment, or an act which is open to public critique and takes into account qualified evidence. Which type of reality offers resistance to activity depends on the good, and the dependence is actualized by the pragmatic engagement.

A central feature of the dynamics of engagement consists in the clues, or marks, or qualities, that the agent uses to take hold of or capture the environment and to evaluate the success of his or her engagement through revision and creation. The analysis of different regimes demands that social researchers pay as much attention to the distinct *formats* through which actors take hold of their material environment (through functions, properties, clues, etc.: Thévenot 1993) as to the ways actors deal with their human environment. The standard notion of information usually obscures this variety of formats because it presupposes a standardized coded form.

It is only after having made clear the ways the good and reality are jointly engaged and *articulated* through a specific form of evaluation that we can turn to the kind of capacity of the principal agent which is involved in each pragmatic regime.[23] Beginning with the mode of engagement, it is possible to infer from it the capacities and agencies that are consistent with this mode.

The conjunction of three main pragmatic regimes

In this final section I shall sketch the conjunction of three principal regimes, suggesting their interconnections and the reasons why human beings have to shift from one to the other.

The regime of familiarity

The liberal notion of 'privacy' does not capture the kind of good involved in the regime of familiarity. Privacy assumes the individuality and autonomy which goes with free will and planning, i.e., with the kind of human agency involved in the next regime. By contrast, the regime of familiarity rests on an accustomed dependency with a neighborhood of things and people. The notion of 'use' grasps this intimate relation to the world but ordinarily lacks the dimension of care which reveals the kind of good engaged in a careful tuning with a nearby environment. Reality is not sliced into clear-cut objects which are ready-made for a regular utilization in accordance to their functional design. Things are worn out and fashioned by personal use. Fragmentary and deeply anchored clues of 'information' are laid down in a web of uses. The resulting integrated capacity is particularly visible in the case of human–machine interaction because it contrasts with the normal way of attributing functional properties to the machine, assuming that it is completely independent of the worker who uses it.[24] Human and nonhuman capacities are entangled: one could either say that the things are personalized or that the personality is consolidated by surrounding things. This regime displays the pragmatic requirements that sustain the format of personality which is among the ones most commonly used to treat other human beings. Such human agency depends on the binding web of familiarity ties illustrated in the first scene of the scenario which takes place at home (*chez moi*; in French, literally, at my self). The web of customized attachments constitutes an extension of an 'attached' personality. It strongly contrasts with the agency of the autonomous individual which is involved in the regime of planned action (and actually depends on the functional capacity of objects). The entities of the regime of familiarity are not detached from the personality which appropriated them; rather, they enlarge his or her surface and secure his or her maintenance. When the things we appropriate are customized, tamed, or domesticated they maintain our intimate being.

This distributed capacity hinders the moral and legal process of attributing responsibility, since such attribution requires an individualized and autonomous agency. The web of customized attachments does not allow the detachment of capable (and eventually culpable) individualized entities, either human or objectal, which is required for imputation. A type of management which fosters local and personal attunement to flexibilize the workplace faces the difficulties of imputation in a 'messy' place. An exemplary contrast is offered by the spatial setup of a workplace which fosters detachment. The physical separation of workstations and the standardization of machines and instructions facilitate imputation of responsibility against a familiar type of collective (Thévenot 1997).

The regime of regular action

The regime of regular planned action mirrors a conception of action which is embedded in everyday language and which has been widely explored in the philosophy of action. What difference does it make to refer to this as a specific regime of engagement?

First, I am looking for a figure which agents use to handle what they do and what others do, in an effective mode of coordination of their activity. It departs from a theoretical debate on 'intentional action' as a general model for all human behavior.[25] I am not considering one theory of action competing with others, but one of the ways people grasp and monitor their engagement with their environment for an effective coordination. In this respect, the idea of regimes of engagement converges partly with the view proposed by Dennett (1987) when he suggests that we treat intentionality as a kind of 'interpretative stance' which the human actor adopts efficiently to deal with certain events and behaviors. Through empirical exploration of the commerce with things, I have found many examples of people who reasonably attribute an intentional planning agency to certain computerized artifacts which are endowed with refined cognitive abilities (Thévenot 1994b).[26] Second, I aim at a more balanced account of the different entities which are engaged, i.e., a principal human agent and his/her environment. The classical view of intentional action concentrates all the attention on the planning capacity of the human agent.[27] In the regime which I identify, the environment is seized in a format of functional capacity and the perspective I adopt brings to light the joint elaboration of both intentional–planning agency and instrumental–functional capacity. Third, I want to relate this regime to a kind of good to which agents are committed. Individual interest is often viewed, in social and political sciences, as the universal cause of human action. By contrast, the analysis in terms of regimes helps to see the pragmatic requirements which sustain an individual agency interested in the success of his/her elementary action. The specific delimitation of the good which governs this engagement is both related to the human individual willing agency, and to the functional preparation of the world. It is the good of a fulfilled planned action.

From the above specification, we can view the limits of this regime. The absence of conventional markers, or qualifications, is an obstacle to generalized evaluations which are needed in public disputes involving critique and justification.

The public regime of justification

The dynamics of the regime of critique and justification are discernible in disputes that display the kind of arguments and proofs which demand the highest degree of legitimacy, as illustrated by the third scene above. Boltanski and I identified the different orders of worth which constitute common forms of public evaluation and which are grounded in the same grammar of the common good (Boltanski and Thévenot 1991). Publicity puts a strain on the judgment which guides action. The critical test to which arrangements are put requires that people and things qualify for this reality test. Qualifying is not only a categorization or the creation of a typology; nor is it merely a convergence of beliefs. It depends heavily on capacities that can be tested in relation to the different orders of worth. The third scene above showed how objects might qualify as efficient tools, or commodities appropriate for marketing, or regulatory devices enforcing civic equality in terms of health or safety in particular, or patrimonial assets that relate to the past and anchor trust. Other qualifications relating to different orders of worth are signs supporting fame or creative innovations which testify to inspiration.[28]

Persons qualify jointly as: professionals or experts; dealers and customers; equal citizens; trustworthy and authoritative people; celebrities, creators. The format of relevant information is always conventional. Reports are much more formalist than the ordinary language used to narrate regular actions.

The three scenes recounted above also suggested the fact that this regime of justification is built on the limitations met in the collective extension of the regime of regular planned action. When large-scale coordination is needed, and this need is combined with the necessity of distant adjustments with anonymous actors, the limited strategic interaction which rests on the mutual attribution of individual plans is no longer appropriate. The dynamics of coordination require a reflexive and judgmental stance which can be viewed in terms of the horizon of a third party.[29]

Conclusion

The concept of 'practice' frequently points to repetitive and collective types of conduct. Bourdieu's social theory offers a systematic picture of society based on a unique model of behavior guided, from one situation to another, by the collective and stable force of the habitus. With Luc Boltanski, I explored an orthogonal avenue of research. We wanted to address an important issue which could not be dealt with by Bourdieu's framework: the capacity demanded by contemporary societies to shift from one pragmatic orientation to another, depending on arrangements specific to the situation. We initially focused on the pragmatic orientations which are required by public critique and justification. My subsequent work has examined other pragmatic requirements in order to investigate other types of agencies and how they are sustained. Emerging from the point of contact between the outline of the good and the format of reality engaged, the pragmatic regimes of engagement supply some analytical tools for a pragmatic sociology that is concerned about the conditions for realizing political and moral goals in a 'furnished' human world.

Notes

I am grateful to Karin Knorr Cetina and Theodore Schatzki for their useful critiques on previous versions of this text. I am indebted to Peter Meyers for linguistic correction or translation of part of the text and for helpful advice on its organization. I also benefited from his fruitful comments resulting from his ongoing work on power, will, and dependence (Meyers 1989, 1998). He is clearly not responsible for the remaining errors of form and content.

1 I owe Peter Meyers the indication of this Emily Dickinson poem which relates qualifying, deeming, shapes, tactics, and practice.
2 See Turner (1994) for a quite comprehensive criticism of the notion of social practice.
3 The Groupe de Sociologie Politique et Morale (EHESS–CNRS, Paris) has been directed by Luc Boltanski and myself, and I developed the framework which is presented here in the continuation of our former work on critique and justification (Boltanski and Thévenot 1991; in translation). For a short presentation in English of this framework, see: Thévenot (1995a), Boltanski and Thévenot (1999). For discussions, see: Bénatouïl (1999); Dodier (1993b); Wagner (1994b, 1999); Wilkinson (1997). For an up-to-date survey of recent moves in French social sciences and humanities, see Dosse (1998). For a US–French comparative study of environmental conflicts built on this framework, see: Thévenot, Moody and Lafaye (2000). On Boltanski's developments about 'régimes d'action' and

particularly 'régime d'agapè,' see in French: Boltanski (1990). For a comprehensive presentation in French of the framework which is introduced in this essay, see: Thévenot (1990a, 1993, 1994b, 1997, 1998, 2001b).

4 *Modernity and Self-Identity* is interestingly dedicated to the interconnection between globalizing influences on the one hand and personal disposition on the other, which Giddens rightly views as a distinctive feature of modernity (Giddens 1991). His developments on 'disembedding mechanism' which separate interaction from the particularities of locales is convergent with my analysis of 'investments in forms.' Giddens's analyses of 'self-actualization' are illuminating but still rest, through his elaboration of 'lifestyles,' on a classical notion of social practice.

5 Winch already noticed the adaptation and local change of custom (Winch 1958).

6 These operations can be designated in terms of 'handling,' 'grasp,' 'seizure' or 'capture.' In French, I have used the generic term *saisir* because it covers manual grip as well as data capture. For a discussion of the vocabulary of 'capture' in relation to the formalization of action in AI, see Agre (1994).

7 Gibbard recently elaborated his moral philosophy on the normative meaning of 'making sense of' (Gibbard 1990).

8 On these issues and an research project of 'empirical political philosophy,' see Wagner (1994a, 1998, 1999).

9 The term 'engagement' might work even better in French where it covers quite concrete material adjustments (a key entering lock, a man moving in a corridor, or a car in a street) as well as a wide range of moral or political commitments.

10 I chose 'environment' as a generic term because of its flexibility. It offers a wider opportunity than 'situation,' 'milieu', 'setting,' or 'surroundings' to permit variations of the scope and format of what might be taken into consideration for the adjustment. These differences are highly significant in the characterization of the engagement. The phenomenological tradition, in particular Heidegger and Merleau-Ponty, contains the most acute insight of the intimate relationship with proximate surroundings. On the relation with the *milieu*, see Berque's stimulating elaboration in terms of 'mediology' (Berque 1986). For a recent and remarkable comprehensive analysis of the engagements involved in 'inhabiting' and 'using,' going back to the classical notion of *khresis*, see Bréviglieri (1998).

11 Ethnomethodologists opened the path with the idea of a 'breaching experiment' which might expose the 'taken-for-granted' in a kind of experimental epoche. With the development of a pragmatic sociology of regimes, we have been able to differentiate the kind of 'breach' which is involved: a critical tension between orders of justification which ground a sentiment of injustice (Boltanski and Thévenot 1991), a critical tension between a regime of justification and regimes of more local arrangements when shift to publicity is required (Thévenot 1990a).

12 But some managers foster this last kind of convenience (Thévenot 1997).

13 For a critique of the consequences in the way to treat objects, see Conein (1997).

14 Among other researchers seeking to overcome this risk, Law and Mol explore three 'theory-metaphors for sociality-materiality' with the idea that materials are relational effects (1995). Rouse's own reflection upon the philosophy of practices is largely dedicated to this issue (1996b).

15 Schatzki recommends that we do not confuse causal mechanism which produces action with practical intelligibility which makes sense of it (1987). But once we pay full attention to the way models of activity are effectively used in modes of coordination, and put to the test, the picture gets more complicated.

16 For rich connections with Durkheim's, Weber's and other authors' uses of the term habitus, see Héran (1987).

17 Schatzki criticizes Bourdieu for conflating corporeal dispositions and a theory of intelligibility (1987). This theory conceived in terms of fundamental oppositions

is actually Bourdieu's anthropological complement to Durkheim's view on social representations which rule practices. For a criticism of the way Bourdieu deals with the 'individualist dilemma,' see Alexander (1988, 1995).

18 I found deep convergence with Rouse's intervention to the seminar which led to this volume. Rouse also refers to 'propriety' to oppose an idea of practice which is grounded in regularity (see his contribution to this volume). I diverge from him by my main interest in acknowledging different kinds of propriety which delineate different pragmatic regimes.

19 Terms from the family 'conven-' do not offer exactly the same possibilities in English and French. Both 'convenience' and *'convenance'* are able to capture the level of personal and local propriety. The English term 'conventional' suggests rather broadly a normal, common, or customary conduct. Although insufficiently specified for my need, it can be used to designate the type of normal plan of action and objectal function involved in the second level of propriety. By contrast, the French *'conventionnel'* implies a more formal and general agreement and is more adapted to the level of most legitimate forms of coordination. Finally, the French *'déconvenue'* designates the rupture of a *'convenance'* and points to our methodological approach to investigate these different modes of propriety.

20 This orientation is surely in accord with the pragmatists', particularly Mead's, view concerning ongoing action and the creative part of the process which Joas has been pointing to (Joas 1993).

21 For a pragmatic analysis of different forms of judgment, see Dodier (1993a).

22 On this point, I depart from Powell and DiMaggio (1991) when they build their convergence with ethnomethodology, Giddens, and Bourdieu, on the 'practicality' as an 'affectively and evaluatively neutral' approach to activity. By contrast, I shift to a notion of pragmatic engagement which highlights the connection between practical material engagement and evaluation.

23 Inversely, Law brings together the concrete conditions necessary for citizen competence in a liberal democracy, showing that such competence excludes 'disabled persons' (Law 1998).

24 For this process of familiarization with things, see Thévenot (1990a, 1994b and, at the workplace, 1997). Karin Knorr Cetina reports convergent observations: because of the 'familiarity with the thing (through a joint biography with the detector), [its responses] may be "understood"' (Knorr Cetina 1993, Chapter 5).

25 On this issue, see Meyers (1989). His ongoing work on the notion of will provides an unusual and illuminating view of the historical construction of this notion, of the various roles it plays, and of an alternative constructions of action. See also Meyers (1995, 1998).

26 For stimulating proposals about 'material agency' and a comprehensive discussion of this issue (including the 'Epistemological Chicken' debate initiated by Collins and Yearly [1992]), see Pickering (1995a).

27 For a discussion on the place of plan in action, situated action, and situated cognition: Conein and Jacopin (1993).

28 Things might have multiple conventional qualifications and not only multiple purposes; in that case they sustain *compromises* between these qualifications (for an empirical analysis on the workplace presenting the methodology, see Thévenot [1989]). In the interactionist paradigm, the literature on 'boundary-objects' highlights the benefits which can result from connections to different social worlds and the translations they foster: Star and Griesemer (1989), Fujimura (1992).

29 This third-party reference traces back to Adam Smith's impartial spectator and informs theories of social interaction and public space through Mead's 'generalized other' (1934) and Habermas (1984). On the impartial spectator, see also Boltanski and Thévenot (1991), Boltanski (1999), Meyers (1991).

5   What anchors cultural practices

Ann Swidler

Recent conceptions of culture as 'practice' have made great headway (see Williams 1973; Ortner 1984; Greenstone 1993; Biernacki 1995). But they have also brought new obscurities in their wake. Most important among these is the question of whether there is some sort of hierarchy among cultural practices, and whether and how some cultural practices organize, anchor, or constrain others.

While it is hard to summarize briefly what scholars of several persuasions, driven by differing questions, have meant by 'practice' or 'practices' (and the two terms alone suggest ambiguities), it is easier to point to some of the problems 'practice theory' has solved.

The problem of the subjectiveness of meaning

The central terms of the older sociology of culture were 'ideas,' Weber's major focus, and 'values,' the term used by Parsons. Both theorists shared the assumption that these cultural elements operated by providing the ends toward which actors (individual or collective) directed their action (see Swidler 1986; Warner 1978). For these theorists, therefore, the influence of culture depended on showing that certain cultural elements, whether ideas or values, actually operated subjectively, in the heads of actors, so that 'the "world images" that have been created by "ideas" have, like switchmen, determined the tracks along which action has been pushed by the dynamic of interest' (Weber 1946: 280). Later theorists, however, had difficulty finding such ideas in any coherent or consensual form in the heads of particular actors (see Wuthnow 1987) or showing that these ideas really influenced action, either through logical implication or by providing the criteria for decisions among alternative lines of conduct (see the critiques in Cancian 1975; Skocpol 1985).

Theories of practice solved these problems in two complementary ways. First, they de-emphasized what was going on in the heads of actors, either individuals or collectivities. Instead these theories emphasized 'practices' understood as routine activities (rather than consciously chosen actions) notable for their unconscious, automatic, un-thought character. Practices can be the routines of individual actors, inscribed in the ways they use their bodies, in their habits, in their taken-for-granted sense of space, dress, food, musical taste – in the social routines they know so well as to be able to improvise spontaneously without a second thought (Sudnow 1978; Bourdieu 1976, 1984). Practices can also be trans-personal, imbedded in the routines organizations use to process people and things, in the taken-for-granted criteria that separate one category of person or event from another – 'art' from what is not art (Williams 1981; Becker 1982), or the sane from the mad (Foucault 1965, 1983). But whether 'practices' refer to individual habits or organizational routines, a focus on practices shifts attention away from what may or may not go on in actors' consciousness – their ideas or value commitments – and toward the unconscious or automatic activities embedded in taken-for-granted routines.

Practice theory moves the level of sociological attention 'down' from conscious ideas and values to the physical and the habitual. But this move is complemented by a move 'up,' from ideas located in individual consciousness to the impersonal arena of 'discourse.' A focus on discourses, or on 'semiotic codes' permits attention to meaning without having to focus on whether particular actors believe, think, or act on any specific ideas. Like language, discourse is conceived to be the impersonal medium through which (with which) thought occurs (Lévi-Strauss's notion that animals are 'good to think with'). A focus on discourse then reintroduces the world of language, symbols, and meanings without making them anyone-in-particular's meanings. Rather the semiotic system is the set of interrelated meanings that constitutes a cultural system. By analogy with the Saussurian distinction between 'parole' and 'langue,' discourse is not the content of what anyone says, but the system of meanings that allows them to say anything meaningful at all.[1]

The old terrain of ideas and actors thus split into two domains, that of practices and that of discourses:

discourse

↑

IDEAS

↓

practices

Finding an observable object for the study of culture

The conceptualization of 'culture' as practices in interaction with discourse solved a second problem as well. By taking culture out of the realm of individual subjectivity (or the realm of transcendent values hovering over or behind social action), the turn to discourse and practices gave the study of culture an empirical object. As Roger Keesing (1974) has observed, Geertz's great accomplishment was to make culture a matter of publicly observable symbols and rituals – the organization, in short, of discourses and practices, rather than something hidden away in individual consciousness (see Wuthnow 1987). To study culture then becomes to observe closely those publicly accessible practices, either through micro observation of largely mute and unnoticed practices (Knorr Cetina 1981; Cicourel 1968; 1974b; Knorr Cetina and Cicourel 1981) or through 'thick description' of the publicly observable symbolic and ritual practices that structure the possibilities of meaning in a given 'cultural system' (Geertz 1973). (Of course, the 'interpretation' of those meanings does take one back into the realm of the subjective, making implicit claims about what symbols mean to individual actors or groups of actors [see Swidler and Jepperson 1994], but such claims are at least focused on description of a clearly observable empirical object: the ritual, practice, symbol, story, or game treated as a 'text'.)

The enormous fruitfulness of the contemporary study of culture, after its older variants seemed to have run out of steam, has come from this renewed focus on a definable empirical object. The interpretation of such objects may vary, and the underlying structure of which these observations are the supposed signs may be debated, but Foucault's (1979) descriptions of the practices of punishment, of diagnosis and confinement of the mentally ill (1965), or of the diagnosis and categorization of sexual 'perversions' (1978), like Geertz's (1973) depictions of Balinese cockfights or Berber tall tales, or Knorr Cetina's (1981) detailing of the routines of scientific laboratories seem to provide direct ways in which social knowledge, or culture, and the implicit logics they contain, can be directly observed. Both discourses and practices are concretely observable in a way that meanings, ideas, and values never really were.[2]

The problem of culture's link to action

The focus on practices and discourse (sometimes 'discursive practices') also solved, or at least transformed, the problem of how to link culture and action. If culture is only practices, the problematic relationship of culture to action disappears. Culture cannot be treated as some abstract stuff in people's heads which might or might not cause their action. Rather cultural practices *are* action, action organized according to some more or less visible logic, which the analyst need only describe. As we shall see below, however, defining the nature of this 'logic' – discerning the structure of a set of practices – becomes a primary challenge for cultural analysis.

Given the difficulty across many contexts and styles of research in linking what people 'say' to what they 'do' (see Swidler 1986; Cancian 1975; Skocpol 1985; Schuman and Johnson 1976; Hill 1981), it is a relief not to have to link ideas and behavior. Rather, if one studies 'practices,' whether linguistic or not, one is already studying behavior, and the problem of the causal connection between one form of behavior and another is at least staved off, if not resolved.

The culture vs. structure distinction

The problem of the causal relationship of culture and action is linked to a larger and more recalcitrant problem, that of the relationship of culture to structure. Sometimes naively cast as the relation between 'ideal' and 'material' interests, the larger problem of the relative weight of 'cultural' vs. 'structural' factors in explaining social outcomes has continued to bedevil the social sciences. Weber treated the distinction as real and tried through his comparative studies to show that 'ideas' made a real, independent difference in shaping social outcomes. If China, like Europe, had the preconditions for capitalist development, but failed to develop capitalism because it lacked the appropriate cultural ethic, the case for the independent importance of culture was strengthened.

Talcott Parsons took this attempt to integrate an understanding of how material and ideal factors interact in processes of social causation to its most sophisticated level. Parsons (1966), followed by Jeffrey Alexander (1983), argued that material and ideal factors are both essential to social causation, but they operate in fundamentally different ways. According to Parsons' 'cybernetic' model, some causal factors (ideas, symbols, values – culture in general) are high in 'information' but low in 'energy.' An example might be an architect's plans, which provide information about how to build a house, but which cannot, by themselves, provide shelter, or even cause a house to be built. Other causal factors, lower down in the 'cybernetic hierarchy,' are higher in 'energy' and lower in information – in essence, they are the unformed matter, like the pile of bricks, boards, and mortar necessary to build a house, or the energy of a potential worker. But without some input of information, these are no more likely to become a house than to become a wall, a set of projectiles, or simply an impediment. So 'material' factors are necessary conditions for action (like the motive energy provided by the engine of interests in Weber's 'switchmen' metaphor), and in that sense they have the greater power in determining action. But ideas (or information) direct action, and in that sense have the final say in shaping the particular kind of action that occurs.

This Weberian/Parsonian effort to integrate cultural and structural factors in the explanation of human action has come under sustained criticism in recent years. Sociologists have increasingly argued that 'culture' and 'social structure' cannot effectively be separated, and that nothing like the classic quasi-experimental maneuver of isolating culture's independent effect by varying culture while holding social structure constant is possible (though see the impressive work of Fulbrook 1983 and Biernacki 1995). On the one hand, theorists have argued that what is taken to be 'social structure' is itself constituted by culture (see Sewell 1985, 1992; Meyer and Rowan 1983; Biernacki 1995). Conversely, both the content and the domain of 'culture' are constituted through a set of undeniably 'material' practices (Williams 1973; Becker 1982). As Sewell (1985: 84) wrote in a kind of manifesto about culture and structure, we must learn to think of 'ideology' as itself a 'structure,' as 'anonymous, collective, and constitutive of social order.'

Sewell extended his analysis of culture and social structure in an important paper, 'A Theory of Structure: Duality, Agency, and Transformation' (1992). It reconfigures the distinction between culture and structure while conceiving of culture itself as a form of structured practice. But in making a substantial advance over earlier formulations, it also reveals the gaps in our understanding of how cultural practices are *organized*.

Sewell (1992) wants to erase, or at least substantially reorganize, the culture–social structure distinction. He follows Giddens (1981: 27) in seeing structures as 'dual,' as 'both the medium and the outcome of the practices which constitute social systems.' Sewell then defines structure itself as enacted cultural schemas, understanding schemas (again following Giddens) as 'generalizable procedures.' Cultural schemas are generalizable 'in the sense that they can be applied in or extended to a variety of contexts of interaction' (Sewell 1992: 8). It is in this sense that, as Giddens notes, schemas are 'virtual.' 'To say that schemas are virtual is to say that they cannot be reduced to their existence in any particular practice or any particular location in space and time: they can be actualized in a potentially broad and unpredetermined range of situations' (Sewell 1992: 8).

Sewell (1992: 13) departs from Giddens in seeing structure as 'composed simultaneously of schemas, which are virtual, and of resources, which are actual.' A schema is what makes a resource meaningful as a resource (to use Sewell's example, what makes Hudson Bay blankets a source of chiefly power for the Kwakiutl rather than simply a means of keeping warm), but resources are actual in the sense that the schema alone will not bring them into being or determine how much of them one can lay hold of. Sewell then argues that '[i]f structures are dual in this sense, then it must be true that schemas are the effects of resources, just as resources are the effects of schemas' (p. 13). This means, he goes on to note, that 'if resources are instantiations or embodiments of schemas, they therefore inculcate and justify the schemas as well. Resources . . . are *read* like texts, to recover the cultural schemas they instantiate' (p. 13). Finally, structures depend on the mutual reproduction of schemas and resources:

> If schemas are to be sustained or reproduced over time – and without sustained reproduction they could hardly be counted as structural – they must be validated by the accumulation of resources that their enactment engenders. Schemas not empowered or regenerated by resources would eventually be abandoned and forgotten, just as resources without cultural schemas to direct their use would eventually dissipate and decay. Sets of schemas and resources may properly be said to constitute *structures* only when they mutually imply and sustain each other over time (p. 13).

The notion that 'structures' such as factories, social class systems, or greeting practices among university colleagues can be 'read' for the (virtual) cultural schemas they embody, and that enacting such schemas in turn generates arrays of resources, finally recasts the culture–social structure distinction. Rather than 'material factors' being a kind of shapeless matter, given form by intangible 'ideal' factors, Sewell has understood that the very structures of material life are structures only because they are patterned by cultural schemas, and he has simultaneously shown that these arrays of resources are 'read' as cultural texts. Structures are reproduced as repeated instantiations of 'virtual' cultural schemas that make the structures what they are.

Practices are structures in just this sense, simultaneously material and enacted, but also patterned and meaningful, both because they enact schemas and because they may be read for the *transposable* schemas they contain. Sewell (pp. 16–19) has brilliantly argued that this revised conception of how structures are formed from schemas and resources allows a substantive account of human agency. Because structures are multiple and intersecting, because schemas can be generalized to new situations and can sometimes generate unpredictable resource outcomes, and most importantly because the schemas implicit in arrays of resources can be 'read' in multiple and sometimes competing ways, transformation as well as continuity of structures is possible.

WHAT STRUCTURES STRUCTURES?

The view of structures and practices as multiple and sometimes inconsistent, and of everything from capitalism to handshakes as structured practice can be liberating, but it can also lead to trouble. If practices are part of unified 'systems' reflecting some single, underlying logic, then we can say a great deal about what any one part of such a system implies about other parts. If we can describe the underlying deep structure, we can understand where the practices we observe come from and we can see how they fit together. But if there is multiplicity, multivocality ('polysemy' in Sewell's terms), and contradiction between structures, which vary from great and enduring to minor and transient, then the reinterpretation of structures may lead to its own dead ends.

Sewell (pp. 22–6) sees the problem, and suggests that structures differ in 'depth' (how pervasive, invisible, and taken-for-granted their schemas are) and in 'power' (how great the resources they generate and depend upon). But this way of categorizing structures, and even the substantive claim that more visible, resource-rich structures may be less stable than others because they become foci of social conflict, does not really help us think about the different kinds of structures and practices and about whether or when some practices govern others.

Are all practices equal, or are some more equal than others?

I proceed inductively here, examining several concrete cases to see how some practices anchor, control, or organize others.

Let us return first to the hypothetical example of an architect's plan for a house versus the materials and labor required to build the house – the kind of example Parsonians would use to illustrate the role of ideal versus material factors in social causation. The Parsonians would see the architect's plans as exerting a 'controlling' influence over the less symbolic, more material ingredients required to build the house. But practice theorists would find this analysis deficient from the start. Like Howard Becker describing *Art Worlds* (1982), practice theorists would note that long before the architect could draw up plans for the house, constraints on the possible design of the house were built into taken-for-granted practices on two fronts. First, the architect assumes the standard kinds of materials that are available, and ignores the potentially infinite set that is unavailable. The standard sizes and properties of bricks and mortar, poured concrete and steel girders, door-frames and skylights, provide the ingredients from which the architect assembles his plans. Like composers who seek to write music for which there are no instruments (Becker 1982), architects will be unable to build houses that require materials no one can make.

Second, the plans any architect draws are inevitably incomplete. Even when the skills of a contractor or builder are added, the plans for a house leave unspecified most of what will be required to build it. Key among the unspecified elements are practices: the informal skills of craft workers (Stinchcombe 1959), the ways workers with different specialties coordinate their activities, and the uses they see as appropriate for standard objects and materials.

Indeed, lying behind the architect's drawings are yet other practices, so taken-for-granted as to be nearly invisible. One, of course, is the implicit knowledge of what a house is and how people use one, including such 'normal' practices as whether people sleep alone or collectively, whether sleep should occur in a room different from that reserved for eating or bathing, etc. Another is the set of social practices against which aesthetic experience is set off, which provides the vocabulary of meanings that an architect, or any artist works with to produce an effect (see Baxandall 1972; Geertz 1976). Yet another is the set of practices that links architects and clients, including who pays whom and which kinds of judgments each party to the transaction is entitled to make (the clients get to decide how many bedrooms they want, but the architect decides whether a given design is technically feasible [see Baxandall, 1985]). And finally, the assumptions that a house is something one can own, that paying wages will mobilize the labor of others such as architects or bricklayers, that how big a house one can have depends on how much money one has, that one has many choices and must decide what one wants – in short, the whole set of practices associated with a capitalist market economy – are necessary to make the architect's plans a meaningful document that could mobilize or direct activities in such a way as to produce a house.

Practices thus lie behind every aspect or level of social causation. And, as Sewell has argued, practices are enacted schemas, schemas which can be transposed from one situation or domain to another and which are expressed in, and can be read from, practices themselves. The question is whether among all these various kinds of practices we can distinguish some that are more central, more controlling, more determinative than others – in given kinds of situations – or whether we are simply awash in practices, each patterned and habitual, each subject to revision as it is transposed or replicated, and none more influential than any other.

Practices that anchor constitutive rules

We take for granted that some structures and their associated practices are, in Sewell's sense, deeper, more fundamental, more powerful than others. So the structures of capitalism and its associated practices, such as paying to buy or build a house which one then owns, are more fundamental – more enduring, more pervasive, more influential in shaping or constraining action – than this year's fad in kitchen countertops, or even the practices of housewifery that make an easy-to-clean countertop desirable. But does such a hierarchy of practices, corresponding roughly to the nested (or un-nested) hierarchy of social organization, really capture the causal significance of cultural practices?

Let me take a concrete example. Elizabeth Armstrong (forthcoming) has studied the proliferation of identities within San Francisco's lesbian and gay community from 1964 to 1994. Having coded identity information for each organization in the community during those years, she first looked at how identities changed substantively, tracing the implicit practices of categorization that defined varieties of gay identity. When did identities based on specific sexual practices emerge? When were identities that combined sexual identifiers with racial or ethnic categories at their height? When were identities that linked standard occupational or leisure activities with sexual identities most common?

After closely examining her data, Armstrong realized that what she was really seeing was a critical change in the larger discourse that made having an 'identity' a crucial feature of membership in the wider lesbian and gay community. She notes a turning point, right around 1971, when attempts to build a single, unifying organization to represent San Francisco's homosexual community were replaced by an organizing strategy that encouraged the proliferation of literally hundreds of organizations focused around diverse identities and interests. The community's diversity was enacted – and celebrated – in the Lesbian/Gay Freedom Day Parade, inaugurated in 1971, with floats, contingents, and marchers representing a panoply of more or less flamboyant identities.

Armstrong's most striking argument is that this understanding of the nature of the 'gay community' (currently, with the proliferation of identity terms, the 'Lesbian/Gay/Bisexual/Transgender Community'), once established, seemed able to resist challenges, reabsorbing them into its discourse about identity. So, for example, the attempt to create a 'queer' politics that would unify the community politically and define its politics as beyond sexual orientation *per se*, was reabsorbed so that 'queer' became just one other identity choice.

How then can we describe this abrupt but apparently resilient change in the implicit rules and associated practices that defined the nature of San Francisco's lesbian/gay community? Roy D'Andrade (1984), the anthropologist, drawing on the work of John Searle, introduces the term 'constitutive rule,' to describe a particular kind of culture – or perhaps we should say a particular kind of cultural *act* – that defines what shall count as what:

> A marriage ceremony, a baseball game, a trial, and a legislative action involve a variety of physical movements, states, and raw feels, but . . . the physical events and raw feels only count as parts of such events given certain other conditions and against a background of certain kinds of institutions . . .
>
> These 'institutions' are systems of constitutive rules. Every institutional fact is underlain by a (system of) rule(s) of the form 'X counts as Y in context C' (Searle [1969] quoted in D'Andrade [1984]: 91).[3]

One way to think about the change Armstrong describes is to say that the 'constitutive rule' defining the gay community changed from a group defined by common interests to a community made up of diverse subgroups. The new constitutive rule then entailed a whole set of new understandings: that diverse identities did not split the community, but united it; that organizers should not aspire to create a single unified organization to represent the community; that the discovery and public assertion of new identities was part of the community-building project.

What anchored this set of 'constitutive rules,' making it so resilient? Why (or how) was it that, once established, the notion that the community consisted of its diverse identities persisted, generating ever more elaborate identity discourses (naturalized by participants, who saw themselves as discovering or expressing their real, authentic identities)?

This situation, in which a set of larger, but implicit 'constitutive rules' anchors an elaborate discourse, like that about identity, creates a real puzzle for cultural explanation. Since the constitutive rules are something no one in the community formulates explicitly, and indeed something they might have trouble seeing even if it were made explicit, what is it that holds the constitutive rule in place, not only reproducing it, but allowing it to drive out competing rules? Bourdieu's (1977) arguments provide a piece, but by no means all of the solution. The idea that the larger rules of the system are reproduced, not by people directly knowing those rules, but by people acting strategically in a world that presumes those rules, fits this situation well. Within the community the way to assert influence, the way to be recognized, the way to matter is to assert an identity; a neglected or demeaned identity creates especially powerful claims on others. But this is hardly a matter of a deeply internalized habitus, inscribed in the body – the system of sense perception, tastes, and so forth. Indeed, the whole discourse is only a couple of decades old, and people latched onto its terms immediately, inventing themselves, and elaborating the discourse, as they went along. Practices are indeed crucial here, but not the sort of deeply internalized, taken-for-granted practices Bourdieu describes.

Armstrong argues that a critical anchor for the constitutive rules that define the lesbian/gay community is the Lesbian/Gay Freedom Day Parade itself. She argues that the practices involved in setting up the parade, in which groups apply to have a contingent or a float included in the parade, and the parade itself, in which the more different groups participating and the more diverse their identity displays the more successful, exciting, and newsworthy the parade is, themselves anchor the definition of the 'community' as composed of multiple identity groups. Thus a practice, of recent origin, and very much a public ritual rather than an inscribed habitus, anchors a larger set of constitutive rules and their attendant discourses. In essence, the parade creates a situation of action in which the enacted schema is that membership in the community equals having a group to identify with, and a set of practices in which asserting one's membership in the community means creating or joining a group which then claims a spot in the parade. Thus a practice encodes the dominant schema – encodes it as a pattern of action that people not only read but enact – a schema that is never explicitly formulated as a rule.

The Lesbian/Gay Freedom Day Parade is a public ritual practice, one that enacts, without explicitly describing, the nature of the community it creates. In Sewell's (1992) terms, as long as it attracts adherents and the adherents manage to bring the event off (the 'resources' part of the equation), the schema the parade actualizes will continue to be available. And in that case, Armstrong argues, it is the practice itself that anchors, and in some sense reproduces, the constitutive rule it embodies.

Why practices dominate

The second example I want to consider is Richard Biernacki's magisterial book, *The Fabrication of Labor: Germany and Britain, 1640–1914* (1995). Using a staggering accumulation of meticulous historical scholarship, this work develops one of the strongest, most original, and most important arguments about culture's influence in recent decades. Biernacki argues that the fundamental difference between British and German labor relations was the way labor was constituted as a commodity. British textile manufacturers purchased labor as it was embodied in commodities, so they worked out payment schemes based on the length and quality of cloth a worker produced. Prussian manufacturers, in contrast, purchased labor power, which they remunerated by measuring how many times the laborer sent the shuttle back and forth to create a given length of cloth. The two systems both rewarded workers for the length and the thread-density of the fabric they produced. But the wage schemes operated on fundamentally different principles, and each produced a scale of remuneration that was linear (that is, created a consistent relationship between remuneration and the quantity of labor) within each country's assumptions but produced irrationalities when transposed to the other country's assumptions.

Biernacki (1995) goes on to show that this difference in the way labor was commodified ramified into the entire system of industrial relations in Prussia vs. Britain, affecting the design of factories, the organization of labor protest (British strikers struck when each weaver finished his piece of cloth and left his loom; German strikers withheld their labor power, staying at their looms but ceasing labor simultaneously at a given hour), and much else.

Biernacki (1995) argues strongly that the difference between the German and British systems did not rest with different *ideas* about labor. Indeed, he argues that the different practices of commodifying labor led theorists from the two traditions to theorize labor very differently. (Marx's understanding that what the worker sold was his labor power was based on German industrial practice.) Biernacki is explicit in separating concrete practices and their influence from the ideas people held about what they were doing. And he gives clear causal priority to practices: 'the schemas encoded in silent practices within the private factory lent workers the concept of labor they used to voice demands in the public sphere' (p. 3). Or again, 'The cultural definition of labor as a commodity was communicated and reproduced, not through ideal symbols as such, but through the hallowed form of unobtrusive practices' (p. 36).

What are these practices to which Biernacki (1995) gives such stark causal priority? He contrasts his approach with views of culture as a 'consistent world view' unifying 'separate cultural beliefs attached to different domains of conduct' or ideas used to legitimate institutions (p. 91). Rather, 'the commodity form of labor constituted from within the form of industrial procedure. In the textile industry, the operation of the weavers' piece-rate scales, the assignment of looms, the replacement of absent workers, the recording of earnings – all these instrumentalities assumed their shape and were reproduced by virtue of the definition of labor as a commodity they sustained' (p. 92). Why did practices have such power – power to define reality such that even when workers were struggling with the irrationalities created by their own wage scales, and even when they had available examples of alternative wage schemes from other countries, they simply could not revise their understandings?

Biernacki develops an argument very close to Sewell's. Practice is culturally constituted, and it directly conveys meaning: 'Comparative study of procedures on the factory shop floor reveals that the micro-practices of production were *constituted* as signs, whether or not they served as the objects of a system of verbal representations' (Biernacki 1995: 93, emphasis in original). He goes on to insist that '[t]he template of labor as a commodity came to life not in the subjective outlooks of individuals but in the orchestration of practice to fulfill a signifying function' (p. 93). If Biernacki is correct, these humble practices, the ones that directly constituted the day-today routines of workers and managers as they negotiated the actual structure of work activity, apparently controlled and provided the model for the more elaborated 'system of verbal representations.' Furthermore, the schemas that were enacted in these day-to-day practices seem to have organized and constrained other schemas.

Because many interconnected practices embodied the same schema for constituting labor as a commodity, the 'established concept of labor' was highly resilient, even when technological changes (for example, a loom imported to England that automatically counted 'labor time' by counting actual shots of the shuttle) altered some of the practices that embodied that concept (Biernacki 1995: 494). On the other hand, the divergent English and German conceptions of labor did not simply persist out of inertial habit or some hidden well of taken-for-granted assumptions. Biernacki makes clear that when the specific practices of wage-setting – the piece-rate scales, the assignment of looms and so forth – were disrupted, the differences in the constitution of labor as a commodity evaporated. Biernacki notes that the German and English conceptions of labor were fundamentally transformed when, during World War I, governments intervened in wage-setting, thus eliminating the practices of piece-rate negotiation that had reproduced the divergent British and German constructions of labor (p. 495).

The extended case Biernacki develops is fundamentally unsettling for traditional understandings of culture. It acknowledges the omnipresence of discourses, but it sees discourses largely as commentaries on concrete realities which are culturally constituted in and through practices. 'Silent' as they are, these practices constitute the unspoken realities upon which more directly symbolic or linguistically mediated activities are based. But the case Biernacki describes is unsettling for 'practice theory' as well. Stephen Turner (1994) has attacked the notion of practices as silent, hidden assumptions, pointing out the insurmountable problems in accounting for both transmission and change of something that is invisible. He proposes substituting the more limited, more economical notion of 'habit,' suggesting that people can learn habits by imitating the public performances of others until they have mastered the capacity to produce those performances, without necessarily having identical internal states or capacities from which those habits flow. But Biernacki's work suggests that this notion of 'habit' and the argument from which Turner derives it is too individualistic. The crucial thing about social practices – and the feature that differentiates them from most habits – is that they are the infrastructure of repeated *interactional* patterns. They remain stable not only because habit ingrains standard ways of doing things, but because the need to engage one another forces people to return to common structures. Indeed, antagonistic interchanges may reproduce common structures more precisely than friendly alliances do. The antagonistic negotiations of workers and owners over wages – the ways workers and employers used piece rates and other work rules to press their own advantage – may have been what held specific conceptions of labor as a commodity so rigidly in place.

This case has in common with the Armstrong example, discussed above, that the anchoring practices operate as enactments of 'constitutive rules,' acquiring their power to structure related discourses and patterns of activity because they implicitly define the basic entities or agents in the relevant domain of social action (defining what constitutes labor as a commodity, or what defines the gay community). But the Armstrong and Biernacki examples are very different in that the anchoring practice of the Lesbian/Gay Freedom Day Parade is a very public ritual, while the practices Biernacki describes are nearly invisible arrangements for organizing everyday tasks and transactions.

What may unite the cases Armstrong and Biernacki describe, however, is that the anchoring practices in both cases constitute socially negotiated realities, so that the practices coordinate basic social relationships. Perhaps practices are more persistent and more likely to structure other domains of thought and action when they constitute social relationships (the negotiations between managers and workers; the relations that are the 'gay community') than when they are simply habits or assumptions held by individual actors.

If we now reexamine Bourdieu's concept of the habitus and Sewell's concept of schemas, we see that both have a remarkably individualistic underlying imagery. Granted, both theorists argue that their core theoretical constructs make no sense except as social products: the habitus is inculcated as the internalization of one's place in a social field; Sewell's schemas are read from prior social practices. Nonetheless, the underlying theoretical imagery leads us to think of an individual person carrying around with her the habitus of her childhood, the skills and dispositions she learned there, mobilizing them strategically as she encounters new social situations. Similarly, Sewell's description of how structures are reproduced allows us to imagine an individual 'reading' the schema from an existing array of resources and attempting to reproduce that structure. Indeed, different individuals can read the existing structure differently and reproduce an altered structure.[4] But perhaps the really persistent practices, those that come to structure wide domains of social life, are those that coordinate actors' actions and thus cannot be changed without disrupting collectively established realities. This, I think, is the implication of Sewell's most recent work on 'events' (Sewell 1996). In an analysis of the storming of the Bastille, Sewell shows that the creation of a new form of social practice – a new constitutive rule that equated the French 'nation' with 'the people' and a new associational pattern for collective behavior – occurred in a highly charged, public ritual occasion, where new meanings were forged and made visible before many people simultaneously. The full working out of the implications of those new patterns awaited the further unfolding of the event and its interpretation, but like the original Gay Freedom Day Parade, the very public event almost immediately established a new form of social practice.

What then can we say about what anchors social practices, or why some social practices seem more firmly anchored – more enduring and more influential – than others? The first claim is that practices of a particular kind –

those that enact constitutive rules that define fundamental social entities – are likely to be central, anchoring whole larger domains of practice and discourse. The second suggestion is that practices may be more firmly anchored when they are at the center of antagonistic social relationships. Third, the establishment of new social practices appears not so much to require the time or repetition that habits require, but rather the visible, public enactment of new patterns so that 'everyone can see' that everyone else has seen that things have changed.

Where are constitutive rules located?

The third example I want to explore is more problematic. I describe a rich set of mutually reinforcing practices and a constitutive rule – voluntarism as the basis for group formation – that might be seen as the 'deep structure' patterning many spheres of American social life. But it is harder to know in this case what specific practices anchor the rule or account for its apparent pervasiveness, coherence, and persistence.

In a recent book, Nina Eliasoph (1998) analyzes the impairment of political discourse in America. In a variety of social action, social service, and recreational groups, Eliasoph finds that even those who claim a political agenda avoid direct discussion of political matters. When such topics are raised, they are typically ignored or met with joking comments to divert the discussion back onto safer ground.

Eliasoph describes many social processes that contribute to silencing political discussion in contemporary America, from the ways news media report political events to the presentation-of-self activists favor (local people concerned about the well-being of their own families). But a central factor inhibiting political discussion appears to be politeness, which makes any topic that could introduce conflict and disagreement seem threatening. Americans have conversational practices, ways of seeming friendly and agreeable in groups, which make any serious discussion that might lead to disagreement problematic. So, at least at first glance, a relatively minor 'practice,' about how informal conversations are supposed to be conducted, can have far-reaching implications for other, apparently more 'important' issues, like the possibilities for political discussion and action. (It is not that people cannot join forces to act politically, but how they act is affected by practices that inhibit open, energetic political discussion even among comrades-in-arms in a movement.) As Europeans always note, Americans like to appear 'friendly,' but that customary friendliness is a practice with important consequences.

There is, however, a deeper 'structural' explanation of the social meaning of these practices. Hervé Varenne (1977) has put in more formal terms what observers since de Tocqueville have noted: American friendliness is related to Americans' tendency to form associations. Varenne speaks of a 'cultural code' (a constitutive rule in the terms we have been using here) in which groups are formed by the voluntary choices of individuals seeking to satisfy their interests. The underlying schema (which in Bourdieu's or Sewell's terms is transposable to new situations and can be used to interpret even highly dissimilar group experiences, like those of families, as well as political groups or garden clubs) is that groups continue to exist only as long as they serve their members' individual needs, and so conflict can easily destroy the group. Thus the norm of polite friendliness is reproduced by the very real fear that conflict in a group can destroy the voluntary participation upon which it depends.

Varenne (1977) thus provides a unifying explanation of both Americans' insistence on their individualism – people need to display distinctive traits, interests, and tastes that make them candidates for affiliation with compatible others – and Americans' conformity – people can remain part of a group only because they share similar interests, needs, or tastes. In this view, then, practices of friendliness are not simply culturally learned skills and habits (Swidler 1986). They are derived from the code for constituting group life according to a particular schema, and they are reproduced by the day-to-day experience of the fragility of group life – the dependence of groups on every-one 'getting along.'

The underlying code according to which what makes an individual unique also makes him or her uniquely valuable to the group is not really tacit. Indeed, while it is not consciously held or frequently explicated as a rule, it is elaborated in paradigmatic myths and stories from *Don't Cry, Big Bird* (Roberts 1981) (Big Bird is too tall to play games with his Sesame Street friends, but when Betty Lou's kite gets stuck in a tree, only Big Bird can save the day) to cowboy movies and hard-boiled detective dramas (Wright 1975; Cawelti 1976).

Many scholars explain America's voluntarist individualism by arguing that America is ideologically an 'individualistic' society, as is evident in its found-ing documents, the religious beliefs of its founding groups, and ideological beliefs of its leaders and publics throughout its history (Hartz 1955; Horwitz 1979; Verba and Orren 1985; Bellah et al. 1985; Lipset 1990). The difficulty with this approach, as many scholars have discovered, is that cultural tradi-tions turn out to contain many competing alternatives (Zuckerman 1982) – in the American case the 'quest for community' as well as the assertion of individualism (see Bender 1978; Hewitt 1989; Swidler 1992).[5]

If an explanation in terms of ideology is unsatisfying, some simple appeal to 'practices' is equally problematic. If Americans indeed learn to think of themselves as autonomous individuals because, for example, from an early age they are expected (indeed, forced) to make choices, so that having preferences and acting on them become part of what defines one as a person (Tobin, Wu, and Davidson 1989), Americans also learn to compete (Dreeben 1968), to both obey and defy authority (Metz 1978), and to feel diminished or enhanced by their position within bureaucratic and status hierarchies (Collins 1981). Americans' typically voluntarist strategies for organizing collective action, and their individualist understandings of their own practice, cannot therefore be due to the fact that they know only one set of practices. They are not doomed to reproduce the dominant structures because of the habits or styles they internalize in childhood.

Then what anchors Americans' voluntarist individualism, and what role do practices play in this process? Another way to describe American voluntarism is to say that Americans act as if there is a constitutive rule that individual agents create groups and, conversely, that groups are the products of their members' choices. A constitutive rule says that something will count as something in a particular context. Practices play a crucial role as repeated ritual confirmations that something is indeed what it is. For example, as John Meyer (1987) and his colleagues have argued, there are increasingly well-institutionalized understandings about what it is to be a nation-state, and the world system is increasingly constituted by nation-states and the abstract individuals those states exist to serve. But concretely, becoming a nation means becoming one of those units that the other units called states recognize as one of themselves. And this is accomplished through conformity to a set of ritual practices. A state has a name, a flag and an anthem (Cerulo 1995), a constitution (Boli-Bennett 1979), and is recognized as a state by the United Nations – with a seat, a vote, and most important recognition in the form of UN membership (McNeely 1995). In a similar way, Erving Goffman (1967, 1971) has delineated the interaction rituals that confirm the status of persons as persons. Moving aside when we pass someone, addressing a person by name, making eye contact, respecting someone's space – all these practices reconfirm the constitutive rules of modern Western selfhood.

Practices also play a key role in recreating the structure of American voluntarism. Varenne himself, who described the underlying code so brilliantly, has focused on discursive practices: the ways in which anything that is said that has 'un-American' content or implications is simply reinterpreted or ignored so as to conform to dominant ways of talking (Varenne 1984, 1987). But I do not think discursive practices in themselves hold the key to the reproduction of such structures. Nor do I think the ordinary practices that instill in Americans a distinctive habitus – the tendency to think of themselves as autonomous selves, their experienced facility in making choices (Tobin, Wu, and Davidson 1989), their expectation that each person will have his or her 'own' opinion on every possible matter (Jepperson 1992), their willingness to advertise their interests and talents to anyone they meet, or their tendency to evaluate others on the basis of moral character more than cultural accomplishments (Lamont 1992) – are the real anchors for the fundamental schema that constitutes persons and groups.

For Americans, the actual creation of groups – establishing church congregations, clubs, support groups, or interest associations – is a recurrent but necessarily intermittent activity. Yet the deep concern with being the kind of self – autonomous, endowed with its own interests and opinions, energetic and ready to take initiative, able and willing to choose – that could form or join a group is a continuing preoccupation (Bellah et al. 1985). For most Americans, the central institutional spheres of action are the market economy, where most people must find places as workers, the bureaucratic state which generates obligations and claims of rights and benefits, and the family where informal as well as legally regulated obligations hold sway. In all modern capitalist societies, encounters with the labor market, in particular, lead individuals to experience themselves as the possessors of skills and capacities which define their social value (see Collier [1997] for an analysis of how labor market experience generates individualized personhood).[6] But none of these are the primary locus of voluntarist individualism. The specific practices that reproduce America's distinctive voluntarist individualism are those people use to negotiate collective action. To act in the wider public sphere, from the neighborhood, to the workplace, to collective political action, to the creation of community alliances and attachments, Americans draw on a diffuse public culture imbued with many elements of the sacred (see Swidler 1992). It is the paradigmatic practices of this wider public sphere, ritual enactments of a civil religion (Bellah 1968), which anchor the fundamental patterns of American voluntarist individualism. Thus when American children choose group activities, or when schools encourage after-school clubs, or when Americans join a church and pay dues, as when on important civic occasions they celebrate 'freedom,' they participate in ritual practices that reinforce voluntarist individualism. This pattern is resilient, I think, precisely because it lies outside the major institutions of bureaucracy, market, and family and thus provides the 'default option' for organizing collective action. In this sense it has something in common with both the 'silent practices' that constituted labor as a commodity in England versus Germany and the public role the Gay Freedom Day Parade played for San Francisco's lesbian/gay community. In all three cases, a practice anchors other forms of practice and discourse because it enacts a constitutive rule that defines a social entity – the 'gay community,' the labor relationship, the 'group' or 'community.'

The notion that certain key practices anchor others and that these anchoring practices may share common features cannot be demonstrated fully with the evidence presented here. I would like, however, to conclude by reemphasizing three points. First, when we invoke the importance of social practices, it is worth asking whether all practices – how scientists in a laboratory turn the lights on and off, how men shave in the morning or how women put on their makeup, whether and where family members gather for dinner, how a social group incorporates new members – are of equal importance in shaping or constraining other social arrangements. I have tried to show that, at least in some cases, there are 'anchoring practices' which play a key role in reproducing larger systems of discourse and practice.

Second, I have suggested that we pay particular attention to the situations in which practices anchor or reproduce constitutive rules, rules that define things as what they are. I have also suggested that while sometimes such practices may be deep, habitual, and taken-for-granted, this need not always be the case. Some public ritual practices seem able to create and then anchor new constitutive rules.

Third, I have tried tentatively to identify kinds of social relationships that might reproduce such constitutive practices. The fact that the differing English and German definitions of labor were central to the ways workers and employers bargained about wages may account for why those defining practices were so enduring and had such wide-ranging ramifications. The examples of the Gay Freedom Day Parade and the many-stranded practices of American voluntarism suggested that ritual practices that define socially central but informally structured social relationships may play an especially important anchoring role. Continued attention to carefully developed empirical cases, where we can see how key structures are constituted by practices, may finally help us to a better understanding of when and how practices anchor or organize systems of practice, discourse, and action.

Notes

1   Sewell (1985: 60) notes a similar shift toward more 'structuralist' thinking about ideology:

> Theorists as diverse as Louis Althusser, Michel Foucault, Clifford Geertz, and Raymond Williams, to name only a few, have shifted the emphasis from highly self-conscious, purposive individuals attempting to elaborate or enact 'blueprints' for change, to the relatively anonymous and impersonal operation of 'ideological state apparatuses,' 'epistemes,' 'cultural systems,' or 'structures of feeling.' For these theorists, the coherence and the dynamics of an ideological formation (under whichever title) are sought in the interrelations of its semantic items and in their relation to social forces, not in the conscious wills of individual actors. Ideologies are, in this sense, anonymous, or transpersonal.

2   The lengths to which cultural analysts had to go to elicit evidence of values, ideas, and meanings illustrate the problem. Scholars like Rokeach (1973) and later Ronald Inglehart (1977) who thought 'values' were important were forced into the uncomfortable position of using respondents' forced-choice rankings of verbal statements of 'terminal' and 'mediating' values as proxies for the deep values that were in theory guiding action. Others used survey-type research, asking respondents how much they agreed or disagreed with various statements as a way of getting at their ideas – their 'beliefs' (like belief in God), 'attitudes' (such as their approval or disapproval of abortion under various circumstances), or their 'values' (like desire for material comfort, versus a clean environment, versus peace on earth). Even brilliant anthropologists like the Kluckhohns were stuck with asking people from different cultural groups about their ultimate values and then trying (without much success) to treat the answers to such decontextualized questions as somehow independent 'causes' of respondents' actions (see Cancian 1975).

3   D'Andrade (1984: 91) develops the concept of a 'constitutive rule,' using marriage as an example:

> Marriage is a culturally created entity – *an entity created by the social agreement that something counts as that entity*. To agree that something will count as something else is more than simply knowing about it, although knowing about it is a necessary precondition. The *agreement* that something

counts as something else involves the *adherence* of a group of people to a *constitutive rule* and to the entailments incurred by the application of the rule (emphasis in original).

He goes on to offer another example:

Games make the most effective illustrations of constitutive rule systems, perhaps because the arbitrary nature of games makes the separation between the physical events of the game and what these events count as quite apparent. When a football player is declared 'out of bounds,' everyone understands that the physical fact of stepping over the line counts as being out of bounds only with respect to the game being played (p. 91).

4 It is significant that in his most recent paper on 'events' that transform structures, Sewell (1996) focuses on a dramatic public ritual, the storming of the Bastille, which loudly, publicly enacted new practices that could coordinate collective action in new ways. See also the argument in Swidler (1992).
5 See the very similar argument in Skocpol (1985) who points to the difficulty of demonstrating that ideologies shaped the outcome of the French Revolution given that leaders of the revolution held inconsistent beliefs and that their actions were often in conflict with their beliefs.
6 Where the institutional order mediates market demands, as in Japan, it can also inhibit the development of many aspects of modern individualism – so that, for example, people may strive to demonstrate individual accomplishment or skill in order to win the favor of a patron or mentor who is the real key to security and success. And of course modern individualisms vary, even among the capitalist democracies (see Stephenson 1989).

Part II
Inside practices

6   Wittgenstein and the priority of practice

David Bloor

§1   There are two salient strategies for defining the relation of theory to practice: one is to give practice priority over theory; the other is to give theory priority over practice. These are not the only possible approaches but they are, arguably, the most stable and difficult to avoid of the options. They have also given rise to identifiable and, to some degree, self-conscious traditions of ideological and philosophical analysis. The tradition according priority to theory over practice is often known as 'rationalism,' while that which – in various ways and at various levels – accords priority to practice over theory is sometimes called 'conservatism.' For better or for worse, these are the labels I shall use here.[1] They are taken from the well-known conservative thinker Michael Oakeshott (1901–90) who articulated a version of this *Weltanschauung* at both the political and psychological levels, developing a detailed social ideology, as well as a characteristic analysis of human thought and action (see Oakeshott 1991). Another representative of conservatism, Ludwig Wittgenstein, only provided a few hints at the more explicit, ideological level. I am thinking particularly of his pessimistic remarks about 'progress,' his interest in Spengler, and his significant, but often overlooked, theological voluntarism.[2] Wittgenstein concentrated his attention on detailed studies of thinking and acting. In the course of these investigations he focused on some of the deepest and most difficult points of conflict between the two traditions. Part of his genius was the ability to distill a problem into a simple, concrete case. This is why his discussion of rule-following is of central importance to anyone wanting to confront the problem of the relation of theory and practice in a fundamental manner.

§2   Rule-following looks like a case where theory has clear priority over practice, where propositional content and meaning precede and determine the action of following the rule. When we think about the compulsion of rules, e.g., the rules of arithmetic, we may be inclined to say, 'The meaning of the rule fixes what we have to do.' If 'doings' count as 'practice' (because they are concrete and take place over time) and if 'meanings' fall under 'theory' (because their nature is abstract and ahistorical) then theory is determining practice. This is why rule-following is so easily taken to be a paradigm case of rationalism. Given the importance attached to logic, mathematics, and calculation in the rationalist tradition, we can see its strategic significance. Wittgenstein's achievement was to win rule-following back for the conservative tradition. He turned it from being a symbol of the priority of theory over practice into an example of the priority of practice over theory.

Here is how he did it. First, he identified the feelings and pictures that sometimes present themselves to us in connection with rule-following as illusions. For example, we may get the feeling that if there is a rule for generating sequences of numbers the sequence is, in some way, already there, waiting for us to trace it out in speech or writing. Wittgenstein insisted there is nothing there. There is no mysteriously preexisting hand-rail to guide us. Second, he explained these pictures and feelings as byproducts of our socialization. The instances of the rule only seem to exist in advance if we are following it in a mechanical, routine and matter-of-course way. These misleading, theoretical pictures are therefore the result of practice, not insights into its cause. Third, he insisted that the only resources we should use for understanding rule-following are naturalistic ones. When we follow rules we act as we do because we are the sort of creature we are, and we have been trained to act in that way: that is all. Explanations of rule-following are not to be grounded in some form of insight into conceptual connections. There is no conceptual or logical 'seeing' that things must be so, just facts about the 'natural history' of human beings in society. (Wittgenstein [1967], *Philosophical Investigations* §25, §415. In subsequent references to the *Investigations* I shall simply cite the relevant paragraph number.)

To drive home the intended exclusion of nonnaturalistic processes, Wittgenstein said that when we follow a rule, ultimately, we act *blindly*: 'Ich folge der Regel *blind*' (§219). There may indeed be intervening processes of interpretation, e.g. using subsidiary rules to follow the original rule, but in the end we just act. This was the famous conclusion in *Investigations* §201. Such routinized behavior does not, of course, by itself necessarily amount to *correct* rule-following. What seems right and what is right are two different things (§258). That aspect of rule-following, the normative aspect, derives from the consensus between different rule-followers. Rule-following is a *practice* (§202). But as far as routine, individual acts of following are concerned, the ultimate basis of the act is blind habit: this is simply what I do (§217). We can see in this argument how Wittgenstein set aside the categories of the rationalist tradition, and reasserted those of the conservative tradition, and how priority was given to practice over theory.

§3   There is, however, a problem with this conservative, antirationalistic account of rule-following. It is a problem which, if it cannot be solved, would allow the defenders of rationalism, once again, to reclaim rule-following as a paradigm case. The problem is that, as it stands, Wittgenstein's account looks as if it has no adequate explanation for a vitally important distinction. I am referring to the distinction between genuinely *following* a rule and merely behaving in ways that outwardly happen to *conform* to the rule.

Nobody thinks the planets 'obey' Kepler's laws in the same sense as a motorist may obey the rules of the road. The planets merely conform; the motorist is capable of more than mere conformity. On a less extreme level, there is a difference between following a custom and unwittingly behaving in ways that happen to fit in with it. To use a familiar example, on the London Underground the custom is to stand on the right-hand side of the escalator, so those in a hurry can pass on the left. Foreigners do not know this, and often stand on the left and block the flow. Some, equally oblivious, happen to stand where they should, on the right. Do these people then 'obey' the custom without knowing it? Our intuitions might differ about whether to use the word 'obey' for these cases. Perhaps mere outward conformity is enough to justify the use of the word, but everyone sees the difference between mere, unwitting obedience, and full, knowledgeable obedience. The underlying causation is different. In one case the action is as it is because of the existence of the custom, and the agent's knowledge of it. In the other case, it is independent of this. Whatever our hesitations over the word 'obey,' regarding laws and customs, intuitions are perhaps closer in the case of following a rule of the kind Wittgenstein typically discussed, e.g., rules generating sequences of numbers. Here, there can be little doubt, the requirement of genuinely following, and not merely conforming, means that we do what we do because of our awareness that it is required by the rule.

§4   To clarify the situation, let me introduce a simple formula derived from Anscombe (1981a and 1981b). We can say that there is a class of actions M, *where M-ing implies that you think you are M-ing.* Conforming does not belong to the class M, because you can conform without thinking you are conforming. Rule-following, however, does belong to the class M, because to follow a rule, you must think you are following it. Our problem may now be expressed sharply as follows: can you do something and simultaneously do it blindly and thinkingly? Does the metaphor of blindness not imply that the behavior is unthinking? There is, at the very least, a prima facie problem in reconciling these two conditions. We must show that we can jointly satisfy *first* the condition that following must be distinguished from conforming, along the lines of Anscombe's formula, and *second* the conclusion of Wittgenstein's attack on the rationalist model, which says that the process of rule-following depends, in the end, on blind action.

How are we to effect a reconciliation – if indeed a reconciliation is possible? Two strategies immediately present themselves: both designed, in their different ways, to close the gap which seems to exist between the self-consciousness of 'following,' with its awareness of the rule, and the 'blindness' of habit. The first strategy is to diminish the 'blindness' of blind rule-following, and inject some thought or propositional content into it. The second is to diminish the 'thinking' needed to make the action the action it is. The less contentful and specified this becomes, the closer it gets to blind rule-following. It will be evident that these two strategies are themselves expressions of divergent commitments on the priority relations between theory and practice. To dilute the blindness of rule-following expresses sympathy to the priority of theory; to dilute the thought that goes into action expresses sympathy to the priority of practice. So one strategy is rationalist, the other conservative. The aim, then, is to see if a sustainably minimal interpretation of thinking can be found which simultaneously allows us to say that rule-following is ultimately blind, and that following a rule is not the same as merely conforming to it. To do this, I shall discuss one of Anscombe' s own examples, and give her own solution, which is, I think, both the right answer, and the Wittgensteinian answer.

§5   Anscombe lists a number of forms of action falling within the class M. As well as following rules the list includes making contracts, playing games, making promises, and getting married. I will stay with the last example for a moment. Getting married implies thinking you are getting married, but what do you have to think? Suppose someone were to go through the ceremony with deliberate, inner reservations. I do not mean the usual doubts, I mean with the intention to deceive. Could such a person argue, on Anscombe-like grounds, that they were not really married because, as they were getting married, they were thinking of themselves as engaged in a deceit, rather than a real marriage? Would that invalidate the marriage? Certainly not. Where does that leave Anscombe' s formula? Has it refuted it? The answer is that it leaves the formula untouched. This is not a counterexample to it. The reason is that the oversubtle deceiver was well aware that it was a marriage he was going through. His being aware of what he was doing was part of what made up the deception. His mistake was to be ill-informed about the requirements making the contract binding. In our imaginary case, the would-be deceiver is in the same position as someone who thinks they can make an expedient marriage, get their hands on their partner's money, and then get a quick and profitable divorce – only to find, too late, that they cannot.

The Anscombe requirement of 'thinking you are getting married' does not, and cannot, properly mean anything like 'knowing the laws of the land.' The requisite thinking does not mean being cognizant of some fitting legal, moral, sociological, or philosophical analysis of the institution. It can only mean something like: knowing that there is such an institution. The thinking involved is the minimal thinking needed to be accepted as a participant in the institution, where such participation ranges from being an expert to being little more than a user of a few relevant words and phrases. Anscombe expresses this by saying that it is a mistake to suppose, 'that the explanation of the thought of M-ing must include an account (of M-ing) as something *contained* in the thought' (1981a: 17). Whatever thinking you are getting married, or thinking you are playing a game, or thinking you are following a rule, consists in, it does not involve a mental state whose propositional content contains an account of the marriage, the game, or the rule-following. But if it does not contain these things, what does it contain? It must have some content if it is to mark a distinction between following and merely conforming. The answer appears to be that it contains an awareness of the existence of the relevant institutions, and an awareness of the actor as currently participating in them.

§6 Let us look at Anscombe's other example, that of playing a game or making a move in a game. Here the question is: if thinking you are making a move is constitutive of making a move, what is 'thinking you are making a move?' Following the line indicated in *Investigations* §197, Anscombe says:

> it is clear that what you do is not a move in a game unless the game is being played and you are one of the players, acting as such in making the move. That involves that you are acquainted with the game and have an appropriate background, and also appropriate *expectations* and *calculations* in connection with e.g. moving this piece from point A to point B. To have these is to think you are playing the game (1981a: 17).

So you are playing, and thinking you are playing, the game, if (i) you are acquainted with the game, (ii) have an appropriate background, i.e., an appropriate degree and depth of acquaintance, (iii) you show the right signs of involvement by forming relevant expectations, and (iv) you are currently responding to a game that is being played. Satisfying conditions (i) to (iv) means you are 'thinking you are playing the game,' even if you cannot give a discursive account of the game, e.g., by formulating its rules.

§7 Have we now resolved the tension between awareness and blindness threatening Wittgenstein's antirationalist account of rule-following? The answer is yes, provided each of Anscombe's constituents of 'thinking' could be enacted 'blindly,' that is, routinely and mechanically.[3] I think they do pass this test. Let us start with being acquainted with the game, and having an appropriate background. Clearly, at some stage, e.g., when we were socialized into game-playing in childhood, games will have been registered in a causal and direct way, where 'direct' means: not mediated discursively by propositional knowledge or interpretive steps. To begin with everything must have depended on what Wittgenstein called 'ostensive teaching' or 'training' (§5–6). We just had to learn by joining in and being told 'do this!' (cf. §143–5). Similar points can be made about the next items on the list concerning background abilities and expectations and calculations. Arguably they are all founded in innate abilities and the routine operation of our normal and inherited cognitive propensities. They are, or depend on, things we simply find within ourselves, or which, as far as we are concerned, simply occur.

Nevertheless, there is still a residual problem: ostensive training is just a form of socialization, and so presupposes an institution into which the learner is being initiated. Where did that institution come from? If we explain it by a prior process of socialization, we are only pushing the problem back rather than solving it. To sustain the priority of practice over theory it must be possible to tell a plausible story about the origin of institutions and practices (such as playing a game). This story must not depend on some prior intention, decision, choice, desire, or belief with a determinate propositional or theoretical content. It must be possible to show how a practice can grow up without depending on some prior 'theory' about it. If that is possible (and if, e.g., Haugeland [1990] is right, it is possible) then ostensive training will take care of the transmission of the institution or practice in an appropriately non-discursive way. Some attention to hypothetical models of the emergence of practices and institutions is needed if a final decision is to be reached on the relative merits of rationalism and conservatism.

§8   So far, I have tried to remove the sense of incompatibility between Anscombe's 'thinking' condition and Wittgenstein's 'blindness' conclusion. It would have been possible, however, to approach this relationship from another direction. Instead of seeing them as potentially conflicting, it could be argued that Anscombe's requirement actually entails Wittgenstein's conclusion. The entailment can be constructed by starting with Anscombe's striking observation that, for the entire class of actions, if M-ing implies thinking you are M-ing, then it is impossible to explain M-ing. This is because explaining M-ing involves mention of thinking you are M-ing, and explaining thinking you are M-ing involves mention of M-ing. The 'explanation' takes us in a circle. This problem is not caused by adopting a rich, or implausibly demanding, construal of 'thinking you are M-ing.' It is not removed by using the minimal definition of 'thinking' that has been defended above. However minimal its specifications, if it is to do the job of distinguishing following from conforming, it will generate the circularity.

If M-ing cannot be explained, how do we ever learn to understand the actions that fall into this class? How, for instance, can we ever learn to follow rules, if Anscombe's impossibility argument is correct? I have already indicated Anscombe's reply, which is that there are other ways of learning apart from explanation. We can be taught how to follow rules, or play games, by example and by doing. We might be told on appropriate occasions, 'you must do this,' or 'you can't do that,' and then, perhaps, be physically made to do things, or physically stopped from doing them. Going along with these requirements would be a precondition for continued participation. At the same time as being made to go through the motions, pupils are also learning how to gloss these moves verbally. They will learn to use, as well as respond to, what Anscombe calls 'stopping modals' or 'forcing modals,' i.e., the language of 'can't' and 'must.' This picture implies the blindness condition because it is the inexplicable character of rule-following which demands ostensive training, and ostensive training is ultimately training in a 'blind' response. Another way to express the point would be to observe that the circularity problem, or the impossibility of explanation, points inevitably to the priority of practice over theory.

We can now see that rule-following has a dual nature. The duality involves, on the one hand, the presence of a certain tendency to act, which will be found, in one form or another, within each individual. On the other hand, alongside this aggregate of dispositions, there will be a shared currency of verbal responses for their evaluation. Both sides of this story capture indispensable features of rule-following. Dispositions alone will not suffice for a proper analysis, because they provide no adequate account of the normative aspect of rules. If our brains were like faultless, pre-programmed machines, which effortlessly coordinated with one another, then no doubt such (ideal) dispositions would achieve everything we currently achieve with our rule-following practices. Under these circumstances, however, there would be no rules because there would be no need for them: it would be the cognitive equivalent of the Golden Age. In reality we need methods for sanctioning and modifying our individual dispositions to keep them in line. This is mediated by verbal commentary, criticism, and evaluation, e.g., by saying 'you can't' and 'you must.'

Verbal glossing practices, on their own, equally fall short. Detached from dispositions to act, they have no real substance. In themselves, they provide no basis for routine rule-following, such as underlies the important phenomenon of noncollusive coordination. We can give six people the task of following the rule '+2,' starting with 0, send them away to work on their own, and when they come back together, they will, for the most part, have produced the same sequence – and be able to agree about its sameness. We cannot understand rule-following as an arrangement which depends on everyone perpetually looking over everyone else's shoulder. It has phases of this character, but it also depends on dispositions, which drive individuals along between face-to-face encounters.

§9   We can now connect what has been said to Wittgenstein's frequently misunderstood claim, in *Investigations* §199, that rule-following is an institution.[4] Wittgenstein never told us what he understood an institution to be, but it is not difficult to construct an account to carry forward the thrust of his argument. My claim will be that, in the case of rule-following, its institutional character depends on exactly those practices of glossing whose role has just been identified. Our habitual responses become instances of rules in virtue of the verbal accounts with which we accompany them as we collectively coordinate our behavior. In general terms, and once again using Anscombe's formula, to think you are M-ing is to be able to account your actions in terms of the institution of M-ing, where that institution itself is constituted by those very accounting practices along with, of course, the accountable patterns of behavior themselves.[5]

As it stands, this is likely to be too compressed a formulation to be illuminating. It presupposes a specific approach to, and analysis of, social institutions and social reality.[6] That approach needs to be brought to the surface so that problems can be addressed. For example, we need to ensure that the interpretation now put on the notion of 'thinking' – in terms of the ability to give a verbal gloss of nonverbal behavior – is consistent with that previously arrived at.

The claim about institutions now being brought into play is that society is the one area of reality amenable to something like an 'idealist' analysis.[7] Social reality, the argument goes, exists and can only exist in virtue of our belief that it exists. When we collectively know about a segment of social reality, the knowing and the thing known are one and the same. In this respect, at least to a first approximation, social objects are different from physical, chemical, or biological objects. Pieces of metal do not exist because we believe in them. By contrast, coins are pieces of metal, but being a coin is a social status attached to the metal. Coins only exist because we treat certain things as coins. (Notice the circularity lingering around such formulations. It is a version of the circularity that made M-ing, as a class, formerly inexplicable.) If everyone were to cease to think of coins, then bits of metal would continue to exist, but coins would vanish into thin air. We can think of all statuses and institutions in this way, i.e., by analogy with currency.

Applying these ideas to the case of rules, the claim is that the rule R exists as an institution in virtue of being referred to for the purposes of glossing those actions which are identified as, or in terms of, instances of following R. The rule R, as an institution, exists only in and through references to R, citing R, describing actions as instances of R, or as not being instances of R, or as attempts to follow R, or as failures to follow R, and so forth through the entire gamut of possible glosses. The institution of the rule is the currency in which the accounting takes place, and its existence is existence as that currency. The self-understanding of rule-followers, their 'thinking' they are following R, is an understanding which invokes the institution of R and, in invoking it, plays its part in constituting the institution as a social reality.

We can now see that the indefinability of Anscombe's class of M-ings is a consequence of the self-referential character of institutions and statuses. Anscombe said that M-ing implies thinking you are M-ing. I recast that into the form: M-ing implies the capacity to gloss or account what is being done as M-ing. Expressed in this way it is easier to exhibit its relation to the self-referential model. The connection is that M-ing must imply the capacity to gloss what is being done as M-ing, because it is the glossing which makes the institution, and it is only in virtue of the institution that the act can have the identity it does – an instance of M-ing can be M-ing only because there is the institution of M-ing. The sequence of dependencies is this: no institution, no M-ing; but no glossing, no institution: so no glossing, no M-ing. This means M-ing and glossing cannot be separated and, as Anscombe noted, that is what produces the circularity and makes explanation impossible. Therefore it is the character of M-ing as an institution, constituted by patterns of self-reference, which generates Anscombe's circle.

§10   There is an immediate connection to be made with Kripke's discussion of rule-skepticism in his *Wittgenstein on Rules and Private Language* (1982). Kripke's skeptic challenges us to say why we have been following the rule for addition rather than another operation, called 'quaddition,' where the quaddition rule is defined so that it is identical to the addition rule for all calculations performed to date. (It diverges for sums which are larger than those performed hitherto.) Intuitively we want to say that we may have been *conforming* to the quaddition rule, but we were actually *following* the addition rule. In Anscombe's terms, we were thinking of addition, not quaddition. The skeptic, reasonably, wants to know what this 'thinking' consists in – what matter of fact about us is involved? The skeptical claim is that (other than by resort to dogmatism) we will not be able to identify this matter of fact, or specify what the thinking consists in. Anscombe's conclusion, that the attempt to explain any instance of the class of M-ing is impossible, and leads us in a circle, is a version of the skeptic's conclusion. The impossibility of explanation means that no matter of fact can be found, at least, not if we confine our attention to the individual rule-follower. Similarly, Anscombe's suggestion that the 'thinking' in question can only be understood by placing the rule-follower in a social context (that is, by their satisfying conditions (i) to (iv) above) is a precursor to Kripke's 'skeptical solution.' Both Kripke's and Anscombe's arguments tell us that the content of the thinking is to be located by reference to the institutions in which the thinker participates. In short, if Anscombe's argument is right, then so is Kripke's.[8]

§11   Wittgenstein's central metaphor of 'language-games' assumes a new and striking importance in this regard. The idea of language-games is, perhaps, the nearest thing Wittgenstein had to a theoretical model, but it was a very significant and suggestive one. The point is that games are instances of institutions, so the metaphor trades on the essentially self-referential character of all social concepts. Wittgenstein's other metaphors can also be seen in this light. For example, at one point he (1978: VII-3) characterized his own philosophical enquiry as follows: 'What I have to do is something like describing the office of a king; – in doing which I must never fall into the error of explaining the kingly dignity by the king's usefulness, but I must leave neither his usefulness, nor his dignity out of account.' Notice how kingship is a phenomenon calling for analysis in terms of the 'idealist,' or self-referential, model of institutions that I have just sketched. At the simplest level, and in its most primitive form, the status of a king is created by everyone's willingness to think of, and refer to, someone as a king, where the thinking and referring is integrated into patterns of deferential action. Again in simple terms, a king nobody accepted as a king, would not be a king, just as money nobody accepted as money would not be money. (See also Wittgenstein 1978: VIII-3, VII-62.)

§12   I have characterized Wittgenstein's achievement as winning back rule-following for the conservative tradition, that is, giving an analysis of rule-following in a way that is consistent with the priority of practice. Superficially, this may seem like an esoteric exercise of interest, perhaps, only to the historian of cultural traditions or to current adherents to the conservative ideology (in Oakeshott's sense). In fact it is a highly consequential achievement of profound significance for contemporary social scientists and historians, particularly historians of science. The basis of its general significance is that it removes one of the major obstacles standing in the way of the sociology of knowledge. Classical sociologists of knowledge, such as Karl Mannheim, were able to offer no guidance on how to think sociologically about rule-following. And that meant they could not help us see how to think sociologically about such important cultural phenomena as mathematics and logic. Wittgenstein shows us how to get around this obstacle. He shows us how to avoid the fatal flaw of saying that the rule itself (thought of as an abstract or formal entity) is responsible for those actions or thoughts that are involved in following it – as if some mysterious mental process of 'grasping the rule' had to be accepted as basic. On this view, the sociologist can only explain deviations from the correct path, or the general preconditions of having the requisite insight and grasp. Only a sociology of error is possible from this standpoint. It is the conservative tradition, as developed so brilliantly by Wittgenstein, which points the way forward to a proper sociological analysis of rule-following and analogous phenomena. Following Wittgenstein we can give substance and depth to the idea that rules are institutions and rule-following is participation in the relevant institutional practices. The great danger here is that of giving too quick and easy assent to Wittgensteinian slogans without an adequate appreciation of the underlying arguments. The arguments alone mark the difference between depth and superficiality in this area. For example, notice that the conclusion is not that rules are institutions merely in the sense of their being widely accepted. The point is that rules are socially constituted, where the manner of constitution can be identified in terms of self-referential processes. The very ontology of rules is social and grounded in patterns of interaction. The detailed arguments have been worked through in order to make this deeper reading available and to prevent the trivialization of Wittgenstein's conclusion.

I want to end by making explicit, and defending, the claim that thinking of rules as institutions – and thinking of institutions along the lines here recommended – is indeed a way of affirming the priority of practice. At first the point may seem counterintuitive. Can an 'idealist' or self-referential model really embody a commitment to the priority of practice? If rule-following is an institution, and institutions are to be understood, as Wittgenstein suggested, on the model of games, which do not answer to any reality outside themselves, how can they be thought of as 'practical'? Practical activity, unlike 'theoretical' activity, implies an engagement with a reality independent of ourselves and our thoughts. This intuition is correct, but it has not been compromised by what has been said about institutions. When we interact for practical purposes with the natural environment, which is indeed profoundly

real service in a virtual world

www.ibooknet.co.uk

lin e

O n

callcentres
eople
wledgeable
Real

ooks
and use
collectable
Real

knet

independent of our thoughts, we do so collectively. This is the crucial point. We are simultaneously interacting with the physical and the social environments. This double modality, as it might be called, is actually a precondition of objective knowledge. The alternative would be a wholly individual and subjective grasp of the world whose characteristics would fall far short of what we take for granted in our shared scientific understanding. An objective understanding is one which is accomplished by and through our cognitive institutions and conventions. The great error is to think that practical and objective cognition must be a response to the physical environment rather than a response to society, as if the two were exclusive. Although under particular circumstances the two can and do trade off against one another, this is not the general case. 'Nature' and 'Society' are not locked into an inevitable zero-sum game. On the contrary, the general case is that we know the physical world with and through society. That is to say: we know the world with our institutions, and by virtue of our institutions, not in spite of them. The self-referential analysis of institutions does not therefore undermine the practicality of our knowledge, but describes a precondition of it. And to say that it is a precondition is simply to say that social practices are an integral part of any other cognitive practices. This is not to compromise the principle of the priority of practice, but merely to articulate and explain it.

Notes

Over the past few years I have had a number of valuable discussions about Anscombe's work with Barry Barnes. We have not always agreed, but the present paper is, in part, the upshot of those discussions. It will be clear how much I have depended on his account of social institutions. I must, however, take responsibility for the shortcomings in my use of these ideas. Celia Bloor and Martin Kusch have read and criticized two earlier drafts of this paper and, where possible, I have done my best to meet their objections. I am most grateful to them, as I am to Konrad Bloor who has, once again, done the typing.

1 Alternatively, the traditions could be called 'Enlightenment' and 'Romantic' respectively. This was the terminology I used in *Knowledge and Social Imagery* (1991). Karl Mannheim (1953) called them the 'Natural Law' and 'Conservative' traditions. The present choice of 'rationalist' and 'conservative' comes from Oakeshott (1991).

2 See Wittgenstein (1980b). For a general discussion of Wittgenstein in relation to Mannheim's category of conservative thought, see Bloor (1983: Chapter 8). His theological voluntarism is discussed in my *Wittgenstein: Rules and Institutions* (1997). On Wittgenstein's ideological and political conservatism see Nyiri (1976, 1982).

3 Wittgenstein's version was this: 'one follows the rule *mechanically*. Hence one compares it with a mechanism. "Mechanical" – that means without thinking. But entirely without thinking? Without *reflecting*' (1978: VII-60).

4 The misunderstandings I have in mind are the individualistic, nonsociological readings exemplified by McGinn (1984) and Baker and Hacker (1984).

5 There is a parallel to be drawn here with a famous argument in Book III of Hume's *Treatise*. Hume said there must be an interest in acting virtuously that was

independent of the sense of duty. A similar argument could be used to claim that we must have a tendency to behave in ways that later become rule-governed, where that original tendency is prior to any sense of a rule demanding such behavior of us. This takes us back to the problem of origins and what Barnes calls 'the problem of priming.'

6   The approach in question is taken from Barnes's important paper 'Social Life as Bootstrapped Induction' (1983). For an account along similar lines but, I believe, a less searching one than Barnes, see Searle (1995). Some important differences between Barnes and Searle are discussed in Bloor (1996a).

7   The label 'idealism,' in this connection, is taken over from Anscombe (1976) who identifies Wittgenstein as a 'linguistic idealist.' For a discussion of Anscombe's difficult but important paper see my 'The Question of Linguistic Idealism Revisited' (1996b). It should perhaps be emphasized that so-called linguistic idealism is not to be confused with a generalized ontological idealism such as the position associated with Berkeley where a thing, such as a tree or a desk, only exists when it is being perceived. Linguistic idealism does not call into question the reality of material things, indeed it presupposes them. It is a doctrine which applies to a limited range of reality, in particular, social 'objects.' Seen in the correct light it is perfectly compatible with a robust materialist ontology. It can be seen as an adjunct to such a materialism in that it provides a way of analyzing realities which might otherwise be granted their own mysterious *sui generis* mode of nonmaterial being. For these reasons it would be wrong to count the position as an expression of a generalized form of nonnaturalism or antnaturalism. One should surely say that social objects were themselves natural phenomena, but ones that can only be understood as the product of collective, self-referential processes. They are, in Hume's terms, artifacts and therefore in a narrow sense of the word 'nature' they are nonnatural, that is, not naturally occurring things, but of course in a broader sense of 'natural' they are indeed part of nature. One merely has to broaden one's view to see just what natural phenomena constitute social objects. Again, Hume's handling of these themes in the *Treatise* provides the correct model.

8   There are criticisms to be made about certain equivocations in Kripke's argument, but it is essentially right. For a thorough discussion see Bloor (1997).

7   What is tacit knowledge?

H. M. Collins

The idea of 'tacit knowledge' has proved fruitful in the sociology of scientific knowledge even while remaining ill-defined and elusive. I will describe and classify what has been done. I will set out some ways in which the idea has been used by practitioners of practice and then offer some comments on the different approaches.[1]

Is this philosophy? Can a mere description of the way a concept has been used by a practitioner stand up to the sharp analysis of philosopher critics?[2] My excuse is as follows: Wittgenstein is the philosopher to whom nearly all theorists of practice defer and I offer my project in terms of the Wittgensteinian sentiment that the meaning of a concept is to be understood through its use. That, of course, is why sociologists are so interested in practices – they are interested in understanding social and conceptual worlds by looking at uses. Here we are merely turning the same principle back on the concept of practice itself.

It follows that I am not terribly interested in the analysis of the term 'tacit knowledge' as it is used in *theories* of practice. Many contributors to this volume consider that terms such as 'tacit knowledge,' or 'tacit rules' are idle wheels in theories, or worse. Some think that to use such terms indicates, misleadingly, that there are hidden structures which underlie practices, whereas all we need to refer to are the practices themselves. I am not trying to make a direct contribution to that debate, at least, not in the terms in which it is usually cast;[3] my contribution is meant to be that of a practicing sociologist, for whom my own (partial) mastering the practices of the communities I study is a very concrete achievement akin to what the members of those communities themselves achieve as they become members. A language describing what I and my respondents do as we move from a state of incompetence to a state of competence seems anything but an idle wheel. Thus, I note that mastery of a practice cannot be gained from books or other inanimate sources, but can sometimes, though not always, be gained by prolonged social interaction with members of the culture that embeds the practice. I note that there are robust indicators of success in grasping a practice: ceasing to commit *faux pas* during interactions with respondents is a good indicator and usually quite an obvious one; the nature of conversations with experts is also a good indicator – if you can get them to listen to you seriously and interestedly when you discuss their subject that means you are getting somewhere; if, on the other hand, all such conversations begin with their explaining principles to you in a pedantic way, you are getting nowhere. These are a few things that are common to all practices. They would remain the same whether or not the term 'tacit knowledge' is replaced by other locutions.[4]

That said, I had better give some indication of the subject area I am going to discuss. It covers those things we know how to do but are unable to explain to someone else. We may not know how to explain them, or we may not even know that we know that we know things of this sort. For example, most native English speakers do not know that they 'know' how to avoid uttering badly formed sentences and have not thought about how they came by this 'knowledge.' They certainly have no idea how to pass the knowledge on in any way except doing a lot of talking.

One way in which I will explore that kind of subject area is to try to destroy my own belief in the tacitness of much of our knowledge by seeing how much of the idea I can dispense with. I will try to 'give away' as much tacitness as I can by looking at ways of making the tacit explicit. I could try to give away the idea to a philosopher (such as Steven Turner 1994), but I am more familiar with the raids on tacit abilities conducted by the 'artificial intelligentsia' – those who believe that all human capabilities can be encoded in machine programs so there can be nothing deeply tacit, or social, about them. Therefore I will try to give as much of the tacit element of tacit knowledge as I can to neural nets – currently the most promising and most 'hyped' candidates for the title of tacit-knowledge-capturing machines. I do not particularly care whether or not I am giving too much because my strategy is to show that however much I try to give away there is still some left which the working sociologist cannot dispense with.[5]

I will divide up the work into three sections which are three approaches to tacit knowledge from which sociologists have set out – from which their practices have begun. I shall then revisit these approaches in turn and try out neural nets against each approach and see what they can gobble up and what, if anything, is still left on the plate. In each case I will conduct a thought experiment and ask whether all the tacit knowledge that is used when scientists try to replicate a difficult experiment could be encoded in a neural net.

Three routes to the idea of tacit knowledge

The motor-skills metaphor

Probably the most influential paradigm case of tacit knowledge, due to Michael Polanyi (1958), is bicycle-riding. Polanyi points out that the physics of bike-riding is complex and counterintuitive,[6] that hardly any bike-riders, if any, know the physics, and that even if they did, they would not be able to use their understanding to master the bike. We learn to ride a bike, then, without knowing how we do it, where 'knowing' is used in the sense of 'being able to formulate the rules.'

What do we mean by 'being able to formulate the rules?' Well, we do know certain rules for riding bikes, such as 'stand the bike on its two wheels'; 'sit on the saddle'; 'turn the pedals with the feet'; 'hold the handlebars with the hands'; 'the size of a bike must be roughly matched to the size of the rider'; and so forth. We also know rules such as, 'it will usually take between ten minutes and a couple of hours to learn to ride the bike and you just have to keep trying even if you fall off a few times'; 'it helps if someone else holds you upright while you are mastering the first aspects of balance'; 'it helps if that person is encouraging'; and 'find a wide level surface to practice on.' Presumably, then, when we follow Polanyi, what we mean by 'being able to formulate the rules,' means something like either 'being able to formulate the rules in a way that would satisfy a physicist,' or 'being able to formulate the rules in a way that would enable another person who read them to be able to ride a bike immediately.'

The second formulation seems to match the intuitive meaning and to be the useful way of looking at the matter. Thus, in this sense, it *is* possible to formulate the rules for the moves of, say, the bishop in chess. Someone who knew how to play draughts (checkers), but not chess – that is, someone who understood how to move tokens around on a squared board – could be taught the legal moves for the bishop, or any other chess token, by being sent a letter inscribed with symbols belonging to a code that they already understood. They could open this letter, read the symbols, and be able to move the bishop immediately without significant error.

Admittedly the last paragraph hides difficulties to do with whether they would be able to move the bishop unerringly without at least a few moments' practice, but if we do not accept this case as a paradigm of nontacit knowledge, we will find that the notion of tacit knowledge has no useful application because all knowledge will be tacit knowledge. So, let us take the bishop's move and the bike-ride as paradigms of explicit and tacit knowledge under the motor skills heading.

This use of the notion of tacit knowledge understood in this way has proved fruitful in the sociology of scientific knowledge. It has proved so useful because many models of science that were in circulation 'before the sociological era' took it that most scientific knowledge could be transferred in nontacit form.[7] For example a common model took it that checking experimental findings was a straightforward matter because it was necessary only for a scientist to write down the 'recipe' for an experiment in order for another scientist to repeat it and verify the result. Informed by the idea that there was a tacit dimension to experimental skill, however, sociologists were able to understand that it was difficult to repeat experiments, that it was, therefore, difficult to test experiments, that scientific skills require continual repair and maintenance provided by the embedding community, and that technical skills might die out if they were not continually refreshed by practice.[8]

The idea of tacit knowledge, understood in the above sense, leads to conse-quences for scientific practice that have been as well corroborated as anything in the social sciences could be.

Note that in the above way of thinking about tacit knowledge the tacitness of *motor skills* is being used metaphorically when we try to understand experimentation because experimentation does not involve the body in the way that bike-riding does. For example, one might try to delegate one's experimental manipulations to technicians in a way that one cannot delegate bike-riding to an assistant. A related problem is that the contrast between the 'bishop's move' example and the bike-riding example is that it seems to suggest that tacitness is essentially to do with manipulative skills and that there is no problem of tacit knowledge that applies to 'cognitive abilities.'

The rules-regress model

In the last section I laid out a route to the idea of tacit knowledge which started with Polanyi's bike-riding example and which, therefore, took motor skills as the paradigm. The sociology of scientific knowledge has also used another paradigm to get to the same place, but this time cognitive abilities are clearly encompassed. This is the Wittgensteinian 'rules do not contain the rules for the their own application' route.[9] One example that has been used frequently is to do with the difficulty of supplying a full set of rules for the continuation of a series. First, there is no mathematical inevitability about the right way to continue a series and therefore what counts as the correct way to carry it on is conventional. Second, it is easy to show that there is no set of rules for continuing a series that cannot be 'followed' in such a way as to break the usual convention for what counts as a proper continuation.[10] Third, a series may have more than one conventional continuation: for example, in the English-speaking world the series 2, 4, 6, 8, can take the continuations '10' or 'Who do we appreciate?' depending on circumstances. The problem of the regress of rules shows up in our inability to describe exactly what are the circumstances under which one convention applies rather than another.

One can equally well use this idea as a metaphor for experimental skills; experimental skills require that one experimenter 'goes on in the same way' as another. The conclusion is, once more, that experimental skills are impossible to transmit in formulaic terms. The same consequences follow for experi-mental method, skills, and replication, as followed from the motor-skills metaphor.

The forms of life approach

A third way of reaching the same conclusions is to start from the observation that people in different social groups take different things to be certain knowledge but they are not aware of the social basis of their certainties. The dizzying aspect of the sociology of knowledge is precisely that if what we take to be certain has more to do with the social groups in which we are embedded than to do with the reasons we provide, our certainties seems groundless. (Or, as I would prefer to put it, we must start using the word 'certainty' in a new way.) As is well known, early sociology of knowledge was taken to have an 'escape clause' where the sciences were concerned; scientific knowledge was universal and the grounds for our scientific beliefs were taken to transcend social convention. The exciting and controversial thing about the sociology of *scientific* knowledge was that it erased the escape clause.

If it is the case that the true sources of our beliefs are in large part the social contexts we inhabit, yet we think that the sources of our beliefs (including beliefs about the natural world), are something else, then the sources of our beliefs are hidden from us. Our beliefs, then, are based on tacit understandings.

We conclude, as before, that there are interesting problems for scientific method and the maintenance and transfer of scientific knowledge. In this case we are inclined to say that the only way to obtain scientific knowledge is through immersion in the relevant social group. This way of looking at things not only explains the difficulty of transfer of knowledge and its consequences but also provides a strategy for gaining it – more social intercourse. The approach leads to the conclusion that common socialization will lead to common solutions to problems.[11]

This way of looking at things also suggests that the grounds of our certainties should be looked for in the histories of the social groups in which we are embedded. To study the emergence of consensus about new scientific facts is to come to understand why those facts are believed. In this way the sociology of scientific knowledge adds a dynamic dimension to the rather static Wittgensteinian picture. When we watch new scientific consensuses emerging we are watching the growth of new bodies of tacit knowledge.

Some features of the first two ways of thinking about tacit knowledge

Motor-skills metaphor revisited

Bike-riding is complicated so let us pick a simpler example for some deeper analysis. Let us consider dancing and its relationship to what psychologists call 'proprioception' – awareness of the position of our own limbs and muscles. Mr Data, a friendly computer in human form portrayed in the TV series *Star Trek: The Next Generation*, has more proprioception than most mortals. In one episode, Mr Data is being taught to dance. Commander Beverley Crusher romps through a set of complicated steps while Mr Data looks on; she is about to start teaching him this dance routine in a 'step-by-step' fashion when Mr Data brushes her aside and repeats the whole sequence flawlessly and in perfect rapid tempo. Somehow, this is what we expect from a computer – to be able to substitute formulaic instruction for practice; Mr Data has translated the dance steps into space–time coordinates and has then used that formula to guide his own dance routine. We are unsurprised that Mr Data can calculate his way through a problem of bodily disposition while we can only struggle to 'internalize' the moves through practice.

It is reasonable to think that the one kind of knowledge can be substituted for the other in the execution of some skills. Humans vary greatly in their ability to use formulaic knowledge. It is a fact, I believe, that some people can have described to them a short sequence of dance steps, in terms of foot movements and so forth, and can then execute them flawlessly. It is a fact, I know, that other people given the same instructions cannot execute the steps without an immense amount of practice. I know the second to be a fact because I am such a person. I do not have much in the way of proprioception. While I am unable to cite much evidence describing my dancing abilities, I am able to cite a great deal of evidence in respect of my abilities to swing a golf club. The basic golf swing is an activity which has been analyzed down to the last detail, and there are endless descriptions available for the proper movement of every muscle in the body and I have read many of them. Like most human golfers, however, I am unable to execute these movements reliably even after more than a decade of trying.

Extending this way of looking at things we can see that much of what is tacit knowledge as far as humans are concerned is tacit only because of the way we are made. Mr Data, no doubt, would be a brilliant golfer from day one. If our brains were as fast as Mr Data's we would probably be able to ride bikes immediately on having the physics explained to us; we would simply put the physics into practice. Given the apparent substitutability of one kind of knowledge for another it seems possible that there is nothing fundamental about the tacitness of this kind of tacit knowledge – its tacitness is just a contingency of how we are made and how difficult certain tasks are in relationship to our brain capacity. (To look at the bike example from the opposite end, it might be quite easy for us to ride a bike on the moon 'calculatively' because everything happens so much more slowly in a reduced gravitational field; in a still weaker gravitational field we might even be able to ride a bike by holding a book of rules in one hand while reading and executing them as we began to topple, ever so slowly, one way or another.)

Even more tempting is to map the two types of motor-skills knowledge onto the two available computer program paradigms – symbolic programs and neural nets.[12] The dancer who can master the steps immediately from a space–time description of foot positions seems, like Mr Data, to be doing something like calculations as processed by a mental digital computer. On the other hand, the dancer (or bike-rider) who needs endless practice and lots of trial and error, seems to be laying down neural pathways which accomplish the dynamics without his or her being able to say exactly what they are doing.[13] So even if we have to master the rules of bodily skills through practice, like a neural net, it does not mean that there is anything *deeply* tacit about them; it does not mean they cannot be represented in symbols, it merely means that it is hard to formulate them in a symbol system with which we are familiar.

So far, then, the motor-skills metaphor does not lead us to the view that those things that are accomplished by tacit knowledge now, might never be managed by explicit knowledge (perhaps stored in big fast digital computers), or as complicated but potentially formulatable knowledge in artificial neural nets. If that is the case, then science, though it may be imperfect now because the problem of tacit knowledge prevents the transfer of enough information to make a perfect test of an experiment possible, should be perfectible in principle. In the distant future, perhaps, an experimenter's task would not have been completed until he or she had transferred everything that there was to be known about an experimental procedure into a digital computer or until he or she had trained a neural net to repeat the work flawlessly. These computers could then be used by other scientists to check an experiment, and everything that was happening in the experiment would be accessible; it would just be a matter of looking at the programs.[14] The 'experimenter's regress' (Collins 1992) would, then, be a matter of human weakness rather than logic.

Rules-regress model revisited

The case of the TEA-laser top lead can be used to look more deeply into the rules-regress model.[15] In the early 1970s laser scientists were unable to build TEA-lasers if their sources of information consisted solely of published sources. Often, however, they were able to build them if they spent some time with another group who had already built functioning lasers. *One* reason why this was so was that the electronics of the laser were not well understood by the laser physicists. In particular, it was not known either by those who had successfully built a laser or by those who were trying to build such a laser, that the high voltage lead to the top electrode had to be short.

This top lead in this design of laser emerged from large and heavy capacitors. It happened that some designers mounted their capacitors on steel frameworks above the laser. This design had the potential to work because the lead would be short. Working from a circuit diagram, however, there would be nothing to suggest that the capacitors should be placed anywhere but beside the laser on the bench, and in that case the laser would not work because the lead would be too long and its inductance would be too great. Successful laser builders could not explain this to novices because they did not know that it was the lead, and the related position of the capacitors, that was responsible for their success. They were successful because their traditional methods worked, but they did not know why. We can say that the fact that the leads had to be short was 'known' by those who used the traditional design, but it was known tacitly. The rule about top lead length became an explicit fact only much later in the history of TEA-lasers.[16]

This example tells us several things. First it illustrates a different kind of tacit knowledge – knowledge not manifested in motor skills but in traditions. The ability to make a violin as good as a Stradivarius is, presumably, something similar.

The second thing the example illustrates is that tacit knowledge of this traditional type *can* turn into explicit knowledge. Once more, this kind of tacit knowledge makes science imperfect in the short term, but what about in the long term?[17] Is it possible in principle to make explicit everything that has to be known in order to make a TEA-laser, given that it is certainly possible to make explicit *some* things that were once tacit?

One is tempted to say 'no' in answer to this question because there are just too many things to be known. There are an indefinite number of things to be said about even the TEA-laser top lead because rules do not contain the rules of their own application. To think one knows all about the top lead once one knows it must be, say, eight inches long, is to miss the huge amount of traditional and conventional knowledge in that statement. For humans to use that rule, they must already know about inches, about 'eight,' about leads, about thicknesses, about how to approximate (for it is impossible to cut a lead to exactly eight inches), about electricity, and so on. To try to express all these things is to run into the rules regress. It may be, then, that while one can make more and more aspects of traditional knowledge explicit, explicit knowledge, however much of it there is, must always rest on unarticulated knowledge.

And yet again, it could be argued that this cannot be a logical problem but a problem of human capacity. It could be argued that the brain's neural circuitry must contain all that we have learned since we were born (and perhaps some 'hard-wired' capacities that were there before we were born). Thus, loose talk of traditions should be replaced with tight talk of, for example, laser builders having images inscribed in their neural circuitry of what a laser should be like, and that this guides their laser-building activities like any other plan – albeit a plan that is more like a mental template than a sequence of 'coordinates' to be followed in sequence. Perhaps humans are not capable of articulating all these images and other aspects of tradition that are laid down in equally non-mysterious ways only because the digital side of their mental apparatus is weak. It may be significant that humans spend some of their time forgetting formal rules, preferring to manage with unarticulated practices instead; this is usually more efficient for humans. One reason is that motor skills seem to be executed more efficiently when we are not thinking about them (i.e., when we are not processing rules self-consciously); a second reason is that an unspoken rule has far more general, if looser, application than an articulated rule which begs a further rule for every individual instantiation; a third reason is that socialization seems a more efficient way of teaching humans than articulation of rules.[18] So, while it seems true that all the rules cannot be spoken by humans, the appearance of an indefinite regress might be an artifact of our limited capacity. Perhaps enough of the rules we know tacitly could be extracted and represented in something with a far larger digital capacity to make the infinite regress of rules seem less of a pressing problem.[19]

Once more, this does not make a difference to the analysis of science as we know it because science as we know it is done by humans as we know them, but it might make a difference of principle to the way we think about knowledge.

Once more, perhaps a neural net could learn enough to be able to carry out a difficult experiment first time through without any practice simply because it can hold so many rules.

The importance of forms of life for understanding tacit knowledge

Neural nets seems to make tacit knowledge tractable. We can now understand how it is that a human may have knowledge and abilities without being able to articulate the corresponding rules. This, as I have argued, makes no difference to sociology of scientific knowledge, nor to science as we know it. Nevertheless, if all there is to tacit knowledge is motor skills and the rules regress, then neural nets seem to promise, at least in the long term, a way to formalize, or at least mechanize, the once mysterious tacit knowledge and thus take the mystery and imperfections out of science.[20] But, even if it is the case that all tacit knowledge as understood via the motor-skills metaphor or the rules-regress model could, in principle, be replaced with something like the programs of artificial neural nets, the *formation* of these rules, which we see as we watch the formation of new scientific consensuses, cannot be so replaced. This is because the history of scientific consensus formation is the history of groups of scientists, and scientists are not artificial neural nets.

Could scientists be replaced with artificial neural nets? No! While we can just about imagine replacing a fixed and final body of tacit knowledge with a neural-net program exposed to human actions fixed by consensual traditions, we cannot imagine such nets having formed these traditions in the same way as humans formed them. To take part in the formation of traditions the nets would need all the status, persuasive power, understanding of what might be credible to others, and so forth, which the sociology of scientific knowledge has shown to be involved in the process of new knowledge formation. In other words, such a neural net would have to be able to take its place in the ongoing flux of social life in the same way as a human. Perhaps one day this will be possible, but no one has the slightest idea how to do it now, not even in principle.

Social embedding

What I have done so far is to consider three ways of approaching the idea of tacit knowledge. In the cases of the first two routes I have taken examples that have allowed me to be prepared to concede that what we call tacit knowledge may have a lot to do with the calculative processing limitations of the human brain and that there is nothing philosophically fundamental about the tacitness. That is to say, I have not found it difficult to imagine that the tacit knowledge involved might be transferred to a subsymbolic computer program and thence, perhaps, to a symbolic computer program. I have argued, however, that even if this is the case, the idea of tacit knowledge is vital for the analysis of science as we know it, and has permanently altered the way we analyze science in so far as anything ever could.

I have then gone on to look at a third way of approaching tacit knowledge and suggested that this creates a new kind of problem – the creation of new consensual knowledge. Even if we allow that all consensual tacit knowledge is potentially transferable to artificial neural nets, the neural nets that would be needed to have taken part in the *creation* of science as we know it would have had to fit into society in the same way as the human scientists fitted, and we do not know how this could have been managed.

Now I want to bring something more puzzling into focus and I will do this by going back to some of my earlier examples. Riding a bike needs to be analyzed into two different kinds of activities. What Polanyi discussed, and what we have discussed so far, should be called 'bike-balancing.' Bike-balancing is maneuvering a bike in a landscape devoid of traffic or the apparatus of traffic management. It is only because bike-riding as discussed by Polanyi is limited to *bike-balancing* that we can talk of a physics of bike-riding and we can imagine this physics being managed by being described or inscribed in one kind of computer program or another, including that of our own brain. (I am assuming that we all agree what bike-balancing consists of and how it is to be managed that the physics of bike-balancing is consensual and frozen.[21])

The other aspect of bike-riding is riding in traffic. This is much more complicated. One might ask of a bicycle rider, 'Why did you cross the junction in front of that car coming from your right?' He or she might reply: 'I exchanged glances with the driver.' But this does not provide a repertoire for junction-crossing since the context is so crucial; it depends on the country in which the bike is being ridden, along with an estimate of the moral integrity of its inhabitants and the particular car driver in question; it depends on whether the rider has a child on board, and, of course, the nature of the glances. Given what are otherwise the 'same' circumstances, the wisdom of the move can change over time and place as the relative status of cars and bikes changes. Thus, this aspect of bike-riding requires embedding in the social milieu from the beginning to the end. It is not just the creative phase of bike-riding that needs social embedding; the need for social embedding is permanent.

The same two aspects can be found in dancing. Mr Data may have learned some steps from Beverley Crusher but putting these into practice on the dance floor is another matter altogether. In the *Star Trek* episode in question, Commander Crusher, impressed by the instantaneous nature of Data's mastery of the steps she has demonstrated, remarks: 'Now all you have to do is improvise.' It is here that *Star Trek* departs from its customary scientific conservatism, for 'improvisation' is exactly what we would not expect Mr Data to be able to manage. Improvisation requires exact attention to, and a very deep understanding of, human society because it is not a matter of following a behavioral repertoire but of making departures from it to a degree that must be consistent with quintessentially unspoken convention. There is little easier to caricature than the gauche dancer desperately trying to impress with inappropriate improvisations, but there is little harder to explain.

When we move to the aspects of human action that are socially embedded it is far harder to imagine them being inscribed in a computer model, whether the computer be symbolic or subsymbolic. These kinds of actions require that behavior be varied, not randomly, but according to the social circumstances. Such actions are what Kusch and I call 'polimorphic actions,' as opposed to the rarer kind of 'mimeomorphic actions' which humans prefer to instantiate with the same behaviors every time.[22]

There seems little hope that the ability to improvise properly, or execute any other polimorphic action properly, could be reduced to settings in a neural net; personally, I think the most economical way of thinking about these things is to see the individual human as a symptom of the social group rather than the other way around, but even if I am wrong, it is certain that, once more, we do not have the faintest idea how to set out these abilities in formulae or programs of any sort, nor do we have the faintest idea how to make an artificial socializable entity; if there are rules for these things, their location is society itself and to know them one has to join in the ongoing flux of social life. For this reason, while I think that all the routes to the idea of tacit knowledge have been, and remain, immensely fruitful in generating a better understanding of science, I believe that the idea of polimorphic action and social embedding is the most fundamental notion. It is the notion that cannot be reduced and dispensed with in our practical study of practices. On the contrary, what we need is a more developed language to discuss its general properties.[23]

Notes

1 To save misunderstanding, in this note I here set out a partial list of what I consider empirical success (the pattern refers to and develops what can be found in the conclusion to Collins and Pinch's book *The Golem* (Collins and Pinch 1993). There we suggest that understanding tacit knowledge, among other things, helps us: understand why forensic science is often misleading and always contestible; understand the interactions of other kinds of experts with other formal institutions; understand why there is a high Ph.D. drop-out rate in the sciences; predict the course of scientific controversies such as that over cold fusion; understand the determination of certain countries to conduct nuclear tests in spite of the pressure for a world-wide ban (see especially MacKenzie and Spinardi 1995); understand the present state and future possibilities of scientific 'discovery' programs written for computers and the prospects for other 'intelligent machines' (see especially Collins 1990 and Collins and Kusch 1998).

2 The philosopher, Steven Turner (1994), has said that the concept of tacit knowledge has been used as a black box into which the residual and unexplained have been dumped while the difficult questions have been avoided. In the course of developing this claim Turner does not deal with the empirical program in the sociology of science which uses the concept of tacit knowledge, nor does he try to show how the empirical findings might be reformulated in the light of his critique.

3 Though I confess to some puzzlement about why philosophers or ethnomethodologists should refuse so adamantly to talk in terms of rules when we have a case before us such as the TEA-laser top lead (Collins 1992, and see below).

4 It also follows that this paper is an implicit critique of analyses of knowledge that reduce society to something like interactions in a network. This paper defends a

notion of society that is very much more than the sum of the interactions of its parts. Certain of the capacities of the members of a society are seen as available to them only because they are members of something larger and irreducible (Collins 1998). In this the paper draws on the philosophy of Wittgenstein (1953; Winch 1958). For related arguments see Schatzki 1996, 1997.

5 Thus, in the conference at which this paper was presented, Eike von Savigny criticized my section on the rules regress on the grounds that I had given away too much. No doubt von Savigny is right and I think my own discomfort with that section probably comes through in the sentences as I have written them. Nevertheless, I think the section can stand unaltered in the light of my overall argumentative strategy.

6 He says, for instance, that if one is falling to the left, the first movement of the handlebars must be to the *right*, whereas we would all think the first movement would be to the left.

7 Of course, most scientists and many other observers of science are still informed by such views of the world.

8 See Collins (1992) on the TEA-laser, the detection of gravitational radiation and the 'experimenter's regress.' See MacKenzie and Spinardi (1995) for a fascinating use of the notion of tacit knowledge in the context of nuclear weapons testing; MacKenzie suggests that if nuclear weapons testing ceases, weapons designers will forget their craft and nuclear weapons will themselves cease to exist.

9 This idea has been used most powerfully by Dreyfus in his critique of artificial intelligence (1972; 1993). For example, Dreyfus writes:

> My thesis . . . is that whenever human behavior is analyzed in terms of rules, these rules must always contain a *ceteris paribus* condition, i.e., they apply 'everything else being equal,' and what 'everything else' and 'equal' means in any specific situation can never be fully spelled out without a regress. Moreover, this *ceteris paribus* condition is not merely an annoyance which shows that the analysis is not yet complete . . . Rather the *ceteris paribus* condition points to a background of practices which are the condition of the possibility of all rulelike activity . . . Thus in the last analysis all intelligibility and all intelligent behavior must be traced back to our sense of what we are, which is, according to this argument, necessarily, on pain of regress, something we can never explicitly *know* (pp. 56–7).

10 See the discussion of the 'awkward student' in Collins (1992: 13–15).

11 The inspiration for my own initial research was the 'form of life' approach and only because a referee drew my attention to Polanyi's tacit knowledge idea did I use that formulation in my 1974 paper. In some ways I have been regretting it ever since because, as I will go on to explain, the form of life approach is the most interesting and fundamental.

12 We know that it is always tempting to model the brain on the latest trend in computerized intelligence, but at this point in this paper there is no need to resist the temptation.

13 Some cute writers deliberately mix up these two types of knowledge to get an amusing effect. For example, Crothers (1987), says: 'The rugby full-back has to know his co-ordinate geometry. His approximate locus for the wider conversion must be a rectangular hyperbola on which the kicker must place his ellipsoid of revolution before sending it on its parabolic way.' On the other hand, a rugby full-back (Webb 1988) said: 'If you tried to write down on paper exactly what you do to kick a ball between two posts with absolute certainty, it would be impossible, you'd still be at it in a million years – but once you've done it just once, your body and mind has the exact formula stored and ready to be repeated.'

14 I believe that once a neural net has stopped 'learning' its program can be expressed as a set of rules amenable to digital treatment and expression in a potentially more comprehensible form. This is, however, a contentious view – Dreyfus, for example, would disagree. Fortunately, because of the argumentative strategy of this paper, it does not matter if I am right or Dreyfus is right for these purposes.

15 Collins (1990: 11–116).

16 For a more complete classification of the sources of tacit knowledge, see Collins on Q of Sapphire: unpublished manuscript obtainable from the author.

17 I mean 'make science imperfect' in the narrow sense of the difficulty associated with the transfer of experimental skills.

18 See Collins (1990: Chapter 6). A little example that illustrates this point is the way that instructions on vending machines become less articulate as such machines enter general use.

19 Douglas Lenat et al. (1986) set up a project which effectively tested whether the rules regress went on for ever or not. Lenat's 'CYC' project was intended to put all the knowledge one needed to know to understand an encyclopedia into explicit form in the program of a computer. Lenat's intention was not only to include the encyclopedia entries, but also the background knowledge required to understand the encyclopedia entries. I do not know what progress CYC has made, but I have not heard of it for several years. My guess would be that any attempt to articulate such as body of knowledge would soon run into difficulties, though whether these are difficulties of a fundamental kind or only a matter of capacity I am not ready to argue here.

20 It may be this that has led critics of artificial intelligence, such as Hubert Dreyfus, to embrace neural nets with more enthusiasm than might have been expected, as though neural nets solve the major problems of putting human abilities into machines, or into formulas (which I believe, *pace* Dreyfus, amounts to the same thing).

21 Even the proper thing to do when bike-balancing is a matter of convention, however – see Bijker (1995). Surprisingly enough, even the golf swing has something of this conventional aspect. It turns out that the paradigm of the proper golf swing has altered markedly over the years, being modeled on first one successful golfer then another, and the argument continues over whether a golfer should try to standardize a swing tailored to him or herself, or try to follow a public standard (Jenkins 1994).

22 (Collins and Kusch 1995a, 1995b, 1998). At this point it might be worth noting exactly how this way of looking at the world differs from that of Dreyfus (e.g., 1993). For Dreyfus an activity like skilled bicycle-balancing is beyond what computers can do because humans do it by what he would call 'intuitive' means. The approach pressed here is that the crucial distinctions do not arise until we get to bicycle-riding proper – including the social elements of riding in traffic, etc. The approach entailed in this paper is in harmony with the AI aficionados' approach that the solution (i.e., at least one possible solution) to bicycle-balancing is more powerful symbol-processing computers. This may not be the most efficient way to do it but there is no reason in principle why it should not be done this way – it would be a matter of fast processing of a number of mathematical functions controlling the relationship between data fed in by sensors attached to various parts of the bike. Where the AI aficionados go wrong is in thinking that this approach can be extended into those aspects of skill where social embedding is involved.

23 Collins and Kusch (1998), an attempt to start on such a language.

8   Throwing out the tacit rule book
Learning and practices

Stephen Turner

'Practices' talk, I have argued elsewhere, gets into trouble over the notion of 'sharing' (1994). The idea that there are 'shared' practices requires some sort of notion of how they come to be shared, and this notion in turn dictates how practices can be conceived. If we decide that these difficulties are insurmountable, I argued, we can dispense with the notion of sharing altogether. Practices without sharing, to use a phrase favored in the nineteenth century, are habits – individual rather than shared. Habits are simply the part of the phenomenon described by the term 'practices' that remains when the idea of people possessing the same shared thing is eliminated. 'Habits,' however, is a potentially misleading term, especially if 'habit' is thought of as a generic alternative explanation rather than simply as the residue of the concept of practices once its objectionable elements have been eliminated. In what follows I will try to avoid this potential misunderstanding by restating my argument against the 'social' conception of practices in somewhat different terms, without appealing to 'habit' as a concept, and by locating the argument in relation to recent work in cognitive science.

'Practices,' for the sake of the following, is defined as those nonlinguistic conditions for an activity that are *learned*. By '*a* practice' I will mean an activity that requires its genuine participants to have learned something of this tacit sort in order to perform. What I intend to discuss are some general features of learning that constrain our conception of practices and therefore of a practice which depends on them. Ordinarily, the tacit stuff is not all there is to a practice. Most cases of a practice involve explicit communication or even explicit rules. Rules are not self-applying, so in the case where there are explicit rules, such as the law, the relevant practices are the practices that enable a person to follow the rules, for a lawyer or judge to interpret the law, for example. Sometimes there are no explicit rules, but there is explicit discussion. Painting a house, for example, can be done correctly or incorrectly, and there is a fairly elaborate vocabulary of evaluation and description of mistakes. Some kinds of 'knowing how' that might be called 'a practice' may have no such elaborate vocabulary of appraisal, and perhaps may have none at all. The practice of flirting, for example, before it was theorized about, presumably lacked such a vocabulary, and small children who flirt presumably have no vocabulary with which to discuss it – but it nevertheless has to be learned. My concern throughout will be with the tacit parts of a practice.

The linguistic analogy

Language has always exercised a regulatory role in discussions of practice. Any account of practice that fails to account for language will be defective, because linguistic practices are part and parcel of many other practices and because linguistic practices are in principle not sufficiently different from other practices to regard them as likely to have a radically different character. The usual understanding of what is involved in the case of language is this: we communicate by virtue of sharing in the possession of this highly structured whole, a language, including the nonlinguistic learned conditions for the use of the language, the practices. This notion can be put in a much more cautious way, as for example Davidson does when he speaks of 'sharing a language, in whatever sense this is required for communication' (1977:166). The 'required sense' of sharing may be minimal, and may not consist of shared tacit rules. In what follows, I propose to deal with the question of what the 'required sense' is, and how it can be squared with a plausible account of learning.

Davidson's remark is fairly conventional stuff in contemporary philosophy, but the argument that informs it is elusive. Is this a kind of unformulated transcendental argument, which amounts to the claim that the 'sharing' of 'language,' in some unspecified sense of these terms, is a condition of the possibility of 'communication' in some unspecified sense of this term? Or is it a kind of inference to the best explanation in which there are no real alternatives – an inference, so to speak, to the only explanation (which is perhaps not a bad definition of transcendental argument)? There are good reasons to be suspicious of arguments of this form. Yet this general picture, of some sort of shared (and presumably tacit) stuff at the basis of language, is highly appealing, and so is its extension to practices generally. The claim that there is some class of things that could not happen, were it not for the existence of some sort of shared practices, is a commonplace, despite, and perhaps because of its vagueness.

Symbolic and connectionist models of higher cognitive processes

As I have said, the Achilles heel of transcendental arguments is that the unique explanation to which the *explanans* point may not be the only explanation. In this case the argument establishes nothing. There is a close analogue to this kind of argument in cognitive science, and it has recently succumbed, at least in the view of many, to the demonstration that an alternative explanation suffices. The argument is this. People have the capacity to reason mathematically and speak grammatically. We can represent mathematical reasoning and the grammatical structure of a language explicitly, in terms of formal proofs and grammatical rules respectively. The fact that people can do in their head what can be done by formal proofs or in accordance with grammatical rules is a fact of the same kind as communication. It is the sort of fact that seems to require that the people who reason mathematically or speak grammatically possess capacities which pretty closely resemble, and operate like, those of formal proof. In short, people, in thinking mathematically or speaking grammatically, must be employing some sort of mental analog to the rules of inference and axioms that go into mathematical proofs. The problem for the cognitive theorist is to model these capacities by identifying the tacit rules and axioms that are employed.

In cognitive science, this problem leads to a specific difficulty, the 'central paradox of cognition,' stated by Smolensky, Legendre, and Miyata as follows:

> Formal theories of logical reasoning, grammar, and other higher mental faculties compel us to think of the *mind* as a machine for rule based manipulation of structured arrays of *symbols*. What we know of the *brain* compels us to think of human information processing in terms of manipulation of a large set of *numbers*, the activity levels of interconnected neurons. Finally, the richness of human *behavior*, both in everyday environments and in the controlled environments of the psychological laboratory, seems to defy rule-based description, displaying strong sensitivity to subtle statistical factors in experience as well as to structural properties of information (1993: 382).

In this case there is an alternative explanation or approach, namely connectionism.

'Connectionism' refers to the claim that the appropriate model for the computation that occurs in the brain is not, as a once dominant viewpoint had it, the operation of logic machines that process symbols, but rather is the parallel distributed processing that is used on a variety of actual computer applications (such as flight simulators) and requires very substantial computing power. The 'symbolic processing' model worked as follows: the mind acquires, either by genetic pre-programming or learning, rules for processing inputs, in a way that is familiar from ordinary computing, in which symbols come in well-defined forms and the computer program operates as if computational 'rules' are 'applied' to them mechanically to produce predictable outputs. Connectionist models work differently. The computer is given a learning algorithm, but no detailed 'rules.' The computer is then 'trained-up' by feeding it data and then giving feedback for 'correct' answers. This is very much a Humean rather than a Kantian machine. Everything that is inside, except for the most basic capacity for forming 'expectations' is a result of inputs, or experience. The inputs are not symbolic, but simply impulses originating from various sensory sources, which are distributed through the brain in pathways made up of 'connections' that are formed statistically, by the association of impulses of one kind with impulses of another kind. These are modeled mathematically as 'weightings' of the impulses, which travel from 'node' or pathway link to 'node' and which modify the link by passing through it, just as a person walking in the forest makes a path, increasing the likelihood of future impulses of a similar kind being distributed in a similar way. The changes in the likelihoods are 'learning.' These computer methods actually work: this is a model based on actual computer achievements, in which parallel distributed processing systems learn to do such things as detect cancers by being trained entirely empirically with inputs of images and feedback for correct predictions. No theory is needed, and no rules are identified or used in this method. The processes are statistical, and the capacities and outputs of the computer depend on what has been fed to it in the form of data and feedback.

The problem for modelers attempting to deal with human cognition is whether this approach is capable of accounting for higher mental processes. The general explanatory problem is the question of 'how . . . competence that is highly systematic, coherent, compositional, and productive' can be achieved with the specific kinds of 'finite and fixed resources' that connectionism employs (Smolensky, Legendre, and Miyata 1993: 383). The highly influential paper by these authors from which these quotations are taken presents some technical results that bear on this problem. Indeed, in the opinion of most cognitive scientists and philosophical observers, these results represent a decisive turning point in the resolution of the issues. Briefly, what Smolensky, Legendre, and Miyata establish is that a connectionist account can be given of certain kinds of grammatical rules previously thought to be impossible to account for without reference to internalized formal rules. Their strategy is to show how 'a fully distributed pattern of numerical activities' of a connectionist kind can be 'the functional near-equivalent of a symbolic structure' (1993: 382). That is, they show how something like 'rules' can be the product of 'learning' through the simple mechanisms of spreading activation employed by connectionist accounts of the brain. The key idea in their analysis is that there is a kind of purposive process which occurs 'when the . . . activation spreading process satisfies certain mathematical properties' (1993: 383), a process they call maximizing Harmony. The strategy of the paper is to make rule acquisition, by which they really mean the acquisition of functional equivalents to a rule, into a special case of connectionist learning generally. This raises an obvious possibility: that practices too may be special cases of this kind, or, alternatively, that practices may be better understood not as a special case of the same kind, but in light of the general properties of connectionist learning. In what follows, I will suggest that the latter is the most plausible conclusion.

I take it that there are two main implications of interest to the study of social practices of connectionism generally, one flowing from the other. The first is that because learning starts from a system state in which some learning has already occurred, we would expect that learning is always a product of a transition between a state A and state B such that the transition between another state in another machine and a state B^n which is functionally equivalent to B will be a transition from a different starting point to a different end point. In short, the mechanisms in question, even if they are governed by the same basic simple mechanisms, are individuated by the history of the mechanism. And, in general, the simpler the mechanism and the longer the chains of links between simple mechanisms the greater the diversity produced by differences in, so to speak, the training history. Like paths from one point in space to another, the connections in a net that produce the 'same' competency may be different in structure.

The implication of this that bears on the theory of social practices or the idea of shared practices is that two individuals with an ability to perform the general kind of task may go about it in ways that are quite different on the level of neuro-cognitive description. Put more simply, if we throw out the idea that there is a rule book that people tacitly master in order to, say, communicate, we also throw out the idea that there is some single thing that people must all have in order to communicate. The approach taken by Smolensky, Legendre, and Miyata modifies this implication, for it suggests that something very much like 'the same' rules of grammar may result from the fact that there is, in effect, a common end point to the process of mastering a grammar, namely maximal Harmony. But the approach also raises the question of when and where this notion of functional equivalence is applicable or relevant.

It suggests the following answer to the question: when information is plentiful and structured in such a way that 'optimizing Harmony' or some other quasi-purposive system goal can lead to the same rule-like results. The general point supported by connectionism is the idea that the simpler the mechanisms that are the building blocks, the longer or more complex the total structure producing the result will be. Unlike rule books, these various complex individual mental structures are built up over time on the basis of different learning events. Ordinarily there will be a significant diversifying effect: the individual facts of the history of the acquisition of many cognitive skills will differ in such a way that the results differ. The question is where the result is rule-like and the rule-like structures are shared, and where it is either not rule-like or not shared. I note, incidentally, that Smolensky, Legendre, and Miyata say nothing about the question of whether more than one individually generated reduction of complexity can be functionally equivalent to a grammatical rule. However, there seems to be no reason that more than one result might be optimally Harmonious. Moreover, actual speakers do vary, so there is no reason to think that there is even one set of rule equivalents that the process of harmonizing would necessarily tend toward in any given language.

We cannot, of course, answer questions about the existence of shared functional rule equivalents directly. But some light can be shed on them by considering the ways in which 'rules' are learned. Consider the child's acquisition of the ability to perform simple arithmetical tasks. What is it to 'be able' to add 2 + 2? Is it merely to parrot the correct answer? Presumably not. Indeed, there may be no 'criteria' in a Wittgensteinian sense for the possession of this competence. Obviously, a child does not master arithmetic immediately or all at once in the sense that the capacity is turned on like a switch. Other things must be mastered first, like counting, and these are often things that it is quite unproblematical to suggest are mastered in different ways. Some children may count on their fingers. Others may learn through singing the numbers, and others may master a great deal of material by rote without knitting it together, and only later make connections between the numbers of a mathematical kind. In short, students come to the learning of $2 \times 2 = 4$ from different starting points. They are then put through a series of experiences, and of course each student's experience is slightly different and each classroom's experience is different.

The differences, however, are not supposed to make a difference in the performance of the capacity. There are right answers, and the point of the various experiences with students having various prior experiences is that the experiences taken together transform the child cognitively in such a way that the child is able to perform the cognitive task correctly. Almost everybody manages to do this. At the period prior to mastery, the cognitive architecture which supports the child's efforts will be, according to the picture I have given here, different. Different children will have different experiences on the way to mastery and the cognitive architecture will be a product of the path and the experiences along this path that the child takes from its starting point to the goal of mastery of the cognitive task. The purposes of children will vary as well. There may be a complex heterogeneity with respect to the goals. Some children may wish to avoid the embarrassment of being brought before the blackboard and humiliated for making mistakes. Other children may have a more positive experience of mastery and pride in achievement. These differences, like differences in the history of learning, do not have any effect on the competence itself.

The question is why? On the account of mastery that fits best with the tacit rule book model, the reason for this is essentially as follows: mastery is no more and no less than 'getting' the basic rules of arithmetic, which are the same for everyone. The student tries this and that, gets corrected, gets told the answer is correct, and does all of this without understanding. But at some point something clicks, and the student 'has' the rule. The history of acquisition is irrelevant because the important moment is the moment of clicking on to the rule, of getting the rule. This model of learning, what I will call the snap-on model, makes the history irrelevant. There is a radical difference of kind between the period before acquiring the rule and the period after, and the learning events of the first period have no effects in the second.

This is obviously an appealing story. It fits well with a certain view of Wittgenstein, and indeed may – though I doubt it – represent the most plausible explication of his notion of rule-following. I do not wish to take the issue up directly here, but I will note that in the history of the reception of the

Philosophical Investigations there was a period in which something like the account I have given here was purveyed by Wittgenstein's students and interpreters.[1] Nevertheless I think it misleads us about practices generally, misleads us into looking for 'criteria' or 'agreements' where there is nothing of the sort to be found. The main reason for this is that mastery – however one wishes to think of it – is in most cases *not* the same thing for different people under different circumstances. It is purpose-relative, and the purposes of individuals involved in the activity vary. It is also situation- or experience-relative, in the sense that it depends on the materials to which the rules are applied.

Differences in purposes lead to differences in experience, and this means differences in the information that is fed into the system. Diversity is the normal result, but diversity is nevertheless consistent with a great many kinds of cooperation, and indeed, I think, with communication. In what follows I will consider some examples, and suggest that most of those we call practices are more plausibly thought of as the common activities of people with diverse learnings than as activities made possible by the sharing of the same rule-like structures. Obviously there is no room here for knock-down arguments. Indeed, the complexity of the processes involved ensure, I think, that they will always be opaque to analysis. But something may usefully be suggested about the probable effects of differences in purposes on the cognitive side of practices.

Notice a few unusual features of instruction in arithmetic. Children are tested on their mastery of multiplication tables and there is clearly a right and a wrong answer to such questions. Children are then disciplined or drilled in these right answers, and indeed in days gone by, the multiplication tables were simply mastered by rote and no attempt was made at giving the child some sort of conceptual understanding of multiplication. This kind of training is anomalous if we consider the universe of 'practices.' Whatever this universe might be taken to consist of, presumably it includes such 'practices' as the standards of etiquette that Norbert Elias describes, the habits of moderation and compromise that are the means of assuring the fruitfulness of parliamentary discussion that thinkers from John Austin to Michael Polanyi and Michael Oakeshott have supposed to operate at the heart of British parliamentary politics, and perhaps many other things as well, such as the means by which laboratory scientists identify objects, as well as the examples I have given here of flirting and house-painting.

Does the snap-on account of learning fit these cases as well? One difference is this: in these more complex cases, perhaps with the exception of flirting, there is a large spoken or explicit element, a vocabulary of appraisal or even theory about the activity, in addition to its tacit base. In the case of elementary arithmetic there are theories, but they are known to mathematicians alone and are not part of the activities of making change and the like in which elementary arithmetic is used. Another difference with the case of arithmetic is that in these 'complex' cases the means by which information about right and wrong are conveyed is different, and the purposes that the parties to the practice have are diverse and lack a common core, like making correct change. So it would be a bit surprising if a model in which these differences had no place made much sense of the learning of the practice. If we see the teaching of arithmetic as the employment of various behavioral technologies that are designed to produce absolute consistency of response, it is no surprise that such things as the differences in purpose between learners have no effect on what is learned – that is one of the incidental consequences of a behavioral technology that is designed to eliminate differences. But the behavioral technologies that serve to convey information about right and wrong with respect to these other bodies of practice do not work in this way.

Grammar is learned without behavioral technologies of the same explicit kind. But, like arithmetic, the effects of diversity of purposes are overwhelmed by the quantity of redundant information and, perhaps, by the structure of the information on which learning operates. Flirting, in contrast, is information-poor, and the starting points of individuals vary enormously. So it would be odd to find functionally equivalent rules there. Nevertheless, flirting, or at least a personal way of flirting and responding to flirting, is learned, and thus fits the model of a practice with which I began. Similarly for politics. One simply does not have the vast amount of experience necessary to overwhelm the diversifying effects of differences in experiences, difference in starting points and differences in purposes. The explicit rather than the tacit parts of politics, the vocabulary of appraisal, the body of political and historical discussion, and explicitly formulated beliefs of various kinds, do the work of making the practice hang together. A practice such as scientific discovery, built around training that is oriented to enabling a person to participate in discussions involving highly specialized terms and employing common apparatus, may in some respects be more like arithmetic, with its explicit behavioral technology of tests, at least with respect to the mastery of techniques. But scientific discussion itself often skates on the border of mutual intelligibility, and not infrequently goes beyond it. And explicit discussion, not the training base, pulls the practice in new directions and toward new goals and experiences.

Practices in the sociological sense: social order

The characteristic way in which sociologists have analyzed social practices in the past has been in terms of patterns which are observed, in which the analyst can say that people behave as if they are following a particular rule, and in which the analyst can point to some sort of sanction or response to violations of the 'as if' rule that indicates that some behavior is deviant. Expressing disapproval is a much different means of conveying information than correcting arithmetic tests. Take the practice of dressing for the beach. Beach-dressing practices differ from country to country and place to place. They differ more or less systematically. What is appropriate in one place, or for one sort of person, is not appropriate for another. There is no place in which one can look up these 'rules.' One may be entitled, from this, to conclude that there is among beach-goers in particular places some sort of tacit 'code' which forbids certain kinds of attire or defines appropriate attire. But this is a very peculiar sort of conclusion. It seems to be little more than shorthand for saying that if one does various things, some people will express disapproval. One can get quite an elaborate account of the whole business of approval and disapproval, of the distinctions that are implicit in the pattern of disapproval and approval, and so forth.

But it is far less clear that we are all attempting to master the same tacit rule book, or indeed that there is some sort of common thing that is being mastered here. Are we simply trying to dress for the beach in accordance with various purposes, one of which may be – but may not be – to avoid disapproval? Could it be that the apparent structure of the activity is simply the results of different people with different purposes and a variety of attitudes acting and expressing approval and disapproval? The tacit rule book model requires us to think that, as with arithmetic exams, we face social life as an exam which we respond to in terms of approval and disapproval. If we meet with approval, we may take it as a sign that we have not violated the tacit rule book. Disapproval represents failure in mastering the tacit rule book. We learn from the experience what is in the tacit rule book or how to apply the tacit rules. If we retain the image that what we have here is a vast tacit rule book of great complexity then we can think of individuals as having, though not very satisfactorily, mastered elements of or approximations of this tacit rule book, that is to say as having incomplete or unsatisfactory mastery.

But this seems rather strange, for a variety of reasons. Go back to the child's performance of addition in a schoolroom. The child's goal may be for the most part to avoid embarrassment. Getting the right answer is simply a means to this and doubtless other ends. Satisfactory performance from the child's point of view is one that manages to achieve enough of the things the child wants to achieve or to avoid the things the child wants to avoid. Of course, children manage to satisfice in the classroom in lots of ways, such as by deflecting embarrassment by becoming the class clown. In short, because goals are heterogenous, 'mastering' is also a heterogenous notion.

With the usual sorts of things we think of as social practices, such as dressing to go to the beach, our goals are heterogenous. What counts as satisfactory will be different for different people. And this has implications for the experiences the person has, and consequently the information that they receive as a result of these experiences. The beach-goer who avoids arrest, who is satisfied with the knowledge that enables him or her to do this, is different from the beach-goer who is satisfied with admiring glances or with being ignored and thus avoiding social disapprobation.

Why should this make any difference to the question of whether there is a tacit rule book of beach attire, or flirting? Arithmetic problems are odd in that optimal mastery is necessary with respect to the large number of usual goals, such as avoiding humiliation, that children bring to the situation of learning elementary arithmetic. Ordinarily matters are different: different goals dictate different results, because the pursuit of the goals leads to experiences that are different in kind. Sometimes, however, there are intermediate goals that are the same, or demand functionally equivalent conduct or understandings. Language seems to be a case like this. Intelligibility is an intermediate goal that is shared by a large number of people. The mastery of a language is necessary for the achievement of this goal. People have very diverse linguistic experiences. But the quantity of linguistic data with which they operate is so immense that it obliterates many of the differences. In the case of beach attire, matters are quite different. It is simply an overstatement of the case to say that people have to internalize a norm of dress in order to participate in the activity. There is no single 'norm' that corresponds to the various 'mastering' strategies that people exhibit in the course of responding to the problem of appropriate beach attire. Not only do people have different explicit ideas about what is appropriate and what is not, they *respond* differently. And their different experiences lead them to have quite different kinds of information on which to operate, information that is different in kind, and not redundant and overwhelming in such a way as to produce the same results. Yet there will be something recognizable to us, as analysts, as a social practice.

If this is a possible explanation, it is a better explanation than the idea of a tacit rule book. The experience of social life, in the absence of a massive amount of information or of highly structured experiences, such as the learning of arithmetic, is simply too diverse, and too thin, for the individual to derive from it anything so determinate as a set of rules that is the same for everyone. Even if there were such rules, and even if individuals optimized in acquiring functional equivalent rule-like responses to the material presented to them, it is reasonable to suppose that the material on which each individual works is too limited – in all but the exceptional cases – for them to acquire the same rule-like response as the next person does.

The domain of practices

If people are 'master' learners who start from different points and acquire what they learn through different sets of experiences and who satisfice according to different goals which may change over time and thus direct the path of experiences and learnings in different ways, it may appear that the real mystery here is how there could be any such things as social practices or 'social order' at all unless there is massively redundant information structured in the appropriate way to produce functional equivalents of the same rule in all parties to the practice. I think that this is indeed the right question and the answer to this question needs to be not that there is a tacit rule book and that the problem is to figure out how people acquire it but rather that the kinds of patterns and regularities we regard as social practices are nothing more than that which people learn, in a rather heterogeneous way, are the best ways or the satisfactory ways to negotiate the paths toward the fulfillment of whatever purposes they might have. What this suggests is that what people acquire that sociologists call practices are lessons that enable them to do particular things, such as go to the beach and be comfortable with the responses of other people or at least get from them responses that they are satisfied with.

This gives us the basis for a crude taxonomy of practices. The learning of some practices is indifferent to the purposes for which they are learned, or, rather, 'optimizing Harmony' makes them the same for everyone. For other practices, in contrast, mastery is purpose-relative. Neither case, I have suggested here, *requires* the model of a common tacit rule book. It is mistaken in the cases in which mastery is purpose-relative because it is simply the imposition of the sociologist – no one learns it, and there is no plausible way for a complex scheme of tacit rules of the hypothesized kind to be learned. It is mistaken in the case in which optimizing Harmony results in the sharing of rules that are functionally the same for everybody because it involves a mistaken inference from the explicit form of an activity to a supposed cognitive basis with a similar form.

Note

1 'We see that we understand one another, without noticing whether our reactions tally or not. *Because* we agree in our reactions, it is possible for me to tell you something, and it is possible for you to teach me something,' as Rhees puts it (quoted in Winch 1958: 85). This is impeccable Wittgenstein (cf. Ambrose 1979: 89), up to a point – the point at which agreeing in our reactions is made into something like a criterion for the existence of a rule.

9 Ethnomethodology and the logic of practice

Michael Lynch

Ethnomethodology is the study of practical action and practical reasoning. Harold Garfinkel's (1967) studies of jurors, coroners, and social science researchers set the agenda by describing the accomplishment of relevant tasks in specific situations. In addition to presenting empirical research on situated practices, Garfinkel's writings develop a praxiological orientation to the classic problems and topics in philosophy and the human sciences.[1] These topics include language, knowledge, trust, reasoning, meaning, normative order, rationality, method, etc. (and 'etc.' itself is a name Garfinkel gives to an ad hoc practice). Simply put, this praxiological orientation is a matter of treating these topics not as ontological entities, foundational processes, parts of society, social structures, cultural systems, behavioral mechanisms, or cognitive faculties, but as situated accomplishments by the parties whose local practices 'assemble' the recurrent scenes of action that make up a stable society. So, for example, when described ethnomethodologically, discourse becomes a practically organized phenomenon: a coordinated assembly of what is said, and by whom, in particular circumstances. When treated in this way, social order becomes an array of practical, self-organizing and self-investigating phenomena. What is at stake is not the theoretical problem of order, but the substantive *production* of order on singular occasions. As Garfinkel (1991: 11) puts it in characteristic fashion, 'sociology's fundamental phenomenon' of the 'objective reality of social facts' is 'every society's locally, endogenously produced, naturally organised, reflexively accountable, on-going, practical achievement, being everywhere, always, only, exactly and entirely, members' work, with no time out, and with no possibility of evasion, hiding out, passing, postponement, or buy-outs.' This 'stunning vision of society as a practical achievement' is not original to ethnomethodology. It is central to the entire tradition of social theory from Hobbes to Parsons.[2] No less central is 'the vexed problem of the practical objectivity and practical observability of practical actions and practical reasoning,' which provides a constant and unfinished task for social theory; a problem that '*because* it was vexed, serve[d] as the standing source and grounds for the adequacy of theorising's claims' (Garfinkel 1991: 11).[3] If reactions to ethnomethodology are any indication, it can be exceedingly difficult to understand the scope and implications of this 'vexed problem of the practical objectivity and practical observability of practical actions and practical reasoning' and, in this essay, I shall discuss how it is brought into relief by the very idea of ethnomethodology. I will then attempt to show how that problem is pertinent to contemporary efforts by social theorists to put practice(s) on the agenda.

Folk methodologies

The word 'ethnomethodology' literally means folk investigations of the principles or procedures of a practice. Already, however, we encounter an ambiguity. Should we suppose that ethnomethodologists are scholars who investigate the methods through which members construct the social world, or should we suppose that the investigations in question are already performed as part of a society's production? In other words, is ethnomethodology a kind of praxiology in which professional scholars investigate the logic or logics of ordinary practices,[4] or do ethnomethodologists suppose that the investigations in question are already performed (or otherwise 'inscribed') before the scholar comes on the scene?

One possible answer to this question is 'both at once.' In conversation analysis, an offshoot of ethnomethodology, professional analysts who examine tape-recorded instances of conversation speak of an 'analysis' that is intrinsic to the production of the talk (Sacks et al. 1974). For conversation analysts, 'analysis' is a pivotal term that identifies their own methodological activity with the objective domain they investigate. The concerted production of intelligible lines of talk is both the subject and the source of such analysis. Professional analysis is thus an effort to *recover* the analytic work that is endogenous to the social production of coordinated talk. So, for example, in one of his transcribed lectures Harvey Sacks describes an incident occurring in a gathering of four young men, Jim, Al, Ken, and Roger. One fellow (Jim) offers some candy, first to Al and then to Ken. Sacks (1992: 293) observes that 'he is observably "not offering candy to Roger".' Sacks then goes on to say that in sociology and anthropology the idea of 'something that didn't happen' has been a persistent source of analytic difficulty: 'if you're going to say that some X hasn't happened, then there's an indefinite list of things that could be said not to have happened at that point. And if that's so, then our case is non-discriminable from the rest of those, and the observation is trivialized' (Sacks 1992: 294). In social and cultural theory, there are a number of familiar examples of 'something that didn't happen' – a nonoccurrence of a workers' revolution, a nonexercise of latent powers, a failure to return a gift in the culturally prescribed fashion, or a failure to choose the most efficient of the available means to a given end – and there are also a number of familiar (and 'vexed') theoretical solutions to the problem of identifying 'something that didn't happen,' but Sacks opts for a characteristic ethnomethodological solution:

What we can perhaps do is see whether there are some methodical ways that persons arrive at such noticings [of 'something that didn't happen'] . . . There are some occasions under which absences are noticed. If we can characterize the bases for them, we can come up with a usable notion of 'absence.' And such a notion could perhaps be generalized beyond the specific occasion that we happened to construct it in relation to (Sacks 1992: 294).

In this instance, Sacks suggests that the notion of a 'round' in conversation might account for the notable absence of an offer to Roger. It is important to see that Sacks proposes that this vernacular notion of 'round' is both a general analytic concept *and* a contingently produced phenomenon which, in the case at hand, provides a basis for seeing that a relevant action does not take place. The notion is not (or not only) a conceptual principle invoked by a professional analyst in order to establish the relevance of the action that did not take place; it is evidently and performatively relevant to the accountable absence. One kind of evidence for the relevance of the local ordering principle is that parties can comment on it: Roger might, for example, complain that Jim failed to offer him any candy. Similarly, evidence for the relevance of an analogous kind of 'round' in an occasion of joke-telling can be found when, after a series of others in the group have told 'their' jokes, a remaining member confesses that he can never remember jokes. Such explicit comments are not, however, required for establishing that the parties to the scene recognize, count on, and contingently enact a projectable order of collective activities. If, as Sacks proposes, rounds of introductions, jokes, stories, offers, etc., exhibit characteristic features – for example, that a first offer in the series will be marked in specific ways (although not necessarily announced in so many words *as* an offer or even as a first in a series of offers), and another offer will be performed in unmarked fashion as a 'next' of the same kind until the round runs to completion – an absence can be noticeable by virtue of its placement in a local context of the *contingently relevant events* (in the case in point, the events making up a 'round' of offers).

In this example, Sacks offers an analytic notion (the 'round' as a contingently produced assemblage of performances by the parties in the scene) which establishes the background condition for a notable absence (the non-offer of candy to Roger). There is a superficial resemblance between this conception of analysis and the more familiar conception of understanding the subjective meaning of action in interpretative anthropology and sociology, but there is also a crucial difference. Consider Weber's classic example of the woodcutter. Weber uses the example to distinguish between two ways of understanding actions. When we see 'the action of woodcutter or of somebody who reaches for the knob to shut a door or who aims a gun at an animal' these are instances of 'rational observational understanding of actions' (Weber 1978: 8). Weber distinguishes this 'direct' mode of understanding from the 'explanatory understanding . . . which consists in placing the act in an intelligible and more inclusive context of meaning' (Weber 1978: 8). So, in the case of the woodcutter, one kind of explanation would place the immediate behavior in one or another motivational context: working for a wage, supplying a store of firewood, getting some exercise, or working off a fit of rage. If one were to apply Weber's distinction to Sacks's example, it might be said that Sacks, as an over-hearer of the conversation, 'directly observed' *that* Jim failed to perform a relevant action. (We shall ignore for the moment that there can be a significant difference between 'directly observing' something and 'directly observing *that*' something (has not) occurred.) If Sacks had drawn inferences about why Jim did not offer the candy to Roger – saying it was done as a joke or a snub – this would be an example of 'explanatory understanding.' It should be clear, however, that Sacks is not primarily addressed to a matter of 'direct' or 'explanatory' *understanding*. Although Sacks's own understanding, and the understandings of Jim, Al, Ken, and Roger, are implicated in the description of the 'something that didn't happen,' according to his analysis the relevant understandings are grounded in the *embodied and concerted production* of a recognizable round of offers. Considered as an interpretative matter, noticing 'something that didn't happen' in a round of offers is not essentially different from noticing that a number is missing in the series 1, 2, 3, 5, 6, 7.[5] In the case of Jim's non-offer to Roger, it is possible to formulate an abstract rule that would account for the (non)event as a transgression (one might even find such a rule in an etiquette manual), but one of the points Sacks makes is that this transgression was made *contingently* relevant by the *production* of a round. Both the observability of the (non-occurring) action and the orderly ground against which it becomes noticeable are produced in and through the practices of composing the round. The rationality in question is not strictly a matter of recognizing what we *see* when we observe the action from a detached vantage point; instead, it is a matter of what we *do* (or, in this case, what Jim, Al, Ken, and Roger evidently do) when engaged in the embodied, here-and-now, production of a scene. The shift in analytic focus is from an observer's interpretation of a scene to a concerted production of the scenic features. By analogy, a 'direct observational understanding' of what is missing in a number series presupposes a conventional use of a rule for counting. If we imagine an unconventional way to continue the series (for example: 1, 2, 3, 5, 6, 7, 9, 10, 11), the number 4 no longer counts as 'absent'; or, rather, its absence is accountable not as a mistake or anomaly, but as a constitutive property of the series. The conventional mode of counting does not originate in an eternal, Platonic realm, but is established through a whole array of daily activities in which we normally and routinely count like *this*: 1, 2, 3, 4, 5, 6. . . . We rely upon the numbers we use, the things we count, and the persons who do the counting to 'behave' in stable and reliable ways. Similarly, the fact that we 'count on' Jim to complete his round of invitations and notice when he fails to do so, is grounded in a practice, in this case not of counting with numbers but of performing a sequence of offers that counts in Al and Ken and counts out Roger. For Sacks, the lesson is not *that* the ordering principle in question originates in a practice, but that the practice is instantiated *in situ*, in a developing production that contingently establishes the recognizability of an incomplete instance of its performance.

The particular example of Jim's non-offer is trivial, especially when compared with such historic nonevents as a workers' revolution, but its very triviality can be considered to be a consequence of the production of a public, mutually recognized, and interactionally organized phenomenon (a round of offers). The theoretical implications of this conception of practice are far from trivial. For many critics of Marxism, the notable absence of workers' revolutions in the most advanced capitalist societies is taken as evidence of a failed theoretical prediction: a failure of empirical events to confirm an alleged historical 'law.' Understood ethnomethodologically, the failure is primarily an organizational production: the concerted actions that would have made the prediction/production 'come true' have not been effectuated (see Sacks 1963: 15, n.3). Or, to put it another way, the relevant organizational production has (thus far?) been effectively negated and resisted as a matter of practical politics. Sacks, of course, is not suggesting that conversation analysts should abandon their ivory towers and take to the streets in order to help effectuate what he calls 'properly-rounded actions' (Sacks 1992: 295). His interest in such phenomena is analytical. Contrary to Marx he argues that 'it is our business to *analyze* how it is that something gets done, or how something is "a something," and not to *employ* it' (Sacks 1992: 295). For Sacks, 'a good deal of the sociological literature' remains inexplicit about how the recurrent events and absences that constitute the events and structures that sociologists describe are actually produced, and he envisaged it as his and his colleagues' task to close the gap in the literature (Sacks 1992: 295).

As Sacks describes it, a round is an abstract phenomenon, because an open series of occasions can be said to be organized into rounds. The notion of contingently relevant events is even more abstract, because it can be used to describe interactional phenomena besides rounds (adjacency pairs, for example). As Sacks (1992: 295) sets it up, the analytic task in the case of the absent offer is to identify and describe the abstract 'apparatus that will give us that usage of "absences."' Consequently, it is possible to identify two distinct places for analysis, one being the local site of conversational production, and the other being a literary space for academic innovation (the gap in the sociological literature). The burden on any conversation analysis project is to demonstrate a link between the two sites.

In conversation analysis, a common way to gloss the difficult task of forging a link between professional and members' analyses is to speak of 'participants' orientations.' Whenever a conversation analysis study employs vernacular categories for persons and actions, the requirement is to demonstrate analytic-ally that those categories are relevantly part of the 'analysis' performed by the participants on the scene. Failures to meet this requirement can be instructive. For example, Schegloff (1987) criticizes a well-known study by Zimmerman and West (1975) about conversations between women and men.

Zimmerman and West employ a mixture of procedures from conversation analysis and experimental social psychology in order to examine male and female speakers' uses of, and responses to, interruptions in conversation. The study's findings confirm what many of their readers may suspect on experiential grounds, that men dominate conversations with women and tend not to listen to what they have to say. Without suggesting that this general proposition is false, Schegloff argues that Zimmerman and West's empirical analysis is irrelevant to the proposition's truth or falsity. He reviews Zimmerman and West's transcribed interchanges between pairs of male and female university students, and criticizes the authors' analytic procedures for identifying 'interruptions' and assigning each interruption to the 'male' or 'female' participant. The vernacular concept of 'interruption' implies that one person speaks before the other has finished and that the cut-off was not warranted. Schegloff argues, on the basis of his own re-analysis of Zimmerman and West's transcripts, that the 'interruptions' they identified in many cases can be characterized more appropriately as locally warranted moves, and he also questions the relevance of the category pair 'male/female' for setting up the accountability of the (alleged) interruptions.

I do not have space to go into the details of Schegloff's argument, but an appreciation of the issues can be gained by reference to the same lecture by Sacks that I have been discussing. Sacks introduces the notion of a 'priority item' to describe one way in which a cut-off of an ongoing action can be locally warranted. A 'priority item' is an action that exhibits 'superseding relevance . . . rights and obligations to be done, perhaps without regard to what it is that has been taking place, under some proper conditions occurring' (Sacks 1992: 296). He adds that one of the features of priority items is that 'when they are properly invoked *they are not interrupting what goes on*, and what goes on ought to cease' (Sacks 1992: 296, emphasis added). One systematic way to claim priority for such an item is to produce it as a 'repair' of a potential mistake or possible misunderstanding in the ongoing activity. The contingent relevance and priority of such an item turns upon 'a systematic categorization of the various personnel present, of locating among them "the one who ought to do the priority item"' (Sacks 1992: 297).[6] The categorization is produced locally by the parties to the scene, and it is intertwined with the recognizable (or in some cases claimable) identity of the priority item as a locally warranted action. An unwarranted 'interruption' is therefore a residual category, in the sense that it cuts off an ongoing utterance without displaying that it is a type of action that should have priority at that moment and/or that the 'interruptor' is locally entitled to perform the action. Almost anyone is eligible to perform some kinds of priority items – for example, stopping someone in order to warn them about an immediate hazard – whereas other actions – for example, stopping a speaker in order to correct their grammar or pronunciation – can be done by persons in restricted social categories (parents, teachers, etc.). Persons who cannot claim the appropriate relational rights are vulnerable to the objection, 'Who are *you* to do that?' One can get a rough appreciation of this issue by imagining an encounter in which one speaker (an adult male teacher) begins speaking before the other (a female child in the teacher's classroom) has finished. A number of alternative characterizations can be made of this moment of interaction: the male interrupts the female; the teacher corrects the student's recitation; the adult dominates the child; the expert identifies the novice's mistake. It might seem reasonable to suppose that each of these descriptions is just as correct as any of the others, and that theoretical assumptions (or ideological presuppositions) will govern any particular attribution the analyst makes. If, as is often argued, there is no avoiding the theory-ladenness of observation, it follows that a responsible analyst should be explicit about her theoretical assumptions in order not to present ideological attributions under the guise of unequivocal characterizations of 'objective' states of affairs. But if, as conversation analysts insist, the intelligibility of the actions in question rests in the first instance on the evident way in which those actions are 'oriented to' in a local pragmatic context,[7] then some theoretical (and operational) criteria can be irrelevant (and even incorrect) for categorizing particular actions and their doers. Although categorizing a pair of interlocutors as 'male' and 'female' may be relevant under some circumstances, and while it might be true that a pupil may not have finished what she was saying before a teacher 'interrupted' her, the demonstrable pairing of personal categories ('male/female') and action ('interruption') can be difficult to support in the face of the locally relevant alternatives: 'teacher/pupil' and 'correction.' Consequently, in order to control such ascriptions, conversation analysts argue that it is necessary to demonstrate that the analyst's characterizations are contingently relevant to the production of the actions under analysis. In particular cases, such demonstrations can themselves be doubtful and disputable, but the point of the policy is to restrain an all-too-familiar interpretative tendency to stipulate identities and actions from a privileged vantage point.

Methods and analyses of method

Theoretical statements on behalf of ethnomethodology often draw a distinction between 'members' methods' employed in the society at large and the ethnomethodological analyses produced by members of a research community.[8] In certain respects this distinction reiterates a long-standing division of labor between practitioners who employ experimental methods and analysts (including some practitioners) who formulate methodological policies and principles. A difference in the case of ethnomethodology is that the varieties of ethno-methods greatly exceed the range of scientific and professional methods that provide subject matter for traditional methodological investigations. The traditional task of formulating methodologies falls to philosophers, logicians, and writers of more specialized pedagogies and protocols. In all of these texts, writers analyze how particular practices are (or should be) done, and this analytic task is distinct from the performance of the practices in question. A key, and perhaps unique, insight from ethnomethodology is that methodologies (and not just methods) themselves come in an immense variety of 'vulgar' forms, including instructions for cooking, gardening, child care, sex, courtship, driving, auto repair, and, in the case of etiquette manuals, conversation. The existence – indeed, the overwhelming abundance – of written instructions, manuals, descriptive schemes, plans, protocols, maps, and so forth, should alert us to the fact that 'methodological' accounts are no less embedded in the world that ethnomethodologists study than are 'methods' themselves. When folk methodologies as well as folk methods are included in the field of study, the relations between social scientists' and members' methodologies can become confusing and contentious.

In certain respects, the conversation analyst's task is like that of other methodologists, but it differs in at least one fundamental respect. Unlike logicians and philosophers, conversation analysts do not suppose that their own formal descriptions identify the basis for a competency that can be abstracted from successful historical performances and used to upgrade the coherence and efficacy of untutored practices. Unlike writers of technical manuals, conversation analysts do not propose to instruct readers on how to perform novel or unfamiliar actions, and unlike writers of etiquette manuals, they do not propose to regulate familiar forms of conduct. In Sacks's analysis of the round of offers, there is no suggestion that Jim needs a methodological lesson. Depending on how Jim's co-participants (and particularly Roger) react to the non-offer, Jim might be given a sharp rebuke, a hurt look, or a playful riposte. If he is given a lesson in etiquette ('Hey, you're supposed to offer candy to all of us!') a conversation analysis description would focus less on the rule ('when offering candy to one party, you should offer it to others present') than on the situated use of that rule on the specific occasion as a complaint, request, or appreciation of a practical joke. Even in a case where a rule stated in an etiquette manual seems to apply, the conversation analysis task is to show just how it applies.

The instructions in etiquette books tend to get written with some specified type of person in mind, given some types of situations, e.g., 'The host at a party ought . . .' There are presumably lots of occasions in which, say, introductions occur, for which there is no 'host at the dinner party.' The question then is, how is it that persons go about picking some class for which the set of integrated rules has been initially written, and replacing the various categories with some available set of categories, and assigning the new categories status with respect to the old, i.e., seeing who is 'like a host' or some such thing; or treating 'the host' as an example from some other class that has some other form, i.e., 'the person in charge here,' or whatever (Sacks 1992: 297)?

From this example, we can see that an opportunity for a distinctive kind of analysis can be found not only in the 'gap in the sociological literature' (the 'gap' created by the sociological literature's inexplicit reliance on common-sense knowledge of how orderly social phenomena are produced), but also in the gap *between* literary accounts of practice and members' actual practices.

The latter gap identifies one of the epistemic frontiers glossed by the notion of tacit knowledge. In the philosophy, history, and sociology of science much has been made of the widely acknowledged fact that 'scientists rarely follow any of the scientific methods that philosophers prescribe for them. They use their common sense.'[9] To this it can be added that scientists also use unformulated 'common sense' when trying to follow the more specific methodological guidelines, recipes, and protocols written in specialized laboratory manuals and research reports. Not only is this fact about science (as well as many other kinds of practice) widely known among scholars in the science studies fields, it is also widely known among the laboratory practitioners they study. Indeed, this fact, together with the fact that is widely known, is an organizational phenomenon. For example, biotechnology firms that conduct pre-natal testing and forensic labs that analyze criminal evidence commonly employ one group of specialists who develop, disseminate, and monitor laboratory protocols, and another group of employees – a graded hierarchy of staff scientists and technicians – who enact the protocols. In line with a familiar factory division of labor between industrial engineers and manual laborers, the work of writing and testing protocols is separated from handling the samples and running the analytic machinery on the shop floor. Despite the impressive efforts to standardize protocols, monitor technicians' compliance, and auto-mate tasks, it is widely acknowledged (especially by the technicians) that there remains a gap between written protocols and local know-how. This gap provides an obscure object of methodological desire and a continual source of frustration for efforts to design and administrate standardized protocols, but the existence of a gap that has not yet been closed implicates many relevant aspects of the organization of work: the organizational hierarchies; the separation of tasks and laboratory spaces; the monitoring of technician's work; the articulation of precautions; the requirements for record-keeping; the recognized roles of 'magic' and 'golden hands' in molecular biology; and the residual allowances for 'common sense' (Cambrosio and Keating 1988; Jordan and Lynch 1993).

When faced with a gap between methodological instructions and practices, many philosophers, social scientists, and technical writers try to bridge the gap by extending and elaborating conventional forms of methodological writing. One common strategy for doing this is to assimilate unformulated methods under principles of the same kind as those used in familiar methodological formulations. For example, in his well-known discussion of tacit knowledge, Michael Polanyi employs a notion of 'hidden rules' to bridge the gap between explicit and inexplicit practices:

> To learn by example is to submit to authority. You follow your master because you trust his manner of doing things even when you cannot analyze and account in detail for its effectiveness. By watching the master and emulating his efforts in the presence of his example, the apprentice unconsciously picks up the rules of the art, including those which are not

explicitly known to the master himself. These hidden rules can be assimilated only by a person who surrenders himself to that extent uncritically to
the imitation of another. A society which wants to preserve a fund of
personal knowledge must submit to tradition (Polanyi 1958: 53).

From reading this passage, it is understandable that Polanyi has been criticized for his conservative emphasis on tradition and scientific authority, but
this is not what concerns me at the moment. Instead, I am concerned with a
series of questions about Polanyi's characterization of the master's and
apprentice's practice as a matter of following hidden rules: How can we know
about rules that neither the master nor the apprentice knows explicitly? How
can a *rule* (as opposed to, say, a habit) be 'unconsciously' learnt and followed?
Are these hidden rules like other rules, except for the fact that they have not
(yet) been made explicit? If we were to write a methodological account of the
rules in question – an analysis that accounts in detail for the unwitting
effectiveness of master's and apprentice's shared 'manner of doing things' –
would this not transform their practice?

Polanyi's reference to hidden, unconsciously mastered rules is a clear
instance of an analytic tendency often found in the cognitive sciences. This is
the tendency to use the language of formal methodology (and especially
experimental methodology) to describe or comparatively analyze nonscien-
tific, unconscious, heuristic, and nonrational modes of reasoning and practice.
Accordingly, the human (or, in some cases, nonhuman) practice in question is
made out in the image of a scientific method, and the agent is endowed with
theories, models, hypotheses, heuristics, protocols, and decision rules,[10] but
the methodological inquiry (the analysis of the method) is the analyst's and
not the agent's prerogative. This way of addressing what Garfinkel (1991: 11)
calls 'the vexed problem of the practical objectivity and practical observability
of practical actions and practical reasoning' reopens the gap between formal
methodologies and situated practices by means of the very effort to close it.
Once again, there is a gap between the analyst's formulation of 'hidden' or
'unconscious' versions of protocols, models, and rules of method and the
practices those protocols, models, and rules allegedly describe or determine.[11]

Conversation analysts do not investigate the competencies of individual
agents by comparing them to, or endowing them with, formulaic accounts of
method. Even where, as discussed earlier, Sacks (1992) deems the instructions in an etiquette manual to be relevant for an analysis of a round of
introductions, he does not propose that a particular instruction ('The host at a
party ought . . .') sufficiently describes or prescribes the methodic actions in
question. Instead, he alludes to a different order of practices through which
the parties locally adapt the instruction (or an instruction like it) to a different
configuration of relational identities. Although Sacks uses expressions like 'a
machinery' and 'an apparatus' to describe the order-productive work performed
on the occasion of talk under analysis, as I understand these expressions, they
do not allude to an internal mechanism that causes compliance to a rule;

instead, they allude to a collectively produced artifact – the round of introductions – that is assembled by the parties at the scene of their action. The methodological task for the conversation analyst is to describe the machinery by formulating a set of instructions for building and operating it on the particular occasion. The grammar of an instruction – describing how you construct and make use of an artifact – differs fundamentally from a deterministic account of how an internal mechanism causes you to behave in a certain way. The grammar of the instruction does not reduce the action to a mechanism operating beneath or behind the public scene of action, but (as Sacks makes abundantly clear with his references to abstract objects like 'rounds' and 'contingently relevant phenomena') neither does it reduce the action to the unique elements of the situation. To a large extent, conversation analysts describe the work of replicating social technologies on singular occasions. The coherence, contingent relevance, and iterable identities associated with 'doing the same thing again' withstand changes in local staff, social circumstances, material resources, and immediate purposes. This ethnomethodological conception of the situated replication of social technologies can be used to relate research in conversation analysis to a topic investigated in the sociology of scientific knowledge (SSK).[12]

Unlike conversation analysts, students of SSK confront the prototypical subject of methodological writing: scientific methods. And unlike conversation analysts, they devote a great deal of attention to criticizing existing philosophical and technical methodologies. Their criticisms should not be confused, as they often are, with attempts to demonstrate the inadequacy of scientific methods. It is not as though the 'failure' of existing experimental protocols to describe the situated uses of experiment implies that experimentation is an inadequate method. Particular experiments *can* be faulted, and the faults can at times be attributed to the incompleteness of protocols, but such faults and such faulting are no less contingently relevant than are determinations of experimental success and technical adequacy. SSK's main lesson about replication is that the situated (re)production of experiments can be shown, when studied empirically, to be a source of greater difficulty, practical struggle, and fractious interpretation than is generally acknowledged in the methodology literature. This lesson has stirred controversy, not because it threatens the adequacy of particular experimental practices and findings, but because it rivals the lessons conveyed by other philosophical and professional accounts of the principles and procedures of experimental practice (Lynch 1996).

Leaving aside the fact that SSK's arguments make abundant use of resources from skeptical philosophy that raise problems of their own, SSK's lesson can highlight a vexed issue for ethnomethodology as well as for traditional conceptions of methodology. If, as I have suggested, conversation analysts describe the work of replicating social technologies on singular occasions, and if, as the literature in the field often seems to suggest, conversation analysts describe such work in the form of members' rules, members' models, and other abstract devices, then 'the problem of replication' will also alert us to an exploitable gap between conversation analysis rules and the situated uses of such rules on singular occasions. As in the case of experimental technologies, when studied closely, the situated (re)production of generic conversational 'apparatus' may turn out to be a source of greater difficulty, practical struggle, and fractious interpretation than is generally acknowledged in the conversation analysis literature.[13]

The logic of practice

Earlier, I discussed how ethnomethodologist Harvey Sacks handled a familiar analytic problem: how do you establish the relevance of 'something that didn't happen?' This problem is familiar to logicians and social scientists, but Sacks treated it in an unusual way. A standard way to handle the problem is to formulate a rule, norm, or empirical proposition that specifies the conditions under which the event in question should take place. Given such normative expectancies, and the nonoccurrence of the event, then it is reasonable to say that the event was notably absent. Sacks's solution was unusual, in that he did not formulate a rule or an empirical proposition but instead described a routine practice, the local production of which established the relevant conditions for noticing 'something that didn't happen.' Although Sacks addressed a general methodological problem (a variant of the problem of relevance), his solution (or rather, the members' solution he described) took the form of a methodic, recurrent, intersubjectively accountable, embodied production in lived time and lived space. In brief, Sacks described a situated, methodic, and embodied solution to a logical problem.

I can imagine that many readers will find the implications of this solution to be less than transparent. One possible implication suggested by Sacks (1992: 294) is that systematic descriptions of the methodic production of logically accountable orders (like the notion of a notable absence) may yield analytically 'usable' notions. One may want to ask, 'usable for whom, and for what purpose?' It seems safe to say that such notions should be usable for other researchers in the community of conversation analysts when they carry out further investigations, but given the generality of the problem of specifying something that did not happen, we might expect there to be broader theoretical implications. I do not believe that there can be a general theoretical solution to the problem. Instead, I think that investigations of how the problem is posed and addressed can have broad *critical* implications. In order to bring such critical implications into relief it may be necessary to put aside any search for 'usable' notions that would foster the development of an analytical discipline. In the remainder of this paper I will suggest that ethnomethodology can radicalize the entire picture of how logic is related to practice. In order to demonstrate how this might be so, I will briefly examine another occasion in which 'something that didn't happen' becomes notable. In this case, however, the methodological use of the notion of 'absence' is both constitutive and tendentious.

During the 1994–5 trial *California* v. *Orenthal James Simpson*, Defense Attorney Barry Scheck carried out an extended cross-examination of Los Angeles Police Department criminalist Dennis Fung. Fung was one of the functionaries who collected blood evidence from the crime scene. In the sequence leading up to the following excerpt from testimony on April 12, 1995, Scheck had been questioning Fung about 'four red [blood] stains' on the door of the defendant's Ford Bronco vehicle:

1 SCHECK: Okay, Mr. Fung. Let me ask you directly, on June 13th in the morning, did Detective Fuhrman point out four red lines, red stains to you on the bottom of the Bronco door?

2 FUNG: I don't recall him doing so.

3 SCHECK: When you say you don't recall, are you saying it didn't happen?

4 FUNG: I'm not saying that. I'm saying I don't recall if he did or if he didn't.

5 SCHECK: All right. If you had seen four red stains on the exterior of the Bronco door on the morning of June 13th, you would have taken a photograph of them; would you have not?

6 FUNG: That would depend, but I don't know. But that would depend on the circumstances.

7 SCHECK: Let's try these circumstances. You were pointed out a red stain by the door handle?

8 FUNG: Yes.

9 SCHECK: You were photographed pointing to that red stain, correct?

10 FUNG: Yes.

11 SCHECK: And you're the person that's supposed to direct the photographer during the collection process?

12 FUNG: Yes.

13 SCHECK: You're supposed to photograph items of evidence of some importance that are pointed out to you by the detectives?

14 FUNG: Yes.

15 SCHECK: In the circumstances of this case, if you had seen four red stains on the exterior of the Bronco door, would you not have directed the photographer to take a picture of it?

16 FUNG: It would be likely. Yes.

17 SCHECK: If you had seen four red stains on the exterior of the Bronco door, would you have not done a presumptive test on June 13th?

18 FUNG: Possibly, I – If it was necessary, I would have.

19 SCHECK: If you had seen four red stains on the exterior of the Bronco door, would you have not swatched them?

20 FUNG: I would – I would possibly have swatched them.

21 SCHECK: If you had seen four red stains on the exterior of the Bronco door, would you not have included that observation in your reports for that day?

22 FUNG: If I thought it was important to the investigation, I would have included it in my notes, yes.

23   SCHECK: Looking back at the circumstances of this case, would not those four red stains have been an important detail that you would have certainly included in your notes?

24   MR. GOLDBERG (PROSECUTOR): Calls for speculation.

25   THE COURT: Overruled.

26   FUNG: From my perspective now?

27   SCHECK: Let's try your perspective then.

28   FUNG: I don't recall my exact state of mind then, but it – I don't know exactly if I would have put it down or not.[14]

In the early part of the sequence, Scheck questions Fung about whether Detective Furman showed him the particular blood stains (described in 'sense data' language as 'four red stains') on June 13, the morning after the murders. Fung professes not to recall, and Scheck then pursues the matter of why Fung has no record (or distinct recollection) of having seen the evidence. The point of the line of question apparently is to impugn Furman's testimony, expose Fung's evasions, and/or imply that Fung collected and recorded the evidence in a sloppy way.

Scheck pursues the matter by asking a series of questions designed with a classic if–then propositional format (lines 5, 15, 17, 19, 21). Each of these questions logically frames 'something that didn't happen' as a notable, and practically contingent, absence. The questions are phrased as variants of the counterfactual conditional form: 'If A had been the case, then B would be the case.'[15] This is one standard form logicians use for stating natural laws, but here the 'law' in question is formulated as a contingent temporal relation between perceiving something and taking an action: 'If you had seen A, you would have done B,' or, interrogatively, 'If you had seen A, would you not have done B?' In this way, the form of an empirical generalization is transformed into *a methodological rule*. Given that Fung (line 2) initially professes not to recall having seen the four red stains in question on June 13, Scheck's repeated questions appear to suggest that if Fung had seen the stains at that time, he would have made sure to record this with photographs, test results, and notes. When Scheck states (and Fung confirms) that Fung was photographed pointing to another blood stain (lines 7–10), he suggests even more strongly that if Fung had seen the four red stains 'under these circumstances,' he would have documented that fact. Scheck's inference from the methodological rule is thus strengthened by an exemplar drawn from Fung's own practice.[16]

Not surprisingly, Fung does not entirely go along with Scheck's account of his practice. Fung prefaces many of his responses with qualifying expressions ('it would be likely' in line 16; 'if it was necessary' in line 18; 'I would possibly have' in line 20; 'if I thought it was important' in line 22). Without entirely contradicting the counterfactuals presented in Scheck's questions – 'If you had seen A, would you not have done B?' – Fung resists each of the implied methodological relationships between circumstance and action. It is not enough to say that these qualifications suggest an uncertain, contingent, or probable mediation between the circumstances at the crime scene and what someone in Fung's position should have (or typically would have) done, they also bring into play the matter of situated judgment. Fung suggests that when he investigates a crime scene he does not simply see particular items of evidence and then document them according to standard protocols, he makes judgments about what is relevant and important (enough) to record and collect. And, presumably, aside from what he did in fact record and collect on June 13, he implies that what he remembers about the crime scene also depends on the judgments he originally made about the salience of particular collectables. In other words, while he acknowledges the salience of the methodological rules Scheck formulates, he also implies that he did not follow those rules mechanically.

This dialogue is but a small fragment of an extended series of methodological debates that consumed large portions of the Simpson trial. In this instance, Scheck and Fung assume different positions in a situated variant of an interminable debate about the logic of practice: where Scheck relies upon a methodological rule to determine what Fung's method must (or should) have been, Fung defends his indistinct recollections by alluding to a method that is thick with judgments about significance and relevance. Neither argument is intrinsically 'right,' though both are subject to the overhearing court's assessments of plausibility and credibility.

It is sometimes presumed that ethnomethodology privileges a 'subjectivistic' view of practice, in opposition to the more deterministic logics promoted in other branches of the social sciences. A different understanding becomes possible when, as I suggested at the outset, methodology itself is regarded as a domain of social phenomena. Accordingly, ordinary ('ethno') methodology consists of situated investigations of practical action and practical reasoning. It is not limited to academic investigations of scientific or other methods. Scheck and Fung together perform a situated methodological investigation, so that in the sense I have just outlined they *perform* a substantive instance of ethnomethodology, not only by performing 'ethnomethods,' but also by contentiously examining the order and logical implications of those methods. Scheck takes the lead in the examination of Fung's methods, and he employs an abstract apparatus (the rules of method expressed in counterfactual form) that sets up the analyzability of 'something that didn't happen' (the fact that Fung recorded no evidence of the four red stains on June 13). Fung, placed in a more reactive position, partly complies with Scheck's examination, but he also resists Scheck's 'analysis' by adding qualifications, giving indistinct recollections, and invoking local judgments. Consequently, the dialogue presented to the overhearing audience itself is a relevant contingency for establishing the descriptive adequacy of the rules of method Scheck formulates. A witness's unqualified confirmation of a question of the form 'If you had seen X, would you not have done Y?' for all practical purposes turns the interrogatory analysis into an oriented-to rule: 'When I see X, I do Y.' A failure to confirm the rule does not necessarily negate its relevance, because, as we can see from the above sequence, the interrogator can reiterate the rule while pursuing the question and challenging the witness's credibility.

This particular excerpt provides an unusually clear instance of an interrogator's situated use of a formal logical device. Scheck struggles to instantiate a normative machinery that determines what the details of Fung's practice should have involved, and his repeated questions insistently reiterate a particular line of logical derivation. Fung, for his part, successively (but not necessarily successfully) resists the logical force of the questions by suggesting that a less mechanistic mode of inference-making is characteristic of his practice. The clarity of this struggle allows us to grasp a radical ethnomethodological lesson on the logic of a practice. It is 'radical' not in the sense that it gets to the roots of the matter, but, instead, in the way it displaces the analytic prerogative to expose such roots. Scheck's methodological rules are stated in a strongly determinate form, but their logical force has yet to be rooted in a methodic, recurrent, intersubjectively accountable, embodied production of courtroom dialogue. It is as though the logical machinery needs to be screwed to the floor before its operation can be effective. In the case of the courtroom 'floor,' the relevant platform is both situated in a room and embodied in a discursive spectacle.[17]

Conclusion

At the beginning of this essay I quoted Garfinkel's (1991: 11) assertion that 'the vexed problem of the practical objectivity and practical observability of practical actions and practical reasoning,' provides a constant and unfinished task for social theory. I then suggested that this problem has to do with the way 'methodologies' as well as 'methods' play a constitutive role in the production of social phenomena. The discussion of the example from Sacks's lecture indicated the existence of an ethnomethodological solution to a classic analytic problem of the observability of 'something that didn't happen.' This solution took the irreducible form of an embodied practice (a 'round' of offers), but I subsequently argued that an abstract account of that practice would be likely to reiterate 'the vexed problem' for social theory: the gap between the methodological literature and the local practices that literature describes, instructs, or regulates. The example from the Simpson trial was used to demonstrate that the gap between a determinate, logical account of a practice and the situated performance of that practice is itself a constitutive, organizational phenomenon for courtroom testimony. The lesson I derive from this example is that it is pointless to seek a general methodological solution to 'the vexed problem of the practical objectivity and practical observability of practical actions and practical reasoning,' because any abstract account of the logic of practice immediately reiterates the problem. The investigative task for ethnomethodology is therefore to describe how the logical accountability of practice is itself a subject of practical inquiry; an inquiry that can involve struggles and fragile agreements. Ethnomethodological descriptions are positioned in academic fields and literatures – they are informed by other case studies, they critically engage extant theories and address social science concepts – but they do not entertain the grand theoretical delusion that 'the logic of practice' is a unitary subject of social analysis. For this reason alone, ethnomethodology offers a valuable form of therapy for contemporary social theorists.[18]

Notes

The research for this paper was partially supported by two research grants: a National Science Foundation Research Grant (Studies in Science, Technology and Society, Ethics and Values Studies Program), 'DNA Fingerprinting: Law and Science in Criminal Processes' awarded to Cornell University (Sheila Jasanoff, Principal Investigator), with subcontract to Brunel University (NSF Award # 9312183, 1993–4), and an Economic and Social Research Council grant, 'Science in a Legal Context: DNA Profiling, Forensic Practice and the Courts' (R000235853, 1995–7).

1 See Garfinkel (1964; 1967, Chapter 1), and Garfinkel and Sacks (1970).
2 Garfinkel (1991: 11). Garfinkel discusses the problem of order more extensively in an unpublished manuscript (Garfinkel 1960).
3 As I understand this passage, Garfinkel is alluding to the problem faced by theories that specify criteria of local production (or, in older language, 'subjective understanding' or 'consciousness') as grounds for adequate characterizations of social actions and social structures. Given the often demonstrated possibility of devising mutually incongruent theories of some state of affairs, criteria of local production seem to enable the selection of a single, relevant description (a description that is demonstrably relevant, pragmatically effective, and sensibly part of the action), but by virtue of being abstract and general, such theories necessarily remain aloof from such local, pragmatic conditions of their own adequacy.
4 For a concise review and discussion of this praxiological view of ethnomethodology, see Coulter (1991).
5 Perhaps a closer analogy can be made with the family of practices associated with 'counting' members of a group. For example, if a lecturer records the attendance in a seminar, all of the students in attendance would expect to have been 'counted.' In the case of a roll call, the member taking the roll systematically records as 'absent' persons whose names are on a list who do not respond when their names are called. Although this is a matter of 'counting,' and even of enumerating, the competencies involved are not limited to numeracy, as illustrated by practical jokes played by students on substitute teachers which wreak havoc on the ordinary routines for identifying who is present, who is absent, and 'who is who' in the classroom.
6 I am reading Sacks out of context here. In the quoted passage, he is not discussing repair, but I believe that what he says is applicable.
7 The 'orientations' in question do not necessarily refer to intentions or psychological states within the individual agents. A more appropriate sense of 'orientation' has to do with the evident relations between expressions and actions in pubic situations. It is possible to describe the complex ways in which an answer is 'oriented to' a question, without assigning analytic priority to whatever may be going on 'in the head' of the answer.
8 For examples, see Heritage and Atkinson (1984); Hilbert (1990); and Zimmerman (1988).

9   The quotation is from Max Perutz (1995: 56). Perutz critically reviews Gerald Geison's (1995) study of Louis Pasteur. In a rejoinder, Geison (1996: 68) quotes the line back to Perutz, adding that his book made that very claim. It seems that these antagonists in the alleged 'culture wars' between relativist social historians and positivist scientists at least agree on the point that philosophical method-ologies do not describe scientists' common practices.

10 For a classic example in behavioral studies of nonhuman animals, see Krechevsky (1932).

11 A similar argument about theoretical uses of 'hidden' versions of explicit ordering principles is made by Turner (1994).

12 See Collins (1992). For representative collections of studies and programmatic arguments see Knorr Cetina and Mulkay (1983), and Pickering (1992a).

13 For more elaborate criticisms along this line, see Lynch (1993) and Lynch and Bogen (1994).

14 Reporter's transcript of proceedings, *The People of the State of California* v. *Orenthal James Simpson*, Superior Court of the State of California for the County of Los Angeles, Case No. BA097211, Volume 124, April 12, 1995.

15 See Hempel (1966: 56), and Goodman (1983: Chapter 1). My descriptive interest in the situated use of counterfactual conditionals differs considerably from Hempel's and Goodman's formal analytic treatments.

16 For a concise exhibit of how lawyers can demonstrably 'know' an expert witness's business, and expose apparent lapses of procedure, see Oteri et al. (1982).

17 For an illuminating discussion of the idea of 'floor,' see Macbeth (1992).

18 This is an allusion to Wittgenstein's (1953) suggestion that his investigations therapeutically renounce the 'craving for generality' that pervaded scientistic philosophy. Ethnomethodology is empirical, but it does not (or, rather, in my view it should not) entertain the logical-empiricist dream of a special form of investigation that uncovers realities that are unknown to (or misrecognized by) 'common sense.'

Part III
Posthumanist challenges

10 How Heidegger defends the possibility of a correspondence theory of truth with respect to the entities of natural science

Hubert L. Dreyfus

Science has long claimed to discover the relations among the natural kinds in the universe that exist independently of our minds and ways of coping. Today, most philosophers adopt an antirealism that consists in rejecting this thesis. Contemporary antirealists argue that the independence thesis is not just false but *incoherent*. Thus, these antirealists say they are as realist as it makes sense to be. Such *deflationary realists*, as I shall call them, claim that the objects studied by science are just as real as the baseballs, stones, and trees we encounter with our everyday coping practices, and no more.[1] In contrast to deflationary realism, I shall defend a *robust realism* that argues that the independence claim makes sense, that science can in principle give us access to the functional components of the universe as they are in themselves[2] in distinction from how they appear to us on the basis of our daily concerns, our sensory capacities, and even our way of making things intelligible.[3]

The deflationary and the robust realist positions are each part of the heritage that Heidegger has left us. Consequently, I shall, in my first section, present the deflationary realist's arguments against independence. Then, in the second section, I shall show that, although Heidegger pioneered the deflationary realist account of the everyday, he sought to establish a robust realist account of science. In the third and final section, I shall draw on Saul Kripke's account of direct reference to work out Heidegger's account of formal indication, and using this worked-out version of Heideggerian rigid designation, I will argue that we do, indeed, have practices for achieving access to things that are independent of all our practices.

The argument for deflationary realism

The argument for deflationary realism turns on the rejection of the traditional Cartesian view of human beings as self-sufficient minds whose intentional content is directed toward the world. Both Heidegger and Donald Davidson, a leading antirealist, reject this view and substitute for it an account of human beings as inextricably involved with things and people. Heidegger holds that human beings have to take a stand on who they are by dealing with things and by assuming social roles. Davidson thinks of human beings as language users who, in order to have any mental content of their own, must take up the linguistic conventions of their community. I call Heidegger and Davidson practical holists because they both claim that meaning depends ultimately on the inseparability of practices, things, and mental contents. Heidegger captures this idea in his claim that human beings are essentially being-in-the-world; Davidson makes the same point in his causal theory of meaning.

Both thinkers claim that their holism enables them to answer the Cartesian skeptic. Heidegger argues that, if human beings are essentially being-in-the-world, then the skeptical question of whether the world and others exist cannot sensibly be raised by human beings, and, as Heidegger asks, 'Who else would raise it?' (Heidegger 1962: 246–7). Heidegger thus claims that any attempt to *answer* the skeptic is mistaken. The attempt to take the skeptic seriously and prove that we can know that there is an external world pre-supposes a separation of the mind from the world of things and other people which defies a phenomenological description of how human beings make sense of everyday things and of themselves. Davidson argues, on the basis of a logical reconstruction of the way people learn a language that, although people may differ concerning the truth of any particular belief, in order for a person to acquire a language at all that person must share most of the beliefs of those who speak the language and most of these shared beliefs must be true.

It follows that we cannot make sense of the question whether the *totality* of things could be independent of the *totality* of our practices or whether things are *essentially dependent* on our practices. To raise these questions meaning-fully requires thinking that we can conceive of the totality of things and of the totality of practices with sufficient independence from each other to claim that one is logically prior. But it turns out that we can get no perspective on our practices that does not already include things and no perspective on things that does not already involve our practices. Thus, practical holism seems to make unintelligible all claims about both things in themselves apart from our practices and the totality of practices apart from things. It seems that, since true statements about objects cannot imply *either* the dependence *or* the independence of objects *vis-à-vis* our practices, these statements must be understood as describing objects as they are in the only sense of 'are' that is left, which is the 'are' of ordinary situations. Thus we arrive at a deflationary view that repudiates both metaphysical realism and transcendental idealism.

Once the deflationary realist has argued that one cannot make sense of transcendental idealism or of metaphysical realism, he is able to accept the results of science at face value so long as he makes neither the robust realist's claim that science gives us an account of the functional demarcations of the universe as it is in itself, on the one hand, nor the extreme constructivist's claim that nature must be a cultural creation, on the other. When asked whether it makes sense to claim that things existed in nature before human beings came along and that they would have existed even if human beings had never existed, the deflationary realist can sound like a scientist, saying, on the basis of empirical findings, that of course it makes sense to claim that some types of entities were there before us and would still be there if we had never existed and others would not. But the Davidsonian practical holist says this on a background of meaning that makes any talk about nature as it is in itself incoherent.

Heidegger's attempt at robust realism

Like Davidson, Heidegger answers the skeptic by showing that our practices and the everyday world are inextricably intertwined. Indeed, he argues at length that 'Dasein is the world existingly'(Heidegger 1962: 416).[4] Moreover, Heidegger seems to agree with the deflationary realists that, while entities show up as independent of us, the being or intelligibility of entities depends on our practices. So any talk of things in themselves must be put in scare quotes. Thus, Heidegger says of natural entities:

> It must be stated that entities as entities are 'in themselves' and independent of any apprehension of them; yet, the being of entities is found only in encounter and can be explained, made understandable, only from the phenomenal exhibition and interpretation of the structure of encounter (Heidegger 1985a: 217).

And he seems even more deflationary when he adds:

> Of course only as long as Dasein [human being] is (that is, only as long as an understanding of being is ontically possible), 'is there' being. When Dasein does not exist, 'independence' 'is' not either, nor 'is' the 'in-itself' (Heidegger 1962: 255).

Joseph Rouse, in his book *Knowledge and Power* (1987), sees the parallel between Heidegger's and Davidson's holistic answer to the skeptic and wonders why I fail to see that Heidegger must therefore be a deflationary realist. But, as I will now seek to show, in *Being and Time* Heidegger describes phenomena that enable him to distinguish between the everyday world and the universe and so claim to be a robust realist about the entities discovered by natural science. Moreover, he has the conceptual resources to turn his description of these phenomena into a persuasive defense of robust realism.

The first two phenomena Heidegger calls to our attention are two different ways of being. He points out that normally we deal with things as equipment. Equipment gets its intelligibility from its relation to other equipment, human roles, and social goals. Heidegger calls the equipmental way of being *availability* (*Zuhandenheit*). But Heidegger also points to another equally important phenomenon; we sometimes experience entities as independent of our instrumental coping practices. This happens in cases of equipmental breakdown. Heidegger calls the mode of being of entities so encountered, *occurrentness* (*Vorhandenheit*). Occurrent beings are not only revealed in breakdown but also revealed when we take a detached attitude towards things that decontextualizes or – in Heidegger's terms – deworlds them. In this detached attitude, we encounter occurrent entities as substances with properties.

This experience of the occurrent is still contextual and meaningful in a weak sense. Were it not for a world in which entities could be encountered, the question of whether there could be entities independent of our concerns could not be asked, and, more importantly, without our giving meaning to the occurrent way of being, the question of independence would not make sense. So Heidegger concludes that the being or intelligibility of even the occurrent mode of being depends on us: '[B]eing "is" only in the understanding of those entities to whose being something like an understanding of being belongs' (Heidegger 1962: 228, with a minor translation correction). But he still insists that, 'entities *are* independently of the experience by which they are disclosed, the acquaintance in which they are discovered, and the grasping in which their nature is ascertained' (Heidegger 1962: 228, with a minor translation correction).

This amounts to the seemingly paradoxical claim that we have *practices for making sense of entities as independent of those very practices*. This intellectual *Gestalt* figure can flip one of two ways depending upon whether one empha-sizes the *dependence* on the practices or the *independence* from those very practices. It has thus led to a three-way debate in the scholarly literature over whether Heidegger is a robust realist, a transcendental idealist, or a deflation-ary realist.[5] I have argued, using the above quotation from *Being and Time* to back me up, that Heidegger is a would-be robust realist (Dreyfus 1991). William Blattner has countered that Heidegger must be understood as a transcendental idealist and that, consequently, all the citations that seem to support robust realism, should be read as supporting merely empirical realism (Blattner 1994). David Cerbone has responded to Blattner with a reading in the spirit of Davidson in which Heidegger's account of the inextricable involve-ment of human beings and the world commits him to the view that neither robust realism nor transcendental idealism is intelligible (Cerbone 1995).

In order to see more clearly why I claim that Heidegger is a would-be robust realist, we must return to the phenomenon of deworlding. As I said, Heidegger points out that in situations of extreme instrumental breakdown, we encounter things as occurrent, as independent of the instrumental world – that is, as having no *essential* relation to our everyday coping practices – and as all along underlying our everyday equipment. '[W]hat cannot be used just lies there; it shows itself as an equipmental thing which looks so and so, and which, in its availableness, as looking that way, *has constantly been occurrent too*' (Heidegger 1962: 102–3, my italics).[6]

Nature is thus revealed as *having been there all along*. In such cases, Heidegger holds, '*The understanding of being* by which our concernful dealings with entities within-the-world have been guided *has changed over*' (Heidegger 1962: 412, Heidegger's emphasis).[7] Our practices for coping with the available are significantly different from our practices for dealing with the occurrent. Thus, Heidegger understands this changeover from dealing with things as available to dealing with them as occurrent as discontinuous. This changeover is crucial for Heidegger's answer to deflationary realism.

The radicality of this discontinuity is often hidden by inadequate phenomenological descriptions of breakdowns. When a hammer is so heavy that the carpenter cannot use it, it is then experienced as too heavy. But since being-too-heavy is context-dependent, it still presupposes the equipmental nature of hammers. But breakdown can be so severe that all that is left in experience is a mere something – 'just occurrent and no more' (Heidegger 1962: 103) – whose properties are not connected to its function in any intelligible way and are thus beyond everyday understanding. Heidegger claims that, among other experiences, anxiety gives us access to this unintelligible occurrent. 'Anxiety,' he writes, 'discloses . . . beings in their full but heretofore concealed strangeness as what is radically other' (Heidegger 1977: 105).[8]

Of course, the uninterpreted beings experienced as radically other are not theoretical entities. Heidegger knows that for us to have access to theoretical entities the beings revealed in total breakdown must be recontextualized or reinterpreted in theoretical terms. Heidegger is thus clear that the data used by science are theory-laden. He says, 'The "grounding" of "factical science" was possible only because the researchers understood that in principle there are no "bare facts"' (Heidegger 1962: 414). He is, unfortunately, not clear how these theory-laden data are supposed to be related to the radically other that is revealed in extreme breakdown; that is, he is not clear about how theoretical recontextualization is supposed to work.[9] The important thing for him is that theoretical entities are taken to be elements of nature, that is, of a universe that is anterior to and independent of our everyday mode of making sense of things. In this important sense, science is, according to Heidegger, about the *incomprehensible*. He writes:

> *Nature is what is in principle explainable and to be explained* because it is in principle incomprehensible. It is *the incomprehensible pure and simple*. And it is the incomprehensible because it is the *'unworlded' world* [i.e. the universe], insofar as we take nature in this extreme sense of the entity as it is discovered in physics (Heidegger 1985a: 217–18).

The point is *not* that the phenomenon of total breakdown, theoretical inspection, or anxiety gives us *sufficient grounds* for believing in the independent existence of natural things none of whose properties we understand. Although the quotation may suggest this, we shall see that the phenomenon of total breakdown cannot supply such grounds. What the phenomenon of total breakdown supports is the more minimal claim that nature can be experienced as independent of our coping practices and as underlying everyday things. If we had only the 'available' mode of encountering entities, we could never encounter entities more independent of our coping practices than particular hammers are. But, if Heidegger is right, we can deworld such entities and be led to see them as occurrent components of the universe.[10]

Heidegger clearly wants to embrace robust realism, for he exceeds the limits of deflationary realism when he writes: '[T]he fact that reality is ontologically grounded in the being of Dasein, does not signify that only when Dasein exists and as long as Dasein exists, can the real be as that which *in itself* it is' (Heidegger, 1962: 255, my italics).

We are now in a position to see that, in defending a robust realism concerning scientific entities, Heidegger makes two significant moves which, although they seem to be the right way to proceed, do not, as Heidegger presents them, fully succeed in supporting robust realism.

1   Heidegger points to two special attitudes (confronting equipmental breakdown and anxiety) that, on the face of it, break out of our everyday, equipment-using practices. Since Heidegger bases his account of meaning on equipment-using practices, he concludes that such special attitudes, by 'deworlding' entities, break out of our everyday meanings altogether and give us access to the 'incomprehensible' as it is in itself. But, if one has a broader conception of everyday meaning that includes perceiving things outside of use-relations, such a 'switchover' would not get one outside the everyday.[11]

2   Heidegger contends that the switchover he describes gives us beings that can be recontextualized in a theory that makes no reference to our everyday practices. But he has no account of how the meaningless beings revealed by breakdown can serve as data for science nor what sort of practices could be left after the switchover that would allow dealing with the incomprehensible while leaving it independent of all our practices. That is, in showing we can encounter things shorn of their everyday *functionality*, Heidegger has not shown that we can encounter them as independent of *all* our practices for making things intelligible. There are still the very peculiar practices of making them intelligible as un-intelligible.

In addition, when Heidegger later investigates how scientific research as an institution works, he claims that research is based on what he calls the projection of a total ground-plan (Heidegger 1977b). Research, he claims, is a modern way of studying nature that proceeds by setting up a *total* theory of how nature works and then dealing with the anomalies that show up when the theory is assumed to cover all phenomena. Thus, normal science has, for Heidegger, the ongoing job of trying to account for anomalies, while revolutionary advances in science occur when resistant anomalies lead scientists to propose a new ground-plan.[12]

What is essential for modern science as research, then, is its totalizing claim. Heidegger argues that this totalizing claim is the modern version of the series of totalizing claims about the beingness of beings that have characterized our metaphysical culture perhaps since Anaximander, certainly since Plato. Thus a pervasive cultural practice of just the sort that the deworlding and recontextualization of the incomprehensible were meant to exclude turns out to be fundamental to Heidegger's account of modern scientific research as an institution. This acknowledgment of the cultural practices of research would seem to undermine robust realism.[13]

We shall soon see, however, that the practices of research could, nonetheless, constitute an institution that could intelligibly be said to get at the functional components of the universe as they are in themselves. To save his robust realism, Heidegger would have to argue that, although the practice-based structure of encounter that gives us access to entities depends on us *essentially*, what we encounter only *contingently* depends on this structure. Then both our everyday and our scientific practices, although ineliminable from an account of the entities revealed by science, could be understood, not as *constitutive* practices, but as *access* practices allowing 'genuine theoretical discovering' (Heidegger 1962: 412).

To do this Heidegger would need, to begin with, to find a practical form of noncommittal reference that could refer to entities in a way that both allowed that they could have essential properties and that no property that *we* used in referring to them need, in fact, be essential. It turns out that Heidegger had discovered such a practice in facing a different problem. In the 1920s he realized he wanted to talk about important features of human being and yet he could not claim at the beginning of his investigation that these were *essential* ones. This methodological requirement put him in opposition to Husserl in two related ways: Husserl held that (1) general terms refer by way of the essential features of the types the terms referred to and (2) that one could have an immediate eidetic intuition of essential structures. Since Heidegger saw that his hermeneutic method deprived Husserl's eidetic intuition of any possible ground, he needed some other way to approach the essential structures of human being. How could he refer to kinds without knowing their essential features?

To solve this problem Heidegger developed an account of 'noncommittal' reference made possible by what he called formal indicators or designators (*formalen Anzeige*). Noncommittal reference begins with contingent features and arrives at essential features, if there are any, only after an investigation.[14] Heidegger explains:

> The empty meaning structure [of the formal designator] gives a direction towards filling it in. Thus a unique binding character lies in the formal designator; I must follow in a *determinate direction* that, should it get to the essential, only gets there by fulfilling the designation by appreciating the non-essential (Heidegger 1985b: 33, translation by Hubert L. Dreyfus with Hans Sluga).

Thus, Heidegger held that reference need not commit one to any essential features; rather, it binds one to investigate, in whatever way is appropriate to the domain, which features, if any, of an object referred to by its inessential features are essential. Heidegger continues:

> [We must] make a leap and proceed resolutely from there! . . . One lives in a non-essential having that takes its specific direction toward completion from the maturing of the development of this having . . . The *evidence* for the appropriateness of the original definition of the object is not essential and primordial; rather, the appropriateness is absolutely *questionable* and the definition must precisely be understood in this questionableness and lack of evidence (Heidegger 1985b: 34–5).[15]

Although he never used this idea of noncommittal reference to defend his realism, this methodological principle – that one can designate something by its contingent properties and then be bound by that designation to search for its essential properties – would have allowed Heidegger to use the switchover to the occurrent and its properties to show how access practices can break free of everyday meaning. One could consider the properties, revealed by theory-driven practices after the switchover, to be strictly *contingent* properties of the entities revealed – properties that could serve as a way of designating entities whose essential properties, if any, would have to be discovered by further investigation. The practices of investigation too would be considered contingent rather than constitutive.

Thus, Heidegger has the basic resources to answer the objections that he can get outside neither everyday practices (in a broad sense) nor culturally determined practices. But he does not use these resources. To do so he would need to admit that our everyday skills survive the switchover and that, indeed, they are necessary for (1) identifying the occurrent entities that the detached attitude reveals and (2) working data over in labs so that they can be taken as evidence for the essential properties of theoretical entities. He could then add that none of these practices, however, was essential to what was revealed in the laboratory. For, after the switchover, everyday practices, as well as the practices of the scientific institution, would be themselves experienced and deployed as questionable or contingent, and so the entities encountered could, in principle, be encountered as essentially independent of us. Heidegger seems to say just this in an interesting passage in *Basic Problems*: 'Intraworldliness does not belong to the essence of the occurrent things as such, but it is only the transcendental condition . . . for the possibility of occurrent things being able to emerge as they are [in themselves]' (Heidegger 1982: 194).

A final phenomenological argument for robust realism

For the most part, we encounter people, equipment, and even natural things as both perceptually and instrumentally familiar and inextricably bound up with our everyday practices. We can, however – though we do it rarely –

encounter things and even people in an attitude of unfamiliarity. A trivial instance of encountering something in this attitude can be produced quite easily. If we say a familiar word over and over, we eventually hear the word switch over into a strange acoustic blast. Let us call this experience *defamiliarization* and the way of being it gives access to *the strange*.[16]

Defamiliarization is the breakdown of everyday coping, and all that remains of intelligibility after defamiliarization are coping practices that enable us to *identify* things in a noncommittal, contingent, prima facie not fully adequate way. Access to entities independent of our practices for making them intelligible is thus secured by a radical switchover in the *role played by everyday practices* so that they become *contingent practices* for identifying objects. If we were to engage in the investigation of the relation between the strange thing and its everyday mode of being, we might be able to describe it in terms of sufficient features to reidentify it, but we cannot even be sure of that. Hence, our everyday practices are understood as inappropriate for defining what shows up. As Heidegger puts it, 'the appropriateness is absolutely *questionable* and the definition must precisely be understood in this questionableness.'[17]

Reference here works as Saul Kripke describes the working of *rigid designation*, particularly the rigid designation of samples of a natural kind (Kripke 1980). So, to take two of Kripke's examples, I start by investigating some shiny golden-colored stuff and eventually find out that its essence is to have an atomic weight of 197. Or, I contingently identify lightning as a flash of light in the night sky and eventually find out that it is an electrical discharge. Thus something is designated by a description or by a pointing that is not taken to get at the thing's essence[18] and such a pointing or description leaves open the possibility that investigation may discover the thing's essence. As we have seen, Heidegger calls this mode of reference 'noncommittal formal designation' and says it is empty but binding.

The practice of rigid or formal designation, as I have described it, shows that we do, indeed, have practices that enable us to read the paradox of our having practices for gaining access to things independent of those very practices in a robust realist way. Moreover, we can make sense of the strange as possibly having some necessary unity underlying the contingent everyday properties by which it is identified.[19] This unity is enough to make intelligible the notion of a natural kind whose essence is independent of our ways of making things intelligible.[20]

Notes

I would like to thank the following people who helped me work out my position, in many cases by arguing against it and writing detailed criticisms: William Blattner, Taylor Carman, David Cerbone, Donald Davidson, Dagfinn Føllesdal, Sean Kelly, Lisa Lloyd, Jeff Malpas, Stephen Neal, Joe Rouse, Ted Schatzki, Mark Wrathall, and especially Charles Spinosa.

1 Crucial essays for the deflationary realist position are: Davidson (1991, 1984). For an independently developed account of deflationary realism, see Arthur Fine's description of what he calls the Natural Ontological Attitude in *The Shaky Game* (Fine, 1986). Jeff Malpas and Joseph Rouse have generalized Davidson's arguments concerning the relation of *beliefs* to things to cover the relation of *all coping practices* to things. Malpas and Rouse have also tried to show, contrary to my view, that Martin Heidegger is a deflationary realist. See Malpas (1992) and Rouse (1987, 1996b).

2 When I speak of 'things in themselves,' I am not referring to Kant's notion of things independent of any conceptual scheme and hence unknowable but rather to the knowable functional components of the universe. Some have thought that a belief in natural kinds requires that the 'lines' in the universe between one kind and another must be sharp. I, however, assume that one needs only to be able to distinguish sharply between paradigm cases of kinds in order to describe the universe as divided into natural kinds.

3 The question – whether the idea of an essential structure of the universe independent of our practices for investigating it makes sense – can be taken up without regard to other important discussions of the natural sciences. I, therefore, do not take a stand on: (1) whether unobservable entities are real (the question of instrumentalism), (2) whether events in the universe are lawful throughout or exhibit a degree of randomness (the question of determinism), and (3) whether there are good arguments for metaphysical realism based solely on conceptual analysis. See, for instance, Searle (1995: 149–97), where he argues for the conceptual necessity of brute facts which are discovered, not constituted.

4 When Heidegger speaks of everyday practices or everydayness, he generally means instrumental coping practices or these practices and what we encounter through them. When I speak of everyday practices, I refer more broadly to our familiar ways of encountering things in general, including therefore our familiar perceptual way. The only practices that I deal with in this paper as *non-everyday* are encounters with what I call the strange and scientific practices. More broadly, for me institutional practices, including scientific, religious, and certain aesthetic practices whose intelligibility is founded on non-everyday experiences, count as non-everyday practices. When, however, I explicitly describe Heidegger's views, I shall use the term 'everyday' as he uses it.

5 Heidegger himself seems to be conflicted on the subject. Eight years after his seemingly realist stand in *Being and Time*, he writes in *Introduction to Metaphysics*: 'Strictly speaking we cannot say: There was a time when man *was* not. At all *times* man was and is and will be, in so far as time temporalizes itself only insofar as man is' (Heidegger 1959: 71). This claim follows from the argument, already in *Being and Time*, that without Dasein there would be no before and after. But Heidegger also says in a lecture given in 1928 and published in 1978: 'The question of the extent to which one might conceive the interpretation of Dasein as temporality in a universal-ontological way is a question which I am myself not able to decide – one which is still completely unclear to me' (Heidegger 1984: 210). I think Heidegger should have realized that the occurrent time of nature escapes idealism since it can be understood not in terms of our everyday sense of a before and after but only as an asymmetrical ordering of states.

6 In his later marginal notes, Heidegger adds that this revealing of the occurrent does not require either actual breakdown or an active disregard of the use aspects of equipment but can also be arrived at by training oneself to focus on properties of entities in a way that is not directly related to our coping activity. See Heidegger (1996: 57, note).

7 Rouse rightly thinks that 'Heidegger is disturbingly vague about the changeover which is said to occur' (Rouse 1987: 74–5).

8 Joseph P. Fell develops this point in his 'The Familiar and the Strange: On the Limits of Praxis in Early Heidegger' (Fell 1992: 65–80).
9 Rouse is again right in demanding Heidegger be more specific on this point. One could ask, for example, by what skills do the scientists interpret their data and, if skills are required, how does the scientist have the right to claim that the theoretical objects confirmed by their data are independent of all human activity?
10 Though Heidegger is a realist with respect to natural entities, he is not a reductionist, or naturalist. He argues at length in Sections 19, 20, and 21 of *Being and Time* that our practical ability to disclose ways of being, and thus to discover beings, cannot be understood in terms of the occurrent, and that therefore the occurrent, even recontextualized in a successful science of nature, could not provide the fundamental building-blocks of reality. Natural science can tell us only what is *causally* real, it cannot account for our ability to make intelligible various ways of being, thereby disclosing various domains of being or realities, one of which includes the entities described by physical science. Thus science cannot be a theory of *ultimate* reality. This is Heidegger's reason for rejecting *reductive* realism. He says: 'Realism tries to explain reality ontically by real connections of interaction between things that are real . . . [But] being can never be explained by entities but is already that which is 'transcendental' for every entity' (Heidegger 1962: 251).
11 Thus, Rouse can reasonably object that:

> It is not that such things, which Heidegger calls 'present-at-hand,' [occurrent] exist independent of the behavioral responses of persons within a configuration of practices and functional equipment. It is that the appropriate behavioral responses to them are carefully shorn of any functional reference (Rouse 1987: 74).

12 Heidegger in 1938, thus, anticipates Thomas Kuhn's account of normal science in *The Structure of Scientific Revolutions*. Heidegger also already recognized in *Being and Time* that science progresses by means of revolutions. 'The real 'movement' of the sciences takes place when their basic concepts undergo a more or less radical revision' (Heidegger 1962: 29).
13 Indeed, Rouse holds that later Heidegger gave up the realism of the *Being and Time* period. He notes Heidegger's Kuhn-like remark back in 1938:

> [We cannot] say that the Galilean doctrine of freely falling bodies is true and that Aristotle's teaching, that light bodies strive upward, is false; for the Greek understanding of the essence of body and place and of the relation between the two rests upon a different interpretation of entities and hence conditions a correspondingly different kind of seeing and questioning of natural events. No one would presume to maintain that Shakespeare's poetry is more advanced than that of Aeschylus. It is still more impossible to say that the modern understanding of whatever is, is more correct than that of the Greeks (Heidegger 1977b: 117).

Here Heidegger is obviously trying to counter the claim that Galileo has refuted Aristotle. But he is not doing so, as Kuhn does in *The Structure of Scientific Revolutions*, by holding that neither theory is true of nature, but rather by holding that *both* are true. This could be the innocuous observation that both are 'illuminating,' but in the context of another of Heidegger's remarks, namely, 'that what is represented by physics is indeed nature itself, but undeniably it is only nature as the object-area, whose objectness is first defined and determined through the refining that is characteristic of physics' (Heidegger 1977c: 173–4), it must be the stronger claim that different theories can reveal different aspects of nature. Of course, if one thinks of Aristotle's theory of natural place as an account of *physical* causality meant to explain, for example, why rocks fall, in the same sense that modern physics claims to explain that phenomenon, his position is untenable. The law-like gravitational account given by modern physics, as far as we know, is right and Aristotle is simply wrong. It may well be, however, as Heidegger holds, that Aristotle and Galileo were *asking different kinds of questions*, and so each could be right about a different kind of causality.

14 See, e.g., *Being and Time* where Heidegger speaks of 'a noncommittal *formal indicator*, indicating something which may perhaps reveal itself as its 'opposite' in some particular phenomenological context' (Heidegger 1962: 152). Henceforth I will translate *Anzeige* as 'designator' rather than 'indicator.'

15 What Heidegger presumably has on his mind here when he says that the phenomenological given is absolutely questionable is the fact that any interpretive investigation has to begin with everyday experience which is likely to be distorted both by individual fleeing and by the tradition. Yet the investigator has to begin where he is and can only hope gradually to work himself out of cover-ups and distortions. The recognition that it is necessary to start with the contingent and distorted if one wants to get to the essential explains Heidegger's enigmatic remark in *Being and Time* concerning the hermeneutic circle: 'What is decisive is not to get out of the circle but to come into it in the right way' (Heidegger 1962: 195).

16 Of course, not all encounters with the strange are alike, and I am not describing the unfamiliar in all its forms. Aesthetic wonder which gives us extraordinary things that are sublime does not give us strange things of the sort I am concerned with here, nor does the religious awe that gives us an experience of a radically other being, nor philosophical wonder that takes us outside the ordinary so we can relate ourselves to the everyday as a whole.

17 Martin Heidegger (1985) *Gesamtausgabe, Band 61, Phänomenologische Interpretationen zu Aristoteles*, Frankfurt, Germany: Vittorio Klostermann, pp. 34–5.

18 I do not believe that the necessity involved in making claims about essences requires claims about David Lewis's possible worlds. Dagfinn Føllesdal, for instance, argues for a form of rigid designation much like Kripke's only with an even more minimal ontology. For Føllesdal, considerations of 'all possible worlds' are resolved into considerations about objects which our language enables us to keep track of although we have many false beliefs about the objects, do not know many of their properties, and do not know how their properties will change over time. (Føllesdal 1986: 97–113, esp. 107; Kripke 1980: 15–21).

19 The claim that essentialism follows from rigid designation is argued by all who care about rigid designation. For the claim closest to mine, see Føllesdal (1996: 356–9).

20 A realist science would have to make sure that it had practices for seeking the essences of objects in its domain that did not depend on everyday canons of what makes sense. Such a realist science could separate itself from the everyday by granting full autonomy to a discipline of puzzle-solving within the theoretical projection. Under such a regime, a solution that solves a puzzle, no matter how perceptually and intellectually counterintuitive, would have the power to force scientists to abandon even their current principles of intelligibility. Quantum physics is a case study of long-accepted principles of intelligibility being cast aside. That solutions to puzzles create more puzzles suggests that puzzle-solving is the activity of letting the nature of the universe guide conceptions of it away from human ways of conceiving toward a view from nowhere, appropriate to the universe as it is in itself.

11 Practice and posthumanism
Social theory and a history of agency

Andrew Pickering

§0   This essay moves from theory to history and back again, exploring some directions in which analyses of scientific practice at the microlevel can be suggestively extended to macrosocial concerns. It aims at opening up spaces for research and reflection rather than rigorous analysis (this is especially the case in §5). I think the topic is interesting and important enough to warrant this approach.

Practice and social theory

§1.1   Marx's aphorism: 'production not only creates an object for the subject but also a subject for the object' (*Grundrisse*, quoted in Schivelbusch 1986: 164). Microstudies of scientific practice help us grasp this thought. Think of Ludwik Fleck's account of the establishment of the Wassermann reaction as a test for syphilis. Fleck describes this as a process of the reciprocal tuning of people and things. The serologists tuned the Wassermann reaction as a material procedure, 'adding now "a little more," now "a little less" of a reagent,' letting the reaction proceed a little longer or a little shorter, and so on, until the success rate of the test increased from 15–20 per cent to 70–90 per cent (1979: 72–3). At the same time a specific social community was formed: the community of disciplined practitioners competent to carry out the Wassermann reaction, having the 'serological touch,' and internally differentiated in the 'quasi-orchestral' (97) performance of the reaction. The Wassermann reaction as material procedure was the object for the community of practitioners, and the practitioners were the subject for the object: each developed and took on a particular shape in relation to the other.

§1.2   Marx's language of 'subjects' and 'objects' is too weak. Scientists and reagents are more active than these words suggest. We need to think about agency – performance, doing things. The establishment of the Wassermann reaction entailed a mutual tuning of social and material agency. This is the general message of studies of scientific practice (Latour 1987; Pickering 1993, 1995a).[1]

§1.3   Much of traditional social theory is *humanist*, in as much as key concepts are located in the distinctively human realm. Attributes of specifically human agency – desires, interests, rules, knowledge, social structure, and whatever – are invoked to explain the phenomena at issue. The general inadequacy of such humanist social theory follows from §§1.1 and 1.2. One cannot account for the specific features of the community of practitioners of the Wassermann reaction by appeal to peculiarly human variables; one has to think about the constitution of this community in relation to struggles with the material world. Neither, of course, can we grasp the properties of this community in antihumanist terms – in terms of scientific accounts of how the Wassermann reaction itself works (if, indeed, such an account exists). Instead we need a *posthumanist* social theory: one that recognizes from the start that the contours of material and human agency reciprocally constitute one another.

§1.4   From a different angle, we can note that social theory has traditionally emulated the natural sciences in seeking to expose hidden structures as the explanation of visible phenomena. Stephen Turner (1994) has criticized this genre very effectively. In contrast, nothing in Fleck's account of the Wassermann reaction is hidden: the mutual tuning of material procedures and human agents is visible. Studies of practice suggest that a *social theory of the visible* is enough (Pickering 1997a): there is no need to invoke hidden structures.

§1.5   Again, while traditional behind-the-scenes explanations in social theory attempt to find explanatory constants underlying the flux of appearances, Fleck's study suggests that there is only flux. In the establishment of the Wassermann reaction, everything from material setups and their performance to the contours of human agency was at stake and subject to redefinition. The only generally reliable and enduring feature of practice that I can discern is the pattern that I have so far called tuning, and elsewhere analyzed in detail as a dialectic of resistance and accommodation: 'the mangle' for short (Pickering 1993, 1995a). And mangling is a *temporally emergent* process: its upshots are not given at all in advance. This means that an adequate social theory can amount, at most, to a set of sensitivities in our encounter with empirical phenomena: we should especially look out for posthumanist intertwinings of the human and the nonhuman – the construction of subjects for objects, as well as vice versa – and we should recognize that in general nothing substantive endures in the encounter of material and human agency. A theory of practice, then, would focus our attention on specificity, on particular interdefinitions of machinic and social fields. This is not, of course, how traditional theory functions. Traditionally, as I have said, the invitation is to extract an invariant skeleton from the flux of appearances. Perhaps we should say that a theory that recognizes temporal emergence is an antitheory in the traditional sense. 'The havoc interpretation wreaks in the domain of appearances is incalculable, and its privileged quest for hidden meanings may be profoundly mistaken,' as Jean Baudrillard once put it (1988a: 149).

A history of agency

§2.1   What use is a posthumanist antitheory that continually returns us to specifics? Is such a thing not 'the death of sociology,' to paraphrase John Dewey on pragmatist philosophy (1960: 68)?

§2.2   This antitheory denies itself the appeal to invisible skeletons; but at the same time it suggests a thematics of the visible. Posthumanism directs our attention to encounters between human and nonhuman agency, and we might therefore be encouraged to write a *history of agency* (or a sociology of agency, or a philosophy – these are no longer very different endeavors), which would center on great, enduring, and conspicuously visible sites of encounter of human and nonhuman agency, such as the factory (standing for the whole field of organized production) and the battlefield (standing for organized destruction) (and even the home in its historic transit from production to consumption).[2]

§2.3   The thematics of a history of agency would thus be close to the thematics of Marxist historiography, and could easily draw upon empirical work in that tradition. A history of agency would, however, differ from Marxist historiography inasmuch as it would abstain from the assumption that any sociological reduction is generally tenable – the reduction to the humanist skeleton of class struggle, for example.[3]

§2.4   The periodization of a history of agency would register discontinuities in modes of production and destruction. In production, the most recent breaks would include the industrial revolution, the second, technoscientific, industrial revolution of the late nineteenth century, World Wars I and II, and the 1980s. In destruction, the periodization of a history of agency is less clear but, for the sake of an example, Manuel De Landa (1991: 64–72) distinguishes between three technosocial fighting formations, which he calls clockwork, motorized and network armies, the first dating back to 1560, the second to the late eighteenth century and post-Revolutionary France, and the third emerging from WWI and exemplified in the German *blitzkrieg* tactics of WWII. Notice that these series of breaks in the histories of production and destruction are not identical; in general a history of agency would have multiple clocks. But notice, too, that the world wars of the twentieth century appear on both lists. It is clear that as we approach the present destructive and productive agencies have become increasingly strongly coupled to one another.

Scenes from a history of agency

The synthetic dye industry and the second industrial revolution

§3.1   In a fascinating essay, Henk van den Belt and Arie Rip (1987) date the emergence of the synthetic dye industry back to William Henry Perkin's discovery of aniline purple in 1856. There followed a period of material tinkering which resulted in the production of a continuing series of new synthetic dyes.

§3.2   This material tinkering was guided by developments in chemical theory, including Kekulé's structure theory of 1859 and his benzene theory of 1865 (van den Belt and Rip 1987: 144), the latter forming the basis of modern organic chemistry. The reciprocal intertwining of material practices and scientific theory needs to be emphasized here. Organic chemistry did not first evolve according to its own autonomous dynamics and then find application in the dye industry. Instead its history is better understood as a reflection upon the existing accomplishments of the industry – material processes and products of synthesis – that aimed at further performative achievements. Here, then, science should be seen as *within the plane of practice*: continually emerging from and returning to enduring sites of encounter of material and human agency such as the factory (though occasionally departing on loops through such places as the university). This, in fact, is in general how we should expect to find that science appears in a history of agency.[4]

§3.3   The history of azo dyes after 1877 is especially interesting. Within contemporary chemical theory, the so-called coupling reaction promised to generate an indefinite series of new dyes in 'an endless combination game' (van den Belt and Rip 1987: 151) of different ingredients. And the response to this recognition was the establishment of a new social institution, the industrial research laboratory, within the German synthetic dye industry. From this point on, chemists appeared in the history of synthetic dyes in two roles: (1) an already established role, as academic researchers in the universities; and (2) their new role as 'scientific mass-labor' located within industry itself, running through the endless combination game of dye syntheses as quickly as they could. The industrial research laboratory thus represented a device through which the dye industry could, as it were, wrap itself around scientists and *enfold* them, as a tactic in the optimization of its own performativity.[5]

§3.4   We thus see how the material, the conceptual and the social evolved together in the history of the synthetic dye industry. The establishment of new material procedures and products (the coupling reaction and azo dyes), new bodies of knowledge (modern organic chemistry) and topological transformations of social institutions (the enfolding of science by industry in the industrial research laboratory) hung together, reinforced one another and reciprocally structured each other's development. To return to Marx, we see how 'production not only creates an object [synthetic dyes] for the subject [industry, science, the consumer] but also a subject [an industry with science now enfolded within it] for the object.'[6]

§3.5   A humanist social theory could not hope to grasp these developments.

One cannot understand the emergence of the industrial research laboratory as a social institution without thinking about transformations in the domain of material processes and products. Again, it is no use searching for a temporally nonemergent behind-the-scenes structure here. No one, for example, could have known in advance of actual practice how material, social, and conceptual developments would go in this story. All that one can do is register the visible and specific intertwinings of the human and the nonhuman. But this is enough; what more could one want or need?

The industrial revolution: railways and shock

§4.1   Schivelbusch (1986: 168):

> [T]he stimulus shield model is so abstract that it can be applied to all possible kinds of stimuli: to technically caused ones (i.e., velocity) as well as cultural ones (laws, customs, etc.). Thus the 'civilizing process' described by Norbert Elias can be understood as the formation of a stimulus shield, just as we have understood the process of rail travel to be one. The 'stimuli' that the individual . . . absorbs during the civilizing process are the social rules that are interiorized by the courtly upper strata . . . A violation or breaking of these rules was commonly described as 'shocking': it was the shattering of a stimulus shield of convention – an analogous event to 'shock' in military clash or railroad accident.

Leaving aside the unappetizing concept of 'stimulus shield' and his endorsement of the dubious notion that social life can be understood in terms of rules, Schivelbusch's project is an intriguing one. He wants to move from the humanist sociology exemplified in Elias's work to a posthumanist sociology of people and things. Further, he wants to explore the inner human experience of technology, specifically the contours of what he calls 'industrialized consciousness' – a terrain little explored in mainstream Anglo-American (or even French) science studies. We can follow him a little way to see what is at stake.

§4.2   Schivelbusch takes the nineteenth-century railway to be a key site for the development of industrialized consciousness, and explores it from several angles. One straightforward example of his way of proceeding concerns the development of what he calls *panoramic seeing* (1986: Chapter 4). His suggestion is that the railway journey makes possible a new way of perceiving the landscape quite different from earlier modes of apprehension, associated, for example, with horse-drawn carriages or walking. Where the latter foster a detailed (and multisensual) engagement with the specifics of the local environment, rail supports a panoramic (and purely visual) grasp of the terrain, in which the immediate foreground vanishes (due to the relative speed of the observer) while the background is seen synthetically, and translations between towns, countryside, and villages are grasped as a whole.

It is as though the landscape appears as a movie projected onto the screen of the window.

§4.3   Schivelbusch thus offers us a rather different take on the reciprocal production of subjects and objects from that discussed in §3. Now inner experience is part of the construction of the subject (the panoramic voyeur) for the object (the railway/the landscape). And it is worth emphasizing that panoramic seeing was not envisaged in the construction and use of the railways – nor was it something actively at stake (subject to tinkering) in the evolution of railway travel. In this sense panoramic seeing was an *emergent phenomenon* – a new way to perceive that just happened to manifest itself in a new material situation.[7]

§4.4   A certain frustration can arise here as elsewhere in Schivelbusch's discussions of industrial consciousness. On the one hand, he certainly does seem to illuminate the specificity of what it is like to be in an industrial society; on the other hand, no special language of inner states is involved. Somehow, Schivelbusch gets at the inner by describing the outer: the landscape rushes past, so of course the foreground becomes an unreadable blur, while the landscape unfolds like a map in the distance. One suspects some sleight of hand. But I think this feeling is mistaken. The point to note is that while there are many ways of describing the motion and relation of bodies and objects in railway travel, Schivelbusch describes outward circumstances from a certain perspective or *subject position* – the embodied position of the fast-moving traveler. The railway journey, then, made available the new subject position at which panoramic seeing emerged.

§4.5   Though Schivelbusch's declared focus is on industrialized conscious-ness, he also explores somatic and psychosomatic phenomena – new ways for bodies (or bodies-and-minds) to be. Railway accidents, perhaps by virtue of their unprecedented violence and lack of forewarning, precipitated the construction of the new psychomedical category of victims of shock – persons showing no severe bodily injuries, but exhibiting unusual mental or physical symptoms some time after the event. Shock, then, was a new form of bodily performance – another truly emergent phenomenon – made possible by the new subject position created by rail.[8] And Schivelbusch thematizes what is at stake here in a nice impure, posthumanist, metaphor, comparing shock with metal fatigue (132–4): just as metal cracked unexpectedly on the railways (a phenomenon subsequently explained in terms of novel and specifically dyna-mical stresses), so human beings cracked unexpectedly in railway accidents (subsequently explained by Freud's stimulus shield theory, as dismissed in passing above).

§4.6   Here, then, we find some more senses in which production creates a subject for its object (shock, panoramic seeing) as well as vice versa. At the very least, Schivelbusch's work is valuable in opening up to analysis the relation between technology, bodily states, and inner human experience: a terrain which, as mentioned above, has been ignored by the science and technology studies mainstream, on one side, and also by the humanist social sciences on the other.

The interface

§5.01 My preceding remarks were made from the perspective of a detached academic observer. But the coupling of the human and nonhuman is often a topic of immediate practical importance and has been taken up as such many times, more or less reflectively.

§5.02 At the unreflective end of the spectrum we find the work of engineers. Schivelbusch, for example, argues that heavily upholstered furniture appeared on the railways as a solution to the problem of matching flesh to metal – specifically, as a response to the discomforts of vibrations induced in the human body by railway travel (122–3). And he suggests that upholstery thus concealed the truly industrial nature of railway travel, functioning, in effect, as an equivalent in the material world to ideology in the world of thought. One could perhaps take this suggestion too seriously, but at the same time it illustrates the heuristic power of posthumanist metaphors in social theory. We may no longer be able quite to credit the notion of false consciousness, but it still points to a topic worthy of analysis, and perhaps thinking about comfy chairs might be a good way to get started (cf. Benjamin 1968; Baudrillard 1988b).

§5.03 Closer to the present, one might think of the problem of matching human brains to silicon chips, and all of the postwar developments connected with computer interfaces, running from the development of higher-level languages which mediate between quasi-natural languages, mathematics and machine code, up to visual interfaces and simulations. These directly tailor objects to subjects, rather than vice versa. But they are part of a project with a long history that simultaneously defines the human and nonhuman in relation to one another. Visual interfaces, for example, emerge in part from the failure of ambitious projects for pattern recognition by machines and the reciprocal acknowledgment that pattern recognition is one of the mental tasks that human beings are especially good at – a defining feature, one might say, of the human.[10]

§5.04 One can develop Schivelbusch's ideas about material ideology a bit further here. Computer interfaces certainly obscure the inner workings of the machine, but still, in scientific applications, for example, they serve to connect the human user to something beyond the screen. A visual simulation of a thunderstorm, say, presents the products of massive computation in graspable form. It makes the inner states of the machine accessible to its human exterior. On the other hand, however, other uses of visualization are intended as pure surface. In entertainment – from video games to virtual reality – the interface achieves its apotheosis as pure thing-in-itself: all that matters is destroying the space invaders as they appear on the screen. This surface/depth contrast is an invitation to talk about postmodernity (Jameson 1991) which I will not take up – except to note that a functioning virtual reality would make possible a fully alienated subject position. Of course, we do not talk about 'alienation' any more, either, but Paul Virilio's (1993) notion of the 'terminal citizen' is still worth thinking about.

§5.05   Upholstery and computer interfaces are material solutions to practical problems encountered in the matching of people to things. Their historical evolution has not hinged upon much general reflection on posthuman couplings, at least until recently.[11] But there is a strand of such reflection that dates back at least to the industrial revolution (Pickering 1997b). The early political economists, from Adam Smith to Karl Marx via Charles Babbage, were intensely and explicitly interested in the coupling of people and machines in the factory, which was remaking society as they wrote. Somehow, however, that line of posthumanist thought has been repeatedly subject to humanist and antihumanist purification as it looped through the academy in the late nineteenth and early twentieth centuries. The proto-posthumanism of early scientific management, for example, seems to have disintegrated in the 1920s and 1930s. As Peter Miller and Nikolas Rose put it: 'The plant [then became] understood as pervaded by an attitudinal and communicative atmosphere, a socio-psychological *overlay* to the actual organization of the productive process itself' (Miller and Rose 1995: 435, emphasis added), and the humanist overlay was claimed by the social scientists, while the 'productive process itself' was retained by the engineers.[12]

§5.06   But then, during and shortly after World War II, a posthumanist or cyborg self-consciousness began to blossom once more at several sites. I think of operations research, systems dynamics, and systems theory, ergonomics and cybernetics as rather unorthodox academic disciplines coming straight out of the war itself; and of the Quality of Working Life, participatory design and computer-supported collaborative work movements as later equivalents addressed specifically to the realm of production. All of these, in one way or another, thematized the reciprocal coupling of the human and the nonhuman, the interactive tuning of subjects and objects.[13]

§5.07   The overall history of the postwar cyborg sciences remains largely to be told; but one particular feature seems especially relevant here: namely the terrible sense of *déjà vu* I get when I look into this history. As far back as the 1950s, I think, people at the Tavistock Institute of Human Relations – the home of the Quality of Working Life movement – were thinking seriously about the open-endedness of practice and cultural transformation, a topic that I started to struggle with only in the late 1980s. Likewise, the phrase 'sociotechnical system' – a well-known term of art in the actor-network approach to science studies – was first coined at the Tavistock (Miller and Rose 1995). And one does not need a Ph.D. in the field to know that in his discussions of technological artifacts like 'sleeping policemen' Bruno Latour (e.g., 1988) is simply doing ergonomics. What should we make of such observations?

§5.08   My own first reaction is one of distaste. I feel very uncomfortable when I discover that people I want to write about actually articulated my own interpretive scheme before I did. A consoling temptation is to say that the coincidence proves we are both right; but my fondness for the symmetry principle of the sociology of scientific knowledge gets in the way of that. Instead this seems like a nasty instance, too close to home, of that collapse of theory into its object which Fredric Jameson (1991) has described as characteristic of postmodernity – that loss of analytical distance, critical and otherwise.

§5.09   More positively, one could try regarding posthumanist social theory as a continuation of the WWII projects listed in §5.06. Again, this is an un-comfortable, though reflexively correct, maneuver. From my perspective, it amounts to locating my present work on the history of agency within a particular strand of the same story, that of the WWII regime, as I call it.[14] This move, of course, precipitates the question of just what a posthumanist social theory or antitheory stands to contribute within the overall development of the cyborg sciences? But there are, fortunately, a couple of straightforward answers to that question. First, an injection of posthumanist sensibilities into the mainstream academic disciplines can hardly do any harm. The resolute humanism of much US sociology, for example, makes it enormously difficult for that field even to recognize the technological and scientific constitution of late twentieth-century society. And, second, the studies of scientific practice mentioned at the beginning of this essay have already carried posthumanist analysis into empirical domains that have been left untouched by other cyborg sciences.

§5.10   One last thought. Amongst the cyborg sciences, I find cybernetics especially interesting, and in my unsystematic reading of the literature, I have been struck by two things: (1) the considerable congruence that exists between the cybernetic world-view and the posthuman, temporally emergent metaphysics which I think goes best with studies of practice; and (2) the fact that cybernetics has nevertheless developed a much more detailed and substantive analytical repertoire than practice theory. Perhaps, therefore, a posthumanist social theory could learn something from cybernetics. I close with three examples.

§5.11   I have already drawn upon one concept which is central to some branches of cybernetic thought: that of an *emergent phenomenon*. When Manuel De Landa (1991: 30), drawing upon Deleuze and Guattari (1987), says that 'tracking the [machinic] phylum . . . involves discovering the "emergent properties" of different combinations of materials: that is, any physical property that arises from an assemblage of parts, but that is not present in the parts taken separately,' he is moving along the same lines as Schivelbusch's remarks on shock and metal fatigue. There is a notion of discontinuity and nonlinearity here in the notion of emergent phenomena that is a useful antidote to the gradualist images that attach themselves to notions like Karin Knorr Cetina's old idea of 'tinkering' (1981), or my metaphor of 'tuning.' Perhaps this is why I prefer the more violent word, 'mangling.' (See also Pickering forthcoming b.)

§5.12   Absolutely central to cybernetics is a notion of *homeostasis*, arising from reflections upon the stability of biological organisms in the face of varying environments. Having found no need or desire to invoke homeostasis in studies of scientific practice, I note this just to register my puzzlement. Does it point to some blind spot in current studies of practice; or to the fact that cybernetics mistakes an important particular (the stability of biological organisms) for the general case; or what?[15]

§5.13   Because of its obsession with feedback loops, cybernetics problematizes the question of *units of analysis* in a clear and important way. In evolutionary theory, for example, cybernetic approaches emphasize that the unit of analysis is not the organism alone, but rather the organism plus its environment: the two evolve in relation to one another (Maturana and Varela 1992). This idea can be seen as reinforcing and extending the domain of an *anticontextualist* argument emerging from analyses of practice – namely, that appeals to explanatory context in the human sciences run the risk of effacing fascinating manglings of 'context' itself. My earlier discussion of the evolution of the synthetic dye industry illustrates what is at stake. The social, for example, cannot there be regarded as explanatory of material and conceptual transformations, just because all three heterogeneous cultural strata were so strongly coupled to one another. Units of analysis, therefore, have in general to be *found* in empirical research (and have no necessary temporal stability); traditional disciplinary schemas and explanatory demarcations often just get in the way.[16]

Notes

This essay is dedicated to the participants in my seminar in the sociology of technology, fall 1995, with thanks for many stimulating discussions and arguments. I also thank Norton Wise for comments on the essay itself, especially his insights into 'emergent phenomena.'

1 As it is of cultural studies of science: see Pickering (1995a: 217–29), where I discuss Baird (1993) and Haraway (1991) at length, as illustrating both convergences and differences between cultural studies and studies of practice.

2 'History of agency' is a clearer description of what I called 'performative historiography' in Pickering (1995a: 230). For further thoughts on the history of agency, see Pickering (1995b, 1997b).

3 Noble (1986) is an important example of such a reduction; for a detailed critique, see Pickering (1995a: Chapter 5).

4 Classic texts situating science in a history of agency would thus include Hessen (1971) and Bernal (1953) on the physical sciences, and Foucault (1979) on the human sciences. For a long list of relevant recent authors and texts, see Pickering (1995a: 221, n.12). Bowker (1994) is a recent fascinating study of the emergence of geophysics from oil fields; Lenoir (1997) includes a series of important historical studies on scientific developments in Germany in the nineteenth and early twentieth centuries (and one study of the postwar US) which point in the same direction.

5 For more on enfolding, see the discussion of operations research and military enterprise in World War II in Pickering (1995b).

6 The transformation of the social in this instance had interesting aspects beyond those just discussed. Most strikingly, the very content of German patent law was mangled in the process of developing azo dyes (van den Belt and Rip 1987: 148–55). For an extensive discussion along the lines laid out above, see Pickering (in prep.).

7 One way to appreciate the significance of panoramic seeing is to reflect upon satellite imagery of the earth as a recent instance of the trend that began with the railways. Elichirigoity (1999) argues that satellite images of the earth as an isolated body floating in space were crucial to the emergence of a distinctive discourse of globality (or planet management) in the late 1960s and early 1970s.

8 Strictly speaking, 'shock' was not novel to rail; it was a phenomenon already recognized on the battlefield (Schivelbusch 1986: 150–8). But that similar phenomena might be connected with rail too was unexpected; and, of course, the connection with the battlefield is interesting in itself from the perspective of a history of agency.

9 It is worth noting that the discussion of railway travel moves us from production toward consumption, a move that needs to be taken further in thinking through the history of agency.

10 For earlier redefinitions of the human in relation to mechanized computation, see Daston (1994) and Schaffer (1994) on the late eighteenth- and early nineteenth-century reconceptualization of 'intelligence' occasioned by de Prony's introduction of mass production methods in calculation and Babbage's difference and analytical engines.

11 For more on the history of computer interfaces, see Rheingold (1991).

12 It would be interesting to compare trends in the West with those in the Soviet Union. I have no systematic information on this comparison, but a reading of Zinchenko and Munipov's history of ergonomics (1989: Chapter 2) suggests that the Western humanist/antihumanist purification did not come naturally in a society where Marx's writings were canonical and industrial labor a matter of direct academic concern. We should then see the 'Great October Socialist Revolution in Russia' (Zinchenko and Munipov 1989: 34) as another key date in the history of agency.

13 On the first part of this list see Pickering (1995b, 1998, forthcoming a) and Zinchenko and Munipov (1989); on the second, see Cooper and Mumford (1979) and Miller and Rose (1995) on the Quality of Working Life movement; Easterbrook

(1993) and Bowker, Star, Turner, and Gasser (1996) on cooperative work; and Asaro (2000) and Jirotha and Gognen (1994) on participatory design. I thank Peter Asaro for enlightening discussions of these bodies of work and guidance on the literature.

14 This is probably historically correct, though it has come as a surprise to me to discover it. To grasp what is going on, I suspect that one needs to think about a wartime and postwar purification of academic social theory, which has served to marginalize the cyborg sciences within the universities. Against this trend, however, it seems possible that cybernetic thinking, broadly construed, has been laundered back into science studies via the work of Bruno Latour (I thank Geof Bowker for this suggestion). Latour (1987), for example, makes some character-istically cybernetic moves. Buck (1985) has some ideas on the purification of the social sciences as it played out in the US; Parsons (1965) is a beautiful lesson in how to humanize and lose what is most interesting in cybernetics. In Marxist terms, Parson's trick was to emphasize the superstructure and forget entirely about the material base of society. One has the image of a pyramid of interlocking social systems resting on nothing. Even Terry Pratchett's Discworld rides through space on the back of a turtle.

15 One can note that notions of homeostasis fit nicely with (typically humanist and nonemergent) sociologies that take social *reproduction* as the key topic for analysis. Studies of scientific practice, by contrast, thematize change.

16 On the critique of contextualism, see Callon and Law (1989), Pickering (1992b, 1997b). On the relation of analyses of practice to evolutionary theory, see Pickering (1995a: 246–52; forthcoming b).

12 Objectual practice

Karin Knorr Cetina

In this paper, I want to develop some concepts designed to capture the affective and relational undergirding of practice in areas where practice is creative and constructive. Current conceptions of practice emphasize the habitual and rule-governed features of practice. Though much debate surrounds the exact specification of the relevant rules and habits (see Bourdieu 1977; Giddens 1984; Lynch 1993; Turner 1994; Schatzki 1996), most authors seem to agree that practices should be seen as recurrent processes governed by specifiable schemata of preferences and prescriptions. Such processes are doubtlessly prominent in many areas of social life; their existence sustains our sense of practices as customary or routinized ways of behaving. However, it is also a characteristic of current times that many occupations and organizations have a significant knowledge base. In these areas, one would expect practitioners to have to keep learning, and the specialists who develop the knowledge base to continually reinvent their own practices of acquiring knowledge. Practice, in this case, would seem to take on a wholly different set of meanings and raise a different set of questions from the ones raised by habitual activities. For example, how can we theorize practice in a way that allows for the engrossment and excitement – the emotional basis – of research work? What characterization of practice might make the notion more dynamic and include within it the potential for change? Research work seems to be particular in that the definition of things, the consciousness of problems, etc., is deliberately looped through objects and the reaction granted by them. This creates a dissociation between self and work object and inserts moments of interruption and reflection into the performance of research, during which efforts at reading the reactions of objects and taking their perspective play a decisive role. How can we conceive of practice in a way that accommodates this dissociation?

In this paper, I want to address these questions by taking as my starting point a particular characterization of knowledge-centered practice – one that can be traced back to Heidegger but that also finds support in scientists' self-understandings of their work. At the core of this characterization lies the assumption that creative and constructive practice – the kind of practice that obtains when we confront nonroutine problems – is internally more differentiated than current conceptions of practice as skill or habitual task performance suggest. The dissociation I have in mind is that between subject and (work) object; though time differentiation is also important, I think subject–object differentiation captures more directly what happens when work ceases to be habitual procedure. What holds differentiated practice together and gives it continuity is the relationship between subject and object; this paper is a first attempt to find the basis of knowledge-centered constructive and creative practice in a relational rather than a performative idiom. In moving in this direction, I assume that the relational idiom adequately captures the dynamic properties of research. The relational idiom can also carry the reflexive and affective aspects of epistemic practice. In addition it will bring into focus nonhuman objects, which dominate much of expert work.

In the next section, I briefly review knowledge society arguments – those which maintain that professional knowledge activities are expanding in current Western societies and constitute the leading edge of postindustrial work. If these arguments are right – if we are confronted with the growth of knowledge-centered and knowledge-based activities in many areas of social life – epistemic practices may come to dominate other kinds of practice. The specific characteristics of these practices then also become interesting from a practice theory viewpoint. In the third section, I discuss reasons for a relational approach to conceptualizing practice. I will briefly revisit Heidegger's perspective on these matters, and also present examples of how experts and scientists themselves view constructive practice.

To specify how object relationships define the flow of practice one needs to discuss in some detail the notion of 'object' relevant to knowledge activities. This will be the topic of the section that follows. Knowledge objects differ in important ways from the commodities, instruments, and everyday things discussed in the literature; the section spells out these differences, conceiving of epistemic objects as defined by their lack of completeness of being and their nonidentity with themselves.

The lack of completeness of being of knowledge objects goes hand in hand with the dynamism of research. Only incomplete objects pose further questions, and only in considering objects as incomplete do scientists move forward with their work. In the fifth section, I turn to the subjects rather than objects in attempting to specify further the relational and affective dynamic of expert practice. This section presents a way of conceiving of the bindingness, reflexivity, and mutuality of experts' object relationships as the backbone of this practice.

The knowledge society argument

What drives one to think about knowledge-creating and -validating or 'epistemic' practice? A recent source of concern with knowledge-centered activities are transformation theory arguments. These arguments conceive of current social transitions in terms of a shift from an industrial to a 'postindustrial' or 'posttraditional' society, in which knowledge is of increased relevance to the economy and other areas of social life. There is a widespread consensus today that contemporary Western societies are increasingly ruled by knowledge and expertise. The proliferation of concepts such as that of a 'technological society' (e.g., Berger et al. 1974), an 'information society' (e.g., Lyotard 1984; Beniger 1986), a 'knowledge society' (Bell 1973; Drucker 1993; Stehr 1994), a 'risk society' or 'experimental society' (Beck 1992; Krohn and Weyer 1994) embodies this understanding. The recent source of this aware-ness is Daniel Bell (1973), for whom the immediate impact of knowledge was on the economy, where it resulted in such widespread changes as shifts in the division of labor, the development of specialized occupations, the emergence of new enterprises and sustained growth. Bell and later commentators (e.g., Stehr 1994) also offer a great many statistics on the expansion of R&D efforts, R&D personnel, and R&D expenses in Europe and the United States. More recent assessments have not changed this argument so much as added further arenas of the impact of knowledge. For example, Habermas's argument about the 'technicization' of the lifeworld through universal principles of cognitive and technical rationality attempts to understand the spread of abstract systems to everyday life (1981). Drucker (e.g., 1993) links knowledge to changes in organizational structure and management practices, and Beck (1992) depicts transformations of the political sphere through corporate bodies of scientists. Finally Giddens, arguing that we live in a world of increased reflexivity mediated by expert systems, extends the argument to the self, pointing out that today's individuals engage with the wider environment and with themselves through information produced by specialists which they routinely interpret and act on in everyday life (e.g., 1990).

The advantage of Giddens's use of the notion expert 'system' is that it brings into view not only the impact of isolated knowledge items or of scientific–technical elites but implies the presence of whole contexts of expert work. These contexts, however, continue to be treated by him and others as alien elements in social systems, elements that are best left to their own devices. Knowledge society arguments consider knowledge as a productive force that – in a postindustrial society – increasingly plays the role that capital and labor played in industrial society. These viewpoints also emphasize the role of experts, of technology and its associated risks, and of electronic infor-mation structures (see also Lash and Urry 1994). But the transition to knowledge societies involves more than the presence of more experts, more technological gadgets, more specialist rather than participant interpretations. It involves the presence of knowledge processes themselves – in the terms chosen here, it involves the presence of epistemic practice.

From the present point of view, then, understanding knowledge societies will have to include understanding knowledge practices. In postindustrial societies, knowledge settings are no longer limited to science. To give an example, every major bank employs scores of 'analysts' and other 'specialists,' who research and represent for the bank the world in which the bank moves.

Hence research and analysis practices of different kinds penetrate many areas of social life; to some degree, these practices become constitutive of these areas. For example, global financial markets could not exist without the symbolic representations and analyses of trading activities and contextual events that are created by specialists in information provider firms and similar organizations. In other words, the reality of global financial markets is an expert-provided and expert-observed 'on screen' reality. The practices of creating this screen reality will need to be analyzed with respect to the specific knowledge-producing and -validating strategies they implement; as earlier work suggests, knowledge-producing activities in different areas entail different epistemic cultures (see Knorr Cetina 1999). But also at stake is the conceptualization of knowledge-centered practice from a theoretical perspective which is the topic of this paper.

The relational undergirding of epistemic practice

I now want to begin to describe this practice, starting with the observation of the dissociative dynamic that comes into play when practice ceases to be a procedural routine. As indicated before, the dissociation relevant here is that between subject and object. What do we mean by this dissociation? How does it come about, and why is it important? The separation between subjects with mental states and independent objects is common to all areas of everyday life. To take an example, a car and its driver are distinct entities in our perception and in much of our experience. Nonetheless, while I am driving, my car becomes what Heidegger calls 'ready-to-hand' and transparent (Heidegger 1962: 98ff.): it has the tendency to disappear while I am using it. In other words, the car becomes an unproblematic means to an end rather than an independent thing to which I stand in relation. It becomes an instrument that has been absorbed into the practice of driving, just as I, the driver, have been absorbed into the practice of driving – I, too, become transparent. When I engage in this practice, I am oriented to the street, the traffic, the direction I have to take. I am not oriented to the car – unless it malfunctions and temporarily breaks down. Nor am I thinking of myself as separate from the immediate activity.

It should be plain that scientific practice, when it is routine or habitual, corresponds to this description. To give an example, consider the following comments of a researcher in a molecular biology laboratory whom I asked about her usage of laboratory protocols (for details see Knorr Cetina 1999: Chapter 4):

DS: You asked about protocols. We not only work with protocols, we think in terms of them. When I am doing the protocol, pipetting say, I don't really think about the objects I am dealing with. When it's a routine, there is, for me, no differentiation between the bacteria that I am using there, and the DNA that I'll extract and the enzyme that I am placing on to cut the DNA. 'A thing to do' is more a protocol than dealing with DNA, it is more in the procedure than in the material.

Or consider another molecular biologist in the same laboratory, who described the practice of cloning in the following terms (see Knorr Cetina 1999: Chapter 6):

HB: Cloning is perhaps one level below what one calls exciting in the lab. You sit down, you think about a particular construct, and then you clone it. That's not very different from deciding to dig a hole in the ground and then to dig it – it's about that exciting.

This sort of practice can perfectly well be described in a performative idiom that conceptualizes it, in Wittgenstein's terminology, as an 'ungrounded way of acting' (Wittgenstein 1969: nos. 110, 17e; see also Dreyfus 1995: 155). Yet it appears equally clear that major portions of knowledge-centered work – those that best epitomize epistemic practice – are not adequately described in just these terms. These portions of scientific practice are not, in the above terms, 'routine procedures'; they occur when problems arise, or when work is new to a researcher. Consider again an example, the first researcher's response, at a later point in our conversation, to a question about the protein she was working on:

KKC: What about your protein?
DS: Well, the protein, because it has previously been a problem, the protein is a bit more moody. I think about it, I get more visual, I treat it differently, in one word, I pay more attention to it, it's more precious. I don't handle it routinely yet.
KKC: How do you visualize it?
DS: I see the protein in a certain size in front of me. I visualize why it is precipitating, then I visualize the solution and I visualize the falling out and the refolding process. I also visualize the protein denaturing, streched out and then coming together, and I visualize how it is being shot into the solution and what it is going through when it starts to fold. With the expression, I visualize the bacteria when they grow in a more anthropomorphic way, why are they happy? I try to visualize them shaking around, I visualize aerobic effects, the shaking, how much they tumble around and what could have an effect.

In this second case, the object (e.g., the protein) is no longer 'invisible' and undifferentiated, an undistinguishable part of an activity script. Instead, it becomes enhanced and in fact enlarged through the researcher's strategy of visualizing it and its environment and behavior under various circumstances. It is important to note not only the subject–object differentiation this entails, but also the researcher's active usage of the means we have to overcome subject–object separation – her deployment of *relational resources*. Not only does this researcher experience herself as a conscious subject that relates to epistemic objects, she draws upon resources that are entailed in 'being-in-relation' in everyday life to help define and continue her research. I take these relational resources to include taking the role or perspective of the other; making an emotional investment (taking an interest) in the other; and exhibiting moral solidarity and altruistic behavior that serves the other person. In the present case, DS can be said to take the role and perspective of the protein and of her bacteria; she also imagines the latters' emotions, engaging in what is perhaps a form of empathy. In the following comment on her protein, DS indicates her own emotional involvement:

KKC: Is it [the protein] like a person? Someone you interact with?
DS: No, not necessarily a person. It takes on aspects of some personality, which I feel, depending on if it has been cooperative or not. If it's cooperative then it becomes a friend for a while, then I am happy and write exclamation marks in my book. But later it becomes material again, it goes back to being in a material state. When it stops doing what I want, then I see a personal enemy and think about the problems.

From the subject–object differentiation and the relational definition of the situation DS reaps, one imagines, insights, clarity about next moves, epistemic dividends. In other words, DS uses relational mechanisms as resources in articulating and 'constructing' an ill-defined, problematic, nonroutine and perhaps innovative epistemic practice.

When Heidegger analyzed our instrumental being-in-the-world as a form of un-self-conscious but nontheless goal-directed employment of equipment in its referential context he also pointed out what happens when equipment becomes problematic (Heidegger 1962: 98ff.): then we go from 'absorbed coping' to 'envisaging,' 'deliberate coping' and to the scientific stance of 'theoretical reflection' on the properties of entities. This characterization recaptures the ones I have given, with perhaps one difference. Heidegger came to characterize knowledge in terms of a theoretical attitude that entails a 'withholding' of practical reason. He gave an important characterization of how the project of science appears derivative of the primordial stance of taking things for granted in everyday life. But, at the same time, his character-ization provided less than an adequate account of knowledge processes – in which the presence of equipment is massive, instrumentality prevails, and theorizing rather appeals to us as being itself a form of practice. With the notion of a theoretical attitude, Heidegger brought back into the picture the subject–object differentiation which he had wanted to drive out of the philosophical discourse with his definition of 'Dasein' as a form of concerned coping ('Self and world belong together in the single entity, Dasein. Self and world are not two entities, like subject and object': cf. Dreyfus 1995: 67ff.). But perhaps as a consequence of his larger project, Heidegger never quite gave situations of subject–object distantiation the same consideration and attention that he gave to concerned coping. Theoretical knowledge, for Heidegger, remained a form of 'thematizing' that objectifies objects from a position of detachment. Heidegger did not develop the idea that this 'detachment' simultaneously makes possible relationships in which one can dwell and which can be extended and unfolded through relational mechanisms and resources. I take the position that Heidegger's detachment should rather be recast in terms of the notion of differentiation (between subject and object); that differentiation entails the possibility of a nexus between differentiated entities which provides for our integration in the world (for a form of being-in-the-world); and that this form of being-in-relation also defines a form of 'practice' – in particular, it defines epistemic practice.

What is an object? Objects characterized by a lack in completeness of being

The 'alien' tissue element of epistemic practice that now needs further discussion is that of an object.[1] How can we characterize knowledge objects and why do they require special attention? One reason for discussing epistemic objects is that our everyday notion of an object (take Heidegger's 'hammer') would seem to contradict the features of objects that scientists and other experts encounter. To spell out these features I want to start from a suggestion by the historian of biology Rheinberger, who means by 'epistemic things' any scientific objects of investigation that are at the center of a research process and in the process of being materially defined. Objects of knowledge are characteristically open, question-generating and complex. They are processes and projections rather than definitive things. Observation and inquiry reveals them by increasing rather than reducing their complexity. Rheinberger also emphasizes that what an object is at present to some degree depends on how its future develops (see below). Rheinberger is interested in the historical structure of research programs which oscillate around objects of knowledge that escape fixation (e.g., Rheinberger 1992).

Building upon Rheinberger's ideas, I want to characterize objects of knowledge ('epistemic objects') in terms of a lack in completeness of being that takes away much of the wholeness, solidity, and the thing-like character they have in our everyday conception. The everyday viewpoint, it would seem, looks at objects from the outside as one would look at tools or goods that are ready to hand or to be traded further. These objects have the character of closed boxes. In contrast, objects of knowledge appear to have the capacity to unfold indefinitely. They are more like open drawers filled with folders extending indefinitely into the depth of a dark closet. Since epistemic objects are always in the process of being materially defined, they continually acquire new properties and change the ones they have. But this also means that objects of knowledge can never be fully attained, that they are, if you wish, never quite themselves. What we encounter in the research process are representations or stand-ins for a more basic lack of object.

From a theoretical point of view, the defining characteristic of an epistemic object is this changing, unfolding character – or its lack of 'object-ivity' and completeness of being, and its nonidentity with itself. The *lack in completeness of being* is crucial: objects of knowledge in many fields have material instantiations, but they must simultaneously be conceived of as unfolding structures of absences: as things that continually 'explode' and 'mutate' into something else, and that are as much defined by what they are not (but will, at some point have become) than by what they are. The idea that 'every component of an organism is as much of an organism as every other part,' uttered by a scientist to whom a particular plant had exploded in that way, can perhaps capture the idea of an unfolding ontology. The *unfolding ontology* of objects foregrounds the temporal structure, and, to put it into the original Freudian terms, the *Nachträglichkeit*[2] in definitive existence of knowledge things (their post-hocness), which is difficult to combine with our everyday notion of an object. I will argue in the next section that it is the unfolding ontology of these objects which accommodates so well the structure of wanting, and binds experts to knowledge things in creative and constructive practice.

There are other characteristics. Epistemic objects frequently exist simultaneously in a variety of forms. They have multiple instantiations, which range from figurative, mathematical, and other representations to material realizations. Take the case of a detector in a high-energy physics experiment. 'It' continually circulates through a collaborating community of physicists in the form of partial simulations and calculations, technical design drawings, artistic renderings, photographs, test materials, prototypes, transparencies, written and verbal reports, and more. These instantiations are always partial in the sense of not fully comprising 'the detector.' 'Partial objects' stand in an internal relation to a whole. The instantiations I have listed should not be conceived of as a halo of renderings and preparatory materials anticipating and representing *another* object, 'the real thing.' It is 'the real thing' itself that has the changing ontology which the partial objects unfold. But do physicists not mean, by a detector, the physical machine *after* it has been built and *when* it is complete and running? Is the object not always an intended, an imagined whole? My point here is simply that as an intended object, a detector is an endlessly unfolding project consistent with the above circumscription of an epistemic object as marked by a lack in completeness of being. We should also consider that the boundaries of a technical instrument such as a 'running detector' are still highly problematic: only parts of the instrument tend to be operational at any one time, the physical machine will not run without remote controls, without computers and other equipment connected to it, and the instrument exists for most practical purposes mainly in the form of detector (component) measurements, representations, and simulations (it is literally put behind lead walls and inaccessable while it is running). Finally, even when such an instrument is officially declared 'finished' and 'complete,' the respective experts are acutely aware of its faults, of how it 'could' have been improved, of what it 'should' have become and did not.

The 'finished,' working detector, then, is itself always incomplete, is itself simply another partial object. The notion of an imagined object captures the ontological difference between current instantiations and a possibly more complete ideal, or in another sense extended object. The imagined object might itself be instantiated in design drawings that project a future or hidden state. In this sense a concrete, imagined object is also a partial object, albeit one that stands in relation to an available, occurrent object state as an object that marks the difference to this state. As historical studies show, scientists sometimes map out ideal objects in publications even when current techniques are not able to produce them (e.g. Borck 1997: 6).[3] But imagined objects can also split and divert current practice by projecting a new possible object, one that calls into question current concerns or simply departs from them in lateral ways. This is how current practice often gets constructively extended into new strands.

To return now to the partial object: I do not conceive of it as a gliding replacement for any presumed 'real' object in the sense of a referent. Partial objects, like epistemic objects in general, do not derive their immediate practical significance from the real. The point I want to draw attention to is the signifying force of (partial) epistemic objects by virtue of the internal articulation of these objects. Consider a transparency containing a curve which indicates the increasing 'downtime' of, say, a computer over its lifetime. The curve does not just 'represent' the unspecific experience that the instrument needs repairs over time. It specifies the exact way in which repair incidences accumulate. It may show that there is a small but steady increase of such incidences in the first years, followed by a steep and bumpy downtime increase during midlife, and a slow increase in a generally high incidence of repair shutoffs during older age. From the curve, one can try to decide at what points to replace the instrument. This will make apparent the need for further information, for example about the level of downtime that is acceptable to a project – the curve is telling, but not (ever) telling enough. What one can decide is what points of the curve to explore further to obtain the missing information. For example, one can calculate the cost of data losses through downtime before and after a steep decline in repair incidences. The signifying force of partial objects (of epistemic objects in general) resides in the pointers they provide to possible further explorations. In this sense these objects are meaning-producing and practice-generating; they provide for the concatenation and constructive extension of practice. One can also say the significance of these entities resides in the lack they display and in the suggestions they contain for further unfolding (for a more complicated theoretical physics example, see Merz and Knorr Cetina (1997: 918)).

Thus in creative and constructive practice, (partial) epistemic objects have to be seen as transient, internally complex, signifying entities that allow for and structure the continuation of the sequence through the signs they give off of their lacks and needs. Their internal articulation is important for the continuation of epistemic practice; not just their differe(a)nce to other objects, as in a Saussurean linguistic universe. I do not see partial epistemic objects as elementary units into which a complex whole is decomposed, but rather as complex links which extend a practical sequence at least partly through being unfoldable into equally complex sublinks. An example from everyday life might be a computer equipped with the relevant software. The computer can be 'unfolded' into signifying screens and subscreens, which stimulates in users an epistemic and affective relationship with the instrument (see also Turkle 1995).

I have been emphasizing the *unfolding, dispersed*, and *signifying (meaning-producing)* character of epistemic objects, and particularly their nonidentity with themselves, to bring out the divergence of this idea of an object from everyday notions of material things. I must now add a word about the role naming plays in relation to these objects. The point I want to remind us of is a simple one: a stable name is not an expression and indicator of stable thinghood. Rather, naming, in the present conception, is a way to punctuate the flux, to bracket and ignore differences, to declare them as pointing to an identity-for-a-particular-purpose. I tend to think that one can see a stable name for a sequence of unfolding objects as a way of translating between different time zones, among others personal and institutional time zones. For example, when a sequence of objects and partial object states is called a 'liquid argon calorimeter,' it is brought into accordance with project-financing requirements, work organization principles, institutional career tracks, and so on. A typical example of constantly changing or unfolding objects (also familiar from everyday life) are computer programs. In expert programming, authors write, run, and update the code to suit their own changing interests. At the same time they serve a community of users for whom they may issue the code in 'versions,' 'updates,' program 'family' members, and so on (see Merz 1997). The packaging of progressive modifications in recognizable 'versions' and 'updates' requires a special effort, which the author makes taking into account user needs. The notion of unfolding refers to the evolution of a sequence of which certain segments (and possibly other segments) are gathered together by applying identical names to them. The process of naming and that of unfolding (and dispersion) are independent of each other, and might even stand in contradiction to one another.

Epistemic practice as sustained by object relations

A number of suggestions about how epistemic practice might be conceived have been implicit in the discussion so far. I now want to address these more directly and systematically. I limit myself to two features of epistemic practice: its underlying relational dynamic and the lateral branching out of this prac-tice. The first feature pertains to a kind of practice that is dynamic, construc-tive (creative), and perhaps conflictual. As indicated before, contemporary accounts favor a conception of practice in terms of habits and routines. As a consequence, these authors seek to explain practice (understood as practices) by an appeal to the embodied acquisition of preferences, perceptual schemes and dispositions to react, and by an appeal to shared tacit rules. The former is more the Bourdieu and Dreyfus line of thinking; in the latter case, the nature of the rules, and their exact relation to practical activity, lies at the core of controversies (see Bourdieu 1977; Dreyfus and Dreyfus 1986; Lynch 1993; Turner 1994; Rouse 1996b; Schatzki 1996). In both cases, practice requires participants to have learned something which they subsequently deploy or enact in concrete situations. In contrast, I see epistemic practice as based upon a form of relationship (see also Knorr Cetina 1997; Greenberg and Mitchell 1983) that by the nature of its dynamic transforms itself and the entities formed by the relationship.

What sort of relationship? Consider once more epistemic objects as described before. I want to maintain that the open, unfolding character of knowledge objects uniquely matches the 'structure of wanting' with which some authors have characterized the self. I derive this idea from Lacan (e.g., 1975), but it can also be linked to Baldwin (1973: 373ff.) and Hegel.[4] Lacan derives wants not as Freud did from an instinctual impulse whose ultimate goal is a reduction in bodily tension, but rather from the mirror stage of a young child's development. Wanting or desire is born in envy of the perfection of the image in the mirror (or of the mirroring response of the parents); the lack is permanent, since there will always be a distance between the subjective experience of a lack in our existence and the image in the mirror, or the apparent wholeness of others (e.g., Lacan and Wilden 1968; Alford 1991: 36ff.). One can also attempt a rendering of the lack in a representational idiom that is closer to the present concern. Accordingly, wants are always directed at an empirical object mediated by representations – through signifiers, which identify the object and render it significant. But these representations never quite catch up with the empirical object; they always in some aspects fail (misrepresent) the thing they articulate. They thereby reiterate the lack rather than eliminate it.[5] To relate this now to epistemic objects, the point I made before is that the representations experts come up with in their search processes are not only partial and inadequate, they also tend to imply what is still missing in the picture. In other words they suggest which way to look further, through the insufficiencies they display. In that sense one could say that objects of knowledge structure desire, and provide for the continuation and unfolding of object-oriented practice.

Let me say a little more about what it is that the notion of a structure of wanting offers; one has some explaining to do when turning to a sociologically arcane language such as the one I choose. The Lacanian ideas I use serve to specify objectual relations, which I see as the touchstone of a practice centered on epistemic objects, as relationships based upon a form of mutuality: of objects providing for the continuation of a chain of wantings, through the signs they give off of what they still lack; and of subjects (experts) providing for the possibility of the continuation of objects which only exist as a sequence of absences, or as an unfolding structure. What need not concern us further is

Lacan's account of the lack in subjectivity as rooted in the child's narcissistic relationship to him/herself rather than to a lost person, or his explanatory trope of the mirror stage. One need not find the Lacanian account of the mirror stage persuasive in order to find the idea of a structure of wanting plausible. The latter is a convenient way to capture the way wants have of continually searching out new objects and of moving on to them – a convenient way, if you wish, to capture the volatility and unstoppability of desire. With regard to knowledge the idea of a structure or chain of wantings brings into view whole series of moves and their underlying dynamic rather than isolated reasons, as the traditional vocabulary of motives, intentions and actions does. It also suggests a libidinal dimension or basis of knowledge activities – which is ignored or denied when we conceive of science and expertise as cognitive endeavors.

I believe that the existence of such a dimension is borne out by the intensity and pleasurability of objectual relations as experienced by experts. It is also 'in tune with' ontological reorientations towards 'experience,' etc., in the wider society as diagnosed by some (Welsch 1996). The notion of a knowledge society is not at odds with, for example, that of an experiential society, or with a turn toward a more visual and visually simulated world – what it is at odds with is an arid and overly cognitively tilted notion of knowledge. The conduct of expertise has long harbored and nourished an experiential *mentalité*, if 'experience' is defined, as I think it should be, as an arousal of the processing capacities and sensitivities of the person. The conjunction of the relational and libidinal dimension gives practice a flavor and quality distinctively different from that of routines and habits.

It remains for me to add a note about the lateral and angular branching off of strands of practice. The notion of unfolding when applied to practice can easily be understood as a forward-pointing sequence of steps driven by the interlocking dynamic of a structure of lacks and wantings. However, this would ignore the frequent splitting of activities into different strands, and the possible displacements of one strand by another. Such lateral shifts imply the transference of wants and relational substance from one chain of objectual involvements to another. As the study of science shows, processes of inquiry rarely come to a natural ending of the sort where everything worth knowing about an object is considered to be known. The idea of a structure of wanting implies a continually renewed interest in knowing that appears never to be fulfilled by final knowledge. But it also implies that interest may turn elsewhere, that it jumps the rails of one line of practice and continues on a different track in a somewhat different direction. The angularity of epistemic practice, its continual lateral divergence from itself, needs further discussion which I cannot offer here. Suffice to say that angular splitoffs add a disruptive element to the conception of practice I advocate, an element of conflictual breaks not generally recognized in current conceptions of practice.

Summary and conclusion

The notion of a knowledge society suggests that knowledge-centered practice focused on epistemic objects becomes a prominent part of all areas of social life. I have characterized the objects involved (which may be natural things, instruments, scientifically generated objects, etc.) in terms of their unfolding ontology, the phenomenon that they may exist simultaneously in a variety of forms, and their meaning-generating connective force. These ideas also suggest a notion of practice that is more dynamic, creative, and constructive than the current definition of practice as rule-based routines or embodied skills suggests. The challenge we face, with the present argument, is to dissociate the notion of practice somewhat from its fixation on human dispositions and habits, and from the connotation of iterative procedural routines. I propose to conceive of the backbone of practice in terms of a relational dynamics that extends itself into the future in creative and also in disruptive ways. This relational dynamics does not simply mean the existence of positive emotional ties between individuals and nonhuman objects. We can theorize the sort of object relations addressed in this paper better through the notion of lack, and of an interlocking structure or chain of wantings, than through positive ties and fulfillments. The notion of a structure of wanting entails the possibility of a deep emotional investment in objects; an involvement that is at the same time congruent with the many flavors and orientations of this investment.

Epistemic environments cannot be understood, I want to maintain in concluding, without understanding expert–object relationships. Knowledge-centered work shifts back and forth between the performance of 'packaged' routine procedures and differentiated practice as described in this paper. It is with respect to differentiated practice that a relational idiom becomes plausible and may help in conceptualizing chains of activity. It may also become relevant to object-oriented practice outside knowledge contexts. In a knowledge society, objects in many areas of social life begin to display the kind of internal complexity and dynamic extendability that they have in science and expertise. Computers, financial instruments (Zelitzer 1994), sophisticated sports equipment are typical examples – these appear on the market in continually changing versions, they are both ready to hand and subject to further development and investigation. As objects in everyday life become high-technology devices some of the relational aspects of their existence in expert contexts also carry over into daily life. Some of the problems these devices raise in everyday contexts may well have to do with the relational demands they make and for which some lay users may not be prepared. Conversely, the appeal these objects have for some users may also consist in the relational opportunities they offer (for computers, see Turkle 1984, 1995). When epistemic objects become epistemic everyday things, the relational approach I have advocated may also become relevant to understanding daily work activities and instrumental action.

Notes

1 If there is one aspect of knowledge cultures on which received viewpoints on science and expertise and the newer studies of science and technology agree then this is that knowledge cultures centrally turn around object worlds to which experts and scientists are oriented (for the new sociology of science, this has been emphasized particularly by Callon [e.g., 1986] and Latour [e.g., 1993]). For interesting attempts to work with these ideas by historians and sociologists of science see, for example, Pickering (1995a), Wise (1993) and Dodier (1995). For an important study of individuals' attachment to computers see Turkle (1995). Thévenot's (e.g., 1994b) concepts provide perhaps the most general sociological perspective on the issue.

2 Freud illustrated the principle for some mental disorders: some childhood experiences turn out to have been profoundly disorienting and disorder-promoting only after a person develops a mental disorder, which may happen decades after the experience occurred.

3 Borck's example refers to Einthoven's publication of an ideal graphic registration of the heart in 1895 as an emblem of the curves of later electrocardiographs.

4 Baldwin's and Hegel's notions of desire are summarized by Wiley (1994: 33).

5 In putting it this way I draw on Baas's rendering of Lacan's notion of a thing – albeit without claiming that my reading here is correct (Baas 1996: 22f.).

13   Two concepts of practices

Joseph Rouse

Practice talk has been rampant within late twentieth-century philosophy, social theory, and science studies. I have myself been among the perpetrators. Yet familiar discussions of practices as the unarticulated (but interpretable) background that would halt regresses of explicit interpretation have recently been subjected to withering criticism by Stephen Turner (1994) and by Steve Fuller (1989, 1992). Turner has argued that appealing to practices to explain regularities, continuities, and commonalities in social life is pseudoexplanatory. According to Turner, the inference from common behavior to its supposedly underlying source in *shared* presuppositions or practices cannot be justified, the causal powers of practices are inevitably mysterious, and the transmission or reproduction of practices over time and from one practitioner to another cannot be accounted for. Fuller's criticism echoes Turner's objections to practice talk as pseudoexplanatory, and adds a political dimension: he argues that recourse to the *geisteswissenschaftliche* interpretation of tacit understanding is deeply conservative and antidemocratic, an argument buttressed at least *ad hominem* by reflection upon the political commitments of Heidegger and Wittgenstein, philosophical precursors of the practice industry.[1]

I take Turner's criticisms very seriously, but argue that he has misunderstood their significance. Turner concludes from his arguments that practice talk is altogether bankrupt in philosophy and social theory, and he consequently attempts to resurrect in its place the long abandoned explanatory appeal to 'habit.' Turner's discussion instead reveals a fundamental ambiguity between uses of the term 'practices,' between practices conceived as *regularities* and a *normative* conception of practices. The two uses roughly correspond to the respective uses of the term in social theory (Durkheim, Weber, Oakeshott, Winch) and in philosophy (Kant, Heidegger, Wittgenstein), a distinction that is nevertheless complicated by the widespread appropriation of Heidegger and Wittgenstein within the social theory tradition. Perhaps because his focus is upon social theory, Turner only identifies one side of the ambiguous usage. I think his arguments are indeed telling objections to the conception of 'practices' (as regularities) that he actually addresses, but their upshot is instead to highlight the importance of conceiving practices normatively.

In the first part of the paper, I work out some of the most significant differences between conceiving practices as regularities and conceiving them normatively. These differences concern what practices are, how they become evident, the significance of language within practices, and the sense in which practices are 'social.' I then go on to consider, quite briefly, two important consequences for science studies if we take scientific *practices* as the principal focus of attention. First, a normative conception of practices challenges familiar reifications of language, knowledge, and power, and encourages attention to the temporality of scientific practices and their meaning, justification, and effects. Second, a focus upon scientific practices as normative relocates the science studies practitioner, both theoretically and politically.

So what are practices? The question arises with some force, because of the diversity of things sometimes included under the term. Turner notes that 'practice' is variously interchangeable with 'tradition,' 'tacit knowledge,' 'paradigm,' 'presupposition,' and much more. Practices are sometimes regarded as tacit propositional attitudes, and sometimes as inarticulable competences or performances. In either case, however, the concept of practices is typically invoked to explain continuities or commonalities among the activities of social groups. Turner argues that to do the *explanatory* work attributed to them, practices must be objectively identifiable regularities. If they are presupposed propositional commitments, they must have some 'psychological reality'; if they are practical competences, they must have some causal efficacy. In either case, moreover, the content or pattern embodied in a practice must be transmissable in ways that would preserve its identity across practitioners. Turner ultimately rejects any explanatory appeal to social practices because of allegedly intractable difficulties in justifying the psychological reality, causal efficacy, or transmissable identity of any regularities 'underlying' more readily manifest human activities.

Turner fails to acknowledge the possibility of an alternative conception of a 'practice,' in which actors share a practice if their actions are appropriately regarded as answerable to norms of correct or incorrect practice. Not all practitioners perform the same actions or presuppose the same beliefs, but some are subject to sanctions for actions or beliefs that are inappropriate or otherwise incorrect. Of course, not all improprieties are *actually* corrected or sanctioned. So the differential responses that would signify the incorrectness of some performances are themselves normative practices. It is always possible that such chains of proprieties come to an end in some kind of objectively recognizable regularity. But, as Robert Brandom has noted, 'we can envisage a situation in which *every* social practice of [a] community has as its generating response a performance which must be in accord with another social practice' (Brandom 1979: 189–90). Such a network of practices need not be identifiable as a regularity, even as a whole. Brandom therefore argues that the difference between regularities and norms should itself be regarded normatively, that is, as a distinction between those patterns *appropriately* explained in causal terms, and those things appropriately understood as subject to interpretation and normative response.

Turner's own arguments against the integrity of practices conceived as regularities ironically often point toward such a normative conception of practices. Turner argues, for example, that Marcel Mauss's identification of culturally distinctive ways of walking could not easily be captured in terms of 'culture-free causal categories,' in part because 'one might acquire the 'same' [external] walk by mimicking or by a kind of training which corrected various untutored walks – and corrected them in different respects – to produce a walk which is externally the same' (Turner 1994: 22). Moreover, Turner claimed, the *description* of practices typically depends upon classification schemes that presuppose acquaintance with other practices: such descriptions are only identifiable by contrast to other local, cultural expectations with which they conflict (1994: 24). They are only identifiable *as practices* at all against a background of other practices, and thus can never be reduced to objective regularities. Turner still fails to grasp a normative conception of practices as a genuine alternative, however; what other practice theorists would regard as normative responsiveness, he dismisses as merely an *instrumentalist* appeal to regularities (1994: 37).

Turner objects to such supposedly instrumentalist appeals to regularities of social practice, because they 'fail to connect the stuff of thought to the world of cause and substance ... [leaving] no basis for using our past understandings or interpretations to warrant future interpretations' (1994: 37). But this objection only makes sense if the domain of practices is conceived too narrowly, in two respects. On the one hand, it presumes that the 'world of cause and substance' is somehow distinct from the 'world' of meaningful practices, the 'social world,' such that the two *need* reconnection. It also presumes, more subtly, that practices are distinct from linguistic representation: practices are ontologically suspect, whereas linguistic meaning and reference are not. I consider first the relation between 'practice' and language.

Practice theorists have often been ambivalent about the significance of language for practices, and vice versa. On the one hand, unarticulated or even inarticulable practices are frequently contrasted to explicit assertions or rules. On the other hand, the domain of practice is often extended to incorporate *conceptual* or linguistic practices, perhaps even as the paradigm case of practices. Shared conceptual schemes or presuppositions are often the focus of practice talk. Once we recognize the difference between conceiving practices as regularities or normatively, however, we can see a fundamental distinction between two conceptions of linguistic practices. Those who identify 'practices' with regularities (including shared beliefs or conceptual schemes) typically situate language outside the domain of practices; shared practices may account for particular beliefs or conceptual schemes that are expressible *within* language, but linguistic intentionality itself is then conceived in terms of a representational semantics instead of a pragmatics of discursive practices. By contrast, a normative conception of practices is best understood as a general conception of intentionality. Brandom (1994) has most explicitly worked out an account of intentionality as altogether pragmatic, but once we are clear about the distinction, Heidegger and

Wittgenstein, and more recently, Donald Davidson, are best understood as conceiving of intentionality as normative rather than representational.

Such a pragmatic account of language, and of intentionality more generally, understands language dynamically, without reifying meanings, reference, or shared languages. Shared meanings or beliefs are not the preexisting facts that would explain the possibility of communication, but the norms presumptively invoked in the course of interpreting someone or something as communicative.[2] Only by interpreting a speaker as mostly making sense (within a field of linguistic and other practical proprieties that enable me to make sense of myself as making sense) can I acknowledge her activity (or my own) as linguistic. Note that this characteristic feature of Davidson's and Brandom's interpretive semantics (namely that truth, meaning, language, and other semantic categories can only be explicated via interpretation in an unanalyzed home language) is precisely the feature of practices that most vexed Turner as unacceptably 'instrumentalist.' Turner complains that,

> The assumptions [one] attributes to [another] are identifiable as assumptions only because [one] is in a position to make a specific comparison [to one's own understanding of the 'same' situation]. Starting from a different comparison ... would produce different misunderstandings, and different assumptions would need to be attributed ... Such 'assumptions,' then, are *not natural facts*, but hypotheses that solve specific comparative problems (1994: 33–4; emphasis mine).

But for Davidson, Brandom (and Wittgenstein and Heidegger, I would argue) linguistic practices are *non-natural* in precisely this sense.

With this background, we can now turn to Turner's worries about the connection between practices and 'the world of cause and substance.' Turner clearly takes practice theory to be objectionably antirealist (either instrumentalist or social constructivist). But a normative conception of linguistic and other practices challenges the shared commitments of realists and antirealists alike to a representationalist semantics.[3] The attitudes and responses that identify a practice (*including* a linguistic practice) are only contentful amidst our intra-actions with the world.[4] We interpret utterances by making sense of what is said when, i.e., on which occasions, in what worldly *circumstances* (e.g., for Davidson, we interpret utterances via prior acquaintance with their *truth conditions*; for Heidegger, interpretation is an aspect of *being-in-the-world*). To ask how our representations can ever get a foothold in the world is to presume, erroneously, that we can ever make or understand representations without already having a foothold in the world.[5]

Thus, if we take seriously a normative conception of practices, we must recognize that there *is* no such thing as 'the social world' (*or* the 'natural world') except as reified abstractions from *the* world.[6] The meanings, agency, institutions, or forms of life with which social constructivists would explain how nature becomes manifest to us are themselves senseless apart from those manifestations; they cannot be an independent explanans. But supposedly natural kinds and their causal capacities only acquire their constitutive *counterfactual* import from their normative application *ceteris paribus* within scientific practices of theoretical modeling and experimental manipulation.

I now take up the second theme of this paper. So far, I have not *defended* a normative conception of practices, but only articulated its conceivability as distinct from regularities of practice. I continue in a similarly programmatic way to sketch some possible consequences of focusing science studies upon scientific practices understood in this way, instead of as regularities of behavior or belief.[7] Two groups of consequences stand out. The first concerns the topics that take center stage in such an account, and how they interact. The second concerns what is sometimes called 'reflexivity,' i.e., the theoretical and political positioning of science studies themselves.

One topic that becomes central when we take scientific practices as normative is their temporality. A central concern of postempiricist philosophy of science has been to understand scientific change in ways that do not render it unintelligible as rational. The problem is that the temporality of scientific practices cannot be adequately conceived in terms of scientific *change*. If one took scientific communities to share specific beliefs, values, conceptual contents, or activities, then it would make sense to ask how that consensus changes over time. But such conceptions presume that there is an already determinate character to a scientific community and to the shared commitments that define its boundaries. Such determinacy cannot be presumed once scientific practices are conceived normatively, for such practices are *constitutively* temporally extended. What those practices are *now* depends in part upon how their normative force is interpreted and taken up in subsequent practice. Their *present* content is subject to reinterpretation and semantic drift. Thus, for example, Rheinberger concludes from his historical study of research on oncogenesis that, 'the virus of 1950 must be seen as the condition of possibility for looking at [Peyton] Rous's [1910] agent as that which it had *not* been: the *future virus*' (Rheinberger 1994: 77). This point is ontological rather than epistemic: present semantic content is comparable to whether a goal in soccer is the game-winning goal, in being not yet settled by any facts, and not merely as yet unknown (Wheeler 1991). Understanding practices normatively helps us see why this is so: what a practice is, including what counts as an instance of the practice, is bound up with its *significance*, i.e., with what is at issue and at stake in the practice, to whom or what it *matters*, and hence with how the practice is *appropriately* or *perspicuously* described.

Adequately accounting for the significance of scientific practices requires dynamic accounts of language, knowledge, and power, or so I argue in *Engaging Science* (Rouse 1996b). In sketching what this claim can mean, I focus here on why dynamic or nonreified conceptions of language, knowledge, and power are *mutually* implicated. In criticizing Turner, I have already pointed toward a conception of language as discursive practices, that is, as dynamic interactions among speakers and their surroundings. Linguistic practices are mediated not by conventional meanings, languages, or beliefs, but by partially shared *situations*, which have a history. One consequence of recognizing their dynamics highlights the importance of tropes, whose contrast class is not 'literal' meanings, but familiar or uncontested *uses*.[8] Within the sciences, models (including mathematical, verbal, physical, pictorial or schematic, and experimental models) are especially important examples of tropes. Models, I argue, should be thought of as simulacra rather than representations. The crucial difference is that 'representation' too often denotes a semantic content that intervenes between knowers and the world, whereas simulacra are just more things in the world, with a multiplicity of relations to other things.[9] What makes them models, with an *intentional* relation to what they model, is their being taken up in practices, ongoing patterns of use that are answerable to norms of correctness.

This constitutive role for norms and sanctions in linguistic interaction thus already shows the indispensability of concepts of 'power' and 'resistance' for understanding language. Whether an unfamiliar way of speaking about or dealing with a situation is taken as an innovation, a mistake, a curiosity, an irony, or a variation on the familiar depends crucially upon asymmetries of authority among those who encounter it. Yet the recognition of models as simulacra extends the interconnection of meaning and power beyond the immediate relation between speakers and their interpreters. To see why this is so, consider a question sometimes asked rhetorically about meaning: how could merely representing things differently possibly have a causal influence on them? A similar question about simulacra cannot have the same rhetorical effect: simulacra *are* transformations of the world, and, more significantly, they transform the available possibilities for human action. They do so both by materially enabling some activities and obstructing others, and also by changing the situation such that some possible actions or roles lose their point, while others acquire new significance.[10]

So far, I have sketched how considerations of 'power' might become relevant to conceptions of language and meaning as emergent from the normativity of discursive practices. If such an account were construed in terms of a *reified* conception of 'power,' the result would be a reduction of meaning to something like rhetorical force, and language to a technology of persuasion, a move that is not unknown within science studies. Reducing meaning or significance to rhetorical effects is nevertheless a fundamental mistake. The mistake can be avoided if we also conceive of *power* dynamically, not as a regularity of social life, a thing possessed or exercised by dominant agents, but as a situated and temporally extended relationship among agents and their surroundings.

Wartenburg (1990) developed a partial model for such a dynamic conception of power. He began by noting how power is mediated by 'social alignments': one agent's actions effectively exercise power over another only to the extent that other agents' actions are appropriately aligned with the actions of the dominant agent. For example, judges exercise power over prisoners only if the actions of bailiffs, guards, appeals courts, and others are *appropriately* aligned with what the judge does. Power relations are dynamic, because the *presence* of an alignment, and its *effectiveness*, depend upon how the alignment is sustained or transformed over time, in response to sub-ordinate agents' efforts to resist or bypass them as well as dominant agents' attempts to utilize, strengthen, or extend them. Power is thus not something possessed or exercised by an agent, or even a relation between two agents, but is instead dispersed and deferred across a field of possibilities. Wartenburg's model is only partial, because he mistakenly restricts the mediation of power to *social* alignments of human agents. A more adequate conception would recognize the *material* mediation of power by its circumstances, such that tools, processes, and physical surroundings more generally all belong to dynamic alignments of dominance, subordination, and resistance. Thus, just as practices should not be reduced to *social* practices, power should not be reduced to *social* power.

It may be initially more difficult to grasp how to understand knowing with-out reifying knowledge. Dynamic accounts of language have helpful precedents in Davidson and Brandom; Foucault likewise familiarized a dynamics of power (even if the significance of a *dynamic* conception has not always been adequately appreciated in either case). Yet Wartenburg's discussion of dynamic power alignments offers a useful analogue to a dynamic conception of knowing.[11] Power is only *effective* in enabling or constraining action through dynamic alignments that bring one action to bear upon another. Knowing is likewise only *informative* through dynamic alignments that enable one thing (a statement, a model, an image, a skillful performance, and so on) to be *about* another. Philosophers of science nowadays emphasize the importance of 'back-ground knowledge' in establishing inferential relations between hypotheses and evidence, but that concept is too homogeneous and static. Knowing is mediated not just by a 'background' of assertional commitments, but also by models, skills, instruments, standardized materials and phenomena, and situated interactions among knowers, in short, by *practices*. Moreover, a dynamic account of language as discursive practices obliterates any clear distinction between the representational *content* of knowledge, and its material or social construction or implementation.

The result is a *deflationary* conception of knowledge, modeled on deflation-ary or semantic conceptions of truth. In the latter case, the truth predicate and its uses are indispensable to linguistic and epistemic practices, even though no underlying nature of truth unifies or reifies the instances of its appropriate application. A deflationary account of knowledge likewise denies that 'know-ledge' or 'scientific knowledge' constitutes a theoretically coherent kind. There are many appropriate ascriptions of knowing within the multifarious practices of assessing, attributing, relying upon, or contesting understanding and justification, but there is no *nature* of knowledge underlying these ascriptions.[12] This claim has farreaching consequences: participation in the wholesale legitimation or critique of scientific claims to knowledge almost

invariably proceeds from a conception of scientific knowledge as a theoretically coherent concept that can be surveyed as a whole. It only makes sense to
claim that scientific knowledge as a whole is approximately true, rationally
arrived at, socially constructed, or interest-relative if there is such a (kind of)
thing.[13]

Conceiving of practices normatively rather than as composed of underlying
regularities, and refusing to reify language, power, and knowledge, thus challenge many of the most familiar philosophical and sociological approaches to
science studies. An important aspect of this challenge concerns the theoretical and political 'location' of science studies themselves, often discussed
under the heading of reflexivity. Philosophers and sociologists alike have
aspired to a standpoint of 'epistemic sovereignty' (Rouse 1996a), a theoretical
position 'outside' or 'above' scientific practices from which to establish or
undermine their legitimacy once and for all. If we understand scientific practices normatively, no such standpoint is available. Davidson's and Brandom's
semantics offer a useful parallel; they take natural language as its own
metalanguage, and explicate language from 'within.' We must likewise, I
argue, recognize 'science' to include its own metapractices, and engage in
epistemic explication from within.

Taking science studies as inescapably 'internal' to the cultures of science
may thereby raise Fuller's principal worry, that interpretive engagement
with scientific practices is necessarily conservative. Fuller (1992) claims
that interpretive engagements with scientific practices abandon any attempt
to hold science accountable to norms not of its own choosing.[14] But Fuller's
criticism only shows his commitment to a conception of practices as regularities: he limits 'science' to the set of practices already conventionally
recognized as science, its 'norms' to the goals and standards to which its
practitioners already subscribe, and *therefore* concludes that critical perspective must come from elsewhere. If one instead recognizes scientific practices
as normative, what science or knowledge *is* is not already determined, but is at
issue in what scientists and others do. Various epistemically significant practices are normatively accountable, but such practices also offer competing
interpretations of the norms within which they are situated. The interpretive
resources for science studies thus include a multiplicity of sciences and
metascientific discourses, together with various marginal and oppositional
epistemic practices. Science studies do not come in from the 'outside' to settle
the differences among these coexisting and competing practices, but are
already situated among them and engaged with them.

Such a conception of critical engagement within the culture of science
nevertheless may cause concern that the exercise of power might not only
foreclose the *effectiveness* of political criticism, but also its rational legitimacy,
if what *is* thus governs the space of reason-giving. One response to this worry
is to acknowledge it. There is no guarantee of adequate resources for the
articulation and realization of compelling epistemic and political criticism.
Recognition that ongoing political and epistemological work is needed to

sustain a space for critical reflection and political transformation is a goa against complacency.

There is a more substantive response, however. Taking seriously the prospect of an overwhelming ideological hegemony that could foreclose the intelligibility of critical alternatives underestimates the diversity and con-testedness of epistemic practices and their political significance. There will always be conflicting interpretations of ascendant scientific disciplines, as well as marginal and alternative ways of knowing, which have at least the potential to support critical perspectives upon dominant practices of justification. Presently accepted justifications can never be finally secured against alter-native interpretations, precisely because there are no self-certifying epistemic foundations immune from criticism. Moreover, the dynamics of linguistic meaning remind us that hegemonic ideologies are open to subversive read-ings, while social and material alignments of power are not self-maintaining. New forms of power and domination invite counteralignments. If epistemic and political criticism must always be located as intelligible responses to past and present practice, we must nevertheless remember that what past and present practice *is* includes its possible futures, which have not yet been fully determined. An appropriate response to worries about irresistible power and seamless ideology is thus not to seek secure grounds for criticism, but to engage the specific forms of domination that seem troubling, to articulate insightful and effective criticisms of them, and to forge specific alignments and solidarities with others who might come to share such concerns.

This conception of the critical positioning of science studies calls for a thicker conception of reflexivity than has usually been articulated in the science studies literature. Reflexivity has moral and political as well as rhetorical and epistemological dimensions: what do our writings and sayings *do*? to whom do we speak? what other voices and concerns do we acknowledge, make room for, or foreclose? which tendencies and alignments do we reinforce and which do we challenge? above all, to whom are we accountable? These questions arise with considerable force, because science studies as such are not politic-ally or epistemically pre-positioned: our work might variously articulate and reinforce dominant epistemic alignments, contribute to or extend opposi-tional discourses, or shift the field to envision new possibilities. A modest and self-critical attentiveness to our own partiality and situatedness, and account-ability for what we say and do, are the political responsibility incurred by our own contingent positionings within the cultures of science.

Notes

An expanded version of this paper is Joseph Rouse (1999) 'Understanding Scientific Practices: Cultural Studies of Science as a Philosophical Program,' in M. Biagioli (ed.) *The Science Studies Reader*, New York: Routledge, 442–56.

1 Turner himself (1989) has argued that the *ad hominem* consideration of Heidegger's politics must be taken as a quite serious prima facie problem for any conception of practices that draws extensively upon Heidegger's work.

2 'Interpretation' (or, as Turner too narrowly construes it, 'attributing assumptions') is here understood in a thoroughly pragmatic way as adopting a practical attitude rather than offering an explicit account: I 'interpret' someone as communicative simply by listening and responding in appropriate ways. A useful parallel is Heidegger's discussion of *Auslegung* in *Sein und Zeit* (*Being and Time*), in which one interprets something as a hammer by hammering with it; no explicit attribution of properties or meanings is required. One can, of course, try to make explicit the practical attitudes adopted when engaging in such interpretation, but such explications always come to an end in further unexplicated *proprieties*: this is what we do. This Wittgensteinian point is often misunderstood by taking 'what we do' as a behavioral regularity, but that cannot be right in the light of his discussion of rules. We appeal to 'what we do' precisely to halt a regress of explications of a regularity. Such a regress *cannot* end in another regularity (explication is needed to determine which one), but only in a propriety (to adapt Samuel Wheeler's example, we should understand 'this is what we do' in the sense of 'we don't hit other children, do we?'). 'What we do' always includes further practices of *correcting* deviant practice.

3 Rouse (1987, Chapter 5; 1991; 1996b: introduction and Chapters 7–8).

4 I follow Barad (1996) in adopting the term 'intra-action' as a substitute for 'interaction,' to avoid the connotation that the things that interact have a determinate identity and character prior to or apart from their intra-actions.

5 The classic philosophical source for this criticism of representationalism, of course, is the Introduction to Hegel's *Phenomenology of Spirit* (1977): the representationalism underlying both realism and antirealism is precisely what Hegel called 'the fear of error that reveals itself as fear of the truth.'

6 Brandom (1994) still identifies practical proprieties as *social* practices, but in a sense he describes as an 'I-Thou' model of social interaction rather than 'I-We.' I would argue that it makes more sense to drop the term 'social,' which inevitably has connotations of supraindividual *entities*. But neither should we think of Brandom's theory as one of *individual* intentionality. Who counts as an agent with 'original intentionality' is itself a normative question, not a factual one.

7 Most of what follows has been developed more extensively in Part II of my recently published book (Rouse 1996b).

8 The *loci classici* for such a conception of metaphor are Davidson (1984) and Wheeler (1991).

9 This concept of simulacra is discussed in Rouse (1996b: Chapter 8). The contrasting sense of 'representation' is indifferent to whether representations are conceived as thoughts accessible to individual minds, or as concepts, conceptual frameworks, languages, or forms of life shared by social groups.

10 These themes have been more extensively discussed in Rouse (1987: Chapters 6–7).

11 The connection is more than just an analogy. Wartenburg's approach to power is deeply influenced by Foucault, whose reflections on the dynamics of power were introduced as an analytics of power/knowledge. Rouse (1993, 1994) argues that Foucault's work of the 1970s projects a dynamics of knowing, even though it is less extensively articulated than his conception of power.

12 Brandom (1994: 201–5) follows a different route, to similar effect; he takes knowledge to denote a *normative status* rather than a factual state of affairs.

13 Rouse (1996b: Introduction and Part I) articulates and criticizes the commitments to the 'legitimation project' that are necessary to make sense of the disagreements among scientific realists, historical metamethodologists, empiricists, and social constructivists.

14 Fuller (1992) provides the clearest and most provocative account of this objection.

14 Derridian dispersion and Heideggerian articulation

General tendencies in the practices that govern intelligibility

Charles Spinosa

There are many fruitful questions one can ask about practices. Philosophers typically ask how practices serve as conditions for the possibility of various kinds of complicated human comportments. Philosophers, for instance, who are interested in cognitive acts will show how shared habitual practices are crucial for the application of any rule. Anthropologists and sociologists interested in instituted aspects of human life such as gender or gift-giving tend to focus on showing that neither systems of belief, nor functional analyses, nor systems of structural difference can account for the improvisational character of such instituted forms of life.[1] Others, frequently with some psychological training, are more likely to ask if practices are more like constantly developing skills or more like rigid habits. Are practices more like developing skills when they are actively deployed toward some particular end or more like stable habits when they ground the recognition of something? Historians, like Foucault, reveal how the same ethical maxims or the same social functions produce quite different forms of life as different kinds of practices, say, monarchical or disciplinary, Stoical or Christian, are in place for enacting the maxims or functions. All of these kinds of analysis are important (and I have only surveyed a small number of fruitful kinds of practice analysis). But I want to focus attention on an aspect of the way practices work which I believe is mostly overlooked and which has significant consequences for any ethics founded on practice. I shall spend the first part of this paper fleshing out the aspect of practices that I am interested in exploring. In the second and third parts of the paper, I shall describe how Derrida and Heidegger give two radically different accounts of this aspect of practice. And in a short fourth part I shall conclude by giving a consideration that suggests why I believe Heidegger's account is preferable and how it could be altered to embed Derrida's insights. My main goal, however, is to open consideration of general tendencies in the way practices work and point out the ethical consequences of identifying such tendencies.

The general tendency of elaboration that governs practices

To see what I am getting at when I speak of a tendency in the way practices work, let me take a simple example. Assuming that social practices are generally matters of skill, note that whenever we learn a new practice, even a very simple one such as jogging, we find ourselves constantly sensitive to new things to which we had paid scant attention before. Or we become sensitive to old things in a new way. In jogging, we become sensitive, for instance, to pains in our legs and lungs, to the racing of our hearts, to how much we perspire, to what interests us as we jog, that is, whether we are more interested in having some intellectual problem to try to work through while we jog or having some beautiful trail to look at. Generally, we elaborate our practice according to whatever new sensitivities appear. And we develop these elaborations with awareness or without. So, we might with full awareness experiment to find out if we notice the pain in our legs so much if we jog while trying to solve an intellectual problem. Or we might discover that we had, without any aware-ness, developed the practice of making the second half of our run with the sea breeze in our faces so that the perspiration would not get in our eyes.[2] In both cases, however, either with awareness or without, we are dealing with some particular issue that arises in the course of jogging simply by engaging in the practice of jogging. As we deal with more and more conditions with more or less awareness, the practice itself will become more elaborated. We will jog, for instance, only when we have thought of a suitable intellectual problem or only in a certain direction. This is only to say that so long as we engage in the practice, we will develop ways of dealing with the wide variety of things that the practice itself opens up to us. There should be little controversial in what I have said so far. I take it that we have all noticed that as we drive or ski or speak in public or teach that we become better at it in ways that go beyond those we explicitly worked at improving. We recognize, for example, that long after we have ceased *trying* to develop our driving skill, we continue improving in smoothing out our ride.

My general point is that practices tend toward their own elaboration. Indeed, that fairly weak and probably uninteresting claim is sufficient for the rest of what I have to say, but I should like to strengthen it because, in its stronger form, its force becomes clearer. I want to say that practices *tend* toward their own elaboration regardless of our explicit intentions. To see that practices have this autonomous tendency, recall that once skills become habitual, they continuously draw us to recognize things relevant to the skill or practice that before we would have passed over. To see that these new recognitions do not depend on the explicit intention to take up the practice, recall that even if I give up jogging, indeed, explicitly and consciously resolve to myself to give up jogging, I will still see this or that trail as looking good for a jog. That is, upon seeing the trail, I will find myself getting my body set to run and wondering where my running shoes are even before realizing that the sight of the trail is enticing me to run. Indeed, I may even realize that the trail enticed me to run at an unaccustomed time, and hence the jogging practice that I sought to curtail was becoming further elaborated despite my intention. Of course, once I catch myself, I will refocus my attention, following whatever practice I have for dealing with irrelevant solicitations to act, and gradually I will become desensitized to attractive running trails. But so long as I have the jogging skill, I will be guided, both with awareness *and without*, by its tendency toward further elaboration of itself.

The question of how to characterize this phenomenon of elaboration has exercised a relatively small number of philosophers. The greatest difference on this point is between Derrida and Heidegger. Derrida argues that the tendency toward elaboration generally involves the production of new ways of deploying a practice that are, in a certain way, discontinuous with the older ways of deploying it. Elaboration is, then, for Derrida, dispersive or disseminating. In contrast, Heidegger argues that this elaboration generally produces a better articulated core practice which we may think of, then, as having a stable (though not a fixed) nature. For Heidegger, then, elaboration is articulative. He sometimes speaks of this articulative nature of practices as gathering and later as *Ereignis*. In developing the Derridian and Heideggerian arguments, we shall see that an account of the nature of elaboration determines whether the stability of things is some sort of imposition that runs against the nature of practice or is the regular tendency of practice. When one considers instituted forms of life such as gender, one can see that arguing for the instability or stability of practices will have large politicoethical consequences.

Dispersion: Derrida on the general tendency of practices

It may seem perverse to connect Derrida to practices. Derrida is associated with deconstructions of structural systems of difference. But, from quite early in his career, Derrida claimed that writing, which for him was a paradigmatic activity for undermining logocentric meaning, and practice were functional equivalents. Practice understood in its ontological structure was the appropriate notion for upsetting the philosophical opposition between theory and practice just as writing understood in its ontological structure was appropriate to upsetting the opposition between speech and writing (Derrida 1981a: 4). More recently, he has claimed that the language system is itself grounded in practices of exchange and that the gift serves the same deconstructive function in social practices generally that writing served in deconstructing metaphysical thinking (Derrida 1992: 80–1).

Since Derrida's claim that practices tend to disperse is less well known than is Heidegger's opposite claim, the argument for it will be deployed in two stages. Leaving out nuances, I will speak of the 'Derridian' argument. First, the Derridian argues for a special sort of externalist decisionism that defeats the Wittgensteinian confidence that habitual practices themselves are sufficient for recognizing stable kinds of things and projecting old meanings into new situations. Second, the Derridian shows that this externalist aspect of practical behavior, which makes practices insufficient for recognizing stable kinds, plays an active role in all of our practical comportments. It is in the second half of this argument that we shall see the Derridian account of practices' dispersive kind of elaboration.

In the first stage of his argument, the Derridian tries to bring out cases where the habitual practices that constitute a context are not sufficient for deciding what some seemingly common kind of thing is. That is to say, habitual practices alone do not determine how we should deal with something familiar. To take a simple case, we may ask if an instance of a door is still an instance of that type when we put it on top of crates and start using it as a desk? Our intuition that the desktop is no longer a door is probably only a little stronger, if it is any stronger at all, than our intuition that it remains a door. To see this, we could change the simple everyday context we start with by weighting more and more details that would strengthen one or the other intuition. We could, for instance, give weight to our sense that the something's origin counts in determining its nature by imagining that we are living in a house full of heirlooms. Or we could add weight to our sense that the function of something determines its nature by imagining that this 'door–desktop' appears in a modern business setting where efficiency is all that counts. The point is to see that we can always give good reasons for giving added weight to considerations that would shift our intuitions concerning this 'door–desktop.'[3]

In these cases where we can give good reasons for seeing something as an instance of either of two incompatible types such as a door or a desktop, we should also see that the way of handling such instances is by an imposition (that could have been directed differently). We run into such impositions in ordinary life when we find that the dissenting opinions of court justices are as compelling as the majority opinions or whenever we, ourselves, must act on very weak intuitions. What determines which type (or law) an instance falls under in such vexed cases is not some determinate detail of the thing or situation. Instead, a determination is made by a speech community (or someone in the authoritative position in the speech community)[4] as to whether the thing will be handled as this or that type of thing.[5] In these kinds of cases, although the context of practices circumscribes the range of the decision, the context of practices alone will not determine under which specific type a given instance falls. To recur to our simple example, in the simple everyday context, no practice will clearly determine whether we have a desktop or a door. But, once the speech community or its representative decides the matter, then we will retrospectively see the situation as a whole in accord with the decision.

So far, though, the Derridian has merely argued that our way of acting *may* include cases where habitual practices do not determine how we deal with something. A decision is then required. To show that the number of such cases is indefinitely large, the Derridian draws on the notion of citationality. *Citationality* is a characteristic of *entities*, namely that they may but need not be taken as instances of the same type in an indefinitely large number of contexts.[6] This property enables people to ask the question: is this entity, which we recognized as an instance of type X in context A still an instance of type X now that we are in context B?[7] And citationality allows that entities that are instances of types may be intelligibly imported with appropriate changes into as many contexts as can be imagined. So citationality allows the door to be taken from the context of practices where we normally encounter it – entering a dwelling – and inserted into such contexts of practices as those for dealing with tables, artworks, and philosophers' examples. And, of course, an indefinitely large number of contexts can be imagined.[8] We only need imagine John Searle asking us about doors inside a whale's stomach to see how far citationality can take us and how unlimited its range is.

But even if there are an indefinitely large number of citationally possible contexts in which practices alone could not tell us how to deal with seemingly common things like doors, one might still argue that Derridian decisionism or imposition is parasitic on situations where habitual practices do succeed in unproblematically determining how to handle something familiar. I take it that a Wittgensteinian would say that if in the cases where imposition occurs, there is a clear choice between two types, then these cases of imposition depend upon the unproblematic cases that determine which types to consider. Consequently, the cases of imposition are logically dependent on the unproblematic, clear cases.[9] That is, one could not recognize the problematic case requiring an imposition if one did not already have the unproblematic cases.

The Derridian, however, believes that, even if there are moments where habitual practices enable determinations without decisions, his arguments show that we have no grounds for attributing logical priority to them. His account of difficult instances where ways of dealing with things must be imposed is supposed to demonstrate that the habitual ways of dealing with things not only underdetermine possible future applications but also underdetermine all our seemingly stable past ways of dealing with things. To see this, we must look to the retrospective nature of impositions.[10] After the fact of any imposition, previous cases are retroactively transformed so as to appear to determine the present case. The second stage of the Derridian argument takes up *why* this reinterpretation of the past takes place. *That* it takes place we may see by reminding ourselves that this kind of revisioning frequently happens when important laws change. In the United States, for instance, when the judicial determination in *Plessy* v. *Ferguson* was the law of the land, then race relations, civil rights, the constitution, and most social situations were generally taken to support the doctrine of separate but equal. Citizenship at its best was, by and large, just seen as in support of *Plessy*. But when the judicial determination of *Brown* v. *Board of Education* came to rule, then the nature of civil rights, the constitution, most social situations, and even being a good citizen were seen by most as supporting the new *Brown*-type equality. At least one of these judicial decisions must have been an imposition.[11] And, with such an example, we see that a present imposition changes the way we deal with the meaning and implications of past cases as well as future ones. We see our past now according to our impositions. Consequently, habitual applications of types are as conceptually dependent on imposed applications as imposed applications are dependent on habitual ones. The nature of both past and future practice depends equally on both habit and imposition. Hence, there is no logical priority for determinations by habitual practices alone.

But so far the Derridian argument has only made claims about the equal logical priority of handling things through habitual practices and handling them by imposing a practice. In the second stage of the Derridian argument, the Derridian shows *why* impositions take place and thereby shows that making impositions is always active in our practical comportment. If we are regularly imposing types, kinds, and so forth, then our dealing with things is always taking into account the discontinuity implicit in making such impositions; consequently, the elaboration of practices would be dispersive not articulative. And so far as we do not recognize this instability in our ethics and elsewhere, we are acting and thinking against our practical natures.

In developing this view, Derrida starts with what he holds to be a basic tendency of all intentional comportment. 'Intention,' he says,

> necessarily can and should *not* attain the plenitude toward which it nonetheless inevitably tends . . . Whether it is a question of prediscursive experience or of speech acts, plenitude is at once what *orients and endangers* the intentional movement, whether it is conscious or not. There can be no intention that does not tend toward it, but also no intention that attains it (Derrida 1988c: 136–7).

This is to say, in roughly Searlean terms, that any directed human comportment has conditions of satisfaction that it seeks to satisfy.[12] So, if someone tries to open the door, she will meet the conditions of satisfaction if she brings it about in a standard way that the door is opened. This is what it means for an intentional comportment or practice to seek full plenitude. But the Derridian says that practices never achieve this full plenitude. Surely he cannot be saying simply that conditions of satisfaction are never met. Rather, he is claiming that so far as each situation in which a habitual practice is deployed is different from previous situations of its deployment, the conditions of satisfaction will have to be amended to fit the differences between situations. In short, Derrida is starting by noting that practices must elaborate themselves in different situations. Since the conditions of satisfaction of intentional comportments must be modified to fit the differences between situations, no previously established conditions of satisfaction will be *simply* met. But why not say, as Heidegger does, that these developments of conditions of satisfaction are merely extensions or refined articulations of the general conditions of satisfaction already implicit in the practice? It seems fair to say that, at least, sometimes such amendments of the conditions must be precisely such extensions. But Derrida thinks that this sort of analysis does not take our coping with the differences between situations seriously.

To take these differences seriously, we must note the following things: first, we could not describe what we were doing as engaging in a practice we have engaged in before unless we were able to respond to the current situation as *different* from past situations. Second, this differentiation requires that something about the situation single it out from other past situations. Third, as soon as this difference is recognized with awareness or not, we must assume that the issue of citationality is raised. That is, the issue is opened of whether the conditions of satisfaction for doing X in past situations count as the conditions of satisfaction in this situation. Or must the conditions of satisfaction be amended by an imposition? For Derrida, this constant openness to imposition is enough to claim that the practices tend toward dispersion, which is to say that they tend toward impositions which could not be projected from earlier states of the practices. In short, if we are constantly ready to make impositions, then there are differences enough from situation to situation for us regularly to do so. Here is how Derrida makes this point:

> What . . . I call iterability [here read iterability as citationality] is at once that which tends to attain plenitude and that which bars access to it. Through the possibility of repeating every mark as the same it makes way for an idealization that seems to deliver the full presence of ideal objects . . . but this repeatability itself ensures that the full presence of a singularity thus repeated comports in itself the reference to something else, thus rending the full presence that it nevertheless announces. This is why iteration is not simply repetition (Derrida 1988c: 129).

So for Derrida any stability in the practices, any sense that the practices elaborate themselves by articulating implicit possibilities within themselves is itself based upon citationality and hence on the possibility of imposed practices. Deconstruction is really little more than increasing sensitivity to this instability. As Derrida puts it, the 'norms of minimal intelligibility are . . . by essence mobile' (Derrida 1988c: 147).

The consequences of this position are that all ways of making things intelligible are essentially unstable. To put the matter as Derrida does, "deconstruction' is firstly this destabilization on the move in . . . 'the things themselves'" (Derrida 1988c: 147). As an ethical or political matter, it follows that one should become, at least, suspicious of institutions and experiences that tend toward the stability of things. For such institutions and experiences would tend to occlude the way in which our own form of intelligibility works, that is, would tend to occlude the way practices elaborate themselves. Also, those accounts of practice that regard practices as enabling us to have stable if not permanent kinds, according to the Derridian, get it wrong. Stable institutions, like stable practices, are stable because force, which the Derridian usually thinks of as *hegemonic* force, makes them so (Derrida 1988c: 137 and 144). So logocentrism (understanding ourselves as in control of our intentions) repeatedly imposes itself through the violent force of the legal, academic, journalistic, and other ethics-promoting institutions. Since such force goes against the way we make sense of things, it presumably arises out of a warping of practice to further special interests at the expense of intelligibility.

Articulation: Heidegger on the general tendency of practices

As Derrida has noted, the cardinal difference between his view and Heidegger's lies in Heidegger's wholehearted approval of such terms as owning, the proper, and appropriateness in contrast to Derrida's outright rejection of such terms in favor of grafting and dissemination (Derrida 1981b: 54). The simplest way to see the difference in focus would be to start with the example of a craftsperson. For Heidegger, the typical way human intelligibility works is exemplified by the craftsperson's way of making things intelligible. As with the craftsperson learning his craft, for Heidegger, practices tend toward a refinement whose goal is producing a craft product that draws people not only to use it but also to understand better how such products are an important part of their lives. In contrast, in looking at the same craftsperson in order to understand the nature of the intelligibility of things, Derrida would focus on the way the craftsperson has to make her practices clear to materials suppliers, employees, tax assessors, accountants, different kinds of customers, and so forth. Increasing intelligibility does not amount, for Derrida, to refining those practices that will give a product a single, determinate, and cared-for place in the lives of users. Rather, for Derrida, increasing intelligibility amounts to managing all the situations in which the product appears with all the different people who are related to it in various contexts. There is no primordial context of the sort Heidegger would have.

To understand more fully how Heidegger characterizes the way practices tend toward elaboration means seeing more clearly what he meant in the 1950s when he wrote about *Ereignis* as the 'governing force . . . [that] brings all . . . beings each into its own' (Heidegger 1971a: 127). For this sense of *Ereignis* is what I have so far described with the more general term 'articulation.' Bringing something into its own means bringing it into the context of those practices where the purpose that the thing is recognized as serving comes out most clearly and worthily. What does it mean for something's purpose to be brought out most clearly and most worthily? And what counts as the purpose which a thing is recognized as serving?

Answering the second question is relatively easy. Most of the time, the purpose which something (especially a piece of equipment) is recognized as serving is the purpose for which it was created or the purpose it has come to serve in those social contexts where its loss would be felt as severely constraining. So, for instance, a hammer is for hammering. A car is for driving on roads to get from one place to another in the course of daily activities. But we all know that there are lots of other uses for hammers and cars. Hammers can serve as paper weights and weapons. Cars can serve for off-road races, bedrooms, and so forth. But, for Heidegger, we mostly understand equipment as having a chief role along with other minor roles.[13] The same goes for things other than equipment, but their roles are not so obvious. So, for someone who casually walks through the woods, the deer are for contemplation; for the hunter, however, the deer are for hunting; for the farmer, they are pests, and so forth. It follows that what is generally recognized as the purpose of something changes both with history and with the community of people involved. Bicycles, for young wealthy people, are for maintaining one's fitness and racing from coffee shop to coffee shop. Bicycles, for younger or poorer people, may be for getting around town to do chores, or to get to and from school or work, and so forth. But the changes of purpose are not hidden within each micro act of, say, observing a deer but come out as we cross communities or as we move from the traditional to the vanguard in our own communities.

Purposes, then, are fairly simple. What does it mean for something to exist within a set of practices such that its purpose is brought out most clearly and most worthily? A thing's purpose is brought out most clearly when, first, the thing is in a situation where it solicits those practices which can, in fact, be deployed at the time and which enable one to use the thing effectively and familiarly according to recognized norms. A bottle of wine, for instance, solicits practices for savoring and drinking slowly when we are relaxed and at dinner with friends. It may solicit similar practices when we see it in the shop or while we are driving, but we cannot deploy the appropriate practices on those occasions.[14] Second, a thing will have its purpose come out most worthily when the practices it solicits are ones with which we have a great deal of familiarity. Drinking the wine with friends on many occasions establishes these practices as those that are familiar and indeed embody one of the goods in our lives. This is the kind of familiarity Heidegger has in mind when he is interested in things being brought out in their own.[15] Third, a purpose is brought out clearly and worthily when, for instance, the wine-drinking draws us to express our identities as friends with intensity. That is, we not only feel at home with our fellows but also recognize the vulnerability of our identities as friends as other situations draw us to do things that would make the familiar wine-drinking situation impossible.[16] Fourth, a purpose is brought out clearly and worthily when the thing is able to solicit a general mood that fits with the practices for using it and enables those involved to be attuned to the kinds of distinctions and solicitations that it promotes. The point here is that we may be drinking wine with our friends on a suitable occasion, in the traditional familiar way, and with a sense of the vulnerability of the situation and of our identities to change, but still not feel fully attuned to what is happening. We might be in a sour or nervous mood. The right mood, when it comes, just descends on us.[17] In general, a thing can be said to reveal its purpose most clearly and worthily when the practices that it solicits are important in one's community, make one feel at home in dealing with the thing, enable one to recognize the vulnerability of one's identity, and provoke the right mood for the situation. And a thing's importance to the community, the familiarity with

ch we engage with the thing, the vulnerability of our identity in the situ-
on of engagement, and the appropriate mood all remain relatively stable.

Heidegger calls *Ereignis* this tendency in the practices to bring things into their own in this way. Thus, the practices for dealing with any thing have a kind of telos; they tend to make the thing connected to the rest of a community's life in such a way that the practices and the personal identities involved are taken as worthy. This telos is relational. It depends upon the rest of the practices in a community, the kinds of identities the community supports, the traditions with which people in the community are familiar, and the kinds of uses that the community holds valuable. Also, this telos is only a tendency, or to put it in Heidegger's terms, it is a gentle law (Heidegger 1971a: 128). The tendency can be constrained by all sorts of contingent circumstances. In times of severe economic stress, for instance, practices for sharing wine with friends, perhaps even practices for having friends just could not get off the ground no matter how the wine bottle and past familiarlization solicited that kind of behavior. But, normally, practices are best understood when they are seen as tending towards the local stability provided by the telos. Such thinking suggests that, as practices elaborate themselves, a stable end is implicit in their elaborations.

Under a Heideggerian view, amendments to conditions of satisfaction that are made in response to differences in situations would be made in the light of a thing's overall telos. This stable telos would govern even if a decision had to be imposed regarding which practices to deploy. Thus, this stable telos shows that the differences between situations are normally *not* what is most important. Of course, significant contingent changes might result in a thing soliciting different practices altogether. But then a new telos would be instituted and the gentle law broken. In general, then, while Derrida treats all differences that occur from situation to situation as always important, Heidegger regards them as mostly, but not always, trivial.

Finally, just as the Derridian calls upon us through deconstruction to come into accord with dispersion, the Heideggerian who sees practices as tending to produce local stabilities calls us, in the name of coming into accord with how human intelligibility works, to preserve those stabilities. And, as Derrida notes, this means defending some notions of property and the proper.

Heidegger's articulation over Derrida's dispersion

There is one important reason for preferring the articulative account to the dispersive account. But to become sensitive to it, we must recall a moment in which we have experienced practices bringing something out in its own. Perhaps we all can recall an experience of a family meal where everyone in the family understood at that moment what it meant to be a family member and that eating the dinner and telling the stories of the day made these identities and the practices of sharing food together at the end of the day clear, important, and worthy. Of course, Derrida, too, can give us an account of how central stabilities – like those involving the nuclear family – could seem valuable to us even if their production ran against the general tendency toward dispersion in the practices. Much of Derrida's discussion of hegemonic forces is meant to explain the seeming value of such stabilities. But the Derridian account suggests that our experience of marginal, non-dominant practices should be dispersive and not articulative. But marginal practices infrequently exhibit a dispersive character. Take, for instance, the marginal example that has already been developed of drinking wine with friends. How could the Derridian account make sense of it being beneficial to the logocentric, phallocentric, carnocentric, or other form of Western centrism still active today that the wine gathers friends together as friends? These meetings of friends over wine seem to do nothing to convince us that our intentions are clearly present to us and fully satisfied. Such meetings sometimes do support the clear bounded identities of phallocentrism, but just as often enable displays of feeling that undermine such identities. Perhaps, in the past, such meetings helped us to dominate animals, but one does not think today that drinking wine with friends involves such domination. If anything, such occasions have more kinship with a kind of nearness that merges intentions and identities so that ownership and dominance are lost rather than anything that fits with one of the hegemonic centrisms Derrida worries about. As a careful reader of Heidegger, Derrida worries about nearness too, but that is because he tends to see it as supporting one of the hegemonies. But though there are no doubt many forms of nearness that do support the various reigning mutually supporting hegemonies, friends gathering to drink wine in no obvious way support this or that current hegemony. Such examples of stabilities that occur when we are engaged in *marginal* practices suggest the superiority of Heidegger's claim that practices usually tend to articulate local stabilities rather than unleash dispersive discontinuities.

On the basis of such marginal situations, a Heideggerian would have us recognize that a telos guides the elaboration of practices around some thing or event. Moreover, the marginality of a practice such as friendship which has never been a central organizing practice in our culture suggests that the telos need not be a trace of some centrism in the general cultural practices that draws us to make impositions of one sort and not another. But, as we noted, Heidegger does not think that the tendency to bring things out in their ownmost is anything more than a tendency. He allows that circumstances override it, but he does not describe such cases. The Derridian analysis can be usefully regarded as an important and fitting addition to Heidegger, one that tells us precisely how such an overriding imposition occurs. A practice engages a new circumstance that cannot be easily accommodated with the considerations of the telos (appropriateness, familiarity, vulnerability, and mood). Hence, an imposition is required, and that imposition is itself retrospectively normalized. Drawing the Derridian account into the Heideggerian account in this way enables the Heideggerian interpreter to account for the development of many new marginal practices and for the discontinuities of change.

The Derridian deconstructionist could reply that all the Heideggerian interpreter has done is uncover the force of a new hegemonic 'centrism' – *Ereignis*, the tendency to bring things out in their ownmost – which has infected Western practice. But to accept this Derridian response requires that we make sense of the revolutionary possibility of dispersive practices giving us the ability to make things and people intelligible without any 'centrism,' telos, or stabilizing practice. While we can conceive of such a Derridian revolutionary possibility, we can ground it only in artistic experiences and in such marginal everyday moments as our experience of shocking moments. For instance, when we find ourselves imposing sense before we can make it in such simple and shocking situations as encountering a fertilized egg or a familiar person in a setting that makes immediate identification difficult. To defend his account, the Derridian would have to go further than allowing that those unusual experiences of change could become a little more usual. The Derridian would have to claim that our common experiences of making sense of the world would be of this sort where imposition is common and stability is rare. For these reasons, it is much more plausible to incorporate the Derridian insights into the Heideggerian interpretation and conceive of stability coming from some aspect of our everyday practices, with breaks in stability arising from the imposed responses to radically unusual contingency to which Derrida draws our attention.

Notes

1   In using the term 'improvisational,' I am recurring to Bourdieu's example of the gift-giving master who is able, in a situation full of unusual contingencies, to act against his habitual training in a completely unusual way and yet be recognized by the community as having done exactly the right thing to preserve both his status and the traditional practice of gift-giving itself. I take it that this improvisation shows that practices are more like skills than habits or habitual dispositions and that they are not in the possession of any individual. For many circumstances – some beyond the master's control – had to line up for the master gift-giver's innovative act to count the giving of a gift. And unless it is recognized as such, the action would not have produced a change in the *gift-giving* practice. See Bourdieu (1990: 98–111, esp. 107).

2   I imagine this on the model of discovering that we have without any awareness developed the distance standing practices typical of our culture.

3   If the example of the 'door–desktop' seems too far-fetched, try considering those cases of 'jokes' that we hesitate to call jokes. I have in mind the case of a public speaker who tells what one imagines he intended as a joke but which not only fails to be funny but is offensive. Is such a humorless offense still a joke? In situations in which such things have occurred – everyday situations – such things have an as undecidable nature as I have tried to claim for the door–desktop. But, if we say that we are going to look at matters strictly in terms of speaker intention, then we can get a clearer intuition of whether the speech act was a joke or not. Also, if we focus on success alone, we can also get a clearer intuition about the speech act. Again, if we focus on listeners' responses, we might be able to get a relatively stronger intuition. But in our simple everyday world, we do not usually give added weight to one of these ways of considering things. If it comes about that we in our

community come up with a determinate way of handling such 'jokes,' it will be due very likely to an imposition, not to some newly discovered detail of that kind of speech act.

4 Derrida sometimes names those in authoritative positions responsible for fixing contexts and determining meaning 'the police' (Derrida 1988b: 105 and 1988c: 134–7). When he speaks of his own fixing of contexts, Samuel Weber translates Derrida's term by the English 'impose' (Derrida 1988b: 103 and 1988c: 137, 145, 149), but when Derrida speaks of the police in general fixing contexts and meaning, he calls the act, again following Weber, a 'performative operation' (Derrida 1988c: 132).

5 See Burge (1979: 73–121) for a well-known analytic form of social externalism which meshes well with Derrida's externalism. Burge argues that the content of concepts such as arthritis is fixed by the authoritative experts in the community.

6 Derrida sometimes speaks as though citationality were another word for iterability as in, 'This citationality, this duplication or duplicity, this iterability of the mark is neither an accident nor an anomaly' (Derrida 1988b: 12 and 1988c: 119). But, more commonly, he thinks of citationality in terms of normal citing – taking the exact words written or spoken in one context and entering them into another context with quotation marks around them – or in terms of grafting, both of which involve dealing with things as simple entities or instances of types, not as types (Derrida 1988a: 12).

7 I think that the distinction between these two characteristics offers a powerful tool for understanding intelligibility. I would claim, following Merleau-Ponty, that if organisms could not recognize *instances of the same type* in many different contexts, they would not have any intelligence at all. If they could not recognize the same *entity* as potentially an instance of a different type in various contexts, they would not have *human* or *higher mammal* intelligence (where the precise line is drawn between human and animal intelligence is a matter for empirical research). See Merleau-Ponty (1983: 175).

8 There are a number of ways to use citationality to defend the claim that one can construct an indefinitely large number of situations. Since citationality enables the grafting of anything into any context and even contexts into contexts, an indefinitely large number of contexts are producible in precisely the same way an indefinitely large number of sentences are producible by recursively using the rules of syntax. Alternatively, so long as human beings go on with individual perspectives – which is to say so long as human intelligibility goes on – then each individual human perspective counts as a new context into which anything may be imaginatively cited.

9 I am using 'logical dependence' in the way Searle used it against Derrida. In explaining the logical dependence of fiction on serious discourse, Searle says, 'One could not have the concept of fiction without the concept of serious discourse.' See Searle (1977: 207).

10 In the controversy that has accompanied Derrida, few have taken the time to point out that Derridian *in*determinacy of meaning (that we cannot completely understand what we mean) follows from the retrospective nature of *under*determination (that we cannot project our meanings into all relevant situations).

11 In his writing on the law, Derrida elaborates the way undecidability occurs and is resolved. See Derrida (1990: 967). Derrida, of course, neither claims that all decisions an actual judge makes are impositions nor that all impositions judges have made can in retrospect be justified. Cases of 'undecidability' occur when the context and types involved imply more than one way of applying the crucial types. Of course, a judge could be so befogged as to follow neither line of implication. But, for Derrida, the cases where we see justice enacted are precisely the ones where a narrowly constrainted imposition occurs.

12   Of course, the conditions of satisfaction of intentionality are not the same as psychological conditions of satisfaction. But so far as intentionality is understood to refer to the way we are directed to things, it refers to a relationship or a comportment to things which can fail in various ways. And that failure cannot just mean that some state of affairs is not in accord with some propositional content, but that a way of relating to the world or of comporting oneself to the world is undermined. Intending, generally, even mere seeing things under an aspect, can always go wrong as a way of being related to the world. For this reason, being directed toward something seeks satisfaction.

13   What I have said here amounts to taking a stand on a rather ambiguous point in *Being and Time* (Heidegger 1962). It may be that Heidegger understands pieces of equipment strictly in terms of their roles. So a hammer used as a paper weight would then be a paper weight. In this way, pieces of equipment are intelligible according to the kind of behavior they afford. In general, I think that the text militates against such an interpretation, but the main points of this paper would remain unchanged regardless of one's stand on this question.

14   This is an interpretation of how a thing thinging gathers what Heidegger calls sky. See Heidegger (1971b: 149 and 1971c: 178).

15   This is an interpretation of how a thing thinging gathers what Heidegger calls earth. See Heidegger (1971b: 149 and 1971c: 178).

16   This is an interpretation of how a thing thinging gathers us as mortals. See Heidegger (1971b: 150 and 1971c: 1978–9).

17   This is an interpretation of how a thing thinging gathers what Heidegger calls divinities or the blessing of divinities. See Heidegger (1971b: 150 and 1971c: 178).

Bibliography

Agre, P. E. (1994) 'Surveillance and Capture: Two Models of Privacy,' *The Information Society* 10: 101–27.

Alexander, J. (1983) *The Modern Reconstruction of Classical Thought: Talcott Parsons*, Berkeley: University of California Press.

Alexander, J. (1988) *Action and its Environments: Towards a New Synthesis*, New York: Columbia University Press.

Alexander, J. (1995) *Fin de Siècle Social Theory: Relativism, Reduction and the Problem of Reason*, London and New York: Verso.

Alexander, J., Giesen, B., Munch, R., and Smelser, N. J. (eds) (1987) *The Micro–Macro Link*, Los Angeles: University of California Press.

Alford, C. F. (1991) *The Self in Social Theory*, New Haven: Yale University Press.

Ambrose, A. (1979) *Wittgenstein's Lectures, Cambridge 1932–35. From the Notes of Alice Ambrose and Margaret MacDonald*, Chicago: University of Chicago Press.

Anscombe, E. (1976) 'The Question of Linguistic Idealism,' *Acta Philosophica Fennica* 28: 188–215.

Anscombe, E. (1981a) 'On Promising and its Justice, and Whether it Need be Respected in *Foro Intemo*,' in E. Anscombe, *Collected Philosophical Papers*, vol. 3, Oxford: Blackwell.

Anscombe, E. (1981b) 'Rules, Rights and Promises,' in E. Anscombe, *Collected Philosophical Papers*, vol. 3, Oxford: Blackwell.

Armstrong, E. (1995) 'Multiplying Identities: Identity Elaboration in San Francisco's Lesbian/Gay Organizations, 1964–1994,' paper presented to the American Sociological Association, Washington DC.

Armstrong, E. (forthcoming) *Multiplying Identities: The Transformation of the Lesbian/ Gay Community in San Francisco, 1960–1994*, Chicago: University of Chicago Press.

Asaro, P. (2000) 'Transforming Society by Transforming Technology: The Science and Politics of Participatory Design,' to appear in *Accounting, Management and Information Technology*.

Baas, B. (1996) 'Die phänomenologische Ausarbeitung des Objekts a: Lacan mit Kant und Merleau-Ponty,' *Riss* 1: 19–60.

Baird, D. (1993) 'Analytical Chemistry and the 'Big' Scientific Instrumentation Revolution,' *Annals of Science* 50: 267–90.

Baker, G. P. and Hacker, P. M. S. (1984) *Scepticism, Rules and Language*, Oxford: Blackwell.

Baldwin, J. M. (1973) *Social and Ethical Interpretations of Mental Development*, New York: Arno Press.

Barad, K. (1996) 'Meeting the Universe Halfway. Realism and Social Constructivism Without Contradiction,' in L. Nelson and J. Nelson (eds) *Feminism, Science, and the Philosophy of Science*, Dordrecht: Kluwer, 161–94.

Barnes, B. (1983) 'Social Life as Bootstrapped Induction,' *Sociology* 4: 524–45.

Barnes, B. (1988) *The Nature of Power*, Urbana IL: Illinois University Press.

Barnes, B. (1995) *The Elements of Social Theory*, Princeton NJ: Princeton University Press.

Barnes, B. (2000) *Understanding Agency: Social Theory and Responsible Action*, Thousand Oaks CA: Sage.

Barnes, B. et al. (1996) *Scientific Knowledge: A Sociological Analysis*, Chicago: University of Chicago Press.

Baudrillard, J. (1988a) 'On Seduction,' in *Jean Baudrillard: Selected Writings*, ed. M. Poster, Stanford: Stanford University Press, 149–65.

Baudrillard, J. (1988b) *America*, New York: Verso.

Bauman, Z. (1989) *Modernity and the Holocaust*, Cambridge: Polity Press.

Baxandall, M. (1972) *Painting and Experience in Fifteenth Century Italy*, Oxford: Oxford University Press.

Baxandall, M. (1985) *Patterns of Intention: On the Historical Explanation of Pictures*, New Haven: Yale University Press.

Beck, U. (1992) *Risk Society: Towards a New Modernity*, London: Sage.

Becker, H. S. (1982) *Art Worlds*, Berkeley: University of California Press.

Bell, D. (1973) *The Coming of Post-Industrial Society: A Venture in Social Forecasting*, New York: Basic Books.

Bellah, R. N. (1968) 'Civil Religion in America,' in W. G. McLoughlin and R. N. Bellah (eds) *Religion in America*, Boston: Houghton Mifflin.

Bellah, R. N., Madsen, R., Sullivan, W. M., Swidler, A., and Tipton, S. M. (1985) *Habits of the Heart: Individualism and Commitment in American Life*, Berkeley: University of California Press.

van den Belt, H. and Rip, A. (1987) 'The Nelson–Winter–Dosi Model and Synthetic Dye Chemistry,' in Wiebe Bijker, Thomas P. Hughes, and Trevor Pinch (eds) *The Social Construction of Technological Systems: New Directions in the Sociology and History of Technology*, Cambridge MA: MIT Press, 135–58.

Bénatouïl, T. (1999) 'Comparing Sociological Strategies; the Critical and the Pragmatic Stance in French Contemporary Sociology,' *European Journal of Social Theory*, special issue 'Contemporary French Social Theory' 2 (3): 379–96.

Bender, T. (1978) *Community and Social Change in America*, New Brunswick: Rutgers University Press.

Beniger, J. R. (1986) *The Control Revolution*, Cambridge MA: Harvard University Press.

Benjamin, W. (1968) 'The Work of Art in the Age of Mechanical Reproduction,' in *Illuminations*, New York: Harcourt Brace Jovanovich, 217–51.

Berger, P., Berger, B., and Kellner, H. (1974) *The Homeless Mind. Modernization and Consciousness*, New York: Vintage Books.

Bernal, J. D. (1953) 'Science, Industry and Society in the Nineteenth Century,' in S. Lilley (ed.) *Essays on the Social History of Science*, special issue of *Centaurus* 3 (1–2): 138–65.

Berque, A. (1986) *Le sauvage et l'artifice. Les Japonais devant la nature*, Paris: Gallimard.

Biernacki, R. (1995) *The Fabrication of Labor: Germany and Britain, 1640–1914*, Berkeley: University of California Press.

Bijker, W. (1995) *Of Bicycles, Bakelites, and Bulbs: Toward a Theory of Sociotechnical Change*, Cambridge MA: MIT Press.

Bittner, E. (1965) 'The Concept of Organization,' *Social Research* 32: 239–55.

Blattner, W. D. (1994) 'Is Heidegger a Kantian Idealist?,' *Inquiry* 37:185–201.

Blattner, W. D. (1995) 'Decontextualization, Standardization, and Deweyian Science,' *Man and World* 28: 321–39.

Bloor, D. (1983) *Wittgenstein. A Social Theory of Knowledge*, New York: Columbia University Press; London: Macmillan.

Bloor, D. (1991) *Knowledge and Social Imagery*, 2nd edn, Chicago: University of Chicago Press.

Bloor, D. (1996a) 'Idealism and the Sociology of Knowledge,' *Social Studies of Science* 26: 834–55.

Bloor, D. (1996b) 'The Question of Linguistic Idealism Revisited,' in H. Sluga and D. Stern (eds) *The Cambridge Companion to Wittgenstein*, Cambridge: Cambridge University Press.

Bloor, D. (1997) *Wittgenstein: Rules and Institutions*, London: Routledge.

Blumenberg, H. (1983) *The Legitimacy of the Modern World*, trans. Robert M. Wallace, Cambridge MA: MIT Press.

Blumer, H. (1969) *Symbolic Interactionism: Perspective and Method*, Englewood Cliffs NJ: Prentice Hall.

Boli-Bennett, J. (1979) 'The Ideology of Expanding State Authority in National Constitutions, 1870–1970,' in J. Meyer and M. Hannan (eds) *National Development and the World System*, Chicago: University of Chicago Press.

Boltanski, L. (1990) *L'amour et la justice comme compétences*, Paris: Métailié.

Boltanski, L. (1999) *Distant Suffering: Morality, Medias and Politics*, trans. Graham Burdell, Cambridge: Cambridge University Press.

Boltanski, L. and Thévenot, L. (1991) *De la justification*, Paris: Gallimard.

Boltanski, L. and Thévenot, L. (1999) 'The Sociology of Critical Capacity,' *European Journal of Social Theory*, special issue 'Contemporary French Social Theory' 2(3): 359–77.

Borck, C. (1997) 'Herzstrom,' in V. Hess (ed.) *Die Normierung von Gesundheit. Messende Verfahren der Medizin als kulturelle Praxis*, Wulfsfurt: Matthiesen.

Bourdieu, P. (1972) *Esquisse d'une théorie de la pratique*, Paris and Geneva: Droz.

Bourdieu, P. (1977) *Outline of a Theory of Practice*, trans. Richard Nice, Cambridge: Cambridge University Press.

Bourdieu, P. (1984) *Distinction: A Social Critique of the Judgement of Taste*, trans. Richard Nice, Cambridge MA: Harvard University Press.

Bourdieu, P. (1990) *The Logic of Practice*, trans. Richard Nice, Stanford: Stanford University Press.

Bowker, G. (1994) *Science on the Run: Information Management and Industrial Geophysics at Schlumbeiger, 1920–1940*, Cambridge MA: MIT Press.

Bowker, G., Star, S. L., Turner, B., and Gasser, L. (1996) *Social Science, Technical Systems, and Cooperative Work*, Princeton NJ: L. J. Erlbaum.

Brandom, R. (1979) 'Freedom and Constraint by Norms,' *American Philosophical Quarterly* 16: 187–96.

Brandom, R. (1994) *Making it Explicit: Reasoning, Representing, and Discursive Commitment*, Cambridge MA: Harvard University Press.

Bréviglieri, M. (1997) 'La coopération spontanée. Entraides techniques autour d'un automate public,' in B. Conein and L. Thévenot (eds) *Cognition et information en société*, Paris: Ed. de l'Ecole des Hautes Etudes en Sciences Sociales (Raisons pratiques 8), 123–48.

Bréviglieri, M. (1998) 'L'usage et l'habiter,' sociology dissertation, Ecole des Hautes Etudes en Sciences Sociales, Paris.

Buck, P. (1985) 'Adjusting to Military Life: The Social Sciences Go to War, 1941–1950,' in M. R. Smith (ed.) *Military Enterprise and Technological Change: Perspectives on the American Experience*, Cambridge MA: MIT Press, 203–52.

Burge, T. (1979) 'Individualism and the Mental,' *Midwest Studies in Philosophy* 4: 73–121.

Callon, M. (1986) 'Some Elements of a Sociology of Translation: Domestication of the Scallops and Fishermen of St. Brieuc Bay,' in J. Law (ed.) *Power, Action and Belief: A New Sociology of Knowledge?*, London: Routledge.

Callon, M. and Latour, B. (1981) 'Unscrewing the Big Leviathan,' in K. Knorr Cetina and A. Cicourel (eds) *Advances in Social Theory and Methodology*, Boston: Routledge and Kegan Paul, 277–303.

Callon, M. and Latour, B. (1992) 'Don't Throw the Baby Out with the Bath School,' in A. Pickering (ed.) *Science as Practice and Culture*, Chicago: University of Chicago Press.

Callon, M. and Law, J. (1989) 'On the Construction of Sociotechnical Networks: Content and Context Revisited,' in L. Hargens, R. A. Jones, and A. Pickering (eds) *Knowledge and Society: Studies in the Sociology of Science, Past and Present*, vol. 8, Greenwich CT: JM Press, 57–83.

Cambrosio, A. and Keating, P. (1988) 'Going Monoclonal: Art, Science, and Magic in the Day-to-Day Use of Hybridoma Technology,' *Social Problems* 35: 244–60.

Cancian, F. M. (1975) *What are Norms? A Study of Beliefs and Action in a Maya Community*, Cambridge: Cambridge University Press.

Cartwright, N. (1983) *How the Laws of Physics Lie*, Oxford: Oxford University Press.

Cawelti, J. G. (1976) *Adventure, Mystery, and Romance: Formula Stories as Art and Popular Culture*, Chicago: University of Chicago Press.

Cerbone, D. R. (1995) 'World, World-entry, and Realism in Early Heidegger,' *Inquiry* 38: 401–21.

de Certeau, M. (1990) *L'invention du quotidien*, vol. 1: *Arts de faire*, new edn, ed. and intro. Luce Giard (1st edn 1980), Paris: Gallimard.

Cerulo, K. A. (1995) *Identity Designs: The Sights and Sounds of a Nation*, New Brunswick: Rutgers University Press.

Cicourel, A. (1968) *The Social Organization of Juvenile Justice*, New York: Wiley.

Cicourel, A. (1974a) *Cognitive Sociology: Language and Learning in Social Interaction*, Harmondsworth: Penguin.

Cicourel, A. (1974b) *Theory and Method in a Study of Argentine Fertility*, New York: Wiley.

Collier, J. F. (1997) *From Duty to Desire: Remaking Families in a Spanish Village*, Princeton NJ: Princeton University Press.

Collins, H. M. (1974) 'The TEA Set: Tacit Knowledge and Scientific Networks,' *Science Studies* 4: 165–86; reprinted (1999) in M. Bagioli (ed.) *The Science Studies Reader*, New York and London: Routledge, 95–109.

Collins, H. M. (1990) *Artificial Experts: Social Knowledge and Intelligent Machines*, Cambridge MA: MIT Press.

Collins, H. M. (1992) *Changing Order: Replication and Induction in Scientific Practice*, Chicago: University of Chicago Press; 1st edn 1985, Beverly Hills and London: Sage.

Collins, H. M. (1998) 'Socialness and the Undersocialised Conception of Society,' *Science, Technology and Human Values* 23 (4): 494–516.

Collins, H. M. and Kusch, M. (1995a) 'Automating Airpumps: An Empirical and Conceptual Analysis,' *Technology and Culture* 36 (4): 802–29.

Collins, H. M. and Kusch, M. (1995b) 'Two Kinds of Actions: A Phenomenological Study,' *Philosophy and Phenomenological Research* 55 (4): 799–819.

Collins, H. M. and Kusch, M. (1998) *The Shape of Actions: What Humans and Machines Can Do*, Cambridge MA: MIT Press.

Collins, H. M. and Pinch, T. J. (1993) *The Golem: What Everyone Needs to Know About Science*, Cambridge and New York: Cambridge University Press.

Collins, H. M. and Yearley, S. (1992) 'Epistemological Chicken,' in A. Pickering (ed.) *Science as Practice and Culture*, Chicago: University of Chicago Press, 301–26.

Collins, R. (1981) 'On the Microfoundations of Macrosociology,' *American Journal of Sociology* 86: 984–1014.

Conein, B. (1997) 'L'action avec les objets. Un autre visage de l'action située?,' in B. Conein and L. Thévenot (eds) *Cognition et information en société*, Paris: Ed. de l'Ecole des Hautes Etudes en Sciences Sociales (Raisons pratiques 8), 25–45.

Conein, B. and Jacopin, E. (1993) 'Les objets dans l'espace; la planification dans l'action,' in B. Conein, N. Dodier, and L. Thévenot (eds) *Les objets dans l'action*, Paris: Ed. de l'Ecole des Hautes Etudes en Sciences Sociales (Raisons pratiques 4), 59–84.

Conein, B. and Thévenot, L. (eds) (1997) *Cognition et information en société*, Paris: Ed. de l'Ecole des Hautes Etudes en Sciences Sociales (Raisons pratiques 8).

Conein, B., Dodier, N., and Thévenot, L. (eds) (1993) *Les objets dans l'action*, Paris: Ed. de l'Ecole des Hautes Etudes en Sciences Sociales (Raisons pratiques 4).

Cooper, C. L. and Mumford, E. (eds) (1979) *The Quality of Working Life in Western and Eastern Europe*, Westport CT: Greenwood Press.

Coulter, J. (1982) 'Remarks on the Conceptualization of Social Structure,' *Philosophy of the Social Sciences* 12 (1): 33–46.

Coulter, J. (1989) *Mind in Action*, Atlantic Highlands NJ: Humanities Press International.

Coulter, J. (1991) 'Logic: Ethnomethodology and the Logic of Language,' in G. Button (ed.) *Ethnomethodology and the Human Sciences*, Cambridge: Cambridge University Press, 20–50.

Crothers, D. (1987) 'How to Pot Black with some Angular Momentum and a Touch of Gravity,' *The Guardian*, August 27, 4.

D'Andrade, R. G. (1984) 'Cultural Meaning Systems,' in R. A. Shweder and R. A. LeVine (eds) *Culture Theory: Essays on Mind, Self and Emotion*, Cambridge: Cambridge University Press.

Danto, A. (1965) 'Basic Actions,' *American Philosophical Quarterly* 2 (2): 141–8.

Daston, L. (1994) 'Enlightenment Calculations,' *Critical Inquiry* 21: 182–202.

Davidson, D. (1977) 'The Method of Truth in Metaphysics,' *Midwest Studies in Philosophy* 2: 244–54.

Davidson, D. (1984) 'On the Very Idea of a Conceptual Scheme', 'The Inscrutability of Reference,' and 'What Metaphors Mean,' in *Inquiries into Truth and Interpretation*, Oxford: Clarendon Press, 183–98, 227–41, and 245–64.

Davidson, D. (1986) 'A Nice Derangement of Epitaphs,' in E. Lepore (ed.) *Truth and Interpretation: Essays on the Philosophy of Donald Davidson*, Oxford: Blackwell, 433–46.

Davidson, D. (1991) 'Three Varieties of Knowledge,' in A. P. Griffiths (ed.) *A. J. Ayer, Memorial Essays*, Royal Institute of Philosophy, supplement 30, Cambridge: Cambridge University Press, 153–66.

De Landa, M. (1991) *War in the Age of Intelligent Machines*, New York: Swerve Editions.

Deleuze, G. and Guattari, F. (1987) *A Thousand Plateaus: Capitalism and Schizophrenia*, Minneapolis: University of Minnesota Press.

Dennett, D. (1987) *The Intentional Stance*, Cambridge MA: MIT Press.

Derrida, J. (1981a) *Dissemination*, trans. Barbara Johnson, Chicago: University of Chicago Press.

Derrida, J. (1981b) *Positions*, trans. Alan Bass, Chicago: University of Chicago Press.

Derrida, J. (1988a) 'Signature Event Context,' trans. Samuel Weber and Jeffrey Mehlman, in *Limited Inc.*, Evanston IL: Northwestern University Press.

Derrida, J. (1988b) 'Limited Inc a b c . . .,' trans. Samuel Weber, in *Limited Inc.*, Evanston IL: Northwestern University Press.

Derrida, J. (1988c) 'Afterword,' trans. Samuel Weber, in *Limited Inc.*, Evanston IL: Northwestern University Press.

Derrida, J. (1990) 'Force of Law: The Mystical Foundation of Authority,' *Cardozo Law Review* 11: 919–1045.

Derrida, J. (1992) *Given Time*, trans. Peggy Kamuf, Chicago: University of Chicago Press.

Desrosières, A. (1998) *The Politics of Large Numbers. A History of Statistical Reasoning*, Cambridge MA: Harvard University Press.

Dewey, J. (1960) 'Need for a Recovery of Philosophy,' in R. J. Bernstein (ed.) *On Experience, Nature, and Freedom: Representative Selections*, New York: Bobbs-Merrill, 19–69.

Dodier, N. (1993a) *L'expertise médicale. Essai de sociologie sur l'exercise du jugement*, Paris: Métailié.

Dodier, N. (1993b) 'Action as a Combination of "Common Worlds,"' *Sociological Review* 41 (3): 556–71.

Dodier, N. (1995) *Les Hommes et les machines*, Paris: Métailié.

Dosse, F. (1998) *Empire of Meaning: The Humanization of the Social Sciences*, Minneapolis: University of Minnesota Press.

Dreeben, R. (1968) *On What is Learned in School*, Reading MA: Addison Wesley.

Dreyfus, H. (1972) *What Computers Can't Do*, New York: Harper and Row.

Dreyfus, H. (1991) *Being-in-the-World: A Commentary on Heidegger's Being and Time, Division One*, Cambridge MA: MIT Press; new edn 1995.

Dreyfus, H. (1993) *What Computers Still Can't Do*, Cambridge MA: MIT Press.

Dreyfus, H. and Dreyfus, S. E. (1986) *Mind over Machine: The Power of Human Intuition*, Oxford: Blackwell.

Drucker, P. G. (1993) *Post-Capitalist Society*, New York: HarperCollins.

Easterbrook, S. (ed.) (1993) *CSCW: Cooperation or Conflict?*, London: Springer-Verlag.

Eglin, P. and Hester, S. (1992) 'Category, Predicate and Task: The Pragmatics of Practical Action,' *Semiotica* 88 (34): 243–68.

Eliasoph, N. (1998) *Avoiding Politics: How Americans Produce Apathy in Everyday Life*, Cambridge: Cambridge University Press.

Elichirigoity, I. (1999) *Planet Management: Limits to Growth, Computer Simulation, and the Emergence of Global Spaces*, Evanston IL: Northwestern University Press.

Fell, J. P. (1992) 'The Familiar and the Strange: On the Limits of Praxis in Early Heidegger,' in H. L. Dreyfus and H. Hall (eds) *Heidegger: A Critical Reader*, Oxford: Blackwell.

Fine, A. (1986) *The Shaky Game*, Chicago: University of Chicago Press.

Fleck, L. (1979) *Genesis and Development of a Scientific Fact*, Chicago: University of Chicago Press.

Føllesdal, D. (1986) 'Essentialism and Reference,' in *The Library of Living Philosophers*, vol. 18: *The Philosophy of W. V. Quine*, La Salle IL: Open Court.

Føllesdal, D. (1996) 'Conceptual Change and Reference,' *Cognitio humana – Dynamik des Wissens und der Werte*, XVII Deutscher Kongreß für Philosophie, Leipzig, September 23–27, 1996, lectures and colloquiums, ed. Christoph Hubig.

Foucault, M. (1965) *Madness and Civilization: A History of Insanity in the Age of Reason*, trans. R. Howard, New York: Random House.

Foucault, M. (1975) *Surveiller et punir*, Paris: Gallimard.

Foucault, M. (1976) *The Archaeology of Knowledge*, trans. A. M. Sheridan Smith, New York: Harper and Row.

Foucault, M. (1978) *The History of Sexuality*, vol. 1, trans. R. Hurley, New York: Pantheon.

Foucault, M. (1979) *Discipline and Punish*, trans. Alan Sheridan, New York: Vintage.

Foucault, M. (1980) *Power/Knowledge*, ed. Colin Gordon, New York: Pantheon.

Foucault, M. (1983) 'Afterword: The Subject and Power,' in H. Dreyfus and P. Rabinow (eds) *Michel Foucault: Beyond Structuralism and Hermeneutics*, 2nd edn, Chicago: University of Chicago Press.

Frisby, D. and Sayer, D. (1986) *Society*, New York: Tavistock–Horwood–Methuen.

Fujimura, J. (1992) 'Crafting Science: Standardized Packages, Boundary Objects, and "Translations,"' in A. Pickering (ed.) *Science as Practice and Culture*, Chicago: University of Chicago Press, 168–211.

Fulbrook, M. (1983) *Piety and Politics: Religion and the Rise of Absolutism in England, Württemberg, and Prussia*, Cambridge: Cambridge University Press.

Fuller, S. (1989) *Philosophy of Science and its Discontents*, Boulder CO: Westview Press.

Fuller, S. (1992) 'Social Epistemology and the Research Agenda of Science Studies,' in A. Pickering (ed.) *Science as Practice and Culture*, Chicago: University of Chicago Press, 390–428.

Garfinkel, H. (1960) 'Parsons' Primer: Ad Hoc Uses,' unpublished manuscript, Department of Sociology, University of California, Los Angeles.

Garfinkel, H. (1964) 'A Conception of, and Experiments with, "Trust" as a Condition of Stable Concerted Actions,' in O. J. Harvey (ed.) *Motivation and Social Interaction*, New York: Ronald Press, 187–238.

Garfinkel, H. (1967) *Studies in Ethnomethodology*, Englewood Cliffs NJ: Prentice Hall.

Garfinkel, H. (1991) 'Respecification: Evidence for Locally Produced, Naturally Accountable Phenomena of Order, Logic, Reason, Meaning, Method, etc. in and as of the Essential Haecceity of Immortal Ordinary Society (I) – An Announcement of Studies,' in G. Button (ed.) *Ethnomethodology and the Human Sciences*, Cambridge: Cambridge University Press, 10–19.

Garfinkel, H. and Sacks, H. (1970) 'On Formal Structures of Practical Actions,' in J. C. McKinney and E. A. Tiryakian (eds) *Theoretical Sociology: Perspectives and Development*, New York: Appleton-Century-Crofts, 337–66.

Geertz, C. (1973) *The Interpretation of Cultures*, New York: Basic Books.

Geertz, C. (1976) 'Art as a Cultural System,' *Modern Language Notes* 91: 1473–99.

Geison, G. (1995) *The Private Science of Louis Pasteur*, Princeton NJ: Princeton University Press.

Geison, G. (1996) 'Pasteur and the Culture Wars: A Critical Exchange,' *New York Review of Books* 43 (April 4) : 68–9.

Gibbard, A. (1990) *Wise Choices, Apt Feelings: A Theory of Normative Judgment*, Oxford: Clarendon Press.

Giddens, A. (1979) *Central Problems in Social Theory*, Berkeley: University of California Press.

Giddens, A. (1981) *A Contemporary Critique of Historical Materialism*, vol. 1, *Power, Property and the State*, London: Macmillan.

Giddens, A. (1984) *The Constitution of Society*, Berkeley: University of California Press; Cambridge: Polity Press.

Giddens, A. (1990) *The Consequences of Modernity*, Stanford: Stanford University Press.

Giddens, A. (1991) *Modernity and Self-Identity*, Stanford: Stanford University Press.

Goodman, N. (1983) 'The Problem of Counterfactual Conditionals,' Chapter 1 of N. Goodman, *Fact, Fiction, and Forecast*, 4th edn, Cambridge MA: Harvard University Press.

Goffman, E. (1967) *Interaction Ritual: Essays on Face-to-Face Behavior*, Garden City NY: Doubleday.

Goffman, E. (1971) *Relations in Public: Microstudies of the Public Order*, New York: Basic Books.

Greenberg, J. R. and Mitchell, S. A. (1983) *Object Relations in Psychoanalytic Theory*, Cambridge MA: Harvard University Press.

Greenstone, J. D. (1993) *The Lincoln Persuasion: Remaking American Liberalism*, Princeton NJ: Princeton University Press.

Habermas, J. (1981) *Theorie des kommunikativen Handelns*, Frankfurt/M.: Suhrkamp.

Habermas, J. (1984) *The Theory of Communicative Reason*, vol. 1, trans. Thomas McCarthy, Boston: Beacon Press.

Habermas, J. (1987) *The Theory of Communicative Reason*, vol. 2, trans. Thomas McCarthy, Boston: Beacon Press.

Hacking, I. (1983) *Representing and Intervening*, Cambridge: Cambridge University Press.

Haraway, D. (1991) 'A Cyborg Manifesto: Science, Technology, and Socialist-Feminism in the Late Twentieth Century,' in D. Haraway, *Simians, Cyborgs, and Women*, London: Free Association Books, 149–81.

Hartz, L. (1955) *The Liberal Tradition in America*, New York: Harcourt Brace and World.

Haudricourt, A.-G. (1987) *La technologie science humaine*, preface F. Sigaut, Paris: Ed. de la Maison des Sciences de l'Homme.

Haugeland, J. (1990) 'The Intentionality All-Stars,' in J. E. Tomberlin (ed.) *Philosophical Perspectives*, vol. 4: *Action Theory and Philosophy of Mind*, Ataxadero CA: Ridgeview.

Heal, J. (1995) 'Replication and Functionalism,' in M. Davies and T. Stone (eds) *Folk Psychology: The Theory of Mind Debate*, Oxford: Blackwell.

Hegel, G. (1977) *Phenomenology of Spirit*, trans. A. V. Miller, Oxford: Oxford University Press.

Heidegger, M. (1959) *Introduction to Metaphysics*, New Haven: Yale University Press.

Heidegger, M. (1971a) 'The Way to Language,' trans. Peter D. Hertz, in *On the Way to Language*, San Francisco: Harper and Row.

Heidegger, M. (1971b) 'Building Dwelling Thinking,' trans. A. Hofstadter, in *Poetry, Language, Thought*, New York: Harper and Row.

Heidegger, M. (1971c) 'The Thing,' trans. A. Hofstadter, in *Poetry, Language, Thought*, New York: Harper and Row.

Heidegger, M. (1977a) 'What is Metaphysics,' in *Basic Writings*, trans. D. Farrel Krell, New York: Harper.

Heidegger, M. (1977b) 'The Age of the World Picture,' in *The Question Concerning Technology and Other Essays*, trans. W. Lovitt, New York: Harper Torchbooks.

Heidegger, M. (1977c) 'Science and Reflection,' in *The Question Concerning Technology and Other Essays*, trans. W. Lovitt, New York: Harper Torchbooks.

Heidegger, M. (1978) *Being and Time*, trans. J. Macquarie and E. Robinson, Oxford: Blackwell; 1962 edn New York: Harper and Row; 1996 edn, trans. J. Stambaugh, Albany: State University of New York.

Heidegger, M. (1982) *The Basic Problems of Phenomenology*, trans. A. Hofstadter, Bloomington: Indiana University Press.

Heidegger, M. (1984) *Metaphysical Foundations of Logic*, Bloomington: Indiana University Press.

Heidegger, M. (1985a) *The History of the Concept of Time*, Bloomington: Indiana University Press.

Heidegger, M. (1985b) *Gesamtausgabe, Band 61, Phänomenologische Interpretationen zu Aristoteles*, Frankfurt: Vittorio Klostermann.

Hempel, C. (1966) *Philosophy of Natural Science*, Englewood Cliffs NJ: Prentice Hall.

Héran, F. (1987) 'La seconde nature de l'habitus. Tradition philosophique et sens commun dans le langage sociologique,' *Revue Française de Sociologie* XXVIII: 385–416.

Heritage, J. (1984) *Garfinkel and Ethnomethodology*, Cambridge: Polity Press.

Heritage, J. and Atkinson, J. M. (1984) 'Introduction,' in J. M. Atkinson and J. Heritage (eds) *Structures of Social Action: Studies in Conversation Analysis*, Cambridge: Cambridge University Press, 1–15.

Hessen, B. (1971) *The Social and Economic Roots of Newton's 'Principia,'* New York: Howard Fertig.

Hewitt, J. P. (1989) *Dilemmas of the American Self*, Philadelphia: Temple University Press.

Hilbert, R. A. (1990) 'Ethnomethodology and the Micro–Macro Order,' *American Sociological Review* 55: 794–808.

Hilbert, R. A. (1992) *The Classical Roots of Ethnomethodology: Durkheim, Weber and Garfinkel*, Chapel Hill NC: University of North Carolina Press.

Hill, R. J. (1981) 'Attitudes and Behavior,' in M. Rosenberg and R. Turner (eds) *Social Psychology: Sociological Perspectives*, New York: Basic Books.

Horwitz, R. H. (ed.) (1979) *The Moral Foundations of the American Republic*, 2nd edn, Charlottesville: University Press of Virginia.

Inglehart, R. (1977) *The Silent Revolution: Changing Values and Political Styles*, Princeton NJ: Princeton University Press.

Jameson, F. (1991) *Postmodernism, Or, The Cultural Logic of Late Capitalism*, Durham NC: Duke University Press.

Jayyusi, L. (1984) *Categorization and the Moral Order*, Boston: Routledge and Kegan Paul.

Jenkins, S. P. R. (1994) 'Conscious and Unconscious Control in Highly Learned Motor Actions,' Ph.D. dissertation, Department of Experimental Psychology, University of Oxford.

Jepperson, R. L. (1992) 'National Scripts: The Varying Construction of Individualism and Opinion across the Modern Nation-States,' doctoral dissertation, Yale University.

Jirotha, M. and Gognen, J. (eds) (1994) *Requirements Engineering: Social and Technical Issues*, London: Academic Press.

Joas, H. (1993) *Pragmatism and Social Theory*, Chicago: University of Chicago Press.

Jordan, K. and Lynch, M. (1993) 'The Mainstreaming of a Molecular Biological Tool: A Case Study of a New Technique,' in G. Button (ed.) *Technology in Working Order: Studies in Work, Interaction and Technology*, London and New York: Routledge, 160–80.

Kalberg, S. (1994) *Max Weber's Comparative Historical Sociology*, Chicago: University of Chicago Press.

Keesing, R. M. (1974) 'Theories of Culture,' *Annual Review of Anthropology* 3: 73–97, Palo Alto: Annual Reviews Inc.

Knorr Cetina, K. (1981) *The Manufacture of Knowledge. An Essay on the Constructivist and Contextual Nature of Science*, Oxford and New York: Pergamon Press.

Knorr Cetina, K. (1992) 'The Couch, the Cathedral, and the Laboratory: On the Relationship between Experiment and Laboratory in Science,' in A. Pickering (ed.) *Science as Practice and Culture*, Chicago: University of Chicago Press, 113–38.

Knorr Cetina, K. (1993) *Epistemic Cultures: How Scientists Make Sense*, Chicago: University of Chicago Press.

Knorr Cetina, K. (1997) 'Sociality with Objects. Social Relations in Postsocial Knowledge Societies,' *Theory, Culture and Society* 14 (4): 1–30.

Knorr Cetina, K. (1999) *Epistemic Cultures. How the Sciences Make Knowledge*, Cambridge MA: Harvard University Press.

Knorr Cetina, K. and Cicourel, A. V. (eds) (1981) *Advances in Social Theory and Methodology: Toward an Integration of Micro- and Macro-Sociologies*, Boston: Routledge and Kegan Paul.

Knorr Cetina, K. and Mulkay, M. (eds) (1983) *Science Observed: Perspectives on the Social Study of Science*, London and Beverly Hills: Sage.

Krechevsky, I. (1932) 'Hypothesis in Rats,' *Psychological Review* 39: 516–32.

Kripke, S. (1980) *Naming and Necessity*, Cambridge MA: Harvard University Press.

Kripke, S. (1982) *Wittgenstein on Rules and Private Language*, Oxford: Blackwell.

Krohn, W. and Weyer, J. (1994) 'Society as a Laboratory: The Social Risks of Experimental Research,' *Science and Public Policy* 21(3): 173–83.

Kuhn, T. (1970) *The Structure of Scientific Revolutions*, 2nd edn, Chicago: University of Chicago Press.

Kuhn, T. (1977) 'Second Thoughts on Paradigms,' in T. Kuhn, *The Essential Tension*, Chicago: University of Chicago Press.

Lacan, J. (1975) *The Language of the Self*, New York: Dell.

Lacan, J. and Wilden, A. (1968) *Speech and Language in Psychoanalysis*, Baltimore: Johns Hopkins University Press.

Laclau, E. and Mouffe, C. (1985) *Hegemony and Socialist Strategy*, London: Verso.

Lamont, M. (1992) *Money, Morals, and Manners: The Culture of the French and American Upper-Middle Class*, Chicago: University of Chicago Press.

Lash, S. and Urry, J. (1994) *Economies of Signs and Space*, London: Sage.

Latour, B. (1987) *Science in Action: How to Follow Scientists and Engineers through Society*, Cambridge MA: Harvard University Press; Milton Keynes: Open University Press.

Latour, B. (1988) 'Mixing Humans and Nonhumans Together: The Sociology of a Door Closer,' *Social Problems* 35: 298–310.

Latour, B. (1993) *We Have Never Been Modern*, Cambridge MA: Harvard University Press.

Lave, J. (1988) *Cognition in Practice: Mind, Mathematics, and Culture in Everyday Life*, Cambridge: Cambridge University Press.

Law, J. (1998) 'Political Philosophy and Disabled Specificities,' submitted, and at http://www.comp.lancs/ac.uk/sociology/soc026jl.html

Law, J. and Mol, A. (1995) 'Notes on Materiality and Sociality,' *Sociological Review* 43: 274–94.

Lenat, D., Prakash, M., and Shepherd, M. (1986) 'CYC: Using Common Sense Knowledge to Overcome Brittleness and Knowledge Acquisition Bottlenecks,' *AI Magazine* 6 (4): 65–85.

Lenoir, T. (1997) *Instituting Science: The Cultural Production of Scientific Disciplines*, Stanford: Stanford University Press.

Leroi-Gourhan, A. (1964) *Le geste et la parole. Technique et langage*, Paris: Albin-Michel.

Lipset, S. M. (1990) *Continental Divide: The Values and Institutions of the United States and Canada*, New York: Routledge.

Lynch, M. (1985) 'La rétine extériorisé,' *Culture Technique* 14: 109–22.

Lynch, M. (1993) *Scientific Practice and Ordinary Action: Ethnomethodology and Social Studies of Science*, New York and Cambridge: Cambridge University Press.

Lynch, M. (1996) 'Detoxifying the 'Poison Pen' Effect,' in A. Ross (ed.) *Science Wars*, Durham NC: Duke University Press, 238–58.

Lynch, M. and Bogen, D. (1994) 'Harvey Sacks's Primitive Natural Science,' *Theory, Culture and Society* 11: 65–104.

Lyotard, J.-F. (1984) *The Postmodern Condition: A Report on Knowledge*, trans. Geoff Bennington and Brian Massumi, Minneapolis: University of Minnesota Press.

Lyotard, J.-F. (1988) *The Differend: Phrases in Dispute*, trans. Georges Van Den Abbeele, Minneapolis: University of Minnesota Press.

Macbeth, D. (1992) 'Classroom 'Floors': Material Organizations as a Course of Affairs,' *Qualitative Sociology* 15: 123–50.

McGinn, C. (1984) *Wittgenstein on Meaning: An Interpretation and Evaluation*, Oxford: Blackwell.

MacIntyre, A. (1981) *After Virtue*, Notre Dame IN: University of Notre Dame Press; London: Duckworth.

MacKenzie, D. and Spinardi, G. (1995) 'Tacit Knowledge, Weapons Design and the Uninvention of Nuclear Weapons,' *American Journal of Sociology* 101: 44–99.

McNeely, C. L. (1995) *Constructing the Nation State: International Organization and Prescriptive Action*, Westport, CN: Garland Press.

Malpas, J. E. (1992) *Donald Davidson and the Mirror of Meaning*, Cambridge: Cambridge University Press.

Mannheim, K. (1953) 'Conservative Thought,' in K. Mannheim, *Essays on Sociology and Social Psychology*, London: Routledge and Kegan Paul.

Maturana, H. R. and Varela, F. J. (1992) *The Tree of Knowledge: The Biological Roots of Human Understanding*, rev. edn, Boston: Shambala.

Mauss, M. (1927) 'Divisions et proportions des divisions de la sociologie,' *Année Sociologique*, new series 2; republished as 'Division concrète de la sociologie,' in M. Mauss (1971) *Essais de sociologie*, Paris: Editions de Minuit, Col. Points, 42–80.

Mauss, M. (1934) 'Les techniques du corps,' *Journal de Psychologie* XXXII (3–4); republished in M. Mauss (1950) *Sociologie et anthropologie*, intro. C. Lévi-Strauss, Paris: PUF, 365–86.

Mead, G. H. (1934) *Mind, Self and Society*, ed. Ch. W. Morris, Chicago: University of Chicago Press.

Merleau-Ponty, M. (1964) *Le Visible et l'invisible*, followed by *Notes de travail*, ed. Claude Lefort with a note and preface, Paris: Gallimard.

Merleau-Ponty, M. (1983) *The Structure of Behavior*, trans. Alden L. Fisher, Pittsburgh: Duquesne University Press.

Merleau-Ponty, M. (1989) *Le primat de la perception et ses conséquences philosophiques*, Grenoble: Cynara.

Merz, M. (1997) 'Multiplex and Unfolding: Computer Simulation in Particle Physics,' paper presented at the Annual Meeting of the Society for Social Studies of Science, Tucson.

Merz, M. and Knorr Cetina, K. (1997) 'Deconstruction in a 'Thinking' Science,' *Social Studies of Science* 27 (1): 73–111.

Metz, M. H. (1978) *Classrooms and Corridors: The Crisis of Authority in Desegregated Secondary Schools*, Berkeley: University of California Press.

Meyer, J. W. (1987) 'The World Polity and the Authority of the Nation State,' in G. M. Thomas, J. W. Meyer, F. O. Ramirez, and J. Boli, *Constituting State, Society, and the Individual*, Beverly Hills: Sage.

Meyer, J. W. and Rowan, B. (1983) 'Institutionalized Organizations: Formal Structure as Myth and Ceremony,' in J. W. Meyer and W. R. Scott, *Organizational Environments: Ritual and Rationality*, Beverly Hills: Sage.

Meyers, P. (1989) *A Theory of Power: Political not Metaphysical*, Ann Arbor: University of Michigan Press.

Meyers, P. (1991) 'A Partial Answer to the Question 'Why is the Private/Public Distinction Important for Politics?',' paper presented to the Annual Meeting of the American Political Science Association.

Meyers, P. (1995) 'Theses on the Genealogy of the Will,' paper presented to the Annual Meeting of the American Political Science Association.

Meyers, P. (1998) 'The 'Ethic of Care' and the Problem of Power,' *Journal of Political Philosophy* 6 (2): 142–70.

Miller, P. and Rose, N. (1995) 'Production, Identity and Democracy,' *Theory and Society* 24: 427–67.

Mitchell, T. (1991) 'The Limits of the State: Beyond Statist Approaches and their Critics,' *American Political Science Review* 85 (1): 77–96.

Noble, D. F. (1986) *Forces of Production: A Social History of Industrial Automation*, Oxford: Oxford University Press.

Norman, D. (1989) *The Design of Everyday Things*, New York: Doubleday.

Nyiri, J. (1976) 'Wittgenstein's New Traditionalism,' *Acta Philosophica Fennica* 28: 503–12.

Nyiri, J. (1982) 'Wittgenstein's Later Work in Relation to Conservatism,' in M. McGuinness (ed.) *Wittgenstein and his Times*, Oxford: Blackwell.

Oakeshott, M. (1975) *Human Conduct*, Oxford: Clarendon Press.

Oakeshott, M. (1991) *Rationalism in Politics and Other Essays*, Indianapolis: Liberty Press.

Oakeshott, M. (1992) 'The Tower of Babel,' in M. Oakeshott, *Rationalism in Politics and Other Essays*, new and expanded edn, Indianapolis: Liberty Press.

Ortner, S. (1984) 'Theory in Anthropology since the Sixties,' *Comparative Study of Society and History* 16: 126–66.

Oteri, J. S., Weinberg, M. G., and Pinales, M. S. (1982) 'Cross-examination in Drug Cases,' in B. Barnes and D. Edge (eds) *Science in Context: Readings in the Sociology of Science*, Milton Keynes: Open University Press, 250–9.

Parsons, T. (1949) *The Structure of Social Action*, New York: Free Press.

Parsons, T. (1965) 'An Outline of the Social System,' in T. Parsons, E. Shils, K. D. Naegele, and J. R. Pitts (eds) *Theories of Society: Foundations of Modern Sociological Theory*, New York: Free Press, 30–79.

Parsons, T. (1966) *Societies: Evolutionary and Comparative Perspectives*, Englewood Cliffs NJ: Prentice Hall.

Perutz, M. (1995) 'The Pioneer Defended,' *New York Review of Books* 42 (December 21): 54–8.

Pickering, A. (ed.) (1992a) *Science as Practice and Culture*, Chicago: University of Chicago Press.

Pickering, A. (1992b) 'The Rad Lab and the World,' essay review of J. L. Heilbron and R. W. Seidel, *Lawrence and his Laboratory: A History of the Lawrence Berkeley Laboratory*, vol. I (Berkeley: University of California Press, 1989), *British Journal for the History of Science* 25: 247–51.

Pickering, A. (1993) 'The Mangle of Practice: Agency and Emergence in the Sociology of Science,' *American Journal of Sociology* 99: 559–89.

Pickering A. (1995a) *The Mangle of Practice: Time, Agency, and Science*, Chicago: University of Chicago Press.

Pickering, A. (1995b) 'Cyborg History and the World War II Regime,' *Perspectives on Science* 3: 1–48.

Pickering, A. (1997a) 'Time and a Theory of the Visible,' *Human Studies* 20: 325–33.

Pickering, A. (1997b) 'History of Economics and the History of Agency,' in J. Henderson (ed.) *The State of the History of Economics: Proceedings of the History of Economics Society*, London: Routledge, 6–18.

Pickering, A. (1998) 'A Gallery of Monsters: Cybernetics and Self-Organisation, 1940–1970,' talk presented at the weekly seminar of the Dibner Institute for the History of Science and Technology, MIT, December 1, 1998.

Pickering, A. (forthcoming a) 'Units of Analysis: Notes on World War II as a Discontinuity in the Social and Cyborg Sciences,' to appear in Esther-Mirjam Sent and Albert Jolink (eds) *Economists at War: The Influence of the Practice of World War II and the Cold War in the Culture of Economics*.

Pickering, A. (forthcoming b) 'On Becoming: Imagination, Metaphysics and the Mangle,' to appear in Niels Viggo Hansen (ed.) *Time, Heat and Order*.

Pickering, A. (in prep.) 'Synthetic Dyes and Social Theory.'

Pleasants, N. (1996) 'Nothing is Concealed: De-centering Tacit Knowledge and Rules from Social Theory,' *Journal for the Theory of Social Behavior* 26: 233–55.

Polanyi, M. (1958) *Personal Knowledge*, London: Routledge and Kegan Paul; Chicago: University of Chicago Press.

Powell, W. and DiMaggio, P. (1991) *The New Institutionalism in Organizational Analysis*, Chicago: University of Chicago Press.

Rheinberger, H.-J. (1992) 'Experiment, Difference, and Writing: I. Tracing Protein Synthesis,' *Studies in the History and Philosophy of Science* 23 (2): 305–441.

Rheinberger, H.-J. (1994) 'Experimental Systems: Historiality, Deconstruction, and the "Epistemic Thing,"' *Science in Context* 7: 65–81.

Rheinberger, H.-J. (1997) *Towards a History of Epistemic Things: Synthesizing Proteins in the Test Tube*, Stanford: Stanford University Press.

Rheingold, H. (1991) *Virtual Reality*, New York: Simon and Schuster.

Roberts, S. (1981) *Don't Cry, Big Bird*, New York: Random House/Children's Television Workshop.

Rokeach, M. (1973) *The Nature of Human Values*, New York: Free Press.

Rouse, J. (1987) *Knowledge and Power: Toward a Political Philosophy of Science*, Ithaca: Cornell University Press.

Rouse, J. (1991) 'Indeterminacy, Empirical Evidence, and Methodological Pluralism,' *Synthèse* 86: 443–65.

Rouse, J. (1993) 'Foucault and the Natural Sciences,' in J. Caputo and M. Yount (eds) *Foucault and the Critique of Institutions*, State College: Pennsylvania State University Press, 137–62.

Rouse, J. (1994) 'Power/Knowledge,' in G. Gutting (ed.) *The Cambridge Companion to Foucault*, Cambridge: Cambridge University Press, 92–114.

Rouse, J. (1996a) 'Beyond Epistemic Sovereignty,' in P. Galison and D. Stump (eds) *The Disunity of Science: Boundaries, Contexts, and Power*, Stanford: Stanford University Press.

Rouse, J. (1996b) *Engaging Science: How to Understand its Practices Philosophically*, Ithaca: Cornell University Press.

Sacks, H. (1963) 'Sociological Description,' *Berkeley Journal of Sociology* 8: 1–16.

Sacks, H. (1972) 'An Initial Investigation of the Usability of Conversational Data for Doing Sociology,' in D. Sudnow (ed.) *Studies in Social Interaction*, New York: Free Press.

Sacks, H. (1974) 'On the Analyzability of Stories by Children,' in R. Turner (ed.) *Ethnomethodology*, Harmondsworth: Penguin.

Sacks, H. (1979) 'Hotrodder: A Revolutionary Category,' in G. Psathas (ed.) *Everyday Language*, New York: Irvington.

Sacks, H. (1992) *Lectures on Conversation*, vol. 1, ed. Gail Jefferson, Oxford: Blackwell.

Sacks, H. and Schegloff, E. A. (1979) 'Two Preferences in the Organization of Reference to Persons and their Interaction,' in G. Psathas (ed.) *Everyday Language*, New York: Irvington.

Sacks, H., Schegloff, E. A., and Jefferson, G. (1974) 'A Simplest Systematics for the Organization of Turn-Taking in Conversation,' *Language* 50: 696–735.

Sartre, J.-P. (1962) *Sketch for a Theory of the Emotions*, trans. Philip Mairet, London: Methuen.

Savigny, E. von (1988) *The Social Foundations of Meaning*, Berlin: Springer-Verlag.

Schaffer, S. (1994) 'Babbage's Intelligence: Calculating Engines and the Factory System,' *Critical Inquiry* 21: 203–27.

Schatzki, T. (1987) 'Overdue Analysis of Bourdieu's Theory of Practice,' *Inquiry* 30–1: 113–35.

Schatzki, T. (1996) *Social Practices: A Wittgensteinian Approach to Human Activity and the Social*, New York and Cambridge: Cambridge University Press.

Schatzki, T. (1997) 'Practices and Actions: A Wittgensteinian Critique of Bourdieu and Giddens,' *Philosophy and the Social Science* 27 (3): 283–308.

Schatzki, T. and Natter, W. (1996) 'Sociocultural Bodies, Bodies Sociopolitical,' in T. Schatzki and W. Natter (eds) *The Social and Political Body*, New York: Guilford Press.

Schegloff, E. A. (1987) 'Between Micro and Macro: Contexts and other Connections,' in J. Alexander, B. Giesen, R. Münch, and N. Smelser (eds) *The Micro–Macro Link*, Berkeley: University of California Press, 207–34.

Schivelbusch, W. (1986) *The Railway Journey: The Industrialization of Time and Space in the 19th Century*, Berkeley: University of California Press.

Schuman, H. and Johnson, M. P. (1976) 'Attitudes and Behavior,' *Annual Review of Sociology* 2: 161–207.

Searle, J. (1969) *Speech Acts: An Essay in the Philosophy of Language*, Cambridge: Cambridge University Press.

Searle, J. (1995) *The Construction of Social Reality*, New York: Free Press; London: Allan Lane.

Searle, J. (1997) 'Reiterating the Differences: A Reply to Derrida,' *Glyph* 1 (1): 198–208.

Sewell, W. H. Jr (1985) 'Ideologies and Social Revolutions: Reflections on the French Case,' *Journal of Modern History* 57: 57–85.

Sewell, W. H. Jr (1992) 'A Theory of Structure: Duality, Agency, and Transformation,' *American Journal of Sociology* 98: 1–29.

Sewell, W. H. Jr (1996) 'Historical Events as Transformations of Structures: Inventing Revolution at the Bastille,' *Theory and Society* 25: 841–81.

Skocpol, T. (1985) 'Cultural Idioms and Political Ideologies in the Revolutionary Reconstruction of State Power: A Rejoinder to Sewell,' *Journal of Modern History* 57: 86–96.

Smolensky, P., Legendre, G., and Miyata, Y. (1993) 'An Integrating Connectionist and Symbolic Computation for the Theory of Language,' *Current Science* 64: 381–91.

Spinosa, C., Flores, F., and Dreyfus, H. (1996) *Disclosing New Worlds: Entrepreneurship, Democratic Action, and the Cultivation of Solidarity*, Cambridge MA: MIT Press.

Start, S. and Griesemer, J. (1989) 'Institutional Ecology, 'Translations', and Boundary Objects: Amateurs and Professionals in Berkeley's Museum of Vertebrate Zoology, 1907–1939,' *Social Studies of Science* 19: 387–420.

Stehr, N. (1994) *Arbeit, Eigentum und Wissen. Zur Theorie von Wissengesellschaften*, Frankfurt/M.: Suhrkamp.

Stephenson, P. H. (1989) 'Going to McDonald's in Leiden: Reflections on the Concept of Self and Society in the Netherlands,' *Ethos* 17: 226–47.

Stern, D. (1994) *Wittgenstein on Mind and Language*, Oxford: Oxford University Press.

Stinchcombe, A. L. (1959) 'Bureaucratic and Craft Administration of Production: A Comparative Study,' *Administrative Science Quarterly* 4: 168–87.

Sudnow, D. (1978) *Ways of the Hand: The Organization of Improvised Conduct*, Cambridge MA: Harvard University Press.

Swidler, A. (1986) 'Culture in Action: Symbols and Strategies,' *American Sociological Review* 51: 273–86.

Swidler, A. (1992) 'Inequality in American Culture: The Persistence of Voluntarism,' *American Behavioral Scientist* 35: 606–29.

Swidler, A. and Jepperson, R. L. (1994) 'Interpretation, Explanation, and Theories of Meaning,' paper presented to the American Sociological Association, Los Angeles.

Taylor, C. (1985) *Philosophy and the Human Sciences. Collected Papers*, vol. 2, Cambridge: Cambridge University Press.

Thévenot, L. (1984) 'Rules and Implements: Investment in Forms,' *Social Science Information* 23 (1): 1–45.

Thévenot, L. (1989) 'Economie et politique de l'entreprise; économies de l'efficacité et de la confiance,' in L. Boltanski and L. Thévenot (eds) *Justesse et justice dans le travail*, Paris: Presses Universitaires de France et Centre d'Etudes de l'Emploi, 135–207.

Thévenot, L. (1990a) 'L'action qui convient,' in P. Pharo and L. Quéré (eds) *Les formes de l'action*, Paris: Ed. de l'Ecole des Hautes Etudes en Sciences Sociales (Raisons pratiques 1), 39–69.

Thévenot, L. (1990b) 'On Propriety. Conventions and Objects in a Theory of Action,' paper presented at the 'Conventions' conference, Ecole Polytechnique (CREA) and Stanford University, Paris, March 26–28, 1990.

Thévenot, L. (1993) 'Essai sur les objets usuels: propriétés, fonctions, usages,' in B. Conein, N. Dodier, and L. Thévenot (eds) *Les objets dans l'action*, Paris: Ed. de l'Ecole des Hautes Etudes en Sciences Sociales (Raisons pratiques 4), 85–111.

Thévenot, L. (1994a) 'Statistique et politique: la normalité du collectif,' *Politix* 25: 5–20.

Thévenot, L. (1994b) 'Le régime de familiarité; des choses en personnes,' *Genèses* 17: 72–101.

Thévenot, L. (1995a) 'New Trends in French Social Sciences,' *Culture* 9 (2): 1–7.

Thévenot, L. (1995b) 'Rationalité ou normes sociales: une opposition dépassé?,' in L.-A. Gérard-Varet and J.-C. Passeron (eds) *Le Modèle et l'Enquête. Les usages du principe de rationalité dans les sciences sociales*, Paris: Ed. de l'Ecole des Hautes Etudes en Sciences Sociales, 149–89.

Thévenot, L. (1997) 'Le savoir au travail. Attribution et distribution des compétences selon les régimes pragmatiques,' in B. Reynaud (ed.) *Les limites de la rationalité*, vol. 2: *Les Figures du collectif*, Paris: La Découverte, 299–321.

Thévenot, L. (1998) 'Pragmatiques de la connaissance,' in A. Borzeix, A. Bouvier, and P. Pharo (eds) *Sociologie et connaissance. Nouvelles approches cognitives*, Paris: Ed. du CNRS, 101–39.

Thévenot, L. (2001a) 'Which Road to Follow? The Moral Complexity of an 'Equipped' Humanity,' in J. Law and A. Mol (eds) *Complexities in Science, Technology and Medicine*, Durham NC: Duke University Press.

Thévenot, L. (2001b) *Sociologie pragmatique: les régimes d'engagement*, forthcoming.

Thévenot, L., Moody, M., and Lafaye, C. (2000) 'Forms of Valuing Nature: Arguments and Modes of Justification in Environmental Disputes,' forthcoming in M. Lamont and L. Thévenot (eds) *Rethinking Comparative Cultural Sociology: Repertoires of Evaluation in France and the United States*, Cambridge: Cambridge University Press.

Tobin, J. J., Wu, D. Y. H., and Davidson, D. H. (1989) *Preschool in Three Cultures: Japan, China, and the United States*, New Haven: Yale University Press.

Toulmin, S. (1958) *The Uses of Argument*, Cambridge: Cambridge University Press.

Toulmin, S. (1972) *Human Understanding: The Collective Use and Evolution of Concepts*, Princeton NJ: Princeton University Press.

Traweek, S. (1988) *Beamtimes and Lifetimes: The World of High Energy Physicists*, Cambridge, MA and London: Harvard University Press.

Turkle, S. (1984) *The Second Self. Computers and the Human Spirit*, New York: Simon and Schuster.

Turkle, S. (1995) *Life on the Screen*, New York: Simon and Schuster.

Turner, S. (1989) 'Depoliticizing Power,' *Social Studies of Science* 19: 533–60.

Turner, S. (1994) *The Social Theory of Practices: Tradition, Tacit Knowledge, and Presuppositions*, Cambridge: Polity Press; Chicago: University of Chicago Press.

Varenne, H. (1977) *Americans Together: Structured Diversity in a Midwestern Town*, New York: Teacher's College Press.

Varenne, H. (1984) 'Collective Representation in American Anthropological Conversations: Individual and Culture,' *Current Anthropology* 25: 281–99.

Varenne, H. (1987) 'Talk and Real Talk: The Voices of Silence and the Voices of Power in American Family Life,' *Cultural Anthropology* 2: 369–94.

Verba, S. and Orren, G. R. (1985) *Equality in America: The View from the Top*, Cambridge MA: Harvard University Press.

Virilio, P. (1993) 'The Third Interval: A Critical Transition,' in V. A. Conley (ed.) *Rethinking Technologies*, Minneapolis: University of Minnesota Press, 3–12.

Wagner, P. (1994a) *A Sociology of Modernity, Liberty and Discipline*, London: Routledge.

Wagner, P. (1994b) 'Action, Coordination, and Institution in Recent French Debates,' *Journal of Political Philosophy* 2 (3): 270–89.

Wagner, P. (1998) 'Certainty and Order, Liberty and Contingency. The Birth of Social Science as Empirical Political Philosophy,' in J. Heilbron, L. Magnusson, and B. Wittrock (eds) *The Rise of the Social Sciences and the Formation of Modernity: Conceptual Change in Context, 1750–1850*, Dordrecht: Kluwer, 241–63.

Wagner, P. (1999) 'After Justification. Repertoires of Evaluation and the Sociology of Modernity,' *European Journal of Social Theory*, special issue 'Contemporary French Social Theory' 2 (3): 341–57.

Warner, R. S. (1978) 'Towards a Redefinition of Action Theory: Paying the Cognitive Element its Due,' *American Journal of Sociology* 83: 1317–49.

Wartenburg, T. (1990) *The Forms of Power*, Philadelphia: Temple University Press.

Webb, J. (1988) *The Guardian*, March 12, 15.

Weber, M. (1946) 'The Social Psychology of the World Religions,' in H. H. Gerth and C. W. Mills (eds) *From Max Weber*, New York: Oxford University Press.

Weber, M. (1978) *Economy and Society*, trans. E. Fischoff, ed. G. Roth and C. Wittich, Berkeley: University of California Press.

Welsch, W. (1996) 'Aestheticization Processes: Phenomena, Distinction and Prospects,' *Theory, Culture and Society* 13 (1): 1–25.

Wheeler, S. (1991) 'True Figures: Metaphor, Social Relations, and the Sorites,' in D. Hiley, J. Bohman, and R. Shusterman (eds) *The Interpretive Turn*, Ithaca: Cornell University Press, 197–217.

Wiley, N. (1994) *The Semiotic Self*, Chicago: University of Chicago Press.

Wilkinson, J. (1997) 'A New Paradigm for Economic Analysis?,' *Economy and Society* 26 (3): 305–39.

Williams, R. (1973) 'Base and Superstructure in Marxist Cultural Theory,' *New Left Review* 82: 3–16.

Williams, R. (1981) *The Sociology of Culture*, New York: Schoken Books.

Winch, P. (1958) *The Idea of a Social Science and its Relation to Philosophy*, London: Routledge and Kegan Paul; (1965) 4th impression.

Winch, P. (1977) 'Understanding a Primitive Culture,' in F. Dallmayr and T. McCarthy (eds) *Understanding and Social Inquiry*, Notre Dame IN: University of Notre Dame Press.

Wise, N. (1993) 'Mediations: Enlightenment Balancing Acts, or the Technologies of Rationalization,' in P. Horwich (ed.) *World Changes. Thomas Kuhn and the Nature of Science*, Cambridge MA: MIT Press.

Wittgenstein, L. (1953) *Philosophical Investigations*, trans. G. E. M. Anscombe, Oxford: Blackwell; (1958) 3rd edn, New York: Macmillan and Oxford: Blackwell; (1967) Oxford: Blackwell.

Wittgenstein, L. (1967) *Zettel*, trans. G. E. M. Anscombe, ed. G. E. M. Anscombe and G. H. von Wright, Berkeley: University of California Press.

Wittgenstein, L. (1969) *On Certainty*, New York: Harper and Row.

Wittgenstein, L. (1978) *Remarks on the Foundations of Mathematics*, 3rd edn, trans. G. E. M. Anscombe, ed. G. H. von Wright, R. Rhees, and G. E. M. Anscombe, Oxford: Blackwell.

Wittgenstein, L. (1980a) *Remarks on the Philosophy of Psychology*, vol. 1, trans. G. E. M. Anscombe, ed. G. E. M. Anscombe and G. H. von Wright, Oxford: Blackwell.

Wittgenstein, L. (1980b) *Culture and Value*, trans. P. Winch, ed. G. H. von Wright, Oxford: Blackwell.

Wright, W. (1975) *Sixguns and Society: A Structural Analysis of the Western*, Berkeley: University of California Press.

Wrong, D. (1994) *The Problem of Order*, New York: Free Press.

Wuthnow, R. (1987) *Meaning and Moral Order: Explorations in Cultural Analysis*, Berkeley: University of California Press.

Zelitzer, V. (1994) *The Social Meaning of Money*, New York: Basic Books.

Zimmerman, D. H. (1988) 'On Conversation: The Conversation Analytic Perspective,' in J. Anderson (ed.) *Communication Yearbook II*, London: Sage, 406–32.

Zimmerman, D. H. and West, C. (1975) 'Sex Roles, Interruptions and Silences in Conversation,' in B. Thorne and N. Henley (eds) *Language and Sex: Differences and Dominance*, Rowley MA: Newbury House, 105–29.

Zinchenko, V. and Munipov, V. (1989) *Fundamentals of Ergonomics*, Moscow: Progress Publishers.

Zuckerman, M. (ed.) (1982) *Friends and Neighbors: Group Life in America's First Plural Society*, Philadelphia: Temple University Press.

Index

All names in bibliographical references in the text and endnotes have been included.

abilities, *see* understanding
actions 48; causal connections between
    48, 53, 76; presupposing practices 54;
    psychological basis of 7; socially
    embedded 115–17; strategic,
    reproducing rules 82
Agré, P. E. 72 n. 6
Alexander, Jeffrey 30, 40 n. 2, 73 n. 17,
    77
agency 56; history of 12, 165, 173 n. 4;
    human 11, 79, 164; nonhuman 11,
    163–6; relation between human, and
    environment 64–6, 163, 172;
    versatility of 57–8
Alford, C. F. 185
Althusser, Louis 91 n. 1
Ambrose, A. 130 n.
Anaximander 157
Anscombe, G. E. M. 9, 97, 106 n. 7
antirealism 65, 151, 192
Aristotle 47, 161 n. 13
Armstrong, Elizabeth 81–3
arrangements: established within
    and across practices 53–4;
    interconnection of meanings/
    identities/relations within
    43–4
articulation: of criticism within culture
    of science 196–7; of objects of
    knowledge 183; of practices 201,
    204–8
Asaro, P. 174 n. 13
Atkinson, J. M. 147 n. 8
Austin, John 126

Baas, B. 188 n. 5
Babbage, Charles 170, 173 n. 10

Baird, D. 173 n. 1
Baker, G. P. 105 n. 4
Baldwin , J. M. 185
Barad, K. 198 n. 4
Barnes, Barry 5, 6, 8, 14 n. 4, 27 nn. 2, 3,
    5, 28 n. 7, 106 nn. 5, 6
Baudrillard, Jean 164, 169
Bauman, Zygmunt 24
Baxandall, M. 80
Beck, U. 177
Becker, Howard 75, 77, 80
being: central to social order 43;
    meanings constituting 44
Bell, Daniel 177
Bellah, R. N. 88, 89
Belt, Henk van den 165–6, 173 n. 6
Bénatouïl, T. 71 n. 3
Bender, T. 88
Beniger, J. R. 177
Benjamin, Walter 169
Berger, P. 177
Berkeley, George 106 n. 7
Bernal, J. D. 173 n. 4
Berque, A. 72 n. 10
Biernacki, Richard 74, 77, 83–5
Bijker, W. 119 n. 21
Bittner, Egon 40 n. 12
Blattner, William 154
Bloor, David 9, 14 nn. 4, 6, 28 n. 7, 105
    n. 2, 106 nn. 6, 8
Blumenberg, H. 10
Blumer, H. 32, 39
Bogen, D. 148 n. 13
Boli-Bennett, J. 89
Boltanski, Luc 14 n. 3, 58, 62, 70, 71 and
    n. 3, 73 n. 29
Borck, C. 183

Bourdieu, Pierre 1, 8, 14 n. 3, 50, 58, 66, 71, 73 n. 22, 75, 82–3, 86, 175, 185, 210 n. 1
Bowker, G. 173 n. 4, 174 n. 13
Brandom, Robert 14 n. 7, 49, 190, 191, 195, 198 nn. 6, 12
Bréviglieri, M. 64, 72 n. 10
Buck, P. 174 n. 14
Burge, Tyler 211 n. 5

Callon, M. 11, 65, 174 n. 16, 188 n. 1
Cambrosio, A. 139
Cancian, F. M. 74, 76, 91 n. 2
'carriers': of action orientations 30–1, 34
Cartwright, N. 68
causality 22, 46–8, 162 n. 13; and action 47, 48–53, 97; in collective action 24, 27 n. 5; multicausality 30–1
Cerbone, David 154
Certeau, M. de 58
Cerulo, K. A. 89
Cicourel, A. 65, 76
citationality 202–3, 211 nn. 6, 8; in dispersion of practices 205
cognition 7–8, 42–3
collective: characterization of 17, 20
collective action: interdependence of social agents 24; paradigmatic practices of 90; requiring modification of habit 23
collective 'self-consciousness' 34–5
Collier, J. F. 90
Collins, H. M. 8, 9, 73 n. 26, 117 n. 1, 118 nn. 8, 10, 119 nn. 15, 16, 18, 22, 23, 148 n. 12
Collins, Randall 40 nn. 2, 10, 88
computer programs 112, 115, 117, 122, 184
computers: artificial intelligence 118 n. 9, 119 nn. 20, 22; model of human activity 9, 111–12, 169, 173 n. 10; as partial objects (of knowledge) 184; subject–object relations with 187, 188 n. 1
Conein, B. 62, 65, 72 n. 13, 73 n. 27
connectionism 9, 122
conservatism: priority of practice over theory 95, 103–4
convenience, personal and local 61–2, 66, 68–9
conventional utility 62–3, 69–70
conventions 63–4, 70, 110, 134, 151–2
conversation analysis 29, 132, 135–7, 138, 140–2

Cooper, C. L. 173 n. 13
coordination 58, 65–6, 69, 71, 72 n. 15; in collective action 23, 25; noncollusive, in rule-following 101; of social relationships 86
Coulter, Jeff 6, 11, 147 n. 4
creativity 58, 66, 183
Crothers, D. 118 n. 13
culture: as practice 17; practices interacting with discourse 75–6, 196; relation to action 76–9; relation to structure 77–8; set of 'material' practices 77
cybernetics 12, 170, 171–2

D'Andrade, Roy 82, 91 n. 3
Danto, Arthur 48
Dasein (Heidegger) 153, 156, 160 n. 5, 180
Daston, L. 173 n. 10
Davidson, D. H. 88, 89
Davidson, Donald 12, 121, 151–3, 160 n. 1, 192, 195, 198 n. 8
De Landa, Manuel 165, 172
deconstruction 201, 205
defamiliarization 12, 159, 162 n. 16 *see also* deworlding; familiarization
Deleuze, G. 172
Dennett, D. 69
Derrida, Jacques 13, 42, 43, 211 nn. 4, 6, 11; dispersive elaboration of practice 201–6; view of intelligibility 206
Desrosières, A. 60
destruction: agency in 165, 171
determination: of social orders 46–8
Dewey, John 8, 165
deworlding 154–6, 181; *see also* defamiliarization
Dickinson, Emily 56, 71 n. 1
DiMaggio, P. 73 n. 22
discourse 5; assembly of practical action 131; commentaries on realities 85; system of interrelated meanings 44, 75; transformed by practice 45, 81–3
dispersion: of objects of knowledge 184; elaboration of practice 201, 204
dispositions 7; globalizing influences on 72 n. 4; in rule-following 101, 105 n. 5
Dodier, N. 65, 71 n. 3, 73 n. 21, 188 n. 1
Dosse, F. 71 n. 3
Dreeben, R. 88
Dreyfus, Hubert 1, 2, 7, 12, 14 n. 8, 55 n. 4, 118 n. 9, 119 n. 22, 154, 179, 180, 185

Drucker, P. G. 177
Durkheim 22, 60, 189

Easterbrook, S. 173 n. 13
economic phenomena 39
Eglin, Peter 41 n. 19
Einthoven 188 n. 3
elaboration, of practices 13, 199–210
Elias, Norbert 126, 167
Eliasoph, Nina 87
Elichirigoity, I. 173 n. 7
embodiment 2–3, 7–8, 134, 168
emergent phenomena 168, 172, 173 nn. 4, 7
engagement, *see* pragmatic engagement
environment 72 n. 10; interaction with physical and social 104–5; taking hold of 59, 66, 68, 69, 72 n. 6; *see also* pragmatic engagement; pragmatic regimes; subject–object relations
epistemic objects, *see* objects: of knowledge
epistemic practices, *see* knowledge-centred practices
Ereignis (Heidegger) 201, 206–8, 210
ethics 199; hegemonic influence on 205–6
ethnomethodology 1, 3, 4, 29, 32, 65, 72 n. 11, 131–47, 148 n. 18; analysis of 'absent' actions 132–5, 142, 145, 146
evaluation, of practice 57; reality test of the good 60, 68; verbal, in rule-following 101, 126, 127
expert systems 177, 186
externalism 201–2, 211 n. 5

familiarization 61–2, 66, 68–9, 207–8
   see also defamiliarization
Fell, Joseph P. 161 n. 8
field of practices 2, 3, 5, 13
Fine, Arthur 160 n. 1
Fleck, Ludwik 163, 164
Flores, F. 14 n. 8
Føllesdal, Dagfinn 162 nn. 17, 18
formal designation 12, 157–8, 162 n. 14
Forms, Platonic 47, 54
forms of life 9, 199, 201; as approach to tacit knowledge 110–11
Foucault, Michel 1, 2, 14 n. 7, 43, 58, 75, 76, 91 n. 1, 173 n. 4, 195, 198 n. 11, 199
Freud 188 n. 2
Frisby, D. 30
Fujimura, J. 73 n. 28

Fulbrook, M. 77
Fuller, Steve 189, 196, 198 n. 14

Galileo 161 n. 13
games 99, 100, 103
Garfinkel, Harold 27 n. 1, 29, 65, 131, 140, 146
Gasser, L. 174 n. 13
Geertz, Clifford 75, 76, 80, 91 n. 1
Geison, Gerald 148 n. 9
Gibbard, A. 72 n. 7
Giddens, Anthony 1, 7, 8, 14 n. 3, 27 nn. 1, 4, 50, 58, 72 n. 4, 73 n. 22, 78, 175, 177
Giesen, Bernhard 40 n. 2
goals 6; heterogenous 128–9; knowledgeable enactment 21; in learning 123, 124, 125, 127; *see also* telos, of practices
Goffman, Erving 89
Gognen, J. 174 n. 13
good, the 57; neutralised in sociology 59–60; specifying relevant reality 66, 68, 70; *see also* ethics; evaluation
Goodman, N. 148 n. 15
Greenberg, J. R. 185
Greenstone, J. D. 74
Griesemer, J. 73 n. 28
Guattari, F. 172

Habermas, Jürgen 4, 48, 73 n. 29, 177
habits 23, 26, 85, 120, 176; insufficient for determining common kinds 202, 203–4
habitus 8, 50, 58, 66, 83, 86, 89
Hacker, P. M. S. 105 n. 4
Hacking, I. 14 n. 6, 68
Haraway, D. 173
harmony, maximizing: 'rule' acquisition by connectionism 123, 124, 130
Hartz, L. 88
Haudricourt, A.-G. 65
Haugeland, J. 100
Heal, J. 49
Hegel 5, 31, 185, 198 n. 5
hegemony: in culture of science 197; in stability of institutions 205–6, 209
Heidegger, M. 12, 13, 14 n. 7, 55 n. 4, 72 n. 10, 160 nn. 4, 5, 162 n. 15, 175, 189, 191, 197 n. 1; articulative elaboration of practice 201, 206–8, 209; knowledge as theoretical attitude 180–1; realism of 151, 153–8, 160 n. 1, 161 n. 10, 13; view of intelligibility 206, 212 n. 13

Hempel, C. 148 n. 15
Héran, F. 72 n. 16
Heritage, J. 27 n. 1, 147 n. 8
Hessen, B. 173 n. 4
Hester, Stephen 41 n. 19
Hewitt, J. P. 88
Hilbert, R. A. 40 n. 3, 147 n. 8
Hill, R. J. 76
Hobbes 4, 131
holism 5; practical 152
homogenization, of people and things 58
Horwitz, R. H. 88
human and nonhuman entities: in posthumanist social theory 164, 165, 169; sensorial data sustaining relationship 62: *see also* environment
human body: bodily doings, as practice 48, 168; connecting individual and social 8; in motor-skills 108–9
humanism 2, 10, 11, 164, 171
Hume, David 105 n. 5, 106 n. 7
Husserl, Edmund 47, 157

idealism (in social analysis) 18, 102–4
identification: categories 34, 35, 81, 138; correctness, and relevance 35, 38–9; discourses about 81–3; newspaper reportage 38, 41 n. 19; occasioned relevance 34, 36; perceptual assignability, and relevance 37; *see also* naming
identities, in arrangements 43–4
ideology 88, 92 n. 5, 169; hegemonic 197; as social structure 78, 91 n. 1; in theoretical assumptions 137
impositions: as response to contingency 210, 211 n. 3; retrospective nature of 203, 205, 209; by speech community 202
improvisation 116, 117, 199, 210 n. 1
individualism 4, 6, 24, 26, 28 n. 7, 92 n. 6; constitutive rule of 87–8, 90; methodological 30, 39
Inglehart, Ronald 91 n. 2
institutions (social) 60, 89–90; origins 99–100, 101–2; self-referential character of 102, 103, 104; systems of constitutive rules 82, 92 n. 6; transformation of 166, 173 n. 6; visibility of 33, 165; with/without self-organization 35
intelligibility 206, 211 n. 7; *see also* practical intelligibility; understanding

intentionality 47, 54, 69–70; conditions of satisfaction 204–5, 212 n. 12; linguistic 191; as normative 191–2, 198 n. 6
interactionism 6
interface, human–nonhuman 169–72
interpretation, pragmatic 133–4, 192, 198 n. 2
iterability, *see* citationality

Jacopin, E. 62, 73 n. 27
Jameson, F. 170, 171
Jayyusi, Lena 35
Jenkins, S. P. R. 119 n. 21
Jepperson, R. L. 76, 89
Jirotha, M. 174 n. 13
Joas, H. 58, 73 n. 20
Johnson, M. P. 76
Jordan, K. 139

Kalberg, S. 31
Kant 189
Keating, P. 139
Keesing, R. M. 75
Kekulé, Friedrich August 166
Knorr Cetina, Karin 10–11, 13, 14 n. 6, 65, 73 n. 24, 76, 148 n. 12, 172, 178–9, 183, 185
knowledge: cultures 178, 188 n. 1; deflationary conception of 195–6; dynamic conception of 195; extrinsic to practice 21; formulaic 109; know-how 7, 139; objective knowledge, preconditions of 105; objects of, *see* objects: of knowledge; power related to 27 n. 3; presupposing practice 12; propositional 6, 95; societies 13, 176, 177, 186, 187; substitutability of 112; *see also* tacit knowledge
knowledge-centred practices 13, 175, 176, 177, 187, 195; ideological hegemony in 197; constructing, through relational resources 179–80, 182, 183–4, 186
knowledge societies 176–8
Krechevsky, I. 148 n. 10
Kripke, Saul 28 n. 7, 102–3, 151, 159
Krohn, W. 177
Kuhn, Thomas 20, 43, 161 n. 12
Kusch, M. 117 and n. 1, 119 n. 23

Lacan, Jacques 185–6
Laclau, Ernesto 44–7, 54
Lafaye, C. 71 n. 3

Lamont, M. 89
language: as discursive practice 1, 3,
44–6, 75, 193–4; of formal
methodology 140; games
(Wittgenstein) 103; learning 129, 152;
macro-level 32–3, 39; meanings
defined by 45; significance of, in
practices 13, 45–6, 61, 63, 121, 191–2;
ordinary-language concepts 32–3, 39,
40 n. 12; as social phenomenon 12;
stopping/forcing modals 100
Lash, S. 177
Latour, Bruno 11, 14 n. 6, 65, 163, 174 n.
14, 188 n. 1
Lave, J. 14 n. 6, 65
Law, J. 72 n. 14, 73 n. 23, 174 n. 16
learning 9–10; connectionist 122–4;
inseparable from enacting 25; of
language 129, 152; by ostensive
training 99, 100; tacit rules model
125–7, 130; without explanation
100
Legendre, G. 122, 123, 124
Lenat, Douglas 119 n. 19
Lenin 35
Lenoir, T. 173 n. 4
Leroi-Gourhan, A. 65
Lévi-Strauss, Claude 75
Lewis, David 162 n. 17
Lipset, S. M. 88
logic: counterfactual conditionals 144;
of practical action 32, 76, 142; of
social structure 79
logo-centrism 201, 205–6
Luhmann 5, 30
Lynch, M. 1, 8, 10, 65, 139, 141, 148 n.
13, 175, 185
Lyotard, Jean-François 1, 14 n. 7, 177

M-ing (Anscombe): blind-and-thinking
action 97–9; circular account of 100,
102, 103
Macbeth, D. 148 n. 17
McGinn, C. 105 n. 4
MacIntyre, Alasdair 14 n. 8, 27 n. 6
MacKenzie, D. 117 n. 1, 118 n. 8
McNeely, C. L. 89
macro-social phenomena 6, 29, 30, 32,
40 n. 11; carriers of meaning of 31–2;
observability of 33; occasional
relevance 36–8, 40 n. 3; ordinary-
language concepts 32–3, 39, 40 n. 12;
praxiological instantiation of 34–5,
36, 39

Malinowski, Bronislaw 5
Malpas, Jeff 160 n. 1
mangle 164, 172; *see also* scientific
practices: tuning of social and
material agency
Mannheim, Karl 104, 105 n. 1
marginal practices 209
Marx 34, 84, 135, 163, 170, 173 n. 12
Marxism 17, 31, 165
materialism 3
mathematics: mathematical reasoning
121–2; rules-regress in 110
Maturana, H. R. 172
Mauss, Marcel 60, 64, 191
Mead, G. H. 8, 14 n. 7, 73 n. 20, 73 n. 29
meanings: and culture 75; everyday,
distinct from essential 156, 158, 159,
162 n. 15; hidden 164; indeterminacy
of 202–3, 211 n. 10; institution of, in
particular arrangements 47–8, 54;
and language 45–6, 47–8, 54; as
norms, through interpretation of
language 192; as positions in
discourse 44; practices as source of
12, 45, 152, 153, 154, 156; semantic
drift 193; of social arrangements 6,
43–5; and subjectivity 74
memory, in social action 21
mental states 7; determining practical
intelligibility 49–50; of participants in
institutions 98–9, 102, 103; states of
affairs in person's world 49
Merleau-Ponty, M. 66, 72 n. 10, 211 n. 7
Merz, M. 183
metaphors, in theoretical understanding
168, 169, 198 n. 8
methods; formulations of 10, 137–8;
judgments about relevance 145
Metz, M. H. 88
Meyer, John 77, 89
Meyers, P. 73 nn. 25, 29
micro-macro distinction 6, 29, 58; false
dichotomy 32
microsocial phenomena 32
Miller, Peter 170, 173 n. 13
mind: constituted within practices 11;
dependent on linguistic conventions
151–2; noncausal organizing of
practices 48–53, 54; *see also* mental
states
Mitchell, S. A. 185
Mitchell, T. 14 n. 8
Miyata, Y. 122, 123, 124
Mol, A. 72 n. 14

Moody, M. 71 n. 3
motor-skills metaphor 9
Mouffe, Chantal 44–7, 54
Mulkay, M. 148 n. 12
Mumford, E. 173 n. 13
Munch, Richard 40 n. 2
Munipov, V. 173 nn. 12, 13

naming 184
Natter, W. 14 n. 5
natural science 151, 153, 155, 156–7, 160
    n. 3, 161 nn. 10, 13, 162 n. 19
naturalization 35, 40 n. 13
nature and society 105, 151, 152–3, 154,
    160 n. 5
neural nets 9, 108, 112, 113, 115, 116,
    117, 119 nn. 14, 20
Noble, D. F. 173 n. 3
nonhuman objects 2, 3, 10–11, 108, 176
Norman, D. 65
normativity, as social phenomenon 12,
    13, 191–3; of discursive practices 194
Nyiri, J. 105 n. 2

Oakeshott, Michael 14 n. 8, 95, 126, 189
object relations, *see* subject–object
    relations
objectivism 10–11, 12–13
objectivity 60, 137, 140, 146
objects: formal designation of 157–8,
    159, 162 n. 14; independent from
    practice 12, 153–6; inseparable from
    practice 152–3, 178–9; of knowledge
    13, 175, 176, 179, 181–4, 185, 187;
    occurrent 153–6, 160 n. 6; rigid
    designation of 159, 162 nn. 17, 18;
    social 106 n. 7; theoretical 155, 161 n.
    9; *see also* nonhuman objects
Orren, G. R. 88
Ortner, S. 14 n. 2, 74
Oteri, J. S. 148 n. 16

paradigms 20; practices as 90
Parsons, T. 4, 5, 30, 42, 74, 77, 131, 174
    n. 14
partial objects 182, 183
Perkins, William Henry 165
Perutz, Max 148 n. 9
phenomenology 72 n. 10
philosophy 3, 151; of science 195;
    skepticism 152
Pickering, A. 1, 10–11, 13, 14 n. 6, 65, 73
    n. 26, 148 n. 12, 163, 170, 172, 173 nn.
    1, 2, 3, 4, 5, 13, 174 n. 16, 188 n. 1

Pinch, T. J. 117 n. 1
Plato 47, 157
Pleasants, N. 14 n. 4
Polanyi, Michael 108, 116, 126, 139–40
political criticism 196–7
polysemy of social structures 79
posthumanism 2, 3, 10–13, 164, 167, 170
Powell, W. 73 n. 22
power, conceptions of 13; as dynamic, in
    (social) alignments 194–5, 197; in
    shared practice 27 n. 2; of social
    structures 79; in understanding
    language 194
powers: as practice competences 20–1
practical consciousness 50–1
practical intelligibility 8, 9; determined
    by teleoaffectivity 47, 52, 54; distinct
    from rationality 47; understanding of
    rules expressed in actions 51–2, 54, 72
    n. 15
practice nexuses 5; material mediation
    11
practice theory 1–4; focus on
    unconscious action 74–5; relation
    with practice 19, 95; oppositions 1–2;
    in science 1, 164
practices: *see also* habits; knowledge-
    centred practices; scientific practices;
    shared practices
practices: actual, distinct from accounts
    of 138–9, 146; anchoring constitutive
    rules 83, 86–7, 90; categories of
    ordering 7; categorizing social
    identities 81; category-bound 38;
    connectionist account 123–4;
    construction of 179–80, 183;
    controlling other practices 79–83; in
    cultural theory 1, 74; discursive 45–6,
    76, 89, 146, 191; human activity 2, 48;
    indicators of success in 107–8;
    knowledge-centred, *see* knowledge-
    centred practice; linguistic 121, 129,
    191; logic of 29, 142, 146–7; marginal
    209; as nonlinguistic conditions of
    activity 120; nonregularized actions 7;
    normative 13, 189, 190, 191; as
    observable objects 76, 131–2, 134–5,
    146; organized by mind 48–53; in
    philosophy 1, 151–2, 153–5; and
    powers 20–1; prioritization of, over
    mind 11–12, 13, 84–5; production of
    social phenomena within 131 n.
    134–5, 141; reaction against idealism
    18; and regularities (or routines) of

practices (*cont.*)
  behavior 13, 49, 74–5, 87, 175, 189,
  190; relation with theory 18–20, 95–6,
  100; relational dynamic of 176,
  178–81; reproduction of 27 n. 4, 78,
  85, 90; silent, as basic realities 84, 85,
  90; in social theory 1; stability of 201,
  205–6, 207–8, 210; structural features
  53; structures of enacted schemas 79,
  80–1; support interactional patterns
  85; transposable 79, 81
pragmatic engagement 56–60, 67–8;
  mode of legitimate collective
  conventions 63–4; mode of conventional utility 62–3; mode of personal
  and local convenience 61–2, 66
pragmatic regimes 7, 56, 67 [table];
  familiarity 61–2, 68–9; governed by
  conceptions of good 59, 66; regime of
  justification 63–4, 70–1, 72 n. 11, 73 n.
  28; regular planned action 62–3,
  69–70; tension of engagement 60
pragmatic versatility 57–9, 61–4, 71
presuppositions 2, 189
Prony, Baron de 173 n. 10
proprieties: of relation between agent
  and environment 66, 73 n. 18; *see also*
  evaluation

Quételet, L. A. J. 60

rational choice theory 4, 24
rationalism 95–6
rationality 5, 50
realism 12, 56; deflationary 151–3; of
  pragmatic engagement 58–9, 66–7,
  68; robust 151, 153, 156
reason 5
reflexivity 13, 177; of science studies
  193, 197
representations 1, 194, 198 n. 9;
  inadequate for language and meaning
  12, 192, 198 n. 5; of incomplete
  objects (of knowledge) 181–2, 185;
  linguistic 191, 192; of skills 8, 21;
  verbal 84, 85
resources: instantiating cultural
  schemas 78–9; relational, in
  constructing practice 179–80
Rhees, Rush 130 n.
Rheinberger, H.-J. 14 n. 6, 181, 193
Rheingold, H. 173 n. 11
rigid designation (Kripke) 159, 162 nn.
  17, 18

Rip, Arie 165–6, 173 n. 6
rituals 83, 86, 89, 90, 92 n. 4
Rokeach, M. 91 n. 2
Rose, Nikolas 170, 173 n. 13
rounds 133–5
Rouse, Joseph 1, 6, 11, 13, 14 n. 3, 72 n.
  14, 73 n. 18, 153, 160 nn. 1, 7, 161 nn.
  8, 11, 13, 185, 193, 198 nn. 3, 7, 9, 10,
  11, 13
Rousseau 60
routine activity: as accomplishment
  23–4; rule-following, as blind habit
  96, 178
Rowan, B. 77
rule-following 95, 104; distinct from
  conformity 96–7; divergence 26, 145;
  dual nature of 101; as institution 9,
  101–4; intuition in 97; language of
  100; sustained by interdependent
  agents 26
rule-skepticism 103
rules: constitutive 82, 86, 87–8, 89, 90,
  91 n. 3; explicit formulations for
  actions 8–9, 51, 109, 126, 127; forcing
  models of 100; grammatical 121–2,
  123; identification categories 34;
  instantiated by verbal accounts
  of collective behavior 101; learning
  124; methodological 144, 145–6; as
  social 104; socially embedded
  116–17; stopping models of 100;
  tacit 9, 109, 110, 114, 125, 128, 130,
  139–40
rules-regress 9, 110, 113–15, 118 n. 9,
  119 n. 19

Sacks, Harvey 35, 38, 132–5, 136, 140,
  142, 147 n. 1
Sartre, J.-P. 49
Savigny, E. von 14 n. 7, 118 n. 5
Sayer, D. 30
Schaffer, S. 173 n. 10
Schatzki, T. 14 nn. 4, 5, 54, 55 n. 3, 72
  nn. 15, 17, 118 n. 4, 175, 185
Schegloff, E. A. 41 n. 16, 135–6
schemas 78–9, 86
Schivelbusch, W. 167–9
Schuman, H. 76
science: as activity 1, 2, 127; cognitive
  122, 186; culture of 196; cyborg 170,
  174 n. 14; human and nonhuman
  agency 3, 166, 167; of natural kinds
  151; scientific consensus 111, 115,
  116, 193

science studies: actor-network approach 171; as internal to culture of science 196–7; reflexive position of 13, 193, 197; theoretical 'sovereignty' of 196

scientific practices: anticontextualist analysis of 172; experiments 141–2; models as simulacra, used in 194; paradigms in 20; tacit knowledge in 9, 109, 113, 118 n. 8, 139; temporality of, when conceived normatively 193; theoretical reflection 157, 180; tuning of social and material agency 163, 164, 166, 170

Searle, John 40 n. 11, 82, 106 n. 6, 160 n. 3, 211 n. 9

semantic drift 193

semantic spaces: interrelated fields of meaning 44–5; practices as contexts for 46

Sewell, W. H. Jr 77–8, 84, 86, 91 n. 1, 92 n. 4

shared practices 2, 17, 18, 21–2; accomplishments by members of collectives 24–5, 131; as collective entities 22; as composites of habits 22; distinguished by competence 26; instantiated in collective production 134–5, 141; linguistic 121; mutual susceptibility in 26; routine activity 23–4

shared rules 121, 124

signification: of objects of knowledge 183–4; overflow 45; practices constituting 84–5

Simpson, O. J., trial 10; excerpt from testimony 143–4

simulacra, in normative practices 194, 198 n. 9

skills 2, 7, 80, 199, 200, 210 n. 1; experimental 110, 113; motor-skills 108–10, 111–13; need for supplementation 8; shared 9; teleoaffectivity of 55 n. 4

Skocpol, T. 74, 76, 92 n. 5

Smelser, Neil J. 40 n. 2

Smith, Adam 73 n. 29, 170

Smolensky, P. 122, 123, 124

social, the 24, 172

social causation 7; interaction of material and ideal factors 77, 80, 91 n. 2; practices dominant in 80–1, 84–5

social constructivism 57, 65, 66, 192–3

social embedding 109, 111, 115–17, 119 n. 22

social order 4–7; cognitive problem 42; determinants of 4–5, 17–18, 58, 127–9; instituted within practices 45, 46–7, 53–5, 131; regularity distinct from 42–3; rooted in body 2–3, 8, 9; *see also* arrangements

social reality 84, 85, 90, 102, 131; constituted by semantic spaces 45, 46

social relationships 85, 86, 87, 91

social structure 77; composed of schemas and resources 78, 79, 86; possible transformation of 79, 86; underlying logic of 79

social systems 30

social theory 3, 131, 14; posthumanist 164, 165, 171; traditional 164

socialization: training in rule-following 96, 99–100; transfer of knowledge 111

society: transformation theory 176–7

sociology 57; of (scientific) knowledge 57, 65, 104, 109, 110–11, 141–2, 171; neutralizing the good 59–60; sociological literature 138–9

Spengler, Oswald 95

Spinardi, G. 117 n. 1, 118 n. 8

Spinosa, Charles 13, 14 n. 8

Star, S. L. 174 n. 13

Start, S. 73 n. 28

Stehr, N. 177

Stephenson, P. H. 92 n. 6

Stern, D. 14 n. 4

Stinchcombe, A. L. 80

structure of wanting 182, 185–6, 187

structures: hidden 164

subject–object relations: in knowledge-centred practices 13, 175, 176, 178, 179, 180–1, 185, 187; mutuality 185; in (scientific) practice 163, 164, 166, 168; *see also* environment

subjectivity 74–5, 145

subjects, human beings as 11, 168, 170, 185

Sudnow, D. 75

Sumner 22

Swidler, Ann 6, 7, 14 n. 3, 74, 76, 88, 90, 92 n. 4

symbolic interactionism 4, 32, 39

symmetry, principle of: between humans and nonhumans 11

tacit knowledge 2, 7, 9, 107–8, 118 n. 8; common sense 139, 148 n. 18; forms of life as approach to 110–11, 115, 118 n. 11; motor-skills metaphor

108–10, 111–13; rules-regress model 110, 113–15; social embedding of 116–17; *see also* rules: tacit

Taylor, Charles 1, 44, 45–6

teleoaffectivity 7, 51; structure of 50, 52

telos, of practices 208, 209; *see also* goals

temporal emergence 164, 167, 171; of objects of knowledge 182

theory 3–4

Thévenot, Laurent 6, 7, 14 n. 3, 57, 58, 60, 65, 66, 69, 70, 73 nn. 24, 29, 188 n. 1

Tobin, J. J. 88, 89

Tocqueville, Alexis de 87

Toulmin, Stephen 5

Träger (Weber), *see* 'carriers'

tropes 194

tuning 163–4, 170, 172

Turkle, S. 184, 187, 188 n. 1

Turner, B. 174 n. 13

Turner, Stephen 2, 6, 9, 13, 22–4, 48–9, 50, 71 n. 2, 85, 108, 117 n. 2, 148 n. 11, 164, 175, 185, 189, 190, 191, 197 n. 1

understanding: as abilities linking actions composing practice 51; conceptual, as feature of practice 54, 55; practical, *see* practical intelligibility; priority over rules 9

units of analysis 172

Urry, J. 177

Varela, F. J. 172

Varenne, Hervé 87–8, 89

Verba, S. 88

Virilio, Paul 170

visibility: social theory of the visible 164, 165

Wagner, P. 71 n. 3, 72 n. 8

Warner, R. S. 74

Wartenburg, T. 194, 198 n. 11

Webb, J. 118 n. 13

Weber, Max 6, 30–1, 39, 74, 77, 189; understanding actions 133–4

Weber, Samuel 211 n. 4

Welsch, W. 186

West, C. 135–6

Weyer, J. 177

Wheeler, Samuel 193, 198 nn. 2, 8

wholism 5

Wilden, A. 185

Wiley, N. 188 n. 4

Wilkinson, J. 71 n. 3

Williams, Raymond 74, 75, 77, 91 n. 1

Winch, P. 5, 72 n. 5, 118 n. 4, 130 n. 1, 189

Wise, N. 188 n. 1

Wittgenstein, Ludwig 1, 8, 9, 14 n. 7, 28 n. 7, 42–3, 49, 54, 107, 118 n. 4, 148 n. 18, 179, 189, 192; conservatism of 95; metaphor of 'language-games' 103; on rule-following 96, 99, 101, 105 n. 3, 125–6

Wrong, Dennis 42

Wu, D. Y. H. 88, 89

Wuthnow, R. 74, 76

Yearley, S. 73 n. 26

Zelitzer, V. 187

Zimmerman, D. H. 135–6, 147 n. 8

Zinchenko, V. 173 nn. 12, 13

Zuckerman, M. 88